Cases in Human Resource Management

Cases in
Human Resource
Management

Edited by

Ann E McGoldrick

Senior Lecturer in Human Resource Management
Manchester Metropolitan University

PITMAN
PUBLISHING

London · Hong Kong · Johannesburg · Melbourne · Singapore · Washington

PITMAN PUBLISHING
128 Long Acre, London WC2E 9AN
Tel: +44 (0) 171 447 2000
Fax: +44 (0) 171 240 5771

A Division of Pearson Professional Limited

First published in Great Britain in 1996

© Pearson Professional Limited 1996

ISBN 0 273 61603 X

British Library Cataloguing in Publication Data
A CIP catalogue record for this book can be obtained from the British Library

10 9 8 7 6 5 4 3 2 1

Typeset by M Rules
Printed and bound in Great Britain by Clays Ltd, St Ives plc

The Publishers' policy is to use paper manufactured from sustainable forests.

CONTENTS

PREFACE

The importance of bringing organisational 'life' into teaching management and business studies has been well established. Case studies are a recognised way of accomplishing this aim. This book is designed to provide a set of human resource management cases which permit lecturers, facilitators and individual students to examine a wide spectrum of organisational issues. It encourages readers to bring together their knowledge and understanding of HR frameworks with the experience of the situations involved.

The cases cover the wide range of circumstances which practitioners currently encounter and must deal with. They have all been provided by experts in the particular areas considered. They cover major areas generally addressed by courses in HRM, as required to attain qualifications awarded by the professional body, the Institute of Personnel and Development. To assist in the selection of the appropriate case, they are presented in four major areas. For convenience of access, these have been arranged to correspond with the sections generally employed by widely used texts in this area of study.

The cases in the first part of the volume relate to the wider organisational scene and the need for effectiveness, necessitating a strategic approach to the management of an organisation's human resources. In the second part, focus is placed upon how organisations are resourced and the need to reward employees appropriately. From here, emphasis moves to the means of developing the human resource at all levels, encouraging adaptability as a response to the changing business environment. Finally, in Part Four the employment relationship is considered, with topical cases assessing problems which have arisen and the future way forward.

It is always important, however, to ensure that the necessary linkages are made between areas. These sections are convenient markers rather than 'barriers', with an emphasis here upon the inter-related nature of problems to be faced if HRM is to achieve strategic rather than operational goals. Ease of access should not, therefore, assume ease of evaluation and interpretation.

To aid in fulfilling the requirements of lecturers, course facilitators and individual readers, each case is organised in a similar format. The case opens with a brief analysis of the problem or problems to be assessed, supported by relevant background material to permit initial parameters to be established. The reader is then encouraged to consider the variety of factors which will be influential in analysing the case to determine possible courses of action. The activity brief and questions are designed to elicit thoughtful response and analysis. Required core reading is suggested.

To assist readers, the stages of the case study process are summarised in the Introduction, with the figure on page 6 suggesting the types of skills potentially introduced or developed at each stage of enquiry. The book is also accompanied by a separate Instructor's Manual which is available to lecturers adopting this book, to further support the use of the cases.

ACKNOWLEDGEMENTS

An edited book cannot be possible without the efforts of the contributors. I have been privileged to work with the authors appearing in this volume, who are experts in their fields and have provided an opportunity to present readers with a set of cases which explore the context of human resource management in relation to specific organisational experiences and the necessity to manage people effectively.

I would like to thank Pat Walker and Sharron Rushton at Manchester Metropolitan University. Their diligence and patience were responsible for the preparation of the publication drafts.

The support and professionalism of the editorial staff at Pitman Publishing were essential. I am particularly grateful to Penelope Woolf, Lisa Howard and Annette McFadyen, who ensured the success of the project.

Ann E McGoldrick
June 1996

NOTES ON CONTRIBUTORS

Catherine Allen, BA, MSc, IPD (Grad), is Employee Relations Officer in the UK division of a leading international company. She was previously a Researcher in the Manchester School of Management, UMIST, investigating the changing nature of human resource management. Her role currently involves the full remit of HRM activities. Her particular areas of expertise are management of absence, discipline and payment systems.

Greg Bamber is Professor and Director of the Graduate Management School at Griffith University, Brisbane, Australia. He has more than 100 publications including *Managing Managers,* Blackwell; *Organisational Change Strategies*, Longman and *International and Comparative Industrial Relations*, Routledge. Several of his publications have been translated into other languages. He is a past-president, Australian and New Zealand Academy of Management. Before moving to Brisbane, he was at the University of Durham. He has won a series of competitive research grants in the UK and Australia and has undertaken major consultancy and mediation assignments for governments, employers, unions and international organisations.

Phil Beaumont, B Econ, PhD, is Professor of Employee Relations in the Department of Social and Economic Research, University of Glasgow. His publications include *Human Resource Management: Key Concepts and Skills* (1993) and *The Future of Employment Relations* (1995). Current research interests include changing customer–supplier relationships and the diffusion of employee relations changes.

John R Berridge, BA (Southampton), MSc Econ (LSE), is Senior Lecturer in Personnel Policy and Director of International Management Programmes at the Manchester School of Management, UMIST, where he has also been Course Director for the Masters Programme in Personnel Management and Industrial Relations. He has taught widely in Europe and North America, is the author of over forty books and articles and since 1991 has been editor of the international journal *Employee Relations*.

Paul Brook is a Senior Lecturer in Industrial Relations in the Faculty of Management and Business at Manchester Metropolitan University. From 1986 to 1991 he was a researcher for the Union of Shop, Distributive and Allied Workers (USDAW, UK). During this time he specialised in assessing the impact of European integration on industrial relations, and consequently the development of USDAW's European policies and educational programmes. His current and principal work is on the political economy of European industrial relations, with particular reference to Britain and Italy.

Cary L Cooper is currently Professor of Organizational Psychology in the Manchester School of Management and Pro-Vice Chancellor (External Activities) of the University of Manchester Institute of Science and Technology (UMIST). He is the author of over 70 books on occupational stress, women at work and industrial and organizational psychology. He has written over 250 scholarly articles for academic journals and is a frequent contributor to national newspapers, TV and radio. He is currently Editor-in-Chief of the *Journal of Organizational Behaviour*, co-Editor of the medical journal *Stress Medicine*, and Fellow of the British Psychological Society, The Royal Society of Arts and the Royal Society of Medicine.

Professor Cooper was also the Founding President of the British Academy of Management and is currently Chair of the Higher Education Funding Council's Panel for the Research Assessment Exercise of all UK business and management schools.

Susan Corby is a Senior Lecturer in Industrial Relations at Manchester Metropolitan University. She has written widely on the NHS but her expertise is not confined to the academic. She was formerly a Senior Industrial Relations Officer of the Royal College of Midwives.

Peter Critten, PhD, is a Senior Lecturer in the Business School of Middlesex University. He teaches HRM and, in particular, individual and organisation development. He has over 25 years' experience designing, implementing and evaluating training systems in a variety of industries. Prior to taking up a teaching position, he was Management Development Manager at the Hotel and Catering Training Company. He has published widely in the area of employee training and development.

John Davison has worked in retail management for companies such as BHS and Asda. He became the UK's first university lecturer in Retail Management in 1989. He now works for IBM (UK) as a consultant in their retail and distribution business.

Rick Delbridge, BSc Econ, PhD, is a Research Fellow in the Human Resource Management Section of Cardiff Business School. He has extensive research experience in the areas of manufacturing and 'Japanese' management. His particular research interests are the role of labour and the development of workplace relations in manufacturing organisations.

Martin Dowling, BSc, Dip Ed Tech, MA, MIPD, is a Senior Lecturer in Human Resource Management at Dundee Business School, a part of the School of Management at the University of Abertay, Dundee. He is Course Leader for the School's MSc in Human Resource Management and Vice Chair of the Mid-Scotland Branch of the Institute of Personnel and Development. His current research interests are in the field of organisational change and human resource management, managerial roles and the application of human resource management in third sector organisations.

Mike Doyle is a Senior Lecturer in the Department of Human Resource Management, Leicester Business School. After some 20 years' experience as a line manager, he joined Leicester Business School as a Management Teaching Fellow and subsequently as a full-time lecturer teaching on postgraduate and post-experience management education programmes. His research and consultancy interests revolve around exploring new approaches to management and organisation development. He is a Member of the Institute of Management and holds a BA in Social and Management Studies and an MA in Human Resource Management.

David Farnham is Professor of Employment Relations at the University of Portsmouth. His most recent books include *Employee Relations* (1993), *The Corporate Environment* (1995), *Understanding Industrial Relations* (1995) (with J Pimlott), *Managing the New Public Services* (1996) (with S Horton), *Managing People in the Public Services* (1996) (with S Horton) and *New Public Managers in Europe* (1996) (with S Horton, J Barlow and A Hondeghem).

Margaret Ferrario, BSc (Hons), MSc, BA, C Psychol, is a consultant organisational psychologist. She has several years' experience working in the area of human factors (applying psychological solutions to health and safety problems). She is also currently working at the Manchester School of Management, UMIST, conducting research on stress management initiatives in organisations.

Colin E J Fielding, MBA, MIPM, MMS, is the Borough Personnel Officer at Tameside Metropolitan Borough Council after spending some time in the textile and rubber manufacturing industry. He has worked in all aspects of human resource management but still regards himself primarily as a business manager.

Lesley Giles, BSc (Hons), MA Industrial Relations, Grad IPD, is currently a Research Fellow at the Institute for Employment Studies, where she is involved in research and advisory work in employment, training and labour market policy and human resource management. Her background and training is primarily within the field of personnel management and industrial relations. Her previous job was as Researcher in the Human Resources Research Unit in the Business School at the University of Portsmouth. Prior to this, Lesley was a Researcher in the Centre for Quality at the University of Central England in Birmingham. Much of her research to date has focused, in particular, on developments in public sector employment and the ways people are managed in the public services.

Ian Glendon, BA, MBA, PhD, AFBPsS, CPsychol, FIOSH, RSP, MIMgt, MErgS, is a Chartered Occupational Psychologist specialising in human factors aspects of risk management. His research, teaching and consultancy activities cover a wide variety of areas within management and applied psychology, including human resource management. His experience includes nine years as a company director and his publications include two major texts – *Individual Behaviour in the Control of Danger* and *Human Safety and Risk Management*. In 1996 he takes up the post of Associate Professor in Applied Psychology at Griffith University, Queensland.

Patrick Gunnigle, B Comm, MBS, PhD, FIPD, is Senior Lecturer in Industrial Relations and Personnel Management and Head of the Department of Personnel and Employment Relations, University of Limerick. His publications include *Personnel Management in Ireland* (1990), *Continuity and Change in Irish Employee Relations* (1994), *New Challenges to Irish Industrial Relations* (1995) and *Industrial Relations in Ireland: Theory and Practice* (1995). A former shop steward, he has held a senior industrial relations post in the semi-state sector and lectured for some years in Zambia.

John Guthrie is the Director of the Retail Studies Group at the University of Otago, Dunedin, New Zealand. The group is currently involved in studies on the value of staff as a source of competitive advantage and the associated training requirements.

Laura Hall, PhD, BSc, FIPD, is Senior Lecturer in Human Resource Management at Manchester Metropolitan University. She is also the associate examiner for Human Resource Planning for the IPD, and her publications include *Personnel Management: HRM in Action*, with Professor Derek Torrington from the Manchester School of Management, UMIST. Laura is currently involved in research, supported by the ESRC, exploring developments in the organisational personnel role and activities.

Pat Hornby, BA, MSc, is trained in occupational psychology at the Applied Psychology Unit, University of Sheffield and is currently lecturing in Applied Psychology at the University of Central Lancashire. Her research concerns are in the area of social networking and decision making in organisations and in organisational research methods.

Fintan Hourihan is chief correspondent with *Industrial Relations News* (IRN) which is published weekly and is the most widely read independent report on employee relations in Ireland. He holds Bachelor of Business Studies and Master of Commerce degrees. He has contributed to numerous books on various aspects of employee relations, especially its European dimension.

Nicholas Kinnie, BSc, MA, PhD, is a Lecturer in Industrial Relations and Personnel Management in the School of Management at the University of Bath. He has researched and published widely in the fields of the decentralisation of bargaining structures, the use of information technology by personnel specialists and the links between new manufacturing strategies and the management of human resources.

Audrey Klesta is Professor of Human Resources at the Lyon Graduate School of Business, France.

She has an MA in Human Resources, and is currently working in the area of Organisational Behaviour. Her professional background includes training at the WHO and consultancy at the ILO. She consults for the Groupe ESC Lyon with many multinational corporations such as Alcatel, British Airways and Thompson. Her research interests are centred on expatriates, especially in Asia.

Danusia Malina lectures at the Faculty of Management and Business at Manchester Metropolitan University, teaching HRM and Industrial Relations. She has previously worked at the University of Lancaster, having escaped public sector management training posts. Her recent publications include research on comparative analysis of HRM in China and UK companies and on cross-cultural methodology. Meanwhile in the background lurks a PhD. She believes we write what we most need to know.

Graeme Martin is Director of the Dundee Business School, University of Abertay, Dundee. After an early career in personnel and industrial relations management in the engineering and construction industries, he has taught, researched and consulted in the field of HRM and organisational change for the past seventeen years, in both this country and overseas. His current research interests are mainly in the field of strategic change and HRM and is working, along with colleagues, on a series of linked case studies of locally-based manufacturing subsidiaries of multinational enterprises.

Hamish Mathieson, BA, MA, MIPD, is Senior Lecturer in Industrial Relations in the Department of Management at Manchester Metropolitan University. He teaches industrial relations across the Department's postgraduate courses, including the MA in Industrial Relations with Labour Law. His research interests are the IR implications of privatisation in public enterprises. He is also engaged in a comparison of the implementation of HRM in the UK and Sweden in collaboration with Ueesola University.

Ann E McGoldrick, BA (Hons), Cert in Ed, MA (Econ), PhD, MIPD, is Senior Lecturer in Human Resource Management at Manchester Metropolitan University. Previously she was a lecturer in the Manchester School of Management, UMIST. Principal research interests have been in retirement, pensions and equal opportunities, supported by funding from the ESRC, EOC, HCFC and industrial sponsors. She has published widely in these areas. Recent collaborative ESRC and Institute of Management research has related to managerial response to older employees, while HCFC projects relate to organisational response to disability.

Sally Messenger, MSc, BSc, is a Lecturer in Hotel Management at the University of Surrey. Her main area of research is vocational education and training and, in particular, the development of competence-based systems. In addition, Sally has research interests in organisational change/innovation and management development. Previous to her appointment at Surrey, Sally worked for the National Council for Vocational Qualifications and City and Guilds of London Institute.

Mike Noon, BA, MSc, PhD, is a Senior Lecturer in the Department of Behaviour in Organisations at Lancaster University. He has researched and published on new technology and organisations, human resource management and equal opportunities. His current major research project is analysing organisational change and the transformation of work at Royal Mail.

Patricia J Ohlott is a Research Associate at the Center for Creative Leadership, Greensboro, North Carolina. Her current research interests include workplace diversity, management development through job assignments and executive impact on organisational design. She has co-authored several reports and has published articles in the *Academy of Management Journal, Journal of Applied Psychology, Human Resource Management* and *Personnel Psychology*. She is a member of the Academy of Management, American Psychological Association and the Society for Industrial/Organisational Psychology. Patricia received her BA in Psychology from Yale University and is a doctoral candidate in Organisation Behaviour at the Fuqua School of Business, Duke University.

Thierry Picq holds a Doctorate in Management Science. He is Professor in Human Resource Management at the Groupe ESC Lyon (France). He has five years' experience as a consultant in a large French consulting group. His particular interests deal with team management, project management, organisational behaviour and organisational learning.

Martin Ridley is responsible for management, organisation and career development for all the Westland business now integrated into the larger GKN organisation. He was previously Resourcing and Development Manager for Westland Group plc and has also worked for 3M Company and British Gas. Martin says that training and development is his 'third' career, the others were journalism and marketing. A 'Cockney' born in London, Martin says he enjoys both the frustration and the reward of helping organisations and individuals develop. He has two grown-up sons, enjoys football (mainly Queens Park Rangers), tennis and the 'atmosphere' of live theatre, because it is like a training programme!

Marian N Ruderman is a Research Scientist at the Center for Creative Leadership in Greensboro, North Carolina. Her research interests are centred on management development, the promotion process and diversity in the workplace. She has published several articles and reports on these topics. She is a member of the American Psychological Association, the Society for Industrial Relations and Organisational Psychology and the Academy of Management. She received her BA in Psychology from Cornell University and her PhD in Organisational Psychology from the University of Michigan.

John Salmon, BA, MA, PhD, currently lectures at Cardiff Business School in Industrial Relations and Japanese Management. He previously taught at Manchester Metropolitan University and was Visiting Professor in Human Resource Management at the University of Grenoble, Associate Professor at the Institute of Social Science in the University of Tokyo, and a Japan Foundation Fellow. His published work covers both the UK and Japan.

Sue Shaw, BA, MSc, FIPD, is a Senior Lecturer in Personnel Management in the Department of Management at Manchester Metropolitan University. She contributes to a wide range of Masters and Postgraduate Diploma programmes and heads up the MA and Postgraduate Diploma in HRM courses. She is a Fellow of the Institute of Personnel and Development and is currently Chair of its Manchester Branch.

David E Simmons, BSc (Hons), MMGmt, is a Research Officer in the Australian Centre of Strategic Management (ACSM), Queensland University of Technology. He recently received funding to investigate the integration of human resource strategy with broader business strategy and the adoption of team based work organisation in Australia. David's fields of research include work organisation, job design, organisational design, HR, industrial relations and quality management. This research has been conducted in the automotive, electronics and telecommunications industries. He is also involved in an Australian Research Council funded project to examine the development of business networks between Australian and South East Asian enterprises. David obtained his Masters of Management from the University of Queensland in 1994 and joined the ACSM shortly thereafter.

Paul R Sparrow, BSc (Hons) (Manchester), MSc (Aston), PhD, is a Reader in International Human Resource Management at Sheffield University Management School. He worked as a freelance consultant, Research Fellow at Aston University and then Senior Research Fellow at Warwick Business School. In 1988 he joined PA Consulting Group working as a consultant and finally a principal consultant. In 1991 he returned to academia, lecturing at Manchester Business School. He has written a number of books including *European Human Resource Management in Transition* and *Designing*

xiv   Notes on contributors

and Achieving Competency and published articles concerning the future of work, human resource strategy, management competencies, the psychology of strategic management and international human resource management. He is an Associate Editor of the *Journal of Occupational and Organisational Psychology*.

Richard Thorpe is Professor in Management in the Department of Management at Manchester Metropolitan University. After ten years in industry, he joined the Pay and Reward Centre at Strathclyde University Business School, where he researched in performance improvement. He has worked as a lecturer in Glasgow University and joined MMU eight years ago. Retaining his interest in the area of remuneration and reward, he is regularly involved in lecturing, consulting and writing on the subject of pay reward and change.

Derek P Torrington, JP, MPhil, CIPD, CIMgt, FRSA, is Dean of Management Studies and Professor of Human Resource Management at Manchester School of Management, UMIST. He has written 27 books, including *Personnel Management: HRM in Action* and *International Human Resource Management*.

Christoph Williams, BSc (Hons) Psychology, MBA, is a member of the Institute of Personnel Management and the British Psychological Society. He has worked for an international oil company, a human resources consultancy, the University of Surrey (as a lecturer in Retail Management) and acted as an independent consultant. He has publications in various books and international journals and is currently working as a Training Officer for Safeway Stores PLC.

Carol Woodhams is a member of the IPD and a Research Officer at Manchester Metropolitan University. She is currently undertaking a PhD in the managerial issues of disability in the workplace. Previous to her current position, she gained five years' experience in a management role within the hotel and catering industry, working in hospitality venues worldwide. Her previous academic background is in psychology and human resource management.

INTRODUCTION

Case studies have for some time been acknowledged as an important teaching method, although the availability of suitable sets of cases within the field of HRM remains limited. This book provides a series of cases relating to HR issues, covering essential subject areas and acknowledging the major changes which have occurred within this area of management, including the emphasis upon its strategic nature in ensuring organisational performance, external and contextual pressures from governmental and legislative sources, as well as the more general organisational requirement to respond to the rapidly changing business environment. This also includes the necessity to view the organisation in terms of wider international competition.

The case study method assists in promoting greater realism within the field of management education, essential for both practising managers and those with less direct organisational experience. Cases are designed to give the reader the opportunity to evaluate a 'real' situation, proceeding through all the stages of analysis, assessment and strategic recommendation which must be faced within the business domain. While it is acknowledged that theoretical considerations remain important, these are not considered in isolation but are closely linked to the practical interpretations and actions arising from the case itself. The approach attempts to assist in redressing the relatively low emphasis on management training and development (e.g. Constable and McCormick 1987, Handy 1987), to better equip HR professionals for their performance in their current and future roles.

THE NATURE OF CASE STUDIES

'A case is a written or filmed description of an actual or imaginary situation which is presented in some detail.' (Huczynski 1983)

'The typical case consists of a number of pages of written description of an actual situation facing an organisation. It will usually describe how the current position developed and what problems key personalities in the case are currently facing.' (Easton 1992)

The case method is not new. It is frequently related to the method used in the teaching of students at Harvard Business School, although its origins are much earlier (Masoner 1988). In this particular situation it was normally used as a large class learning tool, with students pre-preparing analyses of a written case to discuss in class under the guidance of an instructor, who would question students and promote them to discuss, analyse and summarise the issues arising. Cases are, however, very varied and there are many alternative ways in which they can be used to assist in promoting understanding of organisational situations.

Some of the major distinctive features in the composition of cases relate to:

Length

Cases may vary from a short, tight summary to a more expansive discussion document. The former are now frequently seen in written examination papers, where it is considered important to provide students with the opportunity of demonstrating their knowledge of course constructs in respect of actual or likely situations, rather than simply repeating frameworks they have encountered in their studies. In the educational environment it is more frequently appropriate to employ a somewhat more detailed case, which provides the material to stimulate thoughtful analysis and discussion as the basis of the learning experience.

Situation

Cases in HRM are usually based in organisations, although not inevitably so. It may be appropriate to utilise other situations relating to the problems of, for example, individuals, groups or countries, to demonstrate the underlying themes which may be applied back to the organisational context.

Thematic content

A case may relate to one specific operational issue, which readers are asked to analyse in order to suggest an appropriate outcome. It may alternatively involve a wider assessment of inter-related themes, possibly necessitating the crossing of traditional subject area boundaries in the discipline. The latter is frequently the case in HRM cases, reflecting the real world of the organisation.

Presentation medium

The most frequent case presentation method is as a written document. Cases may involve other techniques, including films, audio and video media. The written case predominates in that it is less expensive and more adaptable. Written cases are also much more readily accessible to students, who can work on them at their own pace and convenience, returning to the case as frequently as required to complete their evaluation and analysis.

Truth or fiction

A case may be a true description of a situation which has occurred, it may be entirely fictitious or it may combine elements of both. In some instances it may be appropriate to set out in detail a true reflection of an actual occurrence, since this clearly demonstrates the issues which require consideration. Organisational confidentiality may not permit this and disguise may be necessary.

Likewise it may be relevant to combine the experience of several organisations to demonstrate complexities and contrasting approaches in addressing problems. It may also be necessary to construct an entirely fictitious situation when access to relevant data is unavailable, or cases may combine truth with fiction to emphasise essential learning points.

USING CASE STUDIES

Cases may also be used in a range of different ways and for different levels of analysis, for example:

Class discussion

The traditional Harvard case method involved prior preparation by students on a written case, followed by discussion in relatively large class groups, guided by the expert instructor. This is still appropriate in some educational contexts, particularly where there is limited contact time or students are unfamiliar with the case method and need guidance through the early stages of this approach. It has dangers traditionally associated with classroom learning, in respect of the lack of involvement of all participants and the inability of the facilitator to ensure that all students are fully understanding the issues discussed. It can, however, provide a far more varied and richer experience than 'talk and chalk' methods. The instructor will need to carefully judge the degree of involvement required of them by the particular group.

Case course

Rather than introducing cases from time to time the instructor may elect to operate the entire course around the case method. A book of case studies within the area of study may be an appropriate vehicle for student learning, particularly when dealing with postgraduate and post-experience management students, who do not require direct tutoring in fundamental concepts. The participants will gain more in understanding from their consideration of actual examples, utilising their own organisational experience in the interpretation of the cases, thus extending their knowledge base, whilst deepening their awareness and potential approaches to future problem-solving situations.

Group work

Cases provide an ideal opportunity for group projects. Groups of smaller size may work together with the instructor in analysing the case. It may also be appropriate to provide the opportunity for individual study prior to the group meeting, or to give the group time to work without the facilitator in a self-directed manner. Case studies may provide the instructor with a mechanism to permit larger classes to enjoy the benefits of group work. Smaller self-directed groups may be established to consider the case under discussion or a variety of cases, with the instructor or facilitators available on a more limited basis to each group to provide expert guidance.

Presentations

The case method provides an ideal mechanism to encourage students to participate in providing oral presentations of their interpretation of the issues in a structured manner. These can be organised on an individual or group basis according to class or group size constraints, as well as the level and aims of the course. The development of communication skills is, of course, of paramount importance to the HR function and management education generally. Participants may utilise the range of learning aids, including OHP, video and flipchart support, together with written reports and summaries.

Role play

Course participants may undertake role plays to demonstrate significant areas of the case.

These may be suggested by the writer of the case or by the group facilitator, involving the allocation of roles within the case remit to individual or group players. An alternative is to permit the participants to enact their own interpretations of the case. Facilitators should never underestimate the imagination of their groups or neglect to remember that they are themselves also in a learning situation! Role play can be an enjoyable mechanism to place participants within the reality of the constraints and decision-making potential presented by a case.

'Live' or 'dead' format

Cases may be presented in different ways. All relevant information may be given to students at the outset, including reference to support from library and other sources. This may be necessary with larger groups, when there is limited time for case analysis, or where the approach focuses on individual work. A 'live' case involves the presentation of additional information at stages over a period of time. Students may, for example, only be given a verbal or written outline of the organisation or case initially. After they have themselves discussed the likely issues and/or collected information they believe may be relevant, additional documentation and assistance is provided. The facilitator may choose to introduce several stages to this interactive process, encouraging students to 'rethink' the premises upon which they have been proceeding.

Assessment

Cases are now more frequently used as a basis for student assessment, since they represent a more realistic reflection of the student's ability to apply information than the traditional examination question format. While short case examples may be used as part of the traditional examination paper, there is a move in management education towards replacing tests of memory with more organisationally based techniques of evaluation of understanding. It is not always feasible to place these entirely in the experiential framework through projects and personal organisational enquiry. A case study provides a suitable compromise. It can be used on a prepared basis as part of a programme of continuous assessment. It can be used as a 'seen' or 'unseen' vehicle for a time-constrained examination, dependent on length. Alternatively it can be utilised for examination by group written or oral presentation, encouraging communication and teamwork in assessment to reflect their significance in the organisational environment.

ANALYSING CASE STUDIES

It is important that the reader acquires the skills required to deal with case studies. Frequently instructors and facilitators, who are themselves familiar with the techniques involved, forget that students will initially require guidance and support tackling a case. It is also important for readers to think through the necessary stages involved. Practising managers should reflect on the way in which they proceed in approaching problems within their organisation, while other students may consider the life skills necessary to solve other types of problems they have encountered. In both cases an appropriate mode of approach is essential to arrive at a successful outcome.

The most frequent recommendation for case study analysis is to follow a 'step-by-step' method, as in all situations of complex problem solving (Reynolds 1980). A useful suggested format was presented by Tyson and Kakabadse (1987), which involved five major steps:

1 Problem definition
2 Analysis
3 Generating solutions
4 Evaluating solutions
5 Presenting/implementing solutions

A more detailed approach has been advocated by Easton (1992), which again relies on stages but arranges these as seven progressive steps:

1 Understanding the situation
2 Diagnosing problem areas
3 Generating alternative solutions
4 Predicting outcomes
5 Evaluating alternatives
6 Rounding out the analysis
7 Communicating the results

Easton suggest that readers should commence with an examination of the 'basic meat' of the case study – information. From here it is possible to build a model of the situation to enable them to diagnose problem areas effectively.

They may then proceed to generate alternative solutions, permitting them to examine major strategic alternatives before choosing an appropriate course of action. Finally, the results must be communicated in a manner appropriate to requirements, as discussed in the preceding section.

In the study of HRM we are concerned with a number of outcomes from the management education process, which are relevant for instructors, students and individual readers to consider. Our prime concern is to assist course participants and independent learners to manage effectively. In order to do so they need to develop a range of skills to assist them in managing the change process within organisations. In recent years, the acquisition of skills and competencies has been the focus of professional management bodies. The Institute of Personnel and Development has placed great emphasis on this as part of their professional education and development scheme.

It is necessary for all educational providers, as well as facilitators of in-house training courses, to develop these skills as an integral part of the learning process, balancing the requirements for individual effectiveness and the contribution this makes to organisational performance. The case study method can make a significant contribution.

Figure A suggests a way forward which may be adopted to increase the integration of the use of case studies, demonstrating the linkages which instructors, students and readers should consider. They apply in respect of three major dimensions:

1 *Stage:* the stage of approach or action-oriented behaviour required
2 Process: the process required to accomplish the desired goals
3 Skills: the skills utilised and potentially developed in this phase

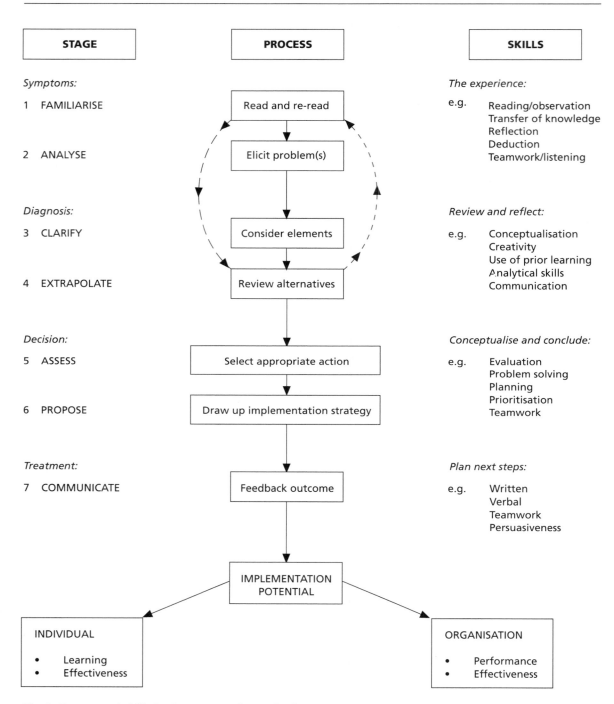

STAGE	PROCESS	SKILLS

Symptoms:

1 FAMILIARISE

Read and re-read

The experience:

e.g.
Reading/observation
Transfer of knowledge
Reflection
Deduction
Teamwork/listening

2 ANALYSE

Elicit problem(s)

Diagnosis:

3 CLARIFY

Consider elements

Review and reflect:

e.g.
Conceptualisation
Creativity
Use of prior learning
Analytical skills
Communication

4 EXTRAPOLATE

Review alternatives

Decision:

5 ASSESS

Select appropriate action

Conceptualise and conclude:

e.g.
Evaluation
Problem solving
Planning
Prioritisation
Teamwork

6 PROPOSE

Draw up implementation strategy

Treatment:

7 COMMUNICATE

Feedback outcome

Plan next steps:

e.g.
Written
Verbal
Teamwork
Persuasiveness

IMPLEMENTATION POTENTIAL

INDIVIDUAL
• Learning
• Effectiveness

ORGANISATION
• Performance
• Effectiveness

Fig A Stages and skills in the case study method

A useful overview for interpreting these layers or stages which must be incorporated in interpreting the case in order to develop managerial effectiveness is found in an analogy used by Charles Handy (1993), which equates managerial problem solving to the procedures of a General Practitioner. The manager is likewise the 'first recipient of problems', which must be dealt with before action can be taken. Both GP and Manager must:

1 Identify the symptoms in any situation
2 Diagnose the disease or cause of the trouble
3 Decide how it might be dealt with – a strategy for health
4 Start the treatment

In addressing the case study students must undertake the first three of these stages, while they must also evaluate how the final stage could proceed, in order to produce a successful outcome in their feedback or communication process. It is useful to review each stage, linking them to initial skills which may be required or which are capable of being developed as part of this learning encounter:

1 Familiarise

It is essential that the student approaches the case with care, reading and re-reading to acquire a sound knowledge of the organisation and the issues to be addressed. In a 'live' case this information may be provided for them on an incremental basis, relying also on their intuitive skills to determine the advance preparation they make. At this stage readers should employ knowledge of organisational procedures to their interpretation, as well as transferring knowledge from previous learning experiences in educational, employment and individual contexts. It is also a phase in which to develop analytical reading skills, to stimulate those utilised by direct observation within the organisation and to elicit the major areas of enquiry upon which the case analysis will be based. Reflection will permit the reader to progress to the analysis stage.

2 Analyse

It is necessary for the reader to employ deductive and analytical skills to transform the raw information obtained into a meaningful and realistic analysis of the situation presented by the case. This will also involve a need to organise and classify available information. Within the organisation it will normally involve the organisational context within which the case is set but be prepared to elicit the main problems which are fundamental to a successful understanding of the case, preparing to make thoughtful propositions at subsequent stages.

3 Clarify

The third phase remains in the reflective mode of operation. Once the problem(s) have been potentially elicited from the case, it is important to ensure that they are clarified to the extent that they can be clearly stated and objectified. Before reaching this goal it is important to ensure that all potentially significant elements have been considered and any available material has been accessed and reviewed. This may involve requesting further information from the facilitator, library or computer search procedures. Analytical and teamworking skills may again be required. Here it is necessary to review the experience of the case before starting to reach outcome conclusions. The real diagnosis now begins.

4 Extrapolate

After clarifying the issues involved, it is time to move to the final stage of diagnosis. It is the time to again ask questions. What is the cause of the trouble or are there several? What are the potential lines of action which can be followed? At this point it is essential to be creative, whilst never losing sight of the factors previously deduced. Alternative courses of action need to be carefully assessed. Prior knowledge and comparative cases need to be taken into account. Teamwork and communication skills may again be of relevance in moving forward within an appropriate decision framework.

5 Assess

Having satisfactorily produced the alternative courses of action by assessing their relevance to the organisation and the principal players, groups and individuals within the situation, the objective is then to select the best action plan upon which to proceed. This is the time to reach conclusions, although they must always be realistic, reflecting the actual difficulties and complexities of the case. It may not be feasible to produce a perfect solution. Contravening factors must be taken into account and, if necessary, be explained at subsequent stages. Skills required at this stage include evaluative abilities, prioritisation and organisational awareness. It is now time to move forward to preparing for implementation.

6 Propose

As a result of previous endeavours the analysis of the case, whether on an individual or group basis, should be ready for the proposal of the implementation or action plan. This is the strategic phase of case analysis, requiring a range of skills. It is now essential to check back through the process engaged in, to ensure that nothing has been missed. It requires an awareness of each stage of the process, as well as reference to future problems which are likely to be faced at the implementation phase. Planning skills are of paramount importance, together with clarity of focus on issues and potential obstacles ahead. It is necessary to consider such factors as time-scales, costs, financial constraints and implications of change for differing groups and individuals.

7 Communicate

Having reached satisfactory conclusions on an individual or group basis it is important in many case study situations to communicate them to others. This may be on an assessed basis. The skills required here are very varied and a group or team may assist in ensuring that all can be fulfilled, as within the organisational domain itself. Quite frequently this will involve writing skills in the preparation of full or short reports on the outcome suggested. These will vary according to the case but students should always consider such factors as: setting the organisational context, defining the problem(s), suggesting the alternatives, focusing upon the potential solution, awareness of constraints, time-scales, cost etc. It may also be necessary to make an oral presentation, which will involve verbal skills and the preparation of supportive and visual material. This is likely to be time constrained, it may involve teamwork and overall must demonstrate a capacity for persuasiveness.

It is not always possible to proceed directly through the stages in a progressive manner, in particular it is necessary to revisit the steps in stages 1–4 of the model as often as required. Identification of causes and appropriate diagnosis are fundamental decision criteria. Unless the factors within the case are fully appreciated and defined it may prove difficult or impossible to continue to the stage of strategic intervention, leading to the implementation plan which will successfully treat the 'ailments' discussed in the case.

While the implementation process cannot be completed within a case study analysis, any final report or presentation should provide evidence of the reader's understanding of all issues involved, realistic assessment of possible courses of action and likely outcomes for the organisation. In this way it provides a direct contribution to organisational performance and effectiveness.

The development of skills or competencies requires further consideration. While this cannot be discussed in detail here, Fig. A demonstrates the association of personal development of learning styles and personal effectiveness potentially resulting in fulfilling organisational goals. The stages of skill development equate to models of learning and management development (Kolb *et al* 1984, Honey and Mumford 1992). They key well with phases of management development, proposing the necessity of immersion in the organisational experience, time for review and reflection, conceptualisation and drawing of conclusions, before planning the next steps in the case or situation to subsequently permit re-engagement individually and at organisational level in the organisational process.

USING THE BOOK

The book contains a collection of 27 case studies, which for convenience have been organised in four parts. This structure broadly follows the format of many HRM courses, although it should always be borne in mind whilst using the cases that dealing with HRM problems frequently requires a far more integrated approach. These are only 'soft' boundaries and there will always be interchange across them. It is essential that the reader is always aware of potential linkages in terms of interpretation of the case, procedures followed, implications arising and recommendations made for action and change.

A major theme underlying all the cases within the book is the focus upon change and development of the organisation, emphasising the strategic role of the HRM function in promoting effective management processes. This is fundamental to each part of the book:

1 Business strategy and effectiveness

The first part of the book presents a series of integrated cases which assess the context within which HR practices must operate. It relates to emergence of the recognition of HRM as a strategic force within organisations and the differences this implies from what used to be termed personnel practice. This is placed within the context of wider organisational goals. Questions raised include those relating to the nature and impact of the function approaches to organisational change, response to environmental pressures, new managerial roles and cultural imperatives.

2 Resourcing and reward

Resourcing the organisation has always been a major HRM role. It is essential that human resourcing requirements are dealt with appropriately, meeting the demands of the organisation, legislation and employee needs. This section addresses important areas for consideration, including recruitment, promotion, discrimination, absence control, reward and employee support programmes. It demonstrates current practice and assesses needs for the future.

3 Employee development

The development of employees is obviously essential to successful business strategy. This is even more essential when organisations are undergoing significant changes in respect of, for example, downsizing, service quality and the need for competitive advantage. The cases in this section consider the underlying issues and responses made. This involves the move towards skills- and competencies-based training, evaluation of training philosophies and programmes.

4 Employee relations

The employment relationship is obviously fundamental to the management of the organisation, dealing with the differing perspectives that various groupings hold. The final set of cases assesses the interaction of these stakeholder groups and the tensions evident as a result of their contrasting aims and interests. As the examples demonstrate, this can lead to dispute and even closure. They also show current changes in approach to employee relations in response to wider societal and government pressures.

The structure of the book also keys in closely with major text books in HRM, which are utilised for IPD Diploma and Masters level courses, permitting links to be made between the principal areas of study and potential case examples. The structure broadly relates to the text provided by Beardwell and Holden (1994), following issues of HRM and its organisational context, organisational resourcing, developing the human resource and the employment relationship. It was considered important to incorporate the international nature of HRM within all sections, encouraging students to consider similarities and differences in the treatment of organisational problems throughout. The cases could, however, be easily related to other leading texts, such as Torrington and Hall (1995). The cases presented here extend the short case synopses contained in the former book, whilst providing access to a recommended form of activity by the authors of the latter text.

Alternatively the case book may stand alone for in-house management development programmes or where instructors wish to base the learning experience on a case course. It can also be used in conjunction with varied readings in HRM, frequently employed at the Masters or MBA level.

The cases provide access to the investigation of a wide spectrum of current issues in HRM and are capable of interpretation at different levels by students at various career stages and with differing organisational involvement. This also permits flexibility in respect of time available to study the case and the selected mode of approach. While cases necessarily vary in respect of content and emphasis, they all provide relevant information for readers to look out for, covering the main dimensions of the situation described. This will include:

● The organisational context
● Background to the case
● Explanation of the situation(s) forming the basis of the case
● Definition of the problem(s) or issue(s) involved
● Information relating to principal actors or groups
● Relevant material to support the reader's interpretation
● Recommended reading in respect of HRM frameworks arising from the case
● A suggested activity brief.

RECOMMENDED READING

Beardwell, I and Holden, L (eds) (1994) *Human Resource Management. A Contemporary Perspective*, London, Pitman.

Constable, J and McCormick, R (1987) *The Manning of British Managers*, London, Institute of Management.

Easton, G (1992) *Learning From Case Studies* (2nd edn), London, Prentice Hall.

Handy, C (1987) *The Making of Managers. Report on Management Education, Training and Development in the United States, West Germany, France, Japan and the UK*, London, NEDO.

Handy, C (1993) *Understanding Organisations*, Harmondsworth, Penguin.

Honey, P and Mumford, A (1992) *Manual of Learning Styles*, Maidenhead, Peter Honey Publications.

Huczynski, A (1983) *Encyclopaedia of Management Development Methods*, Aldershot, Gower.

Kolb, DA, Rubin, IM and McIntyre, JM (1984) *Organizational Psychology: An Experiential Approach* (4th edn), New York, Prentice Hall.

Masoner, M (1988) *An Audit of the Case Study Method*, New York, Praeger.

Reynolds, JI (1980) *Case Method in Management Development*, Geneva, International Labour Office.

Torrington, D and Hall L (1995) *Personnel Management. HRM in Action* (3rd edn), London, Prentice Hall.

Tyson, S and Kakabadse, A (1987) *Case Studies in Human Resource Management*, London, Heinemann.

PART 1

Business Strategy and Effectiveness

It is appropriate that the first case in the book focuses upon the impact of HRM practice in developing effective change processes. In addressing the question 'Organisational change and human resource management: progress to date?', Graeme Martin and Phil Beaumont assess models of change, particularly the ongoing debate regarding organisation-wide, top-down initiatives, compared to more decentralised, incremental approaches.

In 'Life after downsizing at Galenco Healthcare Materials: managing change in a difficult climate', Paul Sparrow examines major responses to financial and commercial pressures. For this particular company this involves structural reorganisation, downsizing and management review in an attempt to develop a service and quality culture.

A topical UK experience is described by Laura Hall in 'Emerging management roles in Westbank Health Centre', which is based upon the journey from a traditional doctor's practice to a fundholding health centre managed as a business. The progress of the business plan introduced is directly linked to the new post of Practice Director, responsible for HR strategy, as well as the newly identified managerial role of the GPs.

'IFI-AUTO' by Thierry Picq deals with the revolution of the Executive Board of a French automobile parts manufacturer, responding to shareholder dissatisfaction regarding their efficiency in maintaining profit and facing competition from Asia. The case underlines the numerous factors which contribute to management quality at the individual, collective, cultural and organisational levels.

A frequent change faced by organisations in attaining effectiveness revolves around the introduction of new technology. In 'First International Bank: the design and introduction of new office technology', Pat Hornby reviews the need for and implementation of a new operating system aimed to improve productivity and avoid the consequences of departmental closure.

The introduction of Compulsory Competitive Tendering (CCT) and public policy initiatives towards customer awareness and quality provision form the basis of 'Adding value to service provision in the public sector'. Sue Shaw and Colin Fielding utilise the experience of a metropolitan authority to demonstrate how this operated as a catalyst for re-evaluating the central HR function.

The final case, 'A re-managed heart in retail change' by Danusia Malina and Paul Brook, represents an original treatment of the experience of change. Within the context of rapid change in a multiple food retail chain, we learn of the internal dilemmas, actions and uncertainties of a Customer Services Manager.

Organisational change and human resource management: progress to date?

Graeme Martin and Phil Beaumont

INTRODUCTION

The 'organisational culture' metaphor has been of growing importance in illuminating the processes of organisational change (Morgan 1986, Brown 1995), although it is not without its critics (*see*, for example, Anthony 1993). The increased popularity of this perspective has had two major effects. First, there has been an enhanced recognition of the fact that the processes of organisational change involve much more than simply changing formal organisational structures; and second, changes in human resource management practices (HRM) have almost invariably been an important dimension of the change programme.

BACKGROUND TO THE CASE

The latter development, however, has not been without its controversies and debates. Initially, attempts to produce organisational 'turnaround' via a new or changed set of HRM practices produced considerable debate regarding what were the individually most powerful levers of change, and in what particular order or sequence they should be used for maximum effectiveness. For example, were changes in compensation/reward practices a more powerful source of change compared to replacement and promotion within the ranks of management (Beaumont 1993, pp 50–1)?

More recently, this debate has entered a new phase, with important questions being asked about the overall approach to or model of the change process. The traditional model of change consisted of the following key elements:

- one sought to change the whole organisation;
- the process was top-down and led by senior management;
- the process involved three, distinct sequential stages: unfreezing, change, and refreezing; and
- a key underlying assumption was the belief that attitude change drove behavioural change.

Increasingly, however, important questions have been raised about the effectiveness of change programmes along these lines. For example, in a widely cited study, three American researchers argued as follows (Beer, Eisenstat and Spector 1990, p 159):

> Most change programs don't work because they are guided by a theory of change that is fundamentally flawed. The common belief is that the place to begin is with the knowledge and attitudes of individuals. Changes in attitudes, the theory goes, lead to changes in individual behaviour. And changes in individual behaviour, repeated by many people, will result in organisational change. According to this model, change is like a conversion experience. Once people 'get religion', changes in their behaviour will surely follow.

According to these researchers, successful organisational change requires a fundamentally different model, namely a much more decentralised, incremental process of change which begins with (and then spreads out from) change initially based in new, small and isolated parts of the organisation which have good potential market prospects and where some naturally occurring change is already underway. A complementary set of ideas emphasises the need for the development of 'learning organisations', which are essentially programmes for continuous rather than 'one-off' change and which place organisational and individual learning at the heart of the change process. According to Pedler and his colleagues, the learning organisation or company is one which facilitates the learning of all of its members and continually transforms itself (Pedler *et al*, 1991). In short, a wholly new approach to organisational change, involving new assumptions, stages and processes, is advocated by both of these groups and researchers.

However, many individuals remain wedded to a more conventional approach to change. This may be because they are committed both by their values and positions to the central tenets of the traditional change model (i.e. focus on the organisation as a whole, senior management-led, and stress on the need for attitude change), although they acknowledge that effective change does not always result. Their explanations for this outcome are more likely to emphasise certain management errors in the change process, rather than shortcomings in the model itself (Dawson 1994). These errors may derive from a variety of sources: too much is attempted too quickly; certain issues do not receive the priority attention which their importance warrants; steps are missed out; the influence of organisational politics, etc. In Table 1.1 we list some researchers' views of the necessary elements of a successful change process which frequently do not receive the management attention they warrant.

This short discussion has highlighted two points. First, many organisations remain committed to the traditional type of change model, and second, in many of these organisations effective and sustained change does not result from the change programme. What remains unclear, however, is the reason for the latter result. Is it because the basic approach or model is inherently flawed, as Beer and his colleagues have argued, or is it that the potential of the model has not been realised through a poor implementation process in which mistakes are made or steps missed out?

The present case study should be seen in the context of this important, ongoing debate over models of change and the role of HRM. The material presented falls into three parts. First, the organisation and its strategy is described. Second, the aims and methods of the change programme are introduced. And third, some evidence of the impact of the programme of change is presented. Readers are then invited to act as consultants to the organisation with a view to identifying the reasons underlying the results of a change audit undertaken two years after the change programme began, and providing some advice to the organisation concerning 'where next?'.

Table 1.1 Factors facilitating successful organisational change

- A receptive context for change together with the managerial ability to create the climate for change

- Establishing a sense of urgency by creating the necessary level of tension within the organisation for change and assembling a powerful group of individuals to lead the change

- Creating a vision which, though it may be imprecise, should nevertheless help direct the change effort

- Using all possible means to communicate the vision deep into the organisation and ensuring that managers 'walk the talk' to demonstrate the new kinds of behaviours

- Empowering others to act by removing structural blockages to change and encouraging risk taking and non-traditional ideas and activities

- Using 'deviants and heretics' to critically evaluate existing practices and bring in fresh ideas

- Planning for and creating short-term wins to encourage long-term persistence with the change initiatives

- Reinforcing changes in culture through changes in structure and changes in reward systems

- Finally, being patient and persistent as major changes in culture and structure may take many years to bring about.

Sources: Pettigrew, AM (1990) 'Is corporate culture manageable?' in Wilson, DC and Rosenfeld, RH, *Managing Organizations; Text, Readings and Cases,* London, McGraw–Hill. Kotter, JP (1995) 'Leading change: why transformation efforts fail', *Harvard Business Review*, Mar–Apr, p 61.

THE LOCAL AUTHORITY: THE LEADERSHIP PLAN

Early in 1993 our medium-sized Scottish local authority (which we refer to as 'the Council') embarked on a large-scale cultural change programme, which involved changes in leadership styles and the introduction of HRM practices such as briefing groups, quality circles and teamworking arrangements, designed to bring about a 'listening culture' which involved a greater organisational sensitivity and response to the users of the Council's services. The Council employs just over 3,000 people in the city, making it one of the largest employers in the region. It is organised on the principles of semi-autonomous divisions, each with its own director; in addition there are a number of departments that provide central services (e.g. personnel, finance, IT). Union density in all divisions is high, with manual workers belonging to the TGWU and GMB, and white collar workers belonging to Unison. National-level collective bargaining operates for all divisions, with COSLA (the Scottish Local Authorities Employers' Association) being heavily involved. Table 1.2 provides some more detailed information concerning employment numbers throughout the Council.

This programme was portrayed in the Council's published literature as a direct response to the larger economic problems of the area which involved a declining population base (197,000 in 1971 to 172,000 in 1992), a substantial decline in manufacturing employment, a relatively high rate of long-term unemployment and a relatively low rate of new firm formation. However, two other influences were also important. The first was

Table 1.2 Structure and employment numbers at the Council

1 *Central support services*
- Administration (149)
- Chief Executive's office (26)
- Finance and computing (96)
- Personnel (20)
- Management services (17)

2 *Divisions*
- Housing (5250)
- Cleansing (9467)*
- Public works (646)*
- Architects, planning and quantity surveying (154)
- Economic development (81)
- Libraries, art and museums (247)
- Leisure and recreation (233)
- Parks (316)*
- Chief engineers (49)
- Environmental health (16)

* These are the major divisions employing manual workers which have been subdivided into client and contractor (DSO) departments.

connected with the reorganisation of local government and the moves towards unitary authorities in Scotland during 1995–6. The region had previously been served by three district authorities and a regional authority. Legislative changes introduced in the early 1990s, together with a subsequent decision taken by the Scottish Office, set out to reduce these four authorities to three by 1995–6. This reorganisation inevitably resulted in competition between the existing authorities in the region for both power and jobs over the period leading up to 1995–6. The Council's new Chief Executive introduced the change programme in 1992 on the basis that not only would it improve existing organisational arrangements which were not thought to be sufficiently customer-oriented, but that it would also place the Council in a much better position in the eyes of the Scottish Office. The new Council, it was hoped, would act as a pacesetter and role model for the others and, in doing so, would enhance the career prospects of the staff whose jobs were threatened by the reorganisation. The second additional influence was legislation extending 'privatisation' to local authorities, particularly the Local Government Act of 1988 that required local authorities to put many of their services out to public tender (CCT). This had the effect of opening up services which they had previously had under direct control to competition with private sector organisations and also of creating separate divisions within local authorities between those who acted in a client role and those who acted as a contractor. Thus large employing divisions like the parks department and housing department (*see* Table 1.2) were split into a client subdivision and a contracting subdivision (a DSO or Direct Service Organisation).

To meet these challenges, the administration of the Council developed a broad vision or mission statement to 'put the heart back into the city'; the tangible steps along these lines included advance factory building, housing and environmental improvements. Within the larger context of this strategic response ('the Leadership Plan') the Council specifically committed itself to (i) maintaining the Council's record in winning CCT contracts, (ii) improving the Council's accessibility and responsiveness via effective communication with citizens and service users, and (iii) 'ensuring that the Council lives up to its mission and values established in the Leadership Plan'.

The Leadership Plan, which was formally launched in March 1992, set out the mission and values framework identified by the Council as a core element of its vision to create 'a strong and vibrant regional centre which attracts and retains people' (*see* Table 1.3 for further details). The leadership strategy, which was developed by a group of officials with the assistance of a management consultant, had the following objectives:

● change from a talking and blame culture to a listening culture;
● introduce a corporate planning system;
● introduce performance measures;
● introduce policies and systems reviews to involve the elected members, employees and citizens.

There was a great deal of emphasis in the Leadership Plan on the importance of HRM and the need to change the 'people culture' with particular emphasis being placed on communication/common language and consistency.

Table 1.3 The Council's mission and values statement

Mission
'We shall lead the way to new horizons for the city of . . ., where the quality of life makes people proud to stay.'

Values

1 *Communications*
   ● We value openness, honesty and understanding in all our communications.
   ● We recognise communication as a positive two-way process which is sensitive and responsive to the views of others.

2 *Change*
   ● We value innovation and recognise the need for continuous improvement.
   ● We recognise that our actions affect others and we value their right to consultation.

3 *Organisation*
   ● The Council values the culture of a caring, listening, developing organisation which adapts to change.
   ● We value the acceptance of authority and responsibility at every level.

4 *Recognition*
   ● We value the recognition of achievement.

5 *People*
   ● We will show respect and consideration for everyone and the environment in which we live.
   ● We value the attainment of fairness, dignity and equality.

6 *Individual*
   ● We value the development of individuals and will support them in reaching their full potential.
   ● We value individuals' knowledge of what is expected of them and their freedom to discuss ideas and views.

7 *Team*
   ● We believe we can only achieve our goals for the city through teamwork.
   ● We value team-building and the fostering of loyalty.

8 *Mission and values*
   ● We value our mission which puts the people of the city at the heart of our actions on which we will be judged.

THE ORGANISATION CHANGE PROGRAMME

The first step here was the development of a heuristic framework of key competencies (the mission and values wheel; *see* Table 1.3) to identify, develop and assess attitudinal and behavioural changes in management and staff throughout the organisation. Using the services of the management consultants, a benchmark survey was undertaken in the period December 1992 to March 1993. This benchmark questionnaire was issued to all Council staff/employees and was designed to evaluate the extent to which staff/employees identified with the Council's mission, and how they felt about existing organisation problems, internal communications, individual development opportunities and training, and the way people were treated, managed and recognised. The response rate to this initial survey was some 42 per cent. Furthermore, a 'leadership working party', consisting of the nine Chief Officers and chaired by the Head of Corporate Planning, was established to steer and progress the programme. The basic aims here were to maximise external publicity and internal involvement in the programmes. To these ends a series of public, corporate and departmental launches were held over time involving presentations, the distribution of documentation and question/answer sessions.

The second step in the change programme involved a variety of policy/practice initiatives concentrated in the two-year period from March 1993 to March 1995. These were essentially as follows:

1 *'Delayering'*. A policy decision was taken to ensure that there were no more than five levels of management between the Chief Executive Officer (CEO) and employees. This involved 'stripping out' between one and three layers of management in all divisions dependent on their size. The delayering has been achieved through non-replacement of managers as they left or retired rather than through compulsory redundancies.

2 *Business planning*. This was introduced into all divisions of the Council with each department within the divisions required to produce an annual Action Plan. These were to be linked to the five-year corporate planning framework. All Chief Officers attended full-day workshops on each of the following: leadership, mission and values, business (or leadership) planning, and performance indicators.

3 *Training and development*. Over 700 managers and team leaders attended a series of seminars on 'action-centred leadership' (three days); 'communication and delegation' (two days); 'problem solving' and 'time management' (one day each).

4 *Team briefing and teamworking*. Team briefing was introduced into all major divisions, and each department was encouraged, with the help of facilitators, to develop high-performance work teams which would involve empowering staff at all levels.

5 *Leadership improvement proposals*. A major programme of employee empowerment was introduced through an elaborate structure for encouraging improvement proposals. These arrangements involved employees being able to make job-specific, divisional or organisation-wide suggestions which would be either implemented immediately or passed on to higher levels of management for consideration. This approach was to be assisted by departmental facilitators and a Leadership Improvement Proposal Steering Group. Targets were set for the programme with the aim being to have each employee on average submitting two proposals per year by 1995–6.

Finally, it is worth noting what the change programmes did *not* involve. Changes in reward/compensation arrangements were absent from the programme, and the degree of change in organisational structures was very limited, at least, beyond that of 'delayering' (*see* Eccles 1994, pp 204–17).

In summary, we have a large-scale, though fairly conventional organisational change programme of the corporate-wide, senior management-led, attitude-change type. The question then becomes, what has been its impact? The initial leadership strategy document had undertaken to audit the changes every two years, and in 1994 the first such assessment was undertaken.

THE ASSESSMENT EXERCISE: KEY FINDINGS

The key findings presented here arise from the staff/employee audit undertaken in late 1994. In considering the findings presented, the following points should be noted.

● This assessment was undertaken by a group of academics, rather than the original management consultants involved in the change programme.
● The questionnaire developed by the academics included many of the same questions used in the original (1992) benchmarking survey so that comparisons over time could be made. However, some additional questions (mainly biographical ones) were included, in order to facilitate examination of any revealed differences across the workforce as a whole (*see* Table 1.5).
● The response rate to the questionnaire in 1994 was 64 per cent (compared to the 42 per cent in the original benchmark survey) although this varied considerably between divisions. In general, a low response rate came from the manual-dominated divisions (e.g. public works 30 per cent, parks 55 per cent), with much higher return rates coming from the white-collar divisions (e.g. housing 78 per cent, planning 80 per cent).

For reasons of space, the full set of tabulated responses to all the questions asked cannot be presented here. However, some of the key findings obtained *for the Council as a whole* are set out in Table 1.4.

In considering the significance and implications of these findings it is worth noting the following observation (Goodman and Dean 1982, p 229):

> An act is not all or nothing; it may vary in terms of its persistence, the number of people in the social system performing the act, and the degree to which it exists as a social fact. The problem in some of the current literature on change is the use of the words *success* or *failure*. This language clouds the crucial issue of representing and explaining degrees or levels of institutionalisation. Most of the organisational cases we have reviewed cannot be described by simple labels of success or failure. Rather we find various degrees of institutionalisation.

In interpreting the results of *any* employee attitude survey there are a number of points which should be borne in mind (Beaumont 1993, pp 165–74). First, such a research instrument can, by definition, produce only a snapshot involving a single-point-in-time set of results. Second, complex, multi-dimensional constructs cannot be probed in any in-depth, qualitative fashion. Third, the overall levels of satisfaction obtained are particularly sensitive to the precise wording of individual questions. And finally, there is likely to be considerable variation in the answers between different parts of the workforce. In general, for instance, women workers and older workers report relatively higher levels of satisfaction – a result which has been attributed to their (lower) levels of expectation. Such variation was certainly a feature of this survey, with some key findings being reported in Table 1.5.

Table 1.4 Assessment of the change programme: some key findings (workforce as a whole)

1 *Overall job satisfaction*

The overall level of satisfaction ranged between 75 per cent and 63 per cent (depending on the particular question answered).

2 *Organisational commitment*

The levels of identification, involvement and loyalty appeared relatively high. For example, 60 per cent articulated an active pride in the Council, only 14 per cent would not recommend a friend to work for the Council, and 77 per cent agreed with the statement that 'In my work, I like to feel I am making some effort not just for myself but for the Council as well'.

3 *Leadership improvement programme*

Eighty-eight per cent of staff were aware of the programme, 41 per cent claimed to have made suggestions for improvement, although only 30 per cent felt that the scheme had been a major factor in encouraging them to make suggestions.

4 *Recognition of achievement*

In general staff/employees felt that their views were listened to and their achievements recognised by supervisors and managers, but not by senior management.

5 *Change and innovation*

In general, employee satisfaction with the level of consultation, communication, encouragement of new ideas and ability to question decisions has, if anything, declined over time.

6 *Teamworking*

Perceptions concerning effective teamworking reveal a decline over time, with little sense of team spirit between managers and workers in departments being reported.

7 *Individual development*

The growth in the content and quality of training is noted and approved of, although dissatisfaction exists concerning longer-term career development and the performance of managers as coaches.

8 *Communication*

Compared to the benchmark surveys, no significant improvement in information flows within departments are reported, and managers are not seen as being more approachable than before.

9 *Mission*

There was no apparent improvement in perceptions concerning the extent to which colleagues and managers understand and act out the mission of the Council.

Table 1.5 Variation in responses within the workforce: some key findings

1   Older staff, senior managers and employees in professional grades were more likely to be imbued with a sense of mission, feel that the public have a positive image of the Council and believe that their department actively listens to feedback from customers.

2   Manual employees in unpromoted posts had significantly more negative perceptions concerning the effectiveness of departmental and interdepartmental communications.

3   Senior managers and professional employees had significantly more positive views of the extent to which new ideas were encouraged.

4   Male workers were more likely to adopt 'extreme' views concerning the recognition of achievement than female workers; this was a general tendency throughout the questionnaire.

5   Improvement suggestions were less likely to have been made by male workers, manual workers and employees in unpromoted posts.

6   The large DSOs employing mainly manual workers whose jobs were dependent on securing contacts in competition with the private sector usually exhibited lower levels of satisfaction than divisions which were mainly staffed by professionals such as art galleries and museums and the architects department.

The contents of Table 1.5 generally suggest that the change programme has most positively impacted on the already 'converted' or the most easily converted groups of employees. In short, the results suggest that the notions of a 'management culture' and an 'organisational culture' are not one and the same thing (Anthony 1993).

THE CURRENT STATE OF PLAY

The material set out in Tables 1.4 and 1.5 was fed back by the academics, albeit in much greater detail than here, to the Council in early 1995. The Leadership Strategy Group of the Council then considered two options. One was to use the Council's usual internal communications media (the staff newsletter and briefing groups) to convey the results and findings back to staff/employees. The other option was to use a more 'specialised' survey feedback approach seeking possible responses and suggestions at the individual departmental level.

ACTIVITY BRIEF

The Council has asked you to act as a consultant to review progress to date.

1 The Council asks you to consider the value of an employee attitude survey as an instrument for assessing the effectiveness of the change programme?

2 The Council asks whether you feel that the change programme has been successful or not? Particular attention should be given to the criteria involved and the time-scale. The quoted observation of Goodman and Dean may be instructive in this regard.

3 You are then asked to review the steps involved in the introduction and implementation of the programme, with a view to identifying any possible errors or weaknesses. (The contents of Table 1.1 may be useful in this regard.)

4 We ended the case with the two options facing the Council. Which approach would you recommend they use, and why?

5 Taking a longer-run perspective, what recommendations would you make concerning 'where next' for the Council? Here you might wish to consider the ideas of Beer and his colleagues or those advocated by the proponents of learning organisations.

RECOMMENDED READING

Anthony, P (1993) *Managing Culture*, Milton Keynes, Open University Press.

Beaumont, PB (1993) *Human Resource Management: Key Concepts and Skills*, London, Sage.

Beer, M, Eisenstat, RA and Spector, B (1990) 'Why change programs don't produce change', *Harvard Business Review*, Nov–Dec.

Brown, A (1995) *Organisational Culture*, London, Pitman.

Dawson, P (1994) *Organisational Change: A Processional Approach*, London, Paul Chapman.

Eccles, T (1994) *Succeeding with Change*, London, McGraw–Hill.

Goodman, PS and Dean, JW (1982) 'Creating long-term organisational change' in PS Goodman and Associates, *Change in Organisations*, San Francisco, Jossey Bass.

Hendry, C (1995) *Human Resource Management: A Strategic Approach to Employment*, Oxford, Butterworth–Heinemann.

IDS Study No. 462 (1990) *Employee Attitude Surveys*, July.

Kotter, JP (1995) 'Leading change: why transformation efforts fail', *Harvard Business Review*, Mar–Apr.

Leach, S, Stewart, J and Walsh, K (1994) *The Changing Organisation and Management of Local Government*, Basingstoke, Macmillan.

Morgan, G (1986) *Images of Organization*, London, Sage.

Pedler, M, Burgoyne, J and Boydell, T (1991) *The Learning Company*, London, McGraw–Hill.

Pettigrew, AM (1990) 'Is corporate culture manageable?' in Wilson, DC and Rosenfield, RH, *Managing Organizations; Text, Readings and Cases*, London, McGraw–Hill.

Wilson, DC (1992) *A Strategy of Change*, London, Routledge.

Life after downsizing at Galenco Healthcare Materials: managing change in a difficult climate

Paul R Sparrow

INTRODUCTION

Galenco Healthcare Materials Ltd has recently experienced a major corporate reorganisation and downsizing. Financial and commercial pressures forced it to refocus on its core activities. A two-stage change process has been embarked upon. The first phase was intended to consolidate the new strategy. A much flatter management structure has been introduced and several supervisory layers abolished. It has introduced a major review and re-evaluation of its management talent in an attempt to change the organisation culture. This has focused around a mission and values culture change programme at management level and an assessment centre to select surviving managers. The second phase of the change process, planned to start in three months, is intended to facilitate growth and develop a stronger customer service and total quality focus. As the time for phase two of the change process approaches, key members of the organisation are involved in a review meeting to judge the potential of the organisation for further changes and to recommend how best to implement a second phase of the change programme.

BACKGROUND TO THE CASE

Galenco Healthcare Materials Ltd is a division of the worldwide medical products group of Galenco plc. The worldwide group operates in 26 countries and has sales in over 90 countries. Last year it made after-tax profits of £100 million on turnover of £840 million. Over the last five years the group has been concentrating on its core businesses in medical products and divesting businesses that do not fit within this portfolio.

Galenco Healthcare Materials Ltd is one of 16 recently formed divisions within the group. It has been identified by the group as one of its poorer performing divisions. It is managed at arms length but is subject to tight financial controls. It produces three major medical products. More than 50 per cent of its components are sold to the Galenco parent group. The industry has recently come under immense competitive pressure. Product cycles are getting shorter, high technology products are increasingly substituting Healthcare Materials' woven products and competition from the Far East (mainly Taiwan, Hong Kong and South Korea) has reduced profit margins to very low levels. For years the industry has seen a steady movement of productive capacity to low-cost countries, seeing the closure of many British mills and factories and drastic cuts in employment. Similar strategies have been pursued by both German and US competitors, who have concentrated production on niche markets in advanced medical fibre markets. Customers in these markets tend to develop long-term and strategic relationships with their suppliers and are driven more by quality and service considerations, rather than just price.

Four years ago Galenco Textiles – as it was then known – operated in five businesses: medical textiles, surgical dressings, knitting and denim, coloured woven products and synthetic fibres. At that time it employed 2500 people. The Textile Division had been managed very traditionally. The structure was hierarchical, relationships and communication were formal and driven top down, workers were closely supervised and the management style was authoritarian. The company had a family atmosphere with several generations of local families being employed there. Managers were production driven with little concern for broader business imperatives. They tended to have worked their way up from the shopfloor. The main criterion for promotion was technical competence. Man-management and strategic skills were not considered essential. Three years ago the coloured woven products and synthetic fibres businesses were sold off, with the loss of around 600 jobs. Other businesses began a long process of rationalisation as sites were closed and costs reduced. Two years ago the overall headcount had fallen to 1300 employees.

There have been six Managing Directors of Galenco Healthcare Materials in ten years. The latest is Mark Henderson, who was appointed 18 months ago. He convinced the Group Board that there was still potential in the business. Together with the Group Chairman and his Divisional Controllers he ironed out a survival strategy. The first phase of this change programme has now largely been implemented. The mission statement of Galenco Healthcare Materials is

'... to be a leading expert provider of fabric and fleece components and products to enhance healing and patient care throughout the world. Through innovation, quality and customer service we will achieve lasting profitability, growth and strategic advantage for Galenco.'

THE GALENCO HEALTHCARE CASE

Phase One of the change process

John Reid was a consultant with Vista Consultants. He recalled his first meeting with Mark Henderson a year ago. The headquarters was sited in a grand old building that used to be a mill. A large double staircase swept up to the first floor, with one side used for going up and one side for going down. When he had entered the Managing Director's office, Mark Henderson smiled at him and asked:

'Did you notice anything unusual about the carpet on the staircase, John? No? Well, on your way out you will notice that the left hand side is very worn but the right hand side is pristine new. I couldn't figure it out until I heard an old story. There used to be a rule here called 'walking on the left'. Only very senior managers above a certain grade could walk down the corridors on the right – because they had the important jobs and needed to scurry about! Now no one has talked about that rule for 30 years, but the carpets tell another story. We have history to contend with. We have problems. This will be no easy task.'

How right he had been. The mission statement seemed far removed from the data they were looking at now. In preparation for his meeting with Mark, John had reviewed the last 18 months which had seen a raft of initiatives within the organisation. The survival strategy had involved the following main elements, which had collectively been combined into what was called Phase One of the change process.

The first change had been a return to core business. The company changed its name from Galenco Textiles to Healthcare Materials. It stopped cotton and yarn spinning and weaving and withdrew from commodity textiles products such as denim manufacture. A new division was established around Healthcare Materials' products and six profit centres that focused on surgical dressing, bandaging, medical and consumer wool products and new healthcare materials were set up.

The second change involved the introduction of new technology. A £6 million investment programme was agreed. Shuttleless looms were being slowly introduced into the production process to improve productivity and quality levels. Automation meant that more employees needed strong cognitive and problem-solving skills. In future the change process would increasingly be driven by the new technical processes and the improvements to productivity and quality that they would bring.

As a consequence of the rationalisation and automation, a year ago the total workforce was reduced from 1211 to 750 employees. Sales per employee were £41,000 before the rationalisation. A further phased headcount reduction to 650 employees will be necessary once the last production processes have been relocated. The target is to reach sales per employee of £90,000 in five years time.

A new organisation structure had been put in place. The four old businesses were rolled into one structure based on functional lines. The new Healthcare Materials Division was run by a Divisional Management Executive comprising the Managing Director, two Divisional Controllers and six profit centre General Managers (*see* Figure 2.1). Below them there was to be a management population of 80 people. The hierarchy had been reduced from seven to four layers.

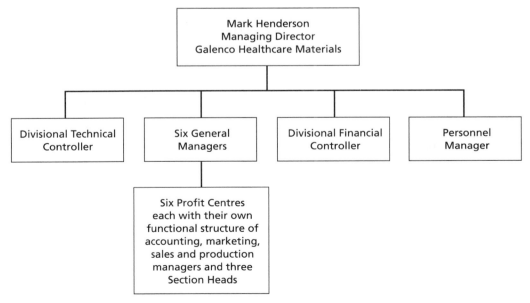

Fig 2.1 Management structure at Galenco Healthcare Materials

The management population therefore had to be reduced from around 160 managers to 80. John had been asked to help out with this downsizing. Mark Henderson had confided in him that under the old regime the 'blue-eyed boys and girls would have been selected. We need something that will treat people fairly and professionally, but will also kick start a culture change process'. Galenco Healthcare Materials wanted to select staff who were adaptable to change and could respond positively to the increased uncertainty of their work environment. Vista Consultants had been brought in to help manage the implementation programme. They had designed an assessment centre for which all 160 managers could volunteer. There were only 80 'positions in the new structure' (rather than pre-determined jobs) available. A set of competencies that were needed to manage the new business were identified. Psychometric testing, work simulations and interviews were used to assess these competencies. The process was run by the new Divisional Management Executive in conjunction with the Personnel Manager and the external consultants. It had been expected that the assessment centre would lead to some difficult selection decisions. To be sure, there would be some incompetent people, but they had to select the best 80 out of 160 people. The reality had been very different (*see* Table 2.1). First, only 96 managers volunteered to go through the process. 64 managers decided this was not for them and accepted redundancy terms without applying for a new position. Second, even by stretching the pass criteria Galenco had managed to appoint only 52 of its own managers out of the 96 who volunteered for the assessment centre.

Table 2.1 Summary results of the assessment centre used to select the final 80 managers

Competency	Management Group	Score in assessment centre					
		1	2	3	4	5	6
Analysis	New recruits	0	0	0	8	11	9
	Surviving managers	0	0	0	18	30	12
Decision making	New recruits	0	0	0	9	12	7
	Surviving managers	0	0	12	15	21	4
Creativity and innovation	New recruits	0	0	0	10	11	7
	Surviving managers	0	0	14	25	9	4
Planning and organising	New recruits	0	0	0	9	17	2
	Surviving managers	0	0	0	17	32	3
Leadership	New recruits	0	0	0	18	5	5
	Surviving managers	0	14	30	6	2	0
Influence	New recruits	0	0	0	16	6	6
	Surviving managers	0	11	29	6	6	0
Team-building	New recruits	0	0	1	14	10	3
	Surviving managers	0	0	14	21	17	0
Communication	New recruits	0	0	5	7	11	5
	Surviving managers	0	4	11	32	5	0
Adaptability	New recruits	0	0	3	8	11	6
	Surviving managers	0	0	15	15	8	4
Customer focus	New recruits	0	0	0	9	10	9
	Surviving managers	0	0	4	28	14	6

NB Managers were scored against a six point scale for each competency (1=poor to 6=excellent). The numbers against each score represent the number of managers who achieved that score. There were 52 surviving managers and 28 new recruits.

Galenco had to go outside the company to recruit another 28 managers, who were also put through the same assessment centres and passed. The new managers had been recruited from key competitors. They were very able and all had experience of total quality management processes. Many of these managers were still joining the company at present. Eventually around 35 per cent of the new management structure would be outsiders.

Partly as a consequence of the findings from the assessment centres, a culture change programme called 'Pride, Mission and Values' was introduced amongst the surviving 80 managers. This involved formal top team-building exercises, analyses of the underlying values of the Division and planning sessions to convert these values into actions. The new culture emphasised flexibility, empowerment, quality and innovation (*see* Table 2.2). Galenco wanted to develop a more participative leadership style amongst their managers. Some of the key features they wanted to develop were confidence and trust in subordinates, listening to subordinates whilst controlling decision making, motivating through reward, involvement and incentives, and using staff ideas and opinions constructively. Most importantly, they wanted to re-instil a sense of pride and assure staff and managers that there was a survivable future.

Table 2.2 The values and behaviours statement accompanying the pride, mission and values culture change programme

Showing commercial awareness

We value employees who are knowledgeable about business performance and who think commercially, by . . .
- communicating the overall business strategy to enable all employees to understand company goals
- trusting people with commercially sensitive information
- sharing information on performance and expecting all employees to understand the contribution their part of the business makes
- developing financial understanding in all employees
- communicating quality issues to everyone involved
- minimising waste in all aspects of the business

Driving for results

We value high achievement and the ability to overcome obstacles and constraints, by . . .
- communicating a clear purpose from the top throughout the organisation
- setting clear and challenging objectives for individuals and teams, monitoring and measuring results and providing regular feedback
- providing determined and enthusiastic leadership, by influencing rather than controlling others
- encouraging high personal standards of performance and providing an example to others
- enjoying change and variety, seeing problems as challenges and opportunities for improvement
- recognising and praising achievement

Satisfying customer needs

We respect the right of our customers to expect high and increasing standards of performance and value employees who put their customers first, by . . .
- putting the requirements of our customers and users first and overcoming any internal obstacles or barriers
- anticipating and seeking out customer and user requirements and responding enthusiastically to change

Table 2.2 continued

- trying to surpass customer expectations of us, and making extra efforts to do so
- working to get it right first time, every time
- recognising and supporting our customer-facing colleagues
- developing and enhancing customer-facing systems

Maximising teamworking

We value the team player and teamworking more than individual results, by . . .
- knowing who our internal 'customers' are and working closely with them
- working across boundaries and taking a cross-functional approach when solving problems
- respecting the expertise and strengths of others and giving positive feedback on contributions made
- giving support to team and project leaders, regardless of status or position
- networking across the Group, sharing ideas for mutual benefit
- communicating both vertically and horizontally, valuing two-way dialogue

Creating technical excellence

We base our competitive advantage on the excellence of our products and processes and the quality of our people, by . . .
- being relentless in our pursuit of product quality and focusing on continuous improvement at all times
- respecting the technical expertise of others and sharing product and process problems with colleagues
- seeking customer feedback and responding quickly to their needs
- investing valuable resources in research and development and communicating this to all employees
- demonstrating our technical leadership and justifying the respect of others within the Group and externally

Encouraging innovation and initiative

We value new ideas, initiative and continued challenge to the status quo, by . . .
- pushing for ever-higher standards through continuous improvement in performance
- trying to work 'smarter rather than harder' to improve our performance, and developing systems which help us
- combining consistency of approach with the adaptability to exploit opportunities
- accepting responsibility for our actions and learning from our mistakes
- not allowing status or position to inhibit our contribution to problem solving
- encouraging fresh ideas and challenge from everyone

Developing individual talents

We value the potential of all employees and the contribution each can make to our business success, by . . .
- actively managing individual performance and stretching people's abilities
- pushing decision making down the organisation whenever possible and offering management support rather than direction
- being committed to personal development, establishing and managing career aspirations and preparing successors for all key roles
- developing people by extending their performance in their current job and encouraging them to take a broad view of their potential contribution

Table 2.2 continued

- expecting people to take responsibility for progressing their own development, making best use of available Company resources
- trusting each other to give of our best at all times and acting as a 'role model' for others

Taking pride in our performance

We value high self-esteem and personal confidence people gain from working for the company, by . . .
- meeting the high personal and ethical standards expected of us
- taking pride in telling people about our products and performance
- being proud to be the 'best' at what we do, but never complacent
- giving extra effort willingly when called for
- having a passion for quality in everything we do and continuously seeking further improvement
- taking genuine pleasure in the achievements of our colleagues and our company

Finally, a top-down communication process using monthly team briefings had been introduced to inform employees of progress. These were run mainly by the Section Heads. A divisional newspaper had also been introduced to communicate the nature of changes taking place.

The planning meeting for Phase Two of the change process

Phase One of the change process had been all about ensuring survival and introducing a degree of stability. Despite what had been achieved by these changes there was no getting away from the fact that the financial situation was still precarious. The Group target was a return on capital employed (ROCE) of 20 per cent. This was a key metric and the new division was currently only providing a ROCE of 4 per cent. Current sales were £47 million, but were running at about £1 million less than the survival plan had estimated. Nevertheless, profits of £1.8 million were now being delivered and were still likely to double in the next year. The company had gone through the first phase of its survival programme which was driven by the logic of consolidation. The new division was now about to enter the growth phase, driven by the logics of total quality management, customer service and continuous improvement.

Phase Two of the change programme was due to be launched in three months time and Mark Henderson and John Reid were meeting to review the latest piece of management research. Mark Henderson had been fairly happy with progress to date, but he knew that Phase One of the change process had only been the beginning. The culture change programme had been well received and amongst his managers he detected a 'we can win' attitude as opposed to the previous sense of institutionalised failure. He was toying with the idea of developing the structure. He had been forced to adopt a functional structure when he consolidated the businesses because a cross-functional structure would have confused an already challenged set of managers. That might have to change when they went down the total quality route. He was not so happy with some of the conflicting information he was looking at this morning. Vista Consultants had run two investigations. The first was a series of interviews with the 80 surviving managers and the second was an attitude survey of over 150 of the shopfloor staff to assess the progress of the change programme. As John read the summary and recalled some of the recent discussions the main findings seemed clear enough (see Appendices 1 and 2 for more detailed findings).

The assessment process that had been used to select surviving managers was criticised. Many technical skills were felt to have been lost. Staff were used to managers having all the answers, but they no longer had them. Managers had low credibility and were reputedly rarely seen on the shopfloor. The new technology was being introduced too slowly and with insufficient training. There was a resentment at making poor quality products. Production needs were being put before customers and quality. This focused on a high rate of machine breakdown and resultant quality problems, which simply added pressure to an already high workload. Yet staff thought that there were many other changes (such as the new structure) that were being introduced too quickly with little creative thought and poor communication. Changes were not being thought through and problem solving was felt to be superficial. They were not learning from their mistakes. They were willing to contribute ideas but felt the team briefings they received were all one way. There was no bottom-up dialogue. In particular, the Section Heads were seen as being too inaccessible. The shopfloor workers were governed by rumours and not by the official organisational lines of communication. In short, the workforce felt that the downsizing strategy had been reactive and simply concerned with cost-cutting. Not surprisingly, although staff had pride in their own performance, they had low pride or trust in the company, were pessimistic about the future and identified more with the sections they worked in rather than with Galenco as a company. They felt they were loyal workers working for a disloyal company.

Given the circumstances, John mused, this was understandable, but didn't they understand how far the company had come in such a short time, but that its future still balanced on a knife edge? Hadn't they already been told that Phase One of the change programme was all about survival and introducing a degree of stability, but Phase Two was going to be all about customers and quality and would address the very concerns they had raised? Clearly, a lot of thought had to be put into the next steps. They had a busy three months ahead planning Phase Two of the change process. A year ago their initial thoughts had been to use the managers to help roll out the original culture change process throughout the entire workforce once the first year of business changes had been worked through. Was this still feasible? The time had come to stand back and work out the jigsaw puzzle revealed by the competency data, values statement and attitude survey data once they were put together.

ACTIVITY BRIEF

As John Reid and Mark Henderson consider what to do next, help them develop answers to the following five questions.

1 What have been the main strengths and weaknesses of the Phase One change programme?

2 How much progress has Galenco made against its pride, mission and values culture change? Which actions to date have been consistent with the espoused culture? Which management and staff attitudes and behaviours still seem inconsistent with the values?

3 In what ways has the downsizing influenced the change process? What problems have been caused solely by the downsizing? What problems have a deeper cause?

4 Is the team of 80 managers competent and ready to cascade the change process down to the next level? Is the workforce ready for this change?

5 What should be the main ingredients of the second phase of the change process? What HRM changes remain to be achieved and how would you attempt to bring them about?

RECOMMENDED READING

Beer, M, Eisenstat, RA and Spector, B (1990) 'Why change programs don't produce change', *Harvard Business Review*, 68,6, pp 158–66.

Schneier, CE, Shaw, DG and Beatty, RW (1993) 'Companies' attempts to improve performance while containing costs: quick-fix versus lasting change,' *Human Resource Planning*, 15,3, pp 1–26.

Vollman, T and Brazas, M (1993) 'Downsizing', *European Management Journal*, 11, 1, pp 18–29.

The case study touches upon a range of HRM tools and techniques. Those wishing to raise awareness of key associated topics should read the following extracts:

Sparrow, PR and Hiltrop, JM (1994) *European Human Resource Management in Transition*, London, Prentice Hall (pp 228–31 on 'Can organisational culture be managed through HRM?'; pp 346–8 on 'Assessment centres'; pp 401–4 and 412–17 on 'The nature of management competencies'; pp 498–500 on participation; and pp 638–44 on downsizing).

APPENDIX 1
SUMMARY DATA FROM MANAGEMENT INTERVIEWS USED TO GAUGE THE SUCCESS OF PHASE ONE OF THE CHANGE PROGRAMME

The views of managers

- 34% believe that short-cuts in work are taken and that staff have a tendency towards 'short-term fixes'.
- 68% believe that good cross-functional co-operation is taking place.
- 56% feel that staff are not fearful of the consequences of owning up to their mistakes.
- 79% feel that their employees are still status-conscious.
- 82% believe that communication has improved greatly with employees aware of how Healthcare Materials is performing and clear about its strategic direction.
- 79% feel that team briefings are useful in helping inform them about changes in the company.
- 38% still feel that communication is plagued by delays, mixed messages and a lack of clarity.
- 70% feel that their own boss is immediately visible and approachable and relationships are open and trusting.
- 22% feel that their contribution is not valued as much as it used to be and that senior managers are not living up to the new culture.
- 86% feel 'stretched' by their own workload.
- 53% find the working environment threatening.
- 51% feel that Galenco Healthcare Materials is loyal to them.
- 58% believe that Galenco Healthcare Materials is in a better commercial position now than it was a year ago.

APPENDIX 2
SUMMARY DATA FROM THE EMPLOYEE SURVEY USED TO GAUGE THE SUCCESS OF PHASE ONE OF THE CHANGE PROGRAMME

The scores shown against each question detail the percentage of staff who were in agreement or strongly agreed with the statement.

Team briefings are necessary.	84%
Team briefings are useful in informing me about changes in the company.	48%
I feel I am loyal to Galenco Healthcare Materials.	50%
I feel I work for/belong to my section.	80%
I feel that Galenco Healthcare Materials is loyal to me.	23%
When managers say things will happen, they generally do.	30%
I would like to be involved in quality improvement projects.	95%
Positive changes have resulted from quality improvement projects.	39%
I often have ideas on how to improve the work that I do.	55%
I have been involved in quality improvement projects.	20%
I believe my boss would give me a fair hearing, even if it was not implemented.	66%
I feel I am consulted about the changes which affect me.	37%
I am well informed about my section's role.	42%
I am well informed about my section's future.	40%
I am well informed about the company's direction.	29%
Galenco Healthcare Materials is in a better commercial position now than it was a year ago.	34%
Product quality has improved over the last year.	40%
Galenco Healthcare Materials is looking for a quick fix.	81%
I am proud to work for Galenco Healthcare Materials.	65%
Changes are being implemented too quickly.	70%
I like to work in teams.	75%
My team is involved in allocating tasks.	38%
I feel the right people get promoted.	27%
I feel managers spend a lot of time on the shopfloor.	25%
The working environment is open.	15%
The working environment is based on trust.	23%
The working environment is friendly.	61%
The working environment is threatening.	36%

Emerging management roles in Westbank Health Centre

Laura Hall

INTRODUCTION

This case study is based on the experiences of a number of health centres and medical centres as they become more business oriented. The case does not represent just one health centre and the individuals identified below are fictitious, although representing commonly found perspectives and issues.

Boaden (1994) describes the changing management focus in doctors' practices:

> The manager is employed by the partners, an arrangement which presented few problems when the role was circumscribed and limited. Under the new arrangements, management includes the partners, who cannot remain unchanged while everyone around them is responding to the changes within practices. This poses a challenge for managers, staff and doctors alike. (Boaden 1994, p 11)

Some practices, recognising the growing importance of the managerial task, are also appointing practice directors with a strategic focus to their managerial role.

BACKGROUND TO THE CASE

Westbank Health Centre was initially founded as a GP's surgery by Dr Argent around 40 years ago. The patient list grew rapidly as the nearest GP's surgery closed due to retirement. This necessitated taking on a partner, Dr Bulmer, within five years. Soon after, the practice was relocated from a small High Street site to Westbank House, a large Victorian house which became both the surgery and the home of Dr Argent. Since that time the practice has continued to grow and there are now six partners, with Westbank House now being devoted entirely to the Health Centre, Dr Argent and his family having relocated their home. In total the Health Centre now employs 22 staff including partners, and has grown so much that the building is now of insufficient size.

Westbank Health Centre is located in a relatively prosperous, and gradually growing community, Westrhodes, on the edge of a major city in the south of England. Employment levels are relatively high compared with the national average. The community itself is slowly growing due to a high number of large family houses, reasonably high levels of local residential building and the conversion of a number of extremely large Victorian properties into family-sized apartments. A large number of retirement homes and homes for the elderly exist in this community. The patient list is currently 7300, and some growth is also anticipated from the retirement of a GP running a surgery two miles away. This growth would mainly consist of younger people with growing families. All partners recognise that the patient list needs to grow as they are concerned that they have a fairly high doctor-to-patient ratio.

The past six years

The past six years have seen considerable changes in the Health Centre. Not only have the patient list, staff numbers, and the range of services offered been growing, the practice is now fundholding. The decision to apply for fundholding status was not made without considerable discussion among the partners over a number of years. Ultimately, it coincided with the retirement of Dr Argent, and his replacement by Dr Bruce. There was a diversity of views at the time, and even now, after fundholding has been implemented, two of the partners, Drs Smith and Bulmer, are not completely reconciled to this way of operating. These two doctors still maintain that their role as GPs is about treating patients and not about business management and balance sheets. They agreed to the decision to become a fundholder, because they could see no real choice in the matter – it was something that had to happen eventually, and finally agreeing did at least mean that the fundholding debate did not always dominate meetings of the partners.

Dr West and Dr Bruce were the key protagonists of fundholding with Dr Main being a strong supporter. Dr Swift was not really interested in the debate itself. Her concern was for adequate funds to run and expand her 'well women' and 'well men' clinics, positive healthcare programmes, and counselling services. As long as fundholding would finance these activities then she was happy to agree. All of the partners agreed that a practice director would be needed in order to implement fundholding.

To the staff of the Health Centre the fundholding decision meant very little and no one explained the 'why' or the 'what'. Although there was a staff meeting once a week this tended to cover short-term operational issues, and attendance was difficult – as most of the Health Centre staff worked different shifts. The meetings were not seen as important, with partners and staff members turning up late and leaving early to attend to other issues.

The staff did notice the pace of activity constantly increasing, and more and more changes taking place. However, despite this, most felt content with their work at the Health Centre. The atmosphere was generally positive with a degree of good-natured humour. The reception and administrative staff, although very busy at times and struggling to cope with an increasing patient list, got on well together and felt they worked well with the practice nurses. They had little direct involvement with the doctors, except when critical paperwork could not be found immediately, and an urgent search was instigated. The paperwork had always been found to date, but the receptionists felt that the doctors did not realise how overworked they were. Administrative tasks and filing were often late being done as patient appointments and patient contact were understandably given priority. There were backlogs, particularly in the sending out of referral letters to hospitals for non-urgent cases, and this was partly due to the fact that there was no dedicated secretary. Repeat prescriptions were also causing a problem as, although the intention was that these would be turned around within 48 hours, they often took a number of days to process and occasionally were overlooked. Typing and telephone work were expected to be shared among all reception and administrative staff. No receptionists felt any particular ownership of the paperwork and if there were still tasks remaining from their shift they assumed that the receptionist on the following shift would try to do them if they had a 'quiet patch'. There were not many quiet patches.

The three practice nurses worked very separately. They each had an appointment book and worked this themselves, explaining to the receptionists that it would be easier this way. The receptionists were pleased not to have more appointments to administer. There was little communication between the nurses and other groups of staff, except occasionally a little banter with the receptionists, and there was also little communication between themselves. The exception to this was the level of contact with Dr Swift as she involved them in her 'well man' and 'well woman' clinics and in the positive healthcare programmes. The nurses were very content in their jobs and the way they had developed them. Turnover was low and all had been in post for over four years. There was some recognition by the partners that nurses operated in different ways and had very differing workloads in terms of amount and type. Although this issue concerned the partners, nothing was done to explore or tackle it, partly because there were no mechanisms in place to assess individual performance, and partly because the partners each felt that his or her own clinical tasks had priority. The only exception to this was Dr West who felt that improving the efficiency and effectiveness of the nurses was critical to the success and expansion of the Health Centre. While recognising this as an important issue he instigated no action with a firm view that this was to be a priority for the new Practice Director.

There were also two health visitors and three community nurses associated with the practice. These were employed by the local Health Trust and were managed by a Trust manager based at the local clinic.

The information technology (IT) systems installed were sophisticated, although the level of use was far below the capacity of the systems. IT use in the Health Centre was very variable. In general the administrative and reception staff were very confident and competent in this area and used the systems reasonably well. The practice nurses, health visitors and community nurses did not use the systems at all, and prepared handwritten notes for the administrative staff to input. The partners in general used the systems increasingly for prescriptions, case notes and referrals. Although there was a lack of consistency with some doctors doing all these things all of the time (Drs West and Bruce), and others doing just some IT activities or doing all but sporadically (Drs Main and Swift). Two partners refused to use IT systems (Drs Smith and Bulmer). It was recognised by all that now fundholding had arrived the use of the computer, consistently by all, was more important, if not essential.

All staff members of the Health Centre were on first-name terms, except that staff referred to all doctors, except Dr Swift and Dr Bulmer, using the title Dr instead of their first name. This created a slight air of unease particularly when meetings of all staff were held.

The consultants' review

Three years ago, at the time it was finally decided to apply to be a fundholding practice, it was also decided to use the services of a consultant to identify issues that needed to be resolved in the management of the Health Centre. The focus of the consultancy exercise was on fundholding, but some of the issues they raised had an impact on the Health Centre more generally. The consultants interviewed each partner, and collected information from each of the other categories of staff by means of focus groups.

Key recommendations made by the consultants were:

● to develop a mission statement and key strategic objectives for the Health Centre;
● to appoint a practice director to implement fundholding and to promote the development of strategy for the Health Centre;

- to co-ordinate and consolidate the use of IT within the Health Centre;
- to reorganise the partners to operate as a Board of Directors and to nominate an executive partner to oversee the management of the Health Centre;
- to restructure the organisation;
- to improve communication;
- to extend the building or move to larger premises;
- to reduce unnecessary costs;
- to focus more services on the increasing number of young families.

Developments in the last two years

A mission statement and key strategic objectives were quickly developed by the partners. A summary of these is shown in Table 3.1. These were developed by the partners on an 'away day' with facilitation from the consultants who were invited back for this activity. The partners agreed at this meeting that they would form themselves as a Board and Dr West put himself forward as the Executive Partner. This was readily agreed. Each of the other partners also took on a nominated management role: these roles were information, accommodation, fundholding and cost effectiveness, communication, and job roles and staff performance. Table 3.2 shows how these responsibilities were allocated. The partners agreed that they would meet regularly as a Board, but to date this had never happened. They continued to act independently and value their clinical expertise and freedom at the expense of developing other roles. They did, of course, continue to meet as partners, but in the usual informal and *ad hoc* way, dealing with immediate rather than long-term issues, except for accommodation.

The patient list had already grown by 5 per cent and arrangements were in hand for the extension of the building with each partner agreeing to invest his or her own money in the programme. There had been no reductions in the drugs budget, or other unnecessary costs, and no progress had been made to date on the IT front.

Staffing was restructured broadly along the lines recommended by the consultants, and the current structure is shown in Fig. 3.1.

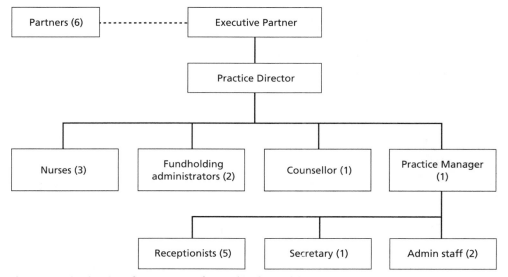

Fig 3.1 Organisational structure of Westbank Health Centre

Table 3.1 Mission statement and strategic objectives for Westbank Health Centre

Mission statement

To promote the physical and psychological well-being of the Westrhodes community by providing excellent medical facilities and services, to a growing patient list, through skilled and well motivated staff

Strategic objectives

1 To be accepted as a fundholding practice and to operate the fund so that the budget is fully and appropriately spent, and not overspent;
2 To eliminate unnecessary costs, and in particular reduce the drugs budget by 25 per cent within the next five years mainly by the increased use of generics;
3 To increase the patient list by 15 per cent within five years;
4 To expand the Health Centre premises by 10 per cent within five years;
5 To improve the range, quantity and quality of services available at the Health Centre, particularly in relation to young families;
6 To have co-ordinated and consistent use of new technology to underpin the business;
7 To develop health promotion and disease prevention programmes, and investigate alternative therapies.

It was recorded that strategies on information technology, drugs and protocols, and human resources were critical to success.

September 1994

Table 3.2 Management responsibilities of partners

Dr West   Executive Partner
Dr Bulmer Job roles and staff performance
Dr Swift   Accommodation
Dr Main   Information
Dr Bruce   Fundholding and cost effectiveness
Dr Smith   Communication

On 1 January 1996, shortly before fundholding was due to start on 1 April, a Practice Director, Jennifer Croft, was appointed. The Practice Director had previous experience of operating as a Practice Director for another health centre in the north-west of England and had three years' fundholding experience. When she was appointed, fundholding was, of necessity, a key activity taking up almost all of her time. However, the role had been described by the partners, when she was interviewed, as having three key areas of responsibility: fundholding, strategy and human resource management. Each of the partners seemed to have a different view of where the balance lay between these three priorities, and what they actually meant in practice.

The Practice Director immediately appointed two staff for dedicated fundholding duties. She appointed them against two carefully drawn up job descriptions, prepared individual training programmes for them and after six months was reasonably happy with their performance. Such an emphasis on training and development was new in the Health Centre. Prior to this, training had been viewed as clinical updating for partners and nurses and the development of IT skills for other staff.

The nurses proved to be a more difficult group to manage. The Practice Director felt that she did not have the technical expertise to manage the nurses effectively. She had begun to identify and explore the issues such as the lack of job definition, the absence of performance standards and assessment, and their independent rather than team-based way of operating. She had also established, however, that they were very resistant to change and felt that they sometimes 'pulled the wool over her eyes' with overly technical jargon and explanations.

The management of the administrative section was more straightforward. Her main concern here was that the Practice Manager, Ann Bale, spent her time managing systems, which she did very effectively, rather than people. The Practice Director noted that one result of this was that she was overburdened with work, doing tasks herself that she might have delegated.

A dedicated secretarial post was created working for the Practice Director, Practice Manager and the partners. The Practice Director quickly found that there was some confusion here as the secretary reported to the Practice Manager and she was not sure of how to deal with her responsibilities to others. In practice she treated any work from the partners as first priority and work from the Practice Director as the lowest priority.

CURRENT SITUATION

It is now September 1996. The fundholding operation is running very successfully, and the Practice Director has decided that it is now time to turn to the other key issues of strategy and staff management.

ACTIVITY BRIEF

1 Identify the training and development needs of the partners. Which are the priority needs and how do you suggest that they might be met?

2 What long-term strategies might you adopt to change the working practices of the nurses, encourage their flexibility and meld them into a team?

3 Identify the development needs of Ann Bale. What short- and long-term approaches can Jennifer Croft adopt to meet these needs? What problems is Jennifer likely to encounter in this area and how can she overcome these?

4 Imagine that you are the Practice Director, Jennifer Croft. You have decided that in order to develop an HR strategy you need to analyse both the present situation and the desired future in order to identify the gap and how this might be bridged.
   (a) Using the culture/people/systems/structures framework in Fig. 3.2, prepare two pictures of the organisation: one of the present situation and one of the desired future.
   (b) Develop an outline HR strategy which is intended to bridge the gap.
   (c) Who would you involve in developing this strategy? In what way and why?

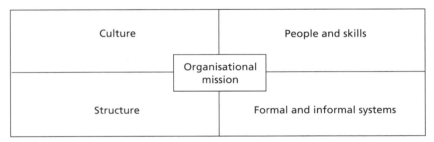

Fig 3.2 Assessing the present and creating a vision of the future

RECOMMENDED READING

Armstrong, M (ed) (1992) *Strategies for Human Resource Management – A Total Business Approach*, London, Kogan Page.

Boaden, M (1994) 'Practice management comes of age', *Health Services Management*, Aug.

Harrison, J and Burns, P (1994) 'GPs: principles and practice', *Health Manpower Management*, 20, 2, pp 16–21.

Kalinauckas, P and King, H (1994) *Coaching: Realising the potential*, London, IPD.

Mabey, C and Mayon-White, B (1993) *Managing Change*, Milton Keynes, Open University Books.

Mumford, E (1993) *Management Development – Strategies for action*, (2nd edn), London, IPD.

Nortier, F (1995) 'A new angle on coping with change: managing transition', *Journal of Management Development*, 14, 4, pp 32–46.

Plant, R (1987) *Managing Change and Making it Stick*, London, Fontana.

Timings, L (1993) 'Management development for GPs and Practice Managers', *Health Manpower Management*, 19, 1.

The firm IFI-AUTO

Thierry Picq

INTRODUCTION

IFI-AUTO manufactures parts for mass-produced cars and is a market leader in the electric and cable field (battery cables, electric caps, light beams, captors and so on). It has a staff of 800, all on one single site in the south-east of France. The firm sells directly to the constructors; IFI-AUTO's customers are well known and sound (Ford, Nissan, Volvo, Renault, Mercedes, etc.) but rather limited in number. In this very competitive and captive market, it is particularly difficult to attract new customers.

IFI-AUTO controls the whole cycle of its products from basic research, development and prototyping to production and commercialisation in France and abroad.

Turnover has been falling steadily for the last three financial years without the overall situation becoming alarming. Trading margins have undergone a marked improvement due to good cost management in the high production areas. The firm's technical know-how is one of its main competitive advantages. A large R&D department is constantly at work improving not only the conception and production processes, but also the development of the technical features of the different products to correspond more closely to the ever-increasing demands of the constructors. The firm was recently awarded its ISO 9001 and has also obtained more specific qualifications required by the different constructors before attaining the status of subcontracting partner ('The Volvo Certificate', 'The Mercedes Quality Contract', and so on).

BACKGROUND TO THE CASE

Asian competition is becoming increasingly strong. The Koreans, in particular, are offering products that are almost the same quality as those of IFI-AUTO and yet at much lower prices. In addition, IFI is suffering from all the current adverse trends typical of the car industry, above all in its new vehicle market. Over the last six months, IFI-AUTO's situation has grown steadily worse, with a noticeable fall-off in sales, reduced profit margins to meet competition and worsening labour relations due to temporary layoffs (the first time the firm has had to take this measure).

IFI-AUTO is a family firm of which Jean T., the founder, has been lord and master for more than 30 years. His son, Patrick T., took over from him less than two years ago. Sixty per cent of the shareholders are either from the founding family or are other private investors who are their close friends. Over the last few years, the number of shares owned by institutions, such as banks, has increased considerably, going from 10 per cent to 40 per cent of the capital. These are the shareholders that are particularly worried about the way the firm is being administered at the present time and they see no measures being taken to improve the situation.

AN AUDIT IS PROPOSED BY THE SHAREHOLDERS

During a particularly heated General Meeting, the external shareholders expressed their concern and openly challenged the efficiency of the management team as well as that of the executives as a whole. We shall quote some of the statements made, that clearly show the seriousness of the accusations:

> ... the firm is bogged down in internal power struggles that prevent it from reacting and taking the collective measures necessary for pulling it round ... the laissez-faire policy which is prevalent encourages cliques and power-groups that work against the common good ... there are no clearly defined strategies for mobilising the staff as a whole behind common objectives ... the management committee is unable to agree, to take decisions together and to resolve the conflicts ...

After a rather turbulent exchange, it was decided to call for a thorough-going audit which should confirm or deny the charges brought. One of the shareholders suggested engaging an independent consultant he knew well. To the surprise of all present, Patrick T., the present Chief Executive Officer (CEO), did not try to counter this proposition and seemed even to be in favour of it.

The consultant accepted the commission of the Board of Directors to evaluate the performance of the management team of IFI-AUTO. For several weeks he had free access to all parts of the firm. Taking full advantage of this freedom, he decided to apply the full range of information-gathering methods:

- individual interviews with the representative members of the executive body;
- collective structured work sessions;
- an analysis of existing official information (documents, notes, etc.);
- observations made by individuals and teams *in situ;*
- an audit of work practices and processes.

THE CONSULTANT'S DIAGNOSIS

The main findings of the consultant's analysis, as they were presented to the shareholders, are listed below.

General statements

The organisation chart of IFI-AUTO as worked out by the consultant is shown in Fig. 4.1. IFI-AUTO has no official organisation chart. This formalised structuring of the hierarchy gives rise to certain comments.

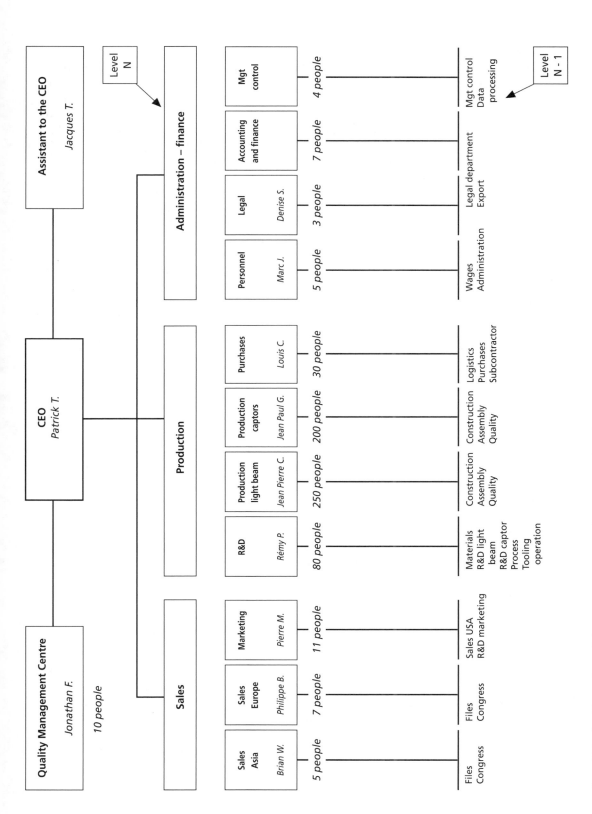

Note. Only the 12 members of the management committee are mentioned.

Fig 4.1 Organisation and chart of IFI-AUTO

- *Patrick T. is the CEO of the firm*. He is both a manager and a member of the Board of Directors. He is in complete charge. But this does not prevent his father, Jean T., who has been officially in retirement for two years and who is a strong charismatic personality and founder of the firm, from making his presence very much felt in the workplace. Patrick T. is aware of the difficulty of his situation. He clearly sees the necessity to improve management practices at IFI-AUTO as rapidly and radically as possible while safeguarding the people and the corporate culture that has led to the success of the firm and of his father. To complete the portrait, it must be added that Patrick T. finds it difficult to take decisions and so to impose himself. The difficulty he encounters in laying down clear strategic guidelines gives free rein to power struggles and inter-departmental strife. Since he is so taken up with solving operational problems, he finds it hard to detach himself sufficiently and take a long-range view of things. His calm acceptance of the audit proposal can be explained by the fact that it represented an opportunity for him to see things from a clearer perspective. Nevertheless, he is recognised by everyone as a good professional at the technical level and a very competent negotiator with important customers (he often goes along with the sales personnel when they are dealing with important cases).
- *The post of Assistant to the CEO is not clearly defined*. At present, it is occupied by Jacques T., Patrick T.'s brother. His young age and his rather diffident personality prevent him from playing a leading role in the firm. For the moment, he is working alone on a certain number of particular projects for Patrick T.
- *The commercial section is divided into three subsections*, each with the same hierarchical importance:
  - the Asian market, with its Commercial Manager, Brian W.
  - the European market, with its Commercial Manager, Philippe B.
  - Administration, commercial consolidation and marketing under Pierre M.

  This last function is responsible for the organisation of all the commercial activity, following up customers, dealing with claims, coordinating sales. It also deals with all the marketing. There are Level N − 1 executives in charge of the smaller specific markets which are not very developed in this firm – the USA and South America, for instance.
- *A Quality Management Centre* was set up recently which is responsible directly to Patrick T. Basically, it consists of a project team responsible for running and co-ordinating the different quality operations. Its role is basically functional; it works with those who have operational responsibilities and those responsible for quality in the different production activities. Jonathan F., who is in charge of this team, co-ordinates the training programmes as well. These programmes are mainly technical and are taught mostly by people brought in from outside. IFI-AUTO does not have its own internal instructors and the practical training given by operational members of the firm has not as yet been developed to any extent.
- *The Research & Development Department* is made up of a team of more than 80 people, spread out in a number of different fields of activity: materials and components, light beam technologies, industrialisation, processes and methods, tooling, etc.
- *Production* is structured around the two main activities of the firm: light beam and captor technologies. The methods, the technologies and the processes concerned with the two products are radically different. The two structures are therefore virtually independent. There is also a very limited cabling section which includes a group of ancillary and heterogeneous products that amount to about 10 per cent of the overall turnover.

- *The logistical and purchasing teams* work for the light beam section as well as for the captors. The personnel is multiskilled and considered to be very competent technically. The manager in charge of subcontracting is part of this function.
- *The administrative section* is made up of four hierarchically equal departments: personnel, legal and labour relations, finance and accounts, management control and computerised management.

Certain obvious points were highlighted by the consultant when considering the organisational structure of IFI-AUTO.

- IFI-AUTO is a firm with both a culture and a set of practices that are basically technical. The actual production process involves more than half the personnel.
- Human resources management just does not exist as a function in itself. Operational decisions concerning human resources management (hiring, promotions, etc.) are dealt with by the appropriate operational executive. Only the basic administrative processes are carried out by the personnel team led by Marc J. The absence of a real, coherent human resources management policy clearly illustrates the attitude the firm has towards human resources. They consider it to be a factor of production like any other, leading to the manufacture of technologically sound products.
- The commercial section is run by a rather small number of people. Philippe B. and Brian W. do have particularly strategic positions, giving them direct contact with the main customers. This is not the case with Pierre M.'s team, however, who feel hard done by and suffer from a blatant lack of recognition.
- R&D, though not short of resources, is really inefficient when it comes to fundamental innovation. With the exception of the old traditional light beam and captor technologies which have enabled IFI-AUTO to develop as it has, R&D just has not come up with any really new products likely to give the firm a boost. It is perhaps too involved in the production processes and short-term operational functioning; its real mission and its precise research objectives are far from clear. It has become more and more a supporting service aiding production, more concerned with improving what exists already than with developing innovative technologies.

The executives' management practices

Everybody in the firm is aware of an evident lack of communication between Levels N (management) and Level N – 1 (executives in charge of technical and commercial teams). The top managers find it very difficult to delegate and admit openly their lack of confidence in the executives who feel at a loss and without any definite responsibilities. Information is usually spread by means of rumour. There are very few formal work-structures, such as project groups or committees, that bring management and the executives together. It is direct contact that constitutes the interface, which is built up on personal affinities. Contacts between people working in sales/marketing, production and administration are infrequent and often confrontational. Thus, the firm is too compartmentalised, both horizontally and vertically, and people at all levels just cannot work together.

At management level (Level N), the most important body is called the management committee which includes 12 people and which meets for a half-day plus lunch once a fortnight. Its objective is to decide on the main strategic options, to work out the corresponding plans of action and to take all the important decisions which guide the firm in its development.

A number of other committees exist, such as the administrative committee, the sales, the production, the quality and the purchasing committees. Their purpose is to prepare the subjects that will be dealt with by the management committee and to take the operational, short-term decisions concerning sales, production, financial management, personnel and so on. They meet usually once a week.

There is a distinct impression that there are too many committees and that they meet far too often. The purposes of each committee are vague, redundant and change continually with all the short-term worries and problems. For example, it is not unusual for a so-called strategic committee to begin tackling urgent operational problems – the launch of some commercial activity or other, the arrival of a customer, dealing with a claim or a hold up in production. Furthermore, practically everybody is a member of nearly all the committees. For instance, the quality committee includes 9 of the 12 members of the management team. In this way, the top managers sometimes seem to spend more time in meetings than on the job.

No formal bodies of this type exist at Level N – 1 (executives). At this level there is a traditional hierarchical structure in which information and decisions move vertically. Likewise there is no committee that links Level N with Level N – 1.

The management committee comes in for particular criticism from the consultant. The meetings are not conducted in an orderly fashion and the agenda is far too long. Informing, problem solving and decision making are not separate functions. It often happens that hasty decisions are taken about important topics without any clear procedure and without all the necessary information being given out. The atmosphere is usually uncongenial; participants try to settle their own disputes, defend their points of view and their own interests rather than striving to be constructive. There is no structure in the way people participate, and so there are frequent clashes. Negativism and power struggles are brought out into the open and take up most of the time. Furthermore, the large number of participants in this management committee impedes its efficiency. Not everyone is concerned about the subjects under discussion, but this committee is the arena where power is lost and won. All the executives believe:

> … the people who count in IFI-AUTO are members of the management committee.

The practical results of these bi-monthly meetings are often disappointing. Few really important decisions are taken there and a lot of time is wasted in undisciplined discussion and personal clashes. The strategic options are rather vague; they are never unanimously agreed upon and, because of this, they are difficult to communicate: 'we don't know where we are going', 'we decide from day to day' are the answers given all the time by the executives (Level N – 1) when they are questioned about strategic decisions in IFI-AUTO.

Personal reactions within the management committee

The consultant gave a shrewd analysis of individual behaviour patterns and personal relationships with the management team. The result of his observations and perceptions is set out in Fig. 4.2.

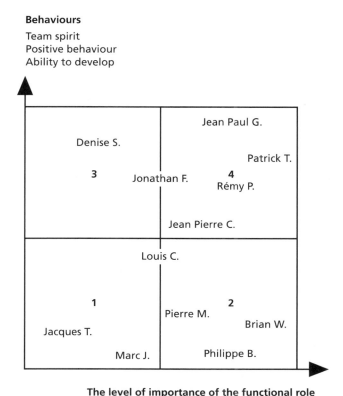

Behaviours
Team spirit
Positive behaviour
Ability to develop

The level of importance of the functional role
Strategic position of the functional role within the firm

Fig 4.2 Behaviour patterns and relationships of management committee members

The horizontal axis measures the degree of importance a certain area of responsibility has within IFI-AUTO. The question asked is, does the person to be placed in the diagram have a function considered as strategic? It is one of the possible ways of assessing the power held by the different players. Considering what has been said already about the technical culture of IFI-AUTO, it is not surprising to find to the right of the diagram those who are responsible for production and sales; the other functions are considered as ancillary activities.

The vertical axis evaluates the personal behaviour of the different players in their roles. To position the person concerned, the following questions must be asked:

● Does he/she usually behave positively?
● Are his/her contributions constructive?
● Is the common good more important to him/her than his/her own stake in his/her own field of competence?
● Does he/she show a real will to get on?

The particularly subjective aspect of this axis must be accepted as such and serves simply to express the consultant's equally subjective judgment.

The general comments that follow arise from the position of the different players in the four squares resulting from the intersection of the axes.

Square 1: weak team spirit, function considered to be secondary.

- Jacques T. is very withdrawn within the management committee and takes no part in the internal power struggles. He is shown very little consideration by the others and his propositions and suggestions are generally hardly listened to.
- Louis C. is one of the most senior members of the firm. He has been there for 27 years. He has come up through the hierarchy and his presence on the management team must be considered as a reward for good and loyal service to IFI-AUTO. He is very efficient in his field, and often not very concerned by the more general questions. For this reason he contributes very little to the different meetings.
- Marc J. has also been in the firm for more than 20 years. He first worked in the sales department and tried for the job of European Manager which was finally given by Jean T. to Philippe B. He was offered as compensation the title of Human Resources Manager with a seat on the management committee. He still shows resentment at being forced to change his career pattern. He often reacts cynically and his negative attitude is often directed against new ideas which he strives quite skilfully to reject.

Square 2: weak team spirit, function considered to be strategic.

- Pierre M. is supposed to co-ordinate the activity of Philippe B.'s and Brian W.'s teams. In practice, this is very difficult to do. Besides the strongly antagonistic personalities, the lack of precision with which the roles and responsibilities have been given out has a deadening effect on the synergy of all effort. Because of this, Philippe B. and Brian W. have restricted their fields of competence and power to correspond to their own personal wishes and at the most they impart a strict minimum of information to Pierre M. about their strategies and activities. The co-ordination between sales and marketing is quite unpredictable. The equivalence existing between the hierarchical levels of the three teams leads to permanent conflict, power struggles and clashes.
- Philippe B. is one of the pillars of the firm having been in it for 25 years. He has a very strong personality and is always 'up front' during any meeting. His strategy is basically defensive and aims at guarding as best he can the prerogatives of his commercial reserve. He often clashes with production, is rarely constructive and totally averse to any change. Having climbed all the rungs of the ladder 'by brute force', as he is wont to say, he refers continually to the past and does his utmost to counter all attempts made to change or question the smooth running of his commercial activity. His impeccable knowledge of the firm and his strong personality make him a particularly difficult character to deal with.
- Brian W. could be described in much the same way, although he arrived much more recently in the firm. He is much more of a manipulator and is considered to be stubborn. He always insists on giving special treatment to his commercial activity and refuses to take production or administration requirements into consideration. His sound knowledge of Asian culture enabled him to sign up some important customers – Nissan and Toyota, for example. He knows he is the only person at IFI-AUTO who can deal with this type of customer and uses this asset as a means of protecting himself.

Square 3: positive attitude, a functional role considered to be secondary.

- Denise S. is the main occupant of this square, officially in charge of the legal department. In practice, her activities include much more than this. She occupies the role of virtual co-ordinator of administrative and financial issues. This unofficial role is not appreciated by the other administrative executives from human resources management, accounts and management control. So relationships tend to be strained, with everyone defending his own territory. On certain specific questions, such as work contracts, legal relationships with the customers, etc., she has taken it upon herself to negotiate with the responsible executives in the technical and commercial sections. This interface function is a difficult one to live with. Since she is not taken seriously as a negotiator of technical questions, her suggestions and ideas about progress are rarely heeded. Though always ready to undertake challenges, she has nonetheless gradually adopted a more withdrawn attitude on the committee.

Square 4: a positive attitude, with a functional role considered to be strategic.

- Apart from Patrick T., the two technical executives are found in this category (one in charge of light beam and the other in charge of captor production) and the executive in charge of R&D. The relationship between these three people is very good. They work together in harmony and have launched a number of projects at their level. The three of them joined the firm fairly recently: Jean Paul G. five years ago, Rémy P. seven years ago and Jean Pierre C. two years ago. They are worried by the lack of clearly defined strategic guidelines and try to launch quite considerable development projects, such as partial delocalisation, breaking into the American market, prospecting for foreign partners, and the partial integration of certain subcontractors. Their actions, however, are somewhat disorganised and most of the time they come up against resistance of different kinds which holds up progress. For instance, the delocalisation project was launched more than a year ago and has not made any significant progress. Their relationship with the commercial section is one of conflict; each of the groups implicitly claims to be the keystone of the firm.

- Finally, Jean Pierre C.'s behaviour is slightly different from that of Jean Paul G. and Rémy P. He is new to the firm, and so he takes on personal challenges – like integrating, acknowledging and marking out his territory – which means that at times he adopts a more individualistic form of behaviour. He is considered to be 'ambitious' by the sales teams since he tends to always look for compensations for his participation in collective projects.

- Jonathan F. has a role all of his own within the context of the management committee. He has been three years with the firm and occupies a functional place, proposing and launching a number of quality development projects at all levels and in every area of the firm. He is very positive and very constructive with his main objective of improving the 'quality culture' within IFI-AUTO. Since many consider him as the 'grey matter' behind Patrick T., his position has given rise to jealousy. Being of English nationality, as is Brian W., he has his own special way of working which is often misunderstood by the other members of the committee, who, nevertheless, don't hesitate to claim the credit for any successes obtained over the last two years in the field of quality within the firm.

ACTIVITY BRIEF

A few weeks after accepting the commission to analyse the firm, the consultant presented the findings of his enquiry to the Board of Directors, just as they have been presented in the preceding pages. With the exception of certain details and certain marginal differences in perception, the shareholders agreed on the whole with the description the consultant gave of the day-to-day functioning of the management team of IFI-AUTO and officially approved his analysis.

Imagine you are the consultant. On the basis of this report, the shareholders ask you to continue your work by helping them to find ways of improving the situation described in the report. After discussion, the shareholders ask you to build into your propositions three major conditions that they consider to be of the utmost importance in the present context of IFA-AUTO. These conditions are:
- that the new system of functioning be brought in smoothly without any great internal upheavals or dire effects on the normal activity of the firm;
- that the proposed solutions on no account involve any layoffs;
- that the changes be as discrete as possible, so that people from outside IFI-AUTO, customers and subcontractors mainly, are virtually unaware of them.

The propositions must provide immediate operational responses to certain key questions:

(a) What ways can be suggested and what strategic concepts can be developed that will give support to Patrick T?
(b) How can Patrick T. be brought to the point where he can better exercise the authority that the power he has gives him?
(c) How can a management committee be made really effective?
(d) How can Level N – 1 be brought into closer co-operation?
(e) How can the desire for progress be freed from the hindrance of personal antagonisms, power struggles and bickering over territory?
(f) How can a real change be brought about that will be accepted as realistic by all the members of the management committee, within the cultural and present human context of IFI-AUTO?

RECOMMENDED READING

Handy, C (1976) *Understanding Organizations*, Harmondsworth, Penguin.

Hendry, C, Arthur, MB and Jones, AM (1995) *Strategy Through People*, London, Routledge.

Katzenbach, J and Smith, D (1993) 'The discipline of teams', *Harvard Business Review*, Mar–Apr, pp 111–20.

Lazarson, MH 'Organisational growth of small firms: an outcome of markets and hierarchies?', *American Sociological Review*, 53, pp 330–42.

Schein, EH 'The role of the founder in creating organizational culture', *Organizational Dynamics*, 11, Summer, pp 13–28.

First International Bank: the design and introduction of new office technology

Patricia Hornby

INTRODUCTION

This case describes the organisational processes, structures and participants involved in the decision to introduce, and the design and implementation of, new technology into the International Department of a major high street bank. The overall title for the new system is, appropriately, the International System (IS). IS has been designed as two interacting subsystems: Business System (BS) and Personal System (PS). BS and PS therefore form IS. BS and PS are meant to operate slightly differently as they are said to be dealing with fundamentally different sorts of accounts and clients: business accounts held by companies and personal accounts held by individual customers respectively.

BACKGROUND TO THE CASE

The Organisation

First International Bank employs over 5000 people, most of whom are based in a centralised headquarters and are involved in one of the five major activities of the bank: *operations* (e.g. processing of transactions and documentation), *administration* (e.g. day-to-day management of customer accounts, dealing with enquiries, etc.), *personnel* (e.g. recruitment, selection and staff development), *computing* (e.g. running and co-ordinating programs on the main computer hardware) or *information technology* (IT) (e.g. development and maintenance of the bank's software). The five areas, briefly described above, are reflected in the structure and design of the organisation and represent the five main directorates (*see* Fig 5.1).

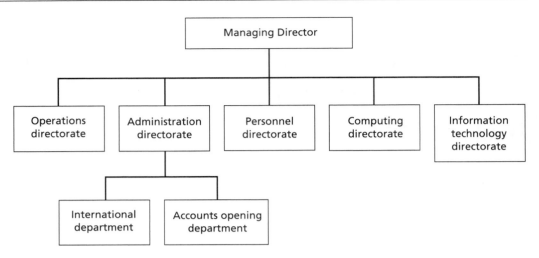

Fig 5.1 Organisational chart of First International Bank

Each of the directorates contains a number of subunits (i.e. departments) which are largely grouped around a functional activity with some further subdivision to allow for a number of functions to face a group of internal or external customers or clients, where necessary. Examples of the functional differentiation of the activities of the departments include the various departments of the operations directorate who deal specifically, for instance, with security and investigations, data processing and post room. Examples of how the departments introduce a degree of flexibility in the basic functional model include accounts branches in the administration directorate who deal with all of the customer enquiries for a particular geographical location and differentiation within branches on the basis of customer business needs, e.g. corporate or private customers, providing some continuity from the perspective of the customer.

This strong tendency to organise by function cascades down through the many layers of the organisation as well as across the directorates, though some directorates clearly lend themselves more easily to the model (e.g. operations and computing), than do others (e.g. personnel and administration). The tendency is a powerful one and observed in almost all areas of the bank. Hierarchically, the bank has modelled itself very much on civil service lines. Responsibility and authority for making decisions flow vertically through several organisational layers punctuated by many and various levels of management. At the very lowest of clerical levels in the bank individual employees may easily find themselves carrying out a very limited number of highly repetitive tasks with little or no discretion over the manner in which the tasks are carried out.

Evidence of this dominant structural model is reflected in the particular instance of the international department (the focus of this case study), described in some detail below.

THE INTERNATIONAL DEPARTMENT

The international department is part of the administration directorate. It processes all international transactions. The work flow is organised according to both function and process. The work of the department is divided between sections.

The business and personal processing sections

These two sections of the department deal with the processing of all international transactions. A very recent change has been made to the organisation of the department in order to reflect the needs of the incoming system – the International System (IS). Prior to the decision to design IS as two separate, though communicating, subsystems – Business System (BS) and Personal System (PS) – the work of processing transactions was carried out in a single section and the work was split between groups on a functional basis, i.e. one group processing only 'in' payments and one group processing only 'out' payments. When the decision was made to design IS as two subsystems, it was also decided to organise the work of the processing section similarly (i.e. business accounts and personal accounts) and then to subdivide the work further in those two subsections into 'in' payments and 'out' payments (*see* Fig 5.2).

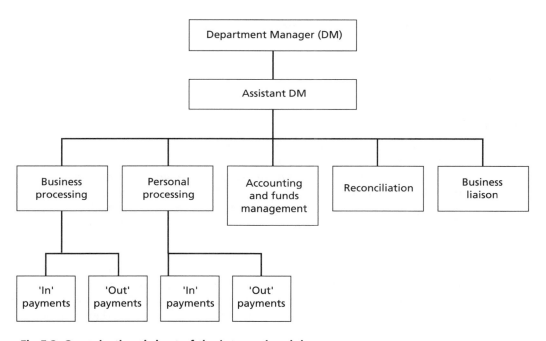

Fig 5.2 Organisational chart of the international department

Accounting and funds management

This section monitors the monies available in the various foreign accounts and decides whether the accounts need funding (i.e. foreign currency should be purchased) or whether they are over-funded (i.e. foreign currency may be sold). This information is derived from the activities of the processing sections and is reported to accounting and funds management via reconciliation.

Reconciliation

This section collects and collates all of the data from the processing sections, carries out the appropriate book-keeping and passes the information to accounting and funds management. The clerks in this section have the most detailed summaries of the transactions that go on in the department, and on the manual system have had a very critical role, being perceived as the 'brain centre' of the department's activities.

Business liaison

This section deals with all business customer enquiries and did not exist before the decision to automate. To some extent it reflects the design of the system (i.e. divided into subsystems specialising in business- and personal-type accounts), which in turn reflects a management decision that the work should be divided in this way as the needs of the two types of account holders and thus through-put of transactions from them is fundamentally different (i.e. business transactions = large denomination, small volume transactions; personal transactions = small denomination, large volume transactions). It was, therefore, argued that the business account holders would need special attention as the loss of a single account would have relatively serious consequences for the business of the branch.

THE PROBLEM IN OUTLINE

Participants/'Stakeholders'

The *Department Manager* (DM) serves as a member of the Process Control Group (PCG – *see* below for details). He arrived late to the project as a replacement to the current User Project Manager as he vacated the department manager's position in order to specialise in project management. The DM admits to feeling very little ownership of the project ('... not my baby') and to being discontented with the functioning of the Process Control Group as little more than a 'talking shop where no real decisions are made. The real decisions are made by the Steering Committee'.

The *Assistant DM* has been in this position in the branch for a number of years and appears to adopt a 'laissez faire' approach in general and in particular with regard to the IS project. He has expressed his unease to the researcher, however, at having to 'sign off' technical reports (such as the specifications documents) as the appointed, senior user. He feels neither technically equipped to present arguments or queries nor powerful enough to insist on delays for clarification.

The *line managers* (5) have responsibility for staff in the five sections of the department described in Fig. 5.2. They are represented in the PCG by the Corporate Liaison Officer. Hers is a fairly new appointment though she is a long-standing member of staff, having progressed through the clerical grades. She is very 'pro' the new system and seen as one of its champions. She is regarded with some suspicion, however, by the other line managers, some of whom expressed opinions to the researcher that she has vested personal interests in seeing the system successfully in place even if it were not the most appropriate move or in the most appropriate form for the department.

In general, the line managers are perceived as a little out of touch with the day-to-day activities of the department. The researcher also discovered that they appear to be unable to see alternatives to the current way of organising work. For instance, when the researcher asked one manager (responsible for one of the processing sections), directly, if he thought the work could be organised differently he said 'There is only one way to organise this sort of work, isn't there? Someone processes payments in, someone processes payments out and someone else balances the books.'

Supervisors (9) have supervisory responsibility for the activities of the clerical workers within the various subunits within the sections. The supervisors have no direct input to the PCG via representatives from their ranks but do have a representative on the User Acceptance Testing team (*see* below). Initially this representation was rotated as each supervisor took a turn in the testing. This became complex to manage however, and latterly one supervisor has been allocated full time to the User Acceptance Testing team.

Clerical staff (officer grade (50) and assistant grade (37)). Although the original plan was to have all users involved in user acceptance testing (*see* below), at the end of the day the User Project Management team decided to retain a small number of clerical and supervisory staff to carry out testing. This team was 'dedicated' to testing during that period and the members were removed from their usual tasks in order to do so. A questionnaire survey (*see* Hornby and Clegg 1992) of the clerical staff revealed that, although contact with the User Project Management team and managers with regard to the project has been reasonably high, users report having made very little contribution themselves to the design process and the majority of users reported some dissatisfaction with the amount and quality of information they have received about the project.

User Project Management Team (2) consisted of the User Project Manager (UPM), who was previously the Department Manager who had subsequently been released from this duty in order to concentrate solely on the role of UPM, plus his assistant. It was on the basis of his original proposals (*see* sequence of events below) that the project came into existence. He appointed his own assistant (internal to the bank, though external to the department) when he was himself appointed full-time to the role of UPM. The UPM Assistant manages the user testing programme in the department.

Information technologists (IT) and external consultants. The information technologists working on designing the system are based in the IT directorate of the bank (see Fig. 5.1). As is usual with large-scale projects of this sort, they employ external consultants, i.e. systems designers, on a short-term contract, who specialise where the internal designers lack expertise. In the case of the IS project, two separate groups of consultants have been employed to work on two separate parts of the project, i.e. the personal and business accounting systems (*see* sequence of events below for further details).

IT staff work closely with the UPM who is, basically, their user representative. In this case they are finding it particularly difficult to manage and integrate the work of two different groups of consultants. This has made an already complex managerial task doubly so from their perspective.

The *Computing Centre (CC)* The CC appears under the operations directorate (*see* Fig. 5.1.) It has a single representative on the PCG (*see* structures and forums below) who is a first-line manager of the change control section within the Computing Centre. The change control section is responsible for ensuring that the new system will operate successfully with the other bank systems. It has a fairly technical role and ideally it should have a good deal of day-to-day contact with the User Acceptance Team who run tests on the system as it is designed. In reality it tends to be central to activities only in the final stages of design once there is something to test. It has a traditionally poor relationship with the information technologists who, it believes, involve it too late, tend to ignore its advice and belittle its contribution in the users' eyes. It has found this project no different from its usual experiences.

STRUCTURES AND FORUMS

Project Steering Committee

This is a small group of senior managers in the bank who authorise all spending and time-scales etc. for the project. The Director of Information Technology and an Operations Director with responsibility for international services in the bank make up the core. The User Project Manager is also a member of the Steering Committee and it is his responsibility to report on the day-to-day progress of the project and to make recommendations.

Project Control Group (PCG)

Representatives of IT, the Computing Centre and the international department's management make up the group which is chaired by the User Project Manager. The group meets fortnightly at critical points in the development of the project (and less often at other times, at the discretion of the UPM) and discusses all aspects of the progress of the project. The group makes recommendations to the Steering Committee, who in practice must authorise any changes to the project plans. A number of the members of the group have expressed their discontent with this part of the process as the group seems unable to make decisions as it has little or no authority to act.

User Acceptance Testing

This is the forum at which the operation of the system is tested by users as parts of it become available from the designers. The stated purposes of the testing are:

- to validate the delivered system against the system functional specification, including screen and report layouts;
- to confirm usability of the system, by simulating all associated interfaces and procedures throughout a normal business cycle;
- to confirm that the selected hardware (including communication links) meets user requirements in terms of capacity and reliability;
- to confirm that the system conforms to operational standards (of the computing centre);
- to confirm that processing can be carried out within the scheduled times and meet user-defined deadlines.

Originally it was envisaged that all users would be involved in the testing. It emerged, however, that only a small core of users were involved and they were removed from their day-to-day responsibilities while testing was carried out.

THE SEQUENCE OF EVENTS IN SUMMARY

March 1994

A new Departmental Manager (DM) is assigned to the international department with a brief to improve the efficiency and productivity of the department or to face the consequence of the closure of the department as it has been returning an overall loss in recent years. This new DM is later to become the User Project Manager as he is removed from day-to-day managerial responsibility for the bank and allocated, full time to the implementation of the new technology in the department.

May 1995

The DM recommends to the bank's General Executive that the outmoded, manual operating systems of the International Department are updated via the implementation of new technology. At the same time the DM instigates an intensive marketing campaign and an examination and development of the department's products with an emphasis on corporate business.

1995 to 1997

- The business of the department increases tenfold in response to the introduction of various new products and the vigorous marketing of all of the department's products. The department is unable to cope operationally with the increase in through-put.
- At the same time an audit of the department's activities is conducted and the subsequent report expresses concern at the ability of the department's management to control its currency position, cash flow and reconciliation time-scales.
- In September 1996 a feasibility study is completed by a set of external consultants who recommend the design of a bespoke computer system, tailored to the exact needs of the department and incorporating all aspects of the work. (*Note.* In order to meet the pressing needs arising from the increase in business some 'off-the-shelf' hardware and software have been purchased and are being used by staff to support their activities.)
- There is some delay as the bank's senior management debate the funding of the scheme.

April to August 1997

- The senior management of the bank agree to the development of a bespoke system for the department and external consultants are appointed to conduct a Systems Functional Specification (SFS), i.e. to define in systems terms the exact needs of the department and the specification of the proposed system.
- A new Assistant to the Department Manager is appointed.

October 1997 to May 1998

- The SFS is completed and a decision is taken that the system (IS) should be designed in two phases: IS1 (an automation of the processing of the day-to-day customer transactions) and IS2 (an automation of the reconciliation, funds management and accounting systems of the department).
- A decision is also taken that IS should be designed as an amalgam of two subsystems: PS – to deal with transactions on personal accounts – and BS – to deal with transactions on business accounts.
- The Branch Manager is transferred full time to deal with the User Project Management (UPM) of the system.

May 1998 to September 1999

- The bank's directors authorise work to commence on the first phase of the IS project. Implementation dates are set: December 1998 for IS1 and April 1999 for IS2.
- A new full-time Departmental Manager is appointed to the department.
- Implementation dates are set back as the bank upgrades its main computing systems.
- An organisational researcher enters the branch to examine the design and implementation process, carries out interviews with all major participants in the project, including representatives of users at all levels in the department, and conducts a questionnaire survey in the user department.

September 1999

- IS1 is implemented in the department and follow-up interviews are conducted by the organisational researcher.

SUMMARY OF RESEARCH FINDINGS

- Reported discontent with the functionality of the system:

    ... it simply carries out some basic processing tasks, it does not really help with management information and has contributed very little by way of reconciliation and funds management. We could have bought an adequate 'off-the-shelf' package at a fraction of the cost.

- The system appears to have '... set in concrete' some inefficient and ineffective organisational features of the department. For instance, there is a long history of rivalry and conflict between the processing functions and the reconciliation, accounting and funds management and, more recently, liaison sections. Largely the conflict stems from errors made at the processing stage that have to be '... mopped up further down the line' by the sections mentioned. The new system has 'cemented' the segmentation of the work of the department by function and done nothing to integrate the tasks and activities of the department into jobs in which individual clerical staff see complete processes through. In so doing, it has failed to reinforce a sense of responsibility in staff who continue to be the last to be made aware of errors they have made and who, in any case, have no power to correct them. In fact this problem has increased with the introduction of the system as the rate of errors has increased with the general increase in speed of through-put. What is more a new clerical post has been created to deal solely with errors arising from processing and identified elsewhere in the system.

- Users in general perceive themselves to have had very little involvement in the development of the system. Many of them appear neither overly concerned nor surprised by that. One user went so far as to comment:

    ... it's no one's fault; it's just how we do things around here. It's their job to manage and ours to do as we are told. If it goes wrong, they're responsible. It suits us all really.

- Despite evidence to the contrary the UPM and his assistant insist that they have adopted an 'open-door policy' with users and that users have participated fully throughout. The UPM has taken up a promotion elsewhere in the bank having established his credibility within the organisation for managing a highly complex and costly project to completion.

- IT continue to bemoan their lack of contact with the 'real' end-users but see this as a perennial problem and are at a loss as to the solution. One analyst commented:

    The problem is, you see, the User Project Management team has to become familiar with the 'jargon' we use and the technological issues in order to take part fully in the process. I have noticed that once this happens they seem to lose touch with the user. It is as if they become 'honorary' technologists.

- The Computing Centre say this is just another example of the analysts and users getting carried away with 'big ideas' and failing to think through the implications for the operation of the system within the total banking systems:

    No doubt there will be operational difficulties and we will be blamed. I just wish they would pay more attention at the design stage and listen when we try to warn them.

ACTIVITY BRIEF

1 How would you define the organisational structures of the department and the organisation in general?

2 What impact, if any, have the structures you have identified had on the decision-making processes and operations described in the case?

3 Consider the major participants in the case. What constraints and/or liberties have been afforded them as a result of their role descriptions? What do you consider have been the major consequences of the roles of the various participants for their engagement in the organisational processes described in the case and the outcomes arrived at?

4 What 'phases' has the change process progressed through and how successfully have they been managed? How could you have improved the change process?

5 To what extent has the new technological system developed and implemented in the case 'mirrored' the structures and operations already in place in the branch prior to the project? Is this a good thing? How could participants have arrived at alternatives? Which particular jobs and processes could have been designed differently and how? What do you consider could have been the results of such changes to organisational practice?

RECOMMENDED READING

Cherns, A (1987) 'Principles of sociotechnical design revisited', *Human Relations*, 40, 3.

Child, J (1984) *Organisation: A Guide to Problem and Practice* (2nd edn), London, Paul Chapman.

Hornby, P and Clegg, C (1992) 'User participation in context: a case study in a UK bank', *Behaviour and Information Technology*, 11, 5, pp 293–307.

Adding value to service provision in the public sector

Sue Shaw and Colin Fielding

INTRODUCTION

Stofford Metropolitan Borough Council (SMBC) is one of six metropolitan authorities in a large conurbation north of Watford. It serves a population of just under a quarter of a million and employs some 9000 employees within ten departments. Its annual revenue budget is £182 million of which 80 per cent is employee costs. It is a Labour-controlled council, organised for decision-making purposes in a typical committee structure. Like all other local authorities, SMBC is currently facing and will continue to face massive and complex changes.

BACKGROUND TO THE CASE

External triggers for change

The overriding trigger for change has been the substantial increase in the involvement of central government, since the Conservatives came to power in 1979. According to Thomson (1992), seven main themes can be detected in government policy since that time:

● Privatisation
● Delegation
● Competition
● Enterprise
● Deregulation
● Service quality
● Curtailment of trade union powers

These are underpinned by the three principles of efficiency, effectiveness and economy. Such principles are not the exclusive preserve of public policy. Efficiency and effectiveness emerged as key components in organisational competitiveness in the 1980s. The notions of quality, both product and service, and customer awareness manifested themselves not only in the writings of such gurus as Porter (1985) and Peters and Waterman (1982) but also in the widescale adoption of such techniques as Total Quality Management, Quality Circles and Customer Care. The importance of the customer and meeting, indeed anticipating, his or her needs is critical. It is in this context that many of the changes in local government must be viewed.

Whatever the espoused principles underpinning government policy, the impact of legislation and the ensuing reforms has been to reduce the power and autonomy of local authorities. Since 1979, there have been over 100 separate pieces of legislation affecting the provision of council services. The government has introduced legislation which has not only regulated the total of local government spending but also that of individual local authorities. Like other authorities, SMBC has experienced successive rounds of budget reduction, capping and restrictions in the way business rates are collected. At the same time, major changes, such as the community charge, have saddled the authority with additional major administrative and cost burdens.

The move to make local authorities more accountable and more efficient using market forces as the driver is at the heart of the changes. The overriding objective is to turn local authorities into enabling authorities which, rather than performing public services, provide a framework through which services can be delivered either by local authority employees (Direct Service Organisations (DSOs)) or privately. The government's main vehicle for achieving this is Compulsory Competitive Tendering (CCT). CCT was first introduced in the Local Government Planning and Land Act 1980 and extended by the Local Government Acts of 1988 and 1992. CCT rests on the principle that services should be provided in-house only if a local authority can demonstrate that it can provide those services as effectively and efficiently as the private sector. For a council to continue to deliver its services in-house, it has to demonstrate that the services have been successfully tendered on the open market against private sector competition on the basis of price and quality.

The activities exposed to CCT under the 1980 and 1988 Acts were essentially blue-collar services (e.g. highways maintenance, refuse collection, catering) and to date SMBC's in-house teams have won all the contracts, including re-tenders. The 1988 and 1992 Acts extended CCT to professional and support services and SMBC is proposing to introduce CCT to these services during the next three years.

The extension of CCT to professional and support services is important because it will significantly increase the proportion of the authority directly affected by the culture of markets, contracts, competition and the discipline of internal accounting frameworks and trading accounts. It is for this reason that CCT is the single most important change facing service provision across all SMBC's ten departments at the current time, with its implications for the size, shape and style of the organisation.

Internal triggers for change

Not all change has been externally driven. While not the first local authority to do so, SMBC was certainly one of the front runners in terms of a changed perspective. The appointment of a new Chief Executive in the late 1980s was important in that it heralded a new philosophy and a move away from highly centralised control, especially in areas such as finance and personnel. Working with the Leader of the Council, the Chief Executive and his deputy were the prime movers in creating a new vision for the future for the authority.

This has manifested itself not only in structural change and devolution but also in a Statement of Values which identifies a number of priorities such as public service, customer care and concern for council employees. The Statement of Values, in turn, is translated into corporate policies in a number of key areas. The period has also seen the introduction of business planning, departmental action plans and project management across departments, hitherto unheard of at Stofford. Central to all this is quality and the influence of Deming is apparent in the Chief Executive's approach.

THE SITUATION AT SMBC

The case focuses on the central human resources function and the implications of the changes outlined above for the function and what it does. It examines how the function has responded to the notion of meeting customer needs.

The human resources function

The function comprises of 30 professional staff who are organised into five functional groupings: training, human resources information and planning, employee relations, health and safety and management services/consultancy. It is headed up by a Director of Human Resources and a Deputy. At the present time, the training team with five professionals is the largest grouping, and employee relations the smallest grouping, reflecting the current focus of activity. The other three groups are broadly similar in size.

Since 1990, parts of the function have been decentralised to service departments with the specific aim of allowing the central function to concentrate on more strategic issues.

Consequently, each department within the authority has got its own personnel section which is there to provide advice on staffing matters such as discipline and personnel information as well as administer basic personnel systems.

The extent to which the decentralised Personnel Officers operate as professionals as opposed to administrators varies across departments. A key strategic development from the central human resources function, however, has been the successful completion of a training initiative with a local college to enable the Personnel Officers to attain the graduate status of the Institute of Personnel and Development (IPD).

The changing role of human resources

The human resources function at SMBC has been at the forefront of the implementation of many of the changes outlined above. At the same time it has been and continues to be subject to the changes as well. During the 1970s and early 1980s, when the emphasis was on the central control of budgets and human resources, the function grew in status. Since the late 1980s, however, with the advent of CCT, local management of schools (LMS), devolved management, service level agreements (SLAs) and the increased emphasis on market forces, there has been a need to re-examine and clarify the relationships within local authorities. Consequently, the users of central services have begun to review the quality, cost and even the need for such central support services. SMBC's central human resources function is no different from many other human resources functions in this respect. In conventional cost accounting terms, any human resources department is non-productive and it is not easy to demonstrate its impact on the bottom line. Since the beginning of the decade, human resources departments have been under increasing scrutiny and growing pressure from their customers to demonstrate the effectiveness and quality of their service in the same way as organisations have been required to examine the quality of service to their external customers.

EVALUATING THE ROLE OF THE CENTRAL HUMAN RESOURCES FUNCTION

The first internal customer survey

The Head of Human Resources has recognised the importance of meeting internal customer needs for some time. The first internal customer survey was undertaken early in 1990 as part of a joint pilot programme initiative with the Local Government Training Board and the regional local authorities employers' organisation.

The first step was to establish a task force. This comprised a team of three people consisting of a representative from each of what were then the three divisions of the human resources department – manpower utilisation, general personnel and human resource development – and from each of the three tiers of the structure. This task force then sought the views of staff within the three divisions on customer perception of the services and ways of improving them. The next step was a customer survey. The key customers were identified as the authority's departmental management teams and the respective Personnel Officer where such a role existed. The survey took the form of a questionnaire and follow-up interview. The questionnaire outlined the personnel services provided and asked recipients to grade each of the services across six quality criteria: reliability, accuracy, responsiveness, timeliness, cost effectiveness and general image, using a five-scale grading system. The services which customers were asked to comment on were:

1 **Manpower utilisation**
   - Review of work to determine necessary manpower resources

2 **General personnel**
   - Advice on conditions of service
   - Advice on industrial relations
   - Grading of jobs
   - Manpower information and planning

3 **Human resource development**
   Employment
   - Recruitment and selection
   - Redeployment/job transfer
   - Equal opportunities
   - Employee services, e.g. welfare/counselling
   - Temporary staff agency
   - Promotion of employment and training opportunities

   Training and development
   - Management of all trainees
   - Provision of in-service training
   - External training including further education
   - Retraining
   - Identification of training
   - Employee development

The questionnaire also provided customers with an opportunity to give their views on the human resources department's mission statement and the extensiveness and relevance of the services offered. A follow-up interview was conducted with members of each departmental management team and the relevant administrative/personnel officers who had responsibility within their own departments for the personnel function.

A number of changes resulted from the 1990 study including:

● Reorganisation of the human resources department into five functional groupings
● Decentralisation of specific human resource activities to Departmental Personnel Officers
● Devolution of routine human resource activities to departmental managers along with the necessary training and provision of management guidelines to equip them in their extended role
● Extension and improvement of the occupational health service;
● Centralisation of the health and safety function;
● Refocusing of the method of training provision away from the menu of training courses to one driven by organisational and individual needs.

Another important finding of the survey was that it helped to identify one of the main customers as being the 'corporate body' in that much of the work of the human resources function was undertaken for the corporate good of the authority. This enabled the function to reconsider where work was charged to. Prior to that time, the cost of the work was directly charged to service departments which partly explained why many customers expressed dissatisfaction with the cost of the services.

The second internal customer survey

As the human resources function moves towards CCT, the focus is once again on the level of service provision. Preparing the department for CCT is an extensive operation ranging from defining the activities, through consideration of the competition requirement (currently 25 per cent for personnel services), preparation for trading, development of internal accounting frameworks and credits for work which has already faced competitive pressure. In the first instance the function will need to decide which aspects of the service it wishes to put out for tender to the private sector.

What is more the Director of Human Resources has recognised that if the function is going to be successful in the tender, it is important that it improves its marketing skills, understands the requirements of customers and provides a relevant and effective service, while at the same time paying consideration to the cost and quality of the service provided. These considerations have resulted in further work being undertaken to establish the quality of the service. The Director firmly believes that there is no point in having a highly efficient personnel service if it is not helping the primary service to deliver better services to the consumer.

The approach taken is based on the concepts of service management and follows Humble's six-step action plan (Humble 1988):

1 Establish a personnel taskforce.
2 Define mission and customers.
3 Study key personnel service issues.
4 Compare with competitors' practices.
5 Review with customers.
6 Implement improvements.

A personnel task force was established comprising the Director, his Deputy and five Principal Officers and its terms of reference were to define the personnel services and design a customer questionnaire. Although the human resources department's mission was considered in the earlier survey, it was not an issue in this second evaluation. Defining the customers is not an easy task. For the purposes of this evaluation the key customers were identified as the Chief Officers who were the decision makers in respect of purchasing the service and the Departmental Personnel Officers who were the main day-to-day contacts. The Chief Executive, the prime purchaser of the corporate activities of the human resource function, was identified as another key customer. The Director of Human Resources argued that it was important to define the services that were provided in a way that internal customers could understand while at the same time taking the government's definition of personnel services into account.

A summary of the services provided was arrived at by involving members of the human resources department and asking them to consider and summarise the services they were responsible for and identify what they thought were the important factors of their service to the customer. It was difficult to get each of the five teams to summarise the services they provided in a succinct way but ultimately a definition of each service was completed and the following eight key areas were identified:

● Corporate and advisory services
● Management consultancy
● Human resource information and planning
● Industrial relations
● Training and development
● Health and safety
● Occupational health services
● Temporary staff agency

Another issue was the quality criteria to be used to measure the human resources function. The Director argued that it was important that customers should define the quality criteria they thought to be important in the delivery of the service. Criteria were arrived at following discussions with the Chief Executive, three other directors, two key elected members – the Chair and Deputy Chair of Personnel – representing the corporate customer and a number of Departmental Personnel Officers. Six key quality factors were identified:

● Reliability/accuracy
● Responsiveness/timeliness
● Sensitivity to the needs of the customer
● Cost effectiveness
● Integrity
● Courtesy

The information was then drawn up into a questionnaire which was circulated to the customers outlined above and subsequently followed up by a semi-structured interview. Four levels of customer satisfaction were identified: excellent; meets requirements; needs improvement; unsatisfactory. Customers were asked to express their level of satisfaction with the overall service and their level of satisfaction for each of the eight services using the six key quality factors.

Subsequently the Director benchmarked the function's services using research undertaken by KPMG Peat Marwick Consultants and APAC National HR Database. The following activities were benchmarked: proportion of training provided externally, cost of human resource function, proportion of decentralised staff, labour turnover and absence.

Results of the customer survey and benchmarking exercise

Results were obtained showing the level of satisfaction by department with the service as a whole and for each of the eight specific services both overall and specifically in terms of the six quality criteria.

The overall satisfaction level was good, although comments were made about the need to market central personnel and training services more effectively (*see* Table 6.1).

Table 6.1 Level of satisfaction with the overall service

	Chief Officer (%)	Dept Personnel Officer (%)	Total (%)
Excellent	20	0	10
Satisfactory	50	90	70
Could improve	30	10	20
Unsatisfactory	0	0	0

Satisfaction levels within the specific service areas varied between very good to extremely mixed satisfaction. The highest degree of satisfaction was felt with training services, which reflected the development and the transformation of that service in the early years of the decade (*see* Table 6.2).

Table 6.2 Level of satisfaction with training services

	Overall satisfaction (%)	Reliability (%)	Responsiveness (%)	Sensitivity (%)	Cost effectiveness (%)	Integrity (%)	Courtesy (%)
Excellent	25	20	30	30	15	30	45
Satisfactory	65	65	45	45	50	55	50
Could improve	10	5	15	15	0	5	0
Unsatisfactory	0	5	5	5	5	0	0
No response	0	5	5	5	30	10	5

Feedback on human resource information and planning and the occupational health unit was generally positive although concern was expressed about accuracy of information and the speed at which it was supplied in the case of the former (*see* Tables 6.3 and 6.4).

In each of three areas, corporate and advisory services, health and safety and industrial relations, at least a third of respondents identified that some improvements could be made. In corporate and advisory services, while there was a feeling that overall human resource strategies were good, adverse comments were made about the relevance of human resource policies to departmental needs and there were also requests for clearer guidelines on policy implementation (*see* Table 6.5).

A similar level of concern was expressed in the area of health and safety where there was a clear feeling of controlling and monitoring rather than advising and helping (*see* Table 6.6).

Table 6.3 Level of satisfaction with the human resource information and planning service

	Overall satisfaction (%)	Reliability (%)	Responsiveness (%)	Sensitivity (%)	Cost effectiveness (%)	Integrity (%)	Courtesy (%)
Excellent	10	5	15	20	0	40	45
Satisfactory	75	65	50	55	50	50	55
Could improve	15	25	30	20	20	0	0
Unsatisfactory	0	5	5	5	0	0	0
No response	0	0	0	0	30	10	0

Table 6.4 Level of satisfaction with the occupational health unit service

	Overall satisfaction (%)	Reliability (%)	Responsiveness (%)	Sensitivity (%)	Cost effectiveness (%)	Integrity (%)	Courtesy (%)
Excellent	10	10	15	10	20	50	50
Satisfactory	65	65	50	65	45	40	45
Could improve	20	20	30	20	10	0	0
Unsatisfactory	5	5	5	5	0	5	0
No response	0	0	0	0	25	5	5

Table 6.5 Level of satisfaction with corporate and advisory services

	Overall satisfaction (%)	Reliability (%)	Responsiveness (%)	Sensitivity (%)	Cost effectiveness (%)	Integrity (%)	Courtesy (%)
Excellent	0	0	0	0	0	25	25
Satisfactory	65	65	30	45	50	60	55
Could improve	35	25	55	45	25	0	5
Unsatisfactory	0	0	10	0	0	0	0
No response	0	10	5	10	25	15	15

Table 6.6 Level of satisfaction with the health and safety service

	Overall satisfaction (%)	Reliability (%)	Responsiveness (%)	Sensitivity (%)	Cost effectiveness (%)	Integrity (%)	Courtesy (%)
Excellent	0	5	10	5	5	25	25
Satisfactory	65	80	65	60	45	65	65
Could improve	25	10	15	25	20	0	10
Unsatisfactory	10	5	10	10	10	5	0
No response	0	0	0	0	20	5	0

Response rates and demarcation between what aspects should be provided centrally and what aspects departmentally were issues in industrial relations, where again there was a mixed level of satisfaction (*see* Table 6.7).

Table 6.7 Level of satisfaction with the industrial relations service

	Overall satisfaction (%)	Reliability (%)	Responsiveness (%)	Sensitivity (%)	Cost effectiveness (%)	Integrity (%)	Courtesy (%)
Excellent	10	15	15	5	20	35	25
Satisfactory	50	55	35	65	35	65	70
Could improve	40	25	40	20	20	0	0
Unsatisfactory	0	0	10	0	0	0	0
No response	0	0	0	10	25	0	5

The Director was concerned to find that 75 per cent of the sample either were not aware of the management consultancy service or had not been using it, or even both (*see* Table 6.8).

Table 6.8 Level of satisfaction with the management consultancy service

	Overall satisfaction (%)	Reliability (%)	Responsiveness (%)	Sensitivity (%)	Cost effectiveness (%)	Integrity (%)	Courtesy (%)
Excellent	0	0	0	0	0	20	20
Satisfactory	15	10	0	5	5	10	5
Could improve	5	15	20	20	10	0	5
Unsatisfactory	5	0	5	0	10	0	0
No response	75	75	75	75	75	70	70

A similar lack of use was demonstrated in the temporary staff agency, although this result was not surprising as the number of clerks employed in this capacity has been drastically cut in the last two years, primarily due to budget cuts (*see* Table 6.9).

Table 6.9 Level of satisfaction with the temporary staff agency

	Overall satisfaction (%)	Reliability (%)	Responsiveness (%)	Sensitivity (%)	Cost effectiveness (%)	Integrity (%)	Courtesy (%)
Excellent	10	5	10	0	5	25	25
Satisfactory	30	35	30	40	25	20	20
Could improve	0	0	0	0	10	0	0
Unsatisfactory	5	5	5	5	5	0	0
No response	55	55	55	55	55	55	55

In addition to the standard data obtained from the questionnaire and interviews, other information was gathered and analysed. This included comments relating to specific services and suggestions for improvement, details of any identified overlaps between the centralised and departmental human resources service or any omissions, use of external suppliers of human resource services, views on the impact of human resources policies and procedures on effective service provision and any new policies that would assist in the provision of services.

In terms of overlaps between the central and departmental human resources functions, two main areas were highlighted:

- demarcation lines in terms of certain procedures such as disciplinary procedure;
- production of management guidelines.

Two main policy areas were seen to be hindering service provision:

- the disciplinary procedure, seen as too lengthy and bureaucratic;
- existing policies such as Maternity and Sick Pay with their additional costs.

While no gaps in service were identified, either centrally or departmentally, respondents did identify five areas where they felt the central function could help them in their provision of a departmental human resources function:

- a more strategic role centrally in assisting departments to implement human resource planning policies;
- the introduction of some form of performance management initiative;
- a reinforcement of flexibility within the organisation, i.e. more inter-departmental staff movement – through secondments, without lengthy recruitment procedures;
- all regradings, to be dealt with by relevant Chief Officers;
- increased use of temporary agency staff for specialised work.

Additionally, the survey showed 80 per cent of departments utilised external consultants mainly for highly specialised work specifically for training, e.g. new legislation training in education and social services.

The Director used a variety of sources of information for the purposes of benchmarking the function's activities. He used the data relating to six other metropolitan districts from within the KPMG Peat Marwick survey for aspects of cash value, credits, staff numbers and externally provided training. Given its population size and annual budget, SMBC can be defined as an average metropolitan district council. SMBC compared favourably with the cash value and staff numbers of the human resources function and was in line with the average for the percentage of credits and externally provided training (*see* Table 6.10).

Table 6.10 Benchmarking cash value, percentage of credits, staff numbers and externally provided training

	Range	*Average*	*SMBC*
Cash value of HR function	£1.6m to £14.2m	£4.8m	£2.7m
Percentage of credits	30% to 49%	34%	35%
Proportion of training			
provided externally	28% to 56%	38%	39%
Staff numbers:			
Centrally provided	18–85	49	43
Decentralised	10–346	105	62

Attempts were also made to benchmark the human resources department's costs, staffing ratios and training costs using the APAC National Human Resource database. However, it proved impossible to analyse the comparative information in any meaningful way.

ACTIVITY BRIEF

1 If you were the Director of Human Resources, what conclusions would you draw from the customer survey and benchmarking exercise results? What actions might you take and why?

2 What aspects of the evaluation of the human resources function does this case highlight?

3 What issues does this case raise for the way human resource services are structured and delivered?

4 Using your own organisation:

   (a) define your customers;
   (b) ask your customers to define the dimensions which make up the general image of the human resource function;
   (c) define the dimensions which you think make up the general image of the human resource function and compare with (b) above.

RECOMMENDED READING

Adams, K (1991) 'Externalisation vs specialisation: what is happening to personnel?', *Journal of Human Resource Management*, 1, 3, pp 40–54.

Burns, D and Thompson, L (1993) 'When personnel calls in the auditors', *Personnel Management*, Jan, pp 28–31.

Humble, J (1988) 'How to improve the personnel service', *Personnel Management*, Feb, pp 30–33.

Peters, TJ, and Waterman, RH (1982) *In Search of Excellence: Lessons from America's Best-Run Companies*, New York, Harper & Row.

Porter, ME (1985) *Competitive Advantage: Creating and Sustaining Superior Performance*, New York, Free Press.

Thomson, P (1992) 'Public Sector Management, in a period of radical change: 1979–1992', *Public Money and Management*, 12, 3, pp 33–41.

A re-managed heart in retail change[*]

Danusia Malina and Paul Brook

INTRODUCTION

Stox Stores is a multiple food retail chain striving to improve its position among the six market leaders. The company's market share has increased at a slow but consistent pace in the early nineties. Employing just under 50,000 staff in 210 locations across the UK, Stox Stores' reputation has been built around its basic pricing and product range, swift service, and down-to-earth approach to customer care. Stox Stores has responded to increased competition among the leading food retailers by directing attention towards consumers and, like others, has sought ways of enhancing its level of customer services. Therefore, energetic efforts have been ploughed into customer-care initiatives throughout the stores. Such drives have centred around management programmes such as Business Empowering Staff Teams (BEST) which encouraged staff to take ownership of their own knowledge of Stox Stores, and as a consequence to suggest improvements to working practice. One of the main components of the BEST programme was the development of Quality Circles. Employee participation in such schemes has reduced, however, as time has passed.

BACKGROUND TO THE CASE

Stox Stores has, for many decades, operated within a managerial style best described as hierarchial, paternalistic and authoritarian with a proud history of guaranteeing 'jobs for life'. Within the past three years, Stox Stores has attempted moves towards HRM, which has overturned the previous approach in a rapid process of change. Hence, the company has shifted emphasis towards a more open and dynamic approach to management. By pursuing a comprehensive strategy of transformation, Stox Stores has described the change as a 'revolution'. The company, like many food retailers, has been unencumbered by a large trade union presence.

The organisation structure remains highly centralised with head office responsible for implementation of core policies and support to branch stores. Due to the vigorous

---

[*]We are indebted to the food retail managers who have helped us in our research. Their willingness to share their thoughts, worries and excitements has proved invaluable in constructing this case. The material presented here is a composite picture of the themes emerging from our many conversations and as such Stox Stores can be seen as a fictitious company.

restructuring programme of the past year, Stox Stores has shed many regional staff responsible for a range of functions, including personnel and training. As a result, the remaining district managers have assumed responsibility for a growing number of stores. At branch level, store managers generally operate with a maximum of three deputy managers reporting to them, while departmental managers cover areas such as fresh foods, dry goods and customer services. Rationalisation at middle-management levels has resulted in low morale in lower grades, due to poor promotion prospects and increased workloads. The sales assistants are employed in the main on a part-time basis with a large proportion of these employees being married women with domestic responsibilities. While Stox Stores has voiced commitment to equality of opportunity for all staff, few female senior managers figure within its hierarchy.

This case study is narrated by and centres on the experiences of Roger Mann, Customer Services Manager in a city branch of the company in the north-east of England. Roger has direct responsibility for 58 members of staff located at the frontline. We join him at a stage when Stox Stores' boldest customer-care initiative is being implemented. Roger's internal dilemmas, actions and uncertainties provoke consideration of the ways in which commitment to an organisation, career and personal life fuse, clash, and are played out within a retailing context.

The case aims to engage students at the experiential and analytical levels simultaneously. It looks to establish identification with the main protagonist, Roger Mann. At the same time, it encourages students to analyse the implications of Roger's experiences for managing the transformation to HRM, via his involvement in a customer-service initiative.

A DRIVE TO WORK

Roger Mann is driving to work on a dull depressing morning. He has a lot on his mind.

Good morning, the time is 6.32. We now turn to the changing world of banking. The long-term shedding of jobs in the industry shows no sign of letting-up. This morning, the National Manchester will announce the loss of a further 10,000 jobs over the next five years as part of the bank's ongoing restructuring. With us to discuss what this continuing large-scale reduction of jobs in banking means for this once secure world are …

Over to Roger …

'When I left school, ten years ago, my parents were keen I went into the "cosy" world of banking – it was a job for life, with good prospects, or so we all thought. I, on the other hand, wanted a job with a bit of excitement where I could deal with people. Sure, I wanted job security and good prospects – Stox Stores seemed to offer what I was looking for, or at least it did until two years ago.

'Why am I thinking like this? Most of my old schoolmates are no better off; a lot are doing worse or are out of work – even those who went to university. Becoming a customer services manager a few years back was just what I wanted. It meant I was at the sharp end, never knowing what would come up next.

'I can't believe Rachel is three months old. Julie is so tired but we keep getting told it gets easier from now on. What really annoys me is that I'm always at work, never around to see Rachel or to help Julie out. What's more, there's so much to do – we're both so tired when we've finished, we don't have any time to be on our own. I didn't mind putting in the hours till we decided to have Rachel, but since then I've started to think differently. After ten years of nothing else bar Stox – we even went on holiday with friends from the company – I want more out of life. I want to enjoy Rachel with Julie, not stand on the sidelines cheering them on.

'The company wants to change in such big ways. They want even more from me. It's not enough that I've "lived, breathed and holidayed" Stox, now I'm told we've all got to be committed to the Board's goals – even my part-timers – and it's my job to make sure they are. Of course, I know it's a lot tougher in food retailing now than in the eighties. All the big companies are pushing hard on customer services to stay competitive. But at the same time, they've not given me enough staff and they're reducing the number of section managers. None of us can be sure we've got futures with Stox anymore. Like banking, there are plenty of redundancies around, and they keep on coming. I can't bear to think of losing my job, not now, not with Rachel.

'I don't know anything other than the Stox way of doing things. I used to know where I stood with them. Sure, I had to watch my back – the "old school" liked the dictatorship style. They're still around and are finding it hard to change. Come to think of it, I'm not finding it easy. I always did what I was told and expected the same when I wanted something doing. Now we're training in "team-building", "challenging behaviour", and "empowering staff". Mind you, I go along with the idea of treating my staff and customers as human beings. It's just that all of this takes time, but I want to give it a go. Anyway, it ought to be more interesting, and with things as they stand at the moment I'm not likely to get promoted in the branches so a bit of excitement won't go amiss.

'But so far these changes and overnight redundancies have killed morale; plus those of us left in jobs are all having to work harder. A lot of the branch managers and senior managers just pay lip service to the new style and culture. Many of them don't even bother making an effort. They carry on as if nothing's changed. At least my store is new, and most of the shopfloor staff don't know what the company used to be like. They're finding it much harder in the older branches, where nobody trusts management and where they reckon they've seen it all before.

'I'll give Sue, my manager, credit – she's always willing to try something new. All the same, she's a hard taskmaster. She expects us to be every bit as committed and hard working as she is. I can't help thinking it all adds up to being committed to her career. I suppose I might be the same if I were in her shoes.

'Here we go again, another week of "hitting the ground running". So much for my 39-hour week.'

With the time at 6.50 here's Florence Bish with news of this morning's batch of traffic delays …

THE BRIEFING

Roger has arrived at the store and has learned that an impromptu management team meeting has been scheduled for later in the morning. Over to Roger …

'I wonder what this morning's management team meeting is about? I guess it's the "next step" in Stox's plan to change. The trouble is, with competition stiff among the big companies, what with their putting more and more effort into cutting queuing time at the checkouts, introducing bag-packers and a "family-friendly" service, none of them seem in control, like each one's running scared. It feels reactive to me, but at the same time we can't afford to stand still. Which is why Stox needs to change.

'One thing is for sure: whatever we've got to do it's going to be really hard work, if only because it'll rely on every last member of staff believing in it. Making sure people are in the right place at the right time is tough enough, but getting them to provide "quality experiences" for customers when I'm not watching feels like having to climb Everest. I don't think I'd be too bothered with "customer satisfaction" if I were on a temporary 15-hour contract and paid peanuts. But we've got to do it, otherwise the company will lose out and have the "City" on its back.

'OK, here we go, it looks as if Sue's ready to spell out what's about to hit us. My goodness, there's an electric feel to the atmosphere here today.'

The Store Manager began:

> This is the biggest challenge yet. If we're to have any chance of maintaining our position with the 'Big Boys', then we have got to involve all staff right from the beginning of this campaign. The training and development we've had over the last couple of years, like working in teams, communicating and delegating responsibility, has got to be made to count. The bottom line is, unlike other customer service initiatives, this one can't work simply because management want it to work. All members of staff have got to have eyes in the back of their heads and be ready and willing to offer and suggest assistance in such a way that the customer believes they really do care.
>
> Roger, you're in the front line but that doesn't mean the rest of us leave you to it. We may be getting more staff but Roger has got to have even more staff if he needs them. I know this is going to leave us short in other departments but we can't afford to deliver high-quality service one day and not the next. If we get it right, our customers will come to expect it and appreciate it. The TV adverts will make it plain what they can demand. If it's not there, we have no excuses … Focus on the …

Back to Roger …

'I think I feel sick – a mixture of fear and excitement. She makes it sound as if it's a World Cup final but without a final whistle. Well at least I know what I'm going to be having nightmares about for the next month or so.

'We all have our pet fears and worries and mine is staff meetings. Not that I don't believe in them – it's just so many good but weird ideas come out of them. I seem to spend most of my time saying, "Yes, that's a great idea, but …". The truth is, a business the size of Stox has to be centralised and that means virtually everything we do is laid down at head office. There's never much room for debate about new ideas. It still feels that at the end of the day we're telling the staff how we want things done. The difference is, we want them to be interested enough so that we can rely on them delivering without being policed.

'What's more, I have the shop steward to contend with. Not that she gives me a hard time; in fact she's one of my best workers. The problem is, since all the change started, the union has grown in influence. There's a growing feeling in the store that the union will only get stronger the longer the change goes on. These days, I get the impression my staff are just as keen to hear what the shop steward has to say, as they are to hear what I have to say. I know there's a lot of quiet talk among junior and middle management in stores about joining the union themselves. I don't know how much of it's talk though. As for me, I'm not against joining the union but I know my manager would take it hard, and she doesn't deserve that. On the other hand, things are not so simple as doing what my manager is happy with anymore. I've more to consider now. When Julie stopped working for Stox, everything suddenly seemed to depend on my getting on here, doing well. Everything's riding on this job – the house, the car – plus now we've Rachel's future to plan for. If these redundancies get any closer to home, I'll have to put my own job and family first, no matter how disloyal my manager and the company think it is.'

The manager continued to address the management meeting:

> Roger, and this goes for the rest of you, we've got ten days before the first TV ad goes out. Personnel will co-ordinate any new training that's needed. Head office are sending a video to use for briefing staff. In the meantime, you'll need to draw up new rotas, arrange a series of meetings with key staff, and hold small but full briefing sessions with all other staff. The meetings are crucial if we're to be ready – get out there and pull your staff round. Each and every one of them must have the opportunity to ask questions and think through what these changes mean for them. We must sell it, and here we will emphasise the extra staffing we're getting. I know you'll be patient, but please try and avoid another flurry of union recruitment. In fact, I will personally talk to the shop steward,...what's her name?

THE SEDUCTION

Roger arranges a series of staff meetings to discuss the changes and to allow staff to voice any concerns …

'Only a couple of staff meetings left to go now. The core staff were OK, if a bit cynical about the company pulling this off. Many of them have learnt to read between the lines. They know full well that all the major food retailers are improving customer service and that it was only a matter of time before Stox tried to get ahead of the others. They want to know whether we're really going to have enough staff and whether we're going to keep them. Of course I'm saying all the right words, as best as I can – after all they need me to be sure of what's going on. Truth is, nothing's certain in Stox these days. I dare not hint that even I'm not convinced we'll have the staff to deal with this scheme.

'The next meeting, with the weekend staff, will be interesting, if tough. With so many rumours flying around I'm going to have my work cut out trying to persuade them that they won't have to do twice the amount of work in the same time. Fridays and Saturdays are frantic enough already.'

Roger addresses the weekend staff:

> Having seen how all of us will greatly improve our customer service, can I ask you for your comments and questions?

'Their faces tell me all I need to know – a mixture of confusion, tiredness and fascination. Sometimes I think these glossy videos do more harm than good. It feels a bit like "Big Brother" talking from a TV screen. If only the company would leave it to me. I know my staff. I know what mood they're in, what gets them going, and what goes down like a lead balloon. Instead, after the video I have to pick up the pieces.'

The staff raise a number of issues:

> Mr Mann, how many staff will we get?

> So, what you're telling us is that, if we get pulled off shelf filling onto checkouts, we won't get

> any hassle from the other manager when we go back to empty shelves!! Is that right, Mr Mann?

> At least we're going to feel more like smiling and being human to the customers if there aren't any queues …

> But suppose we're so busy that there isn't enough of us to keep the queues down, pack bags, trot off to the car park and guide people round the store? Are you really saying that all this comes first rather than getting the goods on the shelf?

'They're right of course, but nobody said the plan was perfect. Other companies seem to manage. The big question is, will it last once it gets going? Never mind if it'll last. As Sue says, "Pull 'em round to Stox's way of thinking, Roger, or we're all out of jobs".'

Roger responded:

> Stox is committed to making sure this initiative works. However, it recognises that it needs your commitment, skill and knowledge to make it work. Unlike previous customer-care campaigns, this one is about putting you at the centre of everything. It's about respecting your experience, and responding to what you need to provide a high-quality service …

'Please, please make sure we have enough staff and don't let this one die a slow death like all the other initiatives. I really want to believe in this one. I'd feel so much better in this job if I knew we were moving forward. I'm not sure I can handle yet another "five-minute wonder". There's no way my staff and I will give all we've got, and do it with a smile, if the resources are not there to help us. The prospect of more and more work, longer hours, and the promise of a few temporary part-timers thrown in, makes me sick, especially since I'm the one left to manage the mess. If I sell it hard enough they might not see how desperate I feel.'

He continued:

> I know I can count on your continuing support … Working as you do on peak trading days makes your part in this all the more important. You show your commitment not only by doing a good job but by giving that bit extra. Stox can only compete, and win, if we extend that extra value to our customers through you. Never underestimate how crucial you are to the business. – OK, thanks for your time – let's get back to work.

'I'll be glad to get home after this. In a way, though, these team briefings are a doddle compared to the tension that's building up with some of my colleagues. Since Stox decided to add a pack-and-carry service it's been a nightmare, because none of us know exactly what it'll mean for managing our own staff. Unless people are bussed in here fast, I'm not going to have any option but to draw staff from other departmental managers to cover the frontline. What's worse is, I know what will happen if this doesn't work. The management team will go for each other's throats, the staff will feel lied to, and from then on they'll just go through the motions. As for me, I'll finish as villain of the piece. All I hope is that head office knows what it's doing.'

THE DEVELOPING SCENE

It is now three months since Stox introduced its latest customer-care initiative. How is Roger faring?

'It's hard to believe it's three months since Stox threw us into running between stocking shelves and packing customers' cars. Those first few weeks were just a case of responding to whatever came up. I mean there were things we could plan for – like the weekends – but no one knew we'd have an amazing week of summer-like weather back in May. That caught us out – queues beyond belief, stocks in fruit and veg. and cool drinks at an all-time low, plus by then the customers had got used to our new services. I've learnt from that scuffle; I know I still need more hours at the front, where it really matters.

'Sure, we've made some gains. Stox brought in a "Hit Team" from other branches and, of course, our supply of agency workers grows when we need it. I've told Sue I think all this is dangerous. We've no time to ensure the quality we say we'll give. It's just a case of keeping things going.

'Right now, I'm getting tired of being pulled between different people. There's Julie itching to get a job back here, now that Rachel's old enough to settle with a minder. And what's more, she's right, we badly need her money again. Then there's checkout staff who keep leaving – it's just how it is in this business – but getting the new ones to understand what we expect is harder now. Let's face it, watching a video isn't going to convince them. I simply don't have the spare hours to see to it myself. Now that we don't have a personnel officer in branch full-time, there always seems to be someone needing to talk to me about their problems too. Yet, I feel things are working out, at a basic level. But I suppose it would help if I knew how senior management thought we were doing. Any day now, the Regional Director will drop in on us. It must be coming up soon and in a way I want it over with. At least then I'll know what I've to do. I just wish Sue had the contacts for a tip-off about the surprise visit then we'd have half a chance of performing well.'

THE VISIT

The Regional Director, Pete Stamore, does indeed pay a visit and does not make Roger's life any more straightforward …

'Who do these Regional Directors think they are, waltzing in here and throwing their weight around? My staff deserve a bit of respect. But that's not Pete Stamore's way. He talks about checkout operators, as he stands over them, as if they were invisible: "Does she know about standards of dress?" he barks as he rushes to inspect the aisles. It's like a pantomime; if it weren't so serious I'd stop and laugh. Sue looks as if she wants to run away; she's white with panic. Bellowing at her, Pete says the queues are not moving quickly enough. I've already pulled staff off the deli, warehouse and the shelves. Now he's complaining they're understaffed.

'As Pete and Sue walk (slowly) down each aisle in silence, panic stations hit the aisles ahead as deputy managers run up and down trying to get rid of cardboard, face up, fill gaps and tidy staff! What happened to the new culture of open communication, of care for staff, of treating people as human beings?

'I hate this attitude yet these top boys set the tone of the company for the rest of us. And Pete's one of the better ones – it's just a fact of life in Stox that good old-fashioned dictatorship comes out in a crisis. I agree we need performance checks of some sort, but surely we don't need the shock treatment and bad-mouthing that come with each visit. If there were any sense of understanding of what we're trying to achieve, Pete Stamore would know that change takes time and patience. It doesn't happen overnight – and we're doing our best here. At least no one's been called to Sue's office for a dressing down. There's still time, I suppose. We all know if you're a Stox manager, "You're only as good as your last visit." '

Later the same day, Roger is summoned to Sue's office where Pete Stamore is waiting to speak to him:

> As I said to Sue earlier, you've done an impressive job here Roger. Your staff are looking good, queues are right down and reports of how you work alongside other departmental managers have filtered through. Good work. We need people like you, who can deliver under pressure, who live up to our expectations. How'd you fancy a move then Roger ? It'd be good for your career, although what I've in mind will be tough …

'How will I break this one to Julie? We've only got settled here lately. It's obvious he means a move away from the area. I'm just winning with the staff here, getting stuck into the job, starting to relax …'

Pete Stamore continued:

> The branch we have in mind is rather stagnant, Roger. We're re-vamping the management structure to allow for people with energy and vision. You fit the bill, from your performance here …

ACTIVITY BRIEF

The following is not intended as an exhaustive list. It is presented merely as a useful starting point for analysis of the case. The experiences of Roger Mann highlight a large number of issues, and it is hoped that users of the case will be encouraged to generate pertinent questions of their own.

1   What is meant by 'commitment' in Stox Stores?

2   What are the main problems facing Roger in trying to 'manipulate' his own and others' commitment?

3   What is the relationship between 'trust' and 'vulnerability' in Roger's experiences?

4   Suggest reasons why Roger may be reluctant to move to a stagnant branch. What pressures are limiting Roger's options? Identify the principal tensions and challenges that are likely to arise in the new post. Specify how the issues may differ from those described in the case above.

5   Why might shop stewards in the branches describe the customer-care initiatives as 'systems of control'?

6   As an independent adviser, you have been asked to monitor the impact of customer-care initiatives. What criteria would you consider for deciding whether the programme has been successful? How would you measure employees' commitment to the scheme?

RECOMMENDED READING

Hochschild, A (1993), *The Managed Heart: the commercialisation of human feeling*, Berkeley, University of California Press.

Legge, K (1994) 'Managing culture: fact or fiction?' in Sisson, K (ed) *Personnel Management: a Comprehensive Guide to Theory and Practice in Britain*, Oxford, Basil Blackwell, pp 397–433.

Marchington, M and Harrison, E (1991) 'Customers, competitors and choice: employee relations in food retailing', *Industrial Relations Journal*, 24, 4, pp 286–99.

Marchington, M and Parker, P (1990), 'Multi-Stores: co-operating with customer care', in *Changing Patterns of Employee Relations*, Hemel Hempstead, Harvester-Wheatsheaf, pp 152–76.

Ogbonna, E and Wilkinson, B (1988) 'Corporate strategy and corporate culture: the view from the checkout', *Personnel Review*, 19, 4, pp 9–15.

PART 2

Resourcing and Reward

This section opens with the case of 'Euroservice', a large French multinational food services organisation. Audrey Klesta investigates the response to a newly acquired American hospital service affiliate, where differences in culture, perception and interpretation create unexpected difficulties for recruitment and performance evaluation at senior management level.

Absence and its control constantly reappears in HR discussions, with ever-changing recommendations about how to deal with it. In 'It all depends on your frame of reference: a study of absence', Catherine Allen and Derek Torrington produce an original analysis of the problem, considering the case of a continuous process plant where they suggest the difference in meaning it has at differing employment levels and the ensuing consequences.

The important area of reward is directly addressed by Richard Thorpe in 'Southern marine remunerations and payment systems'. Rapid company developments lead to management recognition of the need to establish a new wages and salary system, linked to the introduction of job evaluation. The case provides the opportunity to consider the benefits this will bring, as well as problems and pitfalls arising in its implementation.

A further element of reward for employees relates to promotion opportunities, although this may be limited as a result of discrimination on grounds of specific group characteristics. In 'Promotion decisions and management diversity at American Manufacturing', Patricia Ohlott and Marian Ruderman consider how an American company became committed to developing a diverse workforce and relate this to patterns in key selection decisions.

Discrimination and management of diversity themes are again taken up in 'Disabled employees within a local authority', where Carol Woodhams and Ann McGoldrick examine the disproportionate exclusion of disabled people from the workforce. Demographic, social, technological and legislative pressures which are encouraging organisations to consider disabled people as a positive part of the employment pool are used as the basis for examining the adaptation of equal opportunities, strategies and employment practices to encourage awareness and successful integration.

'Justifying an employee assistance programme' by John Berridge presents details of a company's attempt to combat problems of absence, service and quality deficits through the introduction of an EAP programme, replacing their former welfare support scheme. The case addresses the relevance of this change, as well as consequent benefits and pressures involved for individuals, company and the HRM function.

The important theme of employee support is again approached by Margaret Ferrario and Cary Cooper in 'Stress management interventions in organisations', which involves a stress audit in four companies to assess appropriate intervention mechanisms. Comparison is made before, during and subsequent to the initiative, with reference to both individual and organisational levels.

Euroservice

Audrey Klesta

INTRODUCTION

Euroservice is a large, French, multinational service company, which ranks fourth worldwide in the food services industry and employs over 40,000 people. Its major activity is catering for meals in company restaurants, hospitals, hotels, oil rigs and leisure ships.

The company has, in the last decade, expanded its range of services through forward and backward integration.

BACKGROUND TO THE CASE

Euroservice was founded in 1960 by George Cartier in the south-west of France, in the region between Bordeaux and Toulouse. It employed 30 people and its sole activity was the preparation and delivery of food to the ships docked at the port of Bordeaux.

Alain Cartier (George's son) had been a brilliant student in one of Paris' most prestigious business schools (les Grandes Écoles). In 1966, Alain Cartier took over the business from his father and became the President and CEO of Euroservice. His first big client was Aerospatiale in Toulouse. One year later, in 1967, he decided to expand the range of the company's activities in response to the first signs of the growing customer needs in the large cities.

Within a few years, the company had established itself throughout France, but it was only in 1975 that Euroservice began to gain a significant market share in Paris. The visionary Cartier very quickly decided to develop the company's activities linked to large construction sites in France and around the world. He said:

In ten years we will be the industry leader in France.

Indeed, a decade later the prediction had become reality, but Cartier had already defined the company's next ten-year objective :

... we will 'count' in Europe; we will become a worldwide organisation.

Through its opportunist strategy, Euroservice experienced rapid and widespread diversification.

The company's first achievements were in the nuclear industry, at Golfech and at Pierrelatte (in south-eastern France). Euroservice very quickly became the major supplier for several large French and American companies which were setting up factories, and also for large-scale operations such as airports, hospitals and oil rigs in Africa and the Middle

East. The growth environment in the years between 1960 and 1980 was extremely favourable to this kind of company because of the 'explosion' in the demand for services.

The development priorities chosen by Cartier were:

- major investments in the marketing area, and
- considerable revamping of its information technology (which would allow for a more rapid and consolidated reporting system).

On the other hand, until the beginning of the 1990s, there was virtually no policy of either investment or development in human resources within the Euroservice Group .

The above-mentioned context also 'moulded' the company culture, inasmuch as it 'cast' a system of values and behaviours. The following set of 'reflexes' were acquired during that period:

- (superficial) understanding of its customers' industry or business activities (except for the marketing aspect);
- heavy emphasis on the financial aspect of business: intricate budget and quantitative controls, based on short-term profits;
- strongly anchored tradition of decentralisation.

'Closeness' to the client led to a network organisation, made up of profit centres. Each managing director of a profit centre was 'skipper of his own ship'; each operational management team had extensive autonomy – as long as 'the numbers' were good. A 'good' manager was required to have the following competences:

- highly developed sales skills;
- good command of budget controls;
- good understanding of the market and market segments;
- responsive and proactive behaviour.

Some managers demonstrated a tendency to over-react, which led to hasty decisions.

By 1980, Euroservice had become the leader in the French national market and throughout the decade that followed, the company progressively gained a strong foothold in Italy, Belgium, Germany, Spain, Brazil and the United States.

Little by little, the international managers used English for business, especially in the Middle East. Nevertheless, the English language is used only as a 'necessary' communications tool. The company as a whole has not acknowledged the stakes which are represented by their managers having an excellent command of English. Furthermore, with reference to the Anglo-Saxon countries, there doesn't seem to be any worry (on the part of Euroservice) as to the cultural dimension linked to the language. The United States is considered to be a great market opportunity – a 'must' for any company hoping to operate on a global scale. Nevertheless, inasmuch as the company lacks any real corporate policy regarding the languages it uses, French has remained the 'power language', especially concerning the management of the European affiliates.

The company's incredible expansion was made possible by several factors:

- Very rigorous management.
- An 'obsession' with margins and expenses.
- A very strong concern for return on investments.
- A very precise approach to markets, and an organisation by markets. (For example, in the healthcare sector, differentiation in segmentation was made between institutions

which are 'long-stay' (such as convalescence homes) and those which are 'short-stay' (which include those instititions where minor surgery is performed, or maternity homes). The head manager of each segment has an intimate knowledge of how the establishments in his segment function, and how they are financed. In other words, each one of those managers knows where and how to make margins.)

- A culture which is entirely impregnated by its CEO's demanding, innovative and charismatic personality.
- A 'clan' of faithful lieutenants, made up of some 15 managers who were part of the company from the beginning, and who have a close personal relationship with the CEO.

Rapid expansion in profit-oriented markets requires a certain type of professional. At Euroservice, those who worked extensively, knew how to respond quickly to the needs of the customer, and rapidly increased the turnover in their sector, were those who were rewarded. The 'operational' culture which prevailed at Euroservice, characterised by a 'commando' or 'pioneer' spirit, was for a long time the only culture accepted by the company. The model for motivating managers was relatively simple. It was based on the principle of 'stimulus-response', which provided considerable financial rewards (by means of bonuses) to managers who were considered 'effective'.

This method of management was accompanied by a strong pressure 'to belong'. Managers who were considered efficient, were viewed well. Being in 'good grace' with top management, by getting good results, was an important strategy for anyone who wished to be respected 'at the top' and have a long-term career with the company. Unsatisfactory financial results during a one-year period were reason enough for falling out of grace with top management.

In the face of such constraints, the working climate among managers was often characterised by mutual criticism. Many managers tried to defend themselves by criticising their colleagues.

Alongside these very rigorous organisational aspects, Euroservice is, above all, sales-oriented. Alain Cartier quickly realised that the sales flexibility which his managers had could encourage a certain lax attitude, if he were not careful. Therefore, one of Cartier's main worries was trying to prevent any 'sales divergencies' in the operational management practices. As a result, the annual performance evaluations, for example, were always the object of very strict procedures. In order to avoid any risk of bias, in 1980 Alain Cartier took the following position (which is still in effect today):

> The manager must be firm during the appraisal interview. He must evaluate and justify his position. His judgment is non-negotiable! Only the means for improvement are negotiable.

As we have seen, this is a company which, for a long time, favoured purely operational functions. However, the increase in the size of the company made it necessary to create service functions which would forecast, co-ordinate and control. It took a long time and a lot of know-how, however, before these functions were recognised by the head operational managers.

THE AMERICAN AFFILIATE

In 1990, Euroservice had a sizeable amount of liquid assets. Having decided to set up business in the United States, it acquired the Turner Company, which is situated in

Massachusetts, on the East Coast. The history and development of this company can be summarised in a few lines as follows.

In 1965, Harold Turner was the owner of a small restaurant in Massachusetts. The restaurant had an excellent reputation, and, after a few years, the local hospital asked Turner if he would be willing to supply the morning and midday meals to the patients and staff of the hospital.

The demand steadily increased, and soon Turner was asked to also supply the evening meals for the hospital. After a few months the hospital requested that Turner set up and staff a kitchen within the hospital. The operation was a complete success. Within three years, the business had grown considerably. Several hospitals in the area had outsourced their catering needs to the Turner Company. By 1975, over 20 hospitals had become Turner customers. During the 1980s, the number of hospitals involved was over 70 (representing over 1200 people) and encompassing all the New England States.

Mr Turner was representative of many American managers. A self-made man, he built up his business by hard work and perseverance in a new market niche. He possessed no specific financial or management skills; he had acquired what he knew 'on the job', in response to the needs of his growing business. In fact, Turner encouraged his employees to remain flexible – not to become too specialised. Globally speaking, Turner's management style was in many ways representative of American management values in general. For example:

'Anything is possible.'
In the USA, anyone can start a business, and take his chances at becoming rich. The Rockefeller myth is a part of everyday life in America.

'You market yourself every day.'
In a country where initiative and individual risk taking are valued, it's necessary to call attention to oneself, to make known what you know and what you know how to do – otherwise you risk finding yourself out of a job and out on the street!

'The customer is always right.'
Responding to customer needs is an extremely important part of American business practices. Americans know that if they don't respond, someone else will! Rather than being a bunch of techniques, marketing is a state of mind which is widespread in America. Turner knew that competition in his sector was fierce, and that he could lose a contract at any time.

'Service and customer loyalty, depend largely on the quality of the men and women who are employed by the Turner Company ...'
Having learned his line of work on the job, Turner was convinced that the value of the employees made the difference. That's why, for the last several years, careful attention was paid to the training and follow-up of team leaders – those people who were in daily contact with the personnel who served the customer.

When the company reached 300 in size, however, Turner began to recruit a few specialists in the legal and financial departments. The business seemed to 'outgrow' Turner.

Conscious of his strengths and his weaknesses, seeing that profits had been gradually slipping over the last two years, wanting to begin preparing for his retirement, and not having a potential successor in mind, Turner had begun to think about selling his business when he was contacted by Euroservice.

He had never imagined that his business would interest the Europeans. When he was first contacted, Turner was quite surprised. He thought to himself:

> We Americans invented modern management. I can't imagine myself selling my business over to the Europeans. If I leave my company, I ask myself what in the world *they* can teach my employees! I have a hard time imagining my former employees being managed by people who aren't American. I always considered them on an equal basis, very close to me. I wonder how they'll react to Europeans, who have the reputation of being distant, 'stand-offish' and even elitist.
>
> Then there's the language problem! I don't know how people can ever work in a language other than English!

The hospital sector in the United States is managed in a way that differs greatly from the French or European practices. These hospitals are run by directors who are used to operating with several subcontractors at once, dealing with laundry, cooking, cleaning and maintenance. They work at a narrow, fixed margin.

This system allows hospital managers to:

- keep a tight control over the margins suppliers get, and
- to remain in control of the situation by avoiding the overdependency created by a single-supplier situation.

Indirectly, this type of organisation also allows the hospital directors to exercise a certain type of control over their suppliers' employees, through 'bonuses' or other 'advantages' at the workplace. The supplier has virtually no control over this kind of situation.

The management at Euroservice corporate headquarters quickly came to the conclusion that the profitability of their new American affiliate was not up to par with the profitability of their European affiliates. In fact, it only generated about 50 per cent of what the Europeans did. During the first year after the acquisition, the relations between the French corporate management and the American affiliate management showed serious signs of strain.

Alain Cartier appointed one of his 'faithful lieutenants' as President of the new affiliate. Unfortunately, the new President tried to manage the affiliate from Paris! This situation very quickly proved unsatisfactory.

A year later, in order to rectify the situation, Jean Darmet was appointed to head the American affiliate. Darmet had previously headed all of Euroservice's operations in Brazil, as well as having been Regional Director for the Company and Administrative Restaurants Sector in the region of Rhône-Alp (south-east France).

On his flight between Paris and New York, Jean took the time to think about his new assignment and the structure of the American affiliate. Having carefully studied the data made available to him, Darmet decided to reorganise the executive committee of Turner (which was the the real decision-making body of the company). He decided to fire several of the existing managers (who were considered to be poor performers or 'too hostile towards the new French management').

RECRUITMENT

A priority for Darmet was to hire his 'right-hand man' quickly, so that the new affiliate could develop under optimum conditions. In fact, the real reason for this visit to the

States was to interview several candidates for this position. A few candidates had already been shortlisted by the Head of Human Resources at the affiliate.

The major components of the job description had been faxed to the Human Resources Director of Turner two weeks earlier. They included:

● Ensure the liaison between the regional managers of Boston, New York and Washington.
● Represent the interests of the affiliate vis-à-vis the local laws and regulations.
● Conduct an in-depth market study in order to identify new possibilities for penetration into the hospital market.
● Ensure a solid liaison with corporate headquarters in Paris, so as to implement in the USA what appeared to be the most innovative forms of business organisation and marketing in Paris!

ACTIVITY BRIEF

1 Put yourself in Jean Darmet's position. Make a list of the main recruitment criteria. Classify these criteria, beginning with the most crucial. Take into account the job description above.

2 You are the Director of Human Resources of the American affiliate. Draw up a list of the main recruitment criteria. Classify these criteria, beginning with the most crucial. Take into account the job description above.

Jean Darmet asked himself whether he should insist on the use of graphology when selecting the American candidate. Graphology is a technique of handwriting analysis which is regularly used in France for the selection of managers. He knew that when Alain Cartier came to Massachusetts (the following month) he would surely ask for a copy of the graphology report.

Finally, Darmet selected a candidate. His name was John Murphy. He was very surprised when the time came to sign the contract. Each point was discussed in great detail. The candidate felt he shouldn't sign the contract on the spot. He asked for some time to think it over, and to be able to discuss the details with his lawyer. Jean Darmet asked himself if the candidate trusted him!

A SNAPSHOT OF THE FIRST YEAR

On the whole, John Murphy's first few months in his new position went well. It was after about six months, however, that Jean Darmet realised that a certain misunderstanding had permeated the relationship between John Murphy and himself. The two men's offices were adjacent to each other. The more Darmet observed how Murphy worked, the more obvious the misunderstanding appeared to be. Darmet decided to have a talk with Murphy. Several key elements emerged from their discussion.

According to Murphy:

My objectives are totally fuzzy.

In this company, there doesn't seem to be any real set of procedures – except for budgeting.

... Besides, you're so distant and formal. We never seem to be able to roll our sleeves up and really talk business together, even though our offices are right next door to each other!

Also, if you remember, when you hired me, you promised to send me to Paris to get a feel for how the healthcare sector works in France. It was written in my contract.

Even though Jean Darmet was totally shocked by John Murphy's blatent language, he did not show his discontent. Darmet thought to himself:

For the amount of money I pay him, I certainly don't intend to lead him by the hand!

The remark about the lack of procedures had surprised Darmet. He replied to Murphy:

You Americans have the reputation of being entrepreneurial and innovative. So what are you waiting for? Put your money where your mouth is. That's what I hired you for!

Darmet conceded to the fact that he hadn't been of much help to Murphy, and agreed to accompany him to visit their two biggest customers and two other prospects.
Concerning the trip to Paris, Darmet replied:

Look, it's just been a problem of time. I promise to take care of it.

Murphy came back with:

I really feel it's dishonest on your part to have pushed this trip aside. How can you expect me to be efficient in my job, if I've never had a chance to see how things are 'supposed' to be run? I never know exactly what you expect of me in this place! And for your information, I'm not the only one.

It's not a question of a lack of initiative, it's a question of setting clear performance standards.

At the end of their meeting, Darmet carefully spelled out the objectives headquarters had set for the American affiliate: bring the profitability of Turner up to two thirds of that of Euroservice – within the year!

The annual appraisal

John Murphy was certainly not looking forward to this meeting. Darmet began by explaining the reason for their meeting, and then asked Murphy what his present opinion was on the structure of the market within the hospitals.
John replied:

My trip to Paris was very interesting, even though all of the hospital tours that were planned didn't take place. We only actually got to see two of the four hospitals.

In my opinion, the French concept will be very difficult to implement in the States, for a number of reasons. First, it's completely different. Second, in hospitals here, the manager is in the *buyer's seat*. He's used to having several suppliers and making them compete against each other. The guy's power and job security depend on things staying like that!

Third, the public hospital sector is a nightmare. We'd be better off sticking to medium-sized private hospitals.

Darmet had a different point of view:

I totally disagree. Our competitive advantage in Europe is based on offering a total-service package. That's exactly how we outdid our competitors in Belgium, Italy, Germany and Spain. We can't just give up like that. I honestly thought you were more of a fighter!

Now I'd like to tell you what I think about your performance this past year. I've identified the following positive aspects:

- a very strong involvement in your work;
- a good mastery of contacts in the business environment, especially with lawyers;
- respect for budget procedures.

On the negative side :
- you offered very few innovative marketing proposals;
- profitability is only at 4.5 per cent; that's only an increase of a half point. It's insufficient and too slow.

The only way to increase our margin is to have an innovative approach to the market! On the whole, I feel you've lacked a spirit of initiative.

The interview continued. However, the tone had been set. John was surprised and disappointed. He was expecting a dialogue to be established between Darmet and himself, in order to increase his professional development. Instead, he had the distinct feeling that Darmet had played judge and jury. The criticisms Darmet made were more like the results of some kind of test, but what was it based on? He felt the way Darmet had done things was extremely unfair, even unethical! It had been a unilateral judgement. Darmet never even took into consideration John's point of view!

John thought to himself:

Here I am with ten years' work experience, nine of which were with American companies renowned for their avant garde management techniques, and never have I seen someone treated as I just was! Even when I needed serious improvement in certain areas, managers always pointed it out to me in an encouraging way.

I ask myself what he's going to write about me? There's no way he can get me to sign that questionnaire he's filling out on me!

I can't believe he did not say one encouraging thing, even though I busted my back trying to be successful in this job ...

Feeling that the atmosphere was extremely strained, Jean Darmet suggested that they each take some time to think things over, and then get together for another meeting the following week.

ACTIVITY BRIEF (cont.)

3 From a cultural viewpoint, how can you account for the misunderstanding which took place between Jean Darmet and John Murphy?

4 What advice would you give to Jean Darmet for his next meeting with John Murphy?

RECOMMENDED READING

Fatehi, K (1995) *International Management: A Cross-cultural Approach*, London, Prentice Hall.

Harzing, AW and Van Ruyssereldt, J (1994) (eds) *International Human Resource Management*, London, Sage.

Hofstede, G (1980) 'Motivation, leadership and organization: do American theories apply abroad?', *Organizational Dynamics*, Summer, pp. 42–63.

Hofstede, G (1991) *Cultures and Organisations: Software of the Mind*, London, McGraw–Hill.

Pieper, R (1990) (ed) *Human Resource Management: An International Comparison*, New York, Walter de Gruyter.

It all depends on your frame of reference: a study of absence

Catherine Allen and Derek Torrington

INTRODUCTION

Despite the fact that over 250 studies have examined various aspects of the absence phenomenon (Dalton and Mesch 1991), there has been little attention to what this term actually means. The concept of 'absence' has only ever been defined loosely. When researchers offer definitions, they often define tacit theories of absence which are bound to specific measures (Finchman 1984). Consequently our understanding of absence has not progressed much beyond superficial descriptive levels. In practice the meaning and nature of absence varies according to who you are. How absence is construed impacts so heavily on an individual's behaviour regarding absence that an understanding of its meaning to an individual is crucial to understanding that person's behaviour, and is vital to learning how to control that behaviour.

BACKGROUND TO THE CASE

A common assumption is that absence must be a workplace-related phenomenon. This is seen immediately in the widespread use of the term absence *from work*. This assumption is perfectly natural in view of the problems which absence causes management, and yet the logic is incomplete. When people are *absent* from work they must be *present* somewhere else (Johns and Nicholson 1982) Treating absence as a dysfunctional performance at work is only considering one side of the coin. While management may view non-attendance in terms of the employee not being at work, there is no reason to suppose that the non-attender feels the same way. People can only be regarded as absent from their work if they have an ideology of work which requires them to be present at work (otherwise they are not absent from work, they are just not there). In this way, absence can also be seen as a managerial concept which only functions within an ideology of work which defends subordination.

This gives us a clue regarding how people come to view absence in a particular light. There are two major factors which influence a person's view of absence: the orientation to work and the employment contract.

How an individual views absence from work depends largely on how that individual views the work itself. If absence only makes sense within an ideology of work which dictates that a person should attend, then people who do not share that view do not have the same conceptualisation of absence from work. Johns and Nicholson (1982) suggest that where the effort–reward relationship is obscure and the boundary between work and non-work is highly discretionary or blurred by the nature of the task, 'absence' may have an entirely different meaning from that held by those engaged in typical industrial employment.

Workers with an instrumental orientation, whose primary relationship with their employer is money, are likely to take whatever action they feel necessary to achieve their just rewards. Once this has been done, they can concentrate on non-work interests. In terms of attendance the logical implication of this is that the decision to attend rests with the worker. Others, who see their employment as a service to an organisation, have a more complicated relationship with work, imbued with moral obligations which mean that the distinction between work as a money-making encounter and non-work as an interest is not complete. Such workers may feel guilty if they do not attend because their orientation holds that they should be there.

Initially coined by Argyris (1960), the concept of the *psychological contract* has been developed most fully by Schein (1980). He defines it as the set of unwritten reciprocal expectations between an individual employee and the organisation. Gibson (1966) has developed a theory of absence which includes the influence of the contract. He argues that since the psychological contract is probably perceived as more inclusive by those in high discretion roles, managers and professionals would view absence as work-related behaviour, an aspect of individual performance and a fundamental ethical challenge to the contract. Workers in low discretion roles, on the other hand, might have a more restricted view of their obligation to go to work, and see legitimisation as a technical, rather than moral, matter.

The formal contract of employment will also have a bearing on the perception of absence. Payment, for example, is the outward demonstration of the relationship between employer and employee. Employees paid an annual salary are likely to conceive their jobs as having a role in the business with a long-term orientation, with all the moral obligations that this implies. Hourly paid employees, on the other hand, are only paid for the precise hours they work. This impinges on the overall attitude to attendance, for if they are only paid for their time at work, they are the only losers if they do not attend. There has been little research in this area, but such was the attitude of one worker in a recent study. When asked whether he took days off, he replied, 'I suit myself. If I feel like a day off with the wife that's my business.' He argued that if he could afford to lose a day's pay then he had the right to do as he liked with his time, 'After all, we are only paid hourly,' he added (Edwards and Scullion 1982).

Different meanings of absence

For certain employees absence is meaningful because they have a view of work which requires them to be non-absent: absence is deviant behaviour. Without such an attitude towards work, however, non-attendance ceases to have quite the same meaning. The meaning of absence is assumed because it is always approached from a managerial perspective. For managers and management researchers alike, absence is a type of deviant behaviour because it can be seen to cause problems. It imposes direct costs upon both organisational efficiency and productivity. Although logical, this view is not universal.

While we may expect absence to have different meanings for people in contrasting occupations, this does not mean that absence is a behaviour peculiarly characteristic of people lower down the organisational hierarchy. Again, such a supposition is a consequence of defining absence from a managerial point of view. It is largely to do with the 'generalised other'. As Johns and Nicholson (1982) put it, the verb 'to be absent' could be conjugated:

> *I* am sometimes prevented from attending work through no fault of my own. *You* lack motivation to attend work regularly. *They* are lazy malingerers, wilfully milking the system.

One widespread assumption in management thinking is that shopfloor absence by manual workers is much more common ('... lazy malingerers, wilfully milking the system ...') than staff absence among clerical and administrative workers. This can be a vicious circle, for the presumption that staff absence is not a problem means that data referring to staff absence is not even collected; some might say it is part of the privilege of being a member of staff. Consequently staff absence becomes somewhat invisible, and is thus assumed not to represent a problem! Absence occurs throughout the world of work, however. It is frequently found that white-collar staff exhibit lower levels and different forms of absence, and, if this is the case, the difference in attitude and status of the two groups would prove a useful comparison (Edwards and Scullion 1984).

Staff absence also raises further questions as to what we define as absence. Lenz has argued that one of the prerogatives of management is the right to be absent. As Lenz put it:

> 'It is the right to sit around the office and talk, the right to take a slightly longer lunch hour than everyone else, the right to run personal errands during the day while blue-collar workers must wait until Saturday.' (Lenz, quoted in Steers and Rhodes 1984)

Such a comment raises the question of what counts as absence and what does not, for it is one thing to turn up to work each day; it is quite another to work when one gets there! Perhaps one reason why (official) staff absence levels are so low is the fact that staff make up for it with enough absence on the job in the form of non-work. Opportunities for absence at work should not be underestimated in absence research. Edwards and Scullion (1982) point out that 'unrecorded absenteeism' on the shopfloor via an informal rota for periods of time off (up to as much as half a day) was a major factor in keeping absence low in that factory. It can be seen, therefore, that by considering a wider definition of absence which includes 'absence at work', we might uncover some useful pointers as to why people are 'absent from work'.

GLACTEL: FROM TRADITION TO MANAGERIALISM

The case study company is the UK's sole manufacturing site of Glactel, situated in the north-west of England. Until recently the plant had been a staunchly traditional site with a relaxed, 'big happy family' atmosphere. In the 1980s, however, the site faced closure by its European directors, and management felt the need to reassert their authority. Managers proceeded to tighten their control over the workforce, with a view to moving the site towards 'high commitment' and 'high performance'. With this move came an increased managerial focus and clamp down on absenteeism – a behaviour which was viewed by management as being a product of lax management and low commitment. Their control produced few results, however, and a fresh approach was needed.

Glactel is a major multinational business in the fast-moving consumer goods industry, mainly producing personal care products. Its business is based around brand management within a European manufacturing structure, that is, its products are only manufactured in one or two sites and then exported across Europe.

The site in the case study is one of the oldest in Europe. It grew from an old soap-making factory built in 1938, and some of the machinery still dates back to this time. Even though a major renovation process has been underway, the site is still very old-fashioned, both in its structure and in its culture. The dated machinery is a stark reminder that not so long ago the working system was not so different from one which FW Taylor himself might have set up. Management have been trying hard to change this in the last ten years.

The site is now divided into four focus factories: Soaps (160 employees), Bodycare (40 employees), Tubes (150 employees) and Mouthrinse (30 employees). Each focus factory has its own support, while some central support functions such as personnel still remain. Altogether there are 540 employees, 160 of whom are staff. This structure generally works well, except that the competition which it generates between the focus factories has a tendency to become unhealthy. This is in part due to the substantial changes which are being pushed through at the moment.

The move to the HCWS

Management are at present trying to institute a major cultural and structural change. The aim is to move to a team-based, High Commitment Work System (HCWS) whereby the product lines are run by self-managing multi-skilled teams – thus making specialised mechanics and quality departments redundant. The change has not been managed well and there is a lot of ill-will across the site. The first move was in January 1993, when Mouthrinse was set up as a brand new focus factory with new multi-skilled technicians recruited from outside. Since it was the first HCWS factory a lot of training and investment was put into its employees, while the other focus factories were left alone. Moreover, Mouthrinse's special – not to say superior – status was emphasised in the fact that it was a brand new factory with state-of-the-art equipment, set apart physically from the rest of the factory because of hygiene requirements. As a result, Mouthrinse was highly resented. Furthermore the system has not really worked as well as was hoped. The teams within Mouthrinse are still operating fairly traditionally, and a team spirit has not really been formed.

Unfortunately this has not only meant that Mouthrinse employees are frustrated and discontent, but it has also vindicated a lot of the bad feeling across the site. Now the other focus factories are in the process of moving to HCWS, employees are even more unwilling, and tension across the site is high. To make matters worse, management had promised Soaps, the oldest and most traditional factory, that they would stay as they were. Now, however, they have changed their mind and are forcing Soaps to move to HCWS too. (Forcing being the appropriate word here, for, when the employees protested, they were told to 'either move to HCWS or find another job elsewhere'! Needless to say most are moving – reluctantly.)

A workforce unsettled by change

Feelings across the site are far from positive therefore, and the workforce is very unsettled. Lack of communication is rife, with the result that workers are highly suspicious of management, who they feel have hidden agendas. The dismantling of the maintenance function means that there are lot of workers doing jobs for which they are over-qualified (for example, time-served engineers packing on the lines). Employees who have worked as packers all their lives are concerned about the future of their jobs now that multi-skilling is being introduced. Soaps' employees are concerned because the soaps market is declining and much is being lost to European factories. Older workers are dubious now that a period of voluntary redundancies has just swept the site.

This whole situation is made worse by the lack of communication on site and the feeling that workers are powerless to do anything. The two unions are so weak that they are pretty ineffective, and the consultative machinery which is there in name in the form of team briefings has no practical two-way function, focusing mainly on production issues. Not surprisingly, trust is not a plentiful commodity on site.

Does this situation have an effect on absence? According to the occupational health department it has resulted in a lot of workers going off with stress. This is one explanation, but there is another. For while we need to be wary of associating absence with a conscious and motivated behaviour, it has been hypothesised that absence might be used by employees to 'send a message' to management about their unhappiness (Hammer, Landau and Stern 1981). It will be interesting to see if this is happening at Glactel.

Management – employee relations

Although attempts are being made to transform the site, a traditional culture still remains well ingrained. This is fostered by the fact that there are many employees who have worked for the company all their lives. It is further perpetuated by the fact that many of the team managers have been promoted from the shopfloor and have carried a lot of their values with them. Has this led to a tacit acceptance of the absence norm? In an attempt to break out of this vicious circle Glactel has just recruited some new team managers from a company with a much tougher stance towards absenteeism and management in general. What effect will this have? Furthermore, it will be interesting to view whether the culture is any different in the new HCWS system within Mouthrinse, or whether employees who have been transferred from other departments have also transferred their values and assumptions with them.

This situation has been coupled with a fairly lax management stance in general. The Senior Personnel Manager, recruited within the last 18 months, says he was amazed at what he found when he arrived, for this 'blue chip' company was 'still operating in the dark ages'. It is often commentated among higher levels of management that 'this place has been run like a holiday camp for too long', and they are trying to clamp down in general much more. For example, seeing that overtime was too readily available and was having an effect on normal production times (people working slower to get more overtime) they tried to introduce a non-overtime site. This met with limited success, however, since a boost in production in Tubes forced weekend overtime sky high, while the Soaps' business is declining so they have no overtime, and what is more are all being shipped into Tubes! Measures such as these (and the much hated new non-smoking policy) are far from popular, and it is often commented by old-timers that Glactel 'isn't such a nice place to work anymore'.

After all, Glactel had had a reputation as a caring, reasonably paying organisation. Effort levels had not been very demanding and there was a generous set of welfare and fringe benefits, including free health and dental treatment in a brand new occupational health department and an extremely generous sick pay scheme. This tradition, along with a 'job for life' mentality, meant that workers felt pretty secure. This feeling of security has been transformed to one of conflict in the past few years as management have instituted the above-mentioned changes.

Payment and overtime

Workers on the shopfloor are paid by the hour. There are no incentives – at least no incentives to work harder – apart from an annual bonus based on company profits. There is, on the other hand, quite a large incentive to work more slowly, since production quotas not met in the week need to be met at weekends, when workers are paid time-and-a-half and double-time. There is still a very strong overtime culture in the factory, even though it is meant to be moving towards a non-overtime site. The reality is that vast fluctuations in production mean that some departments can be doing quite large amounts of overtime in a given period which can often last for months. These same fluctuations often leave some departments vastly over-crewed. In the Soaps factory at the moment, for example, there are only a few lines working. 'Spare' employees are either shipped onto other lines or left to do the cleaning. Once again, what effect does this have on attendance?

Sick pay, notification and certification

The Company Sickness Benefit Scheme pays sick pay from the first day of sickness at a rate which, after state benefits are taken into account, keeps take-home pay at basic earning levels. This very generous scheme operates for six weeks, when the employee then receives half pay for a further six weeks. Since 1982 when self-certification was brought in, workers no longer need a doctor's note for illnesses under seven days. They now 'self-certify' for shorter absences, though they have to have a doctor's note for longer illnesses and possibly see the company nurse. As far as notification is concerned, the company has a 'sick call line', whereby sick employees phone up an answering machine in the administration centre. As long as the self-certification form is signed off by the team manager (and it invariably is) the employee will receive full pay as normal for the period of absence.

Absence control

In line with the traditionally lax managerial approach, the line taken as regards absence has been far from tough. Indeed until a few years ago absence levels were not even measured! Correspondingly there is no coherent strategy for dealing with absence. Control has tended to be *ad hoc*, individualised, and very irregular indeed. Team managers have been left to handle it as they see fit, but, of course, the pressures of production have tended to mean that it was not handled at all. Consequently absence really has not been an issue until very recently.

Absence levels started to be monitored from about 1992, which prompted an understanding that absence was an issue, but little more. Individuals with appalling attendance records were warned, but little was done with the great majority of employees. May 1993 saw the arrival of a new Senior Personnel Manager from a firm which had been very strict in terms of absence, which was to change the company's attitude to absence. He capitalised on the growing awareness that absence was important and made supervisors clamp down on it.

Absence data analysis

Trend data were calculated over the 18-month period from January 1992 to June 1994. It was analysed using time lost, attitudinal and frequency indexes, and analysed for both hourly paid employees and staff. Patterns were also investigated concerning the days on which one-day absence fell, and the effect of gender and shift patterns.

Site absence levels for hourly paid employees

Figure 9.1 shows the overall level of absence steadily increased during 1992–3, rising to a peak in Sept–Dec 1993 of around 10 per cent. The average over the 18 months is about 6 per cent, which is on the high side for its market sector. (In 1993 the industry average for its category 'other manufacturing' was 4.7 per cent (Industrial Society 1993).) It is interesting that the absence levels had been drifting upwards over the period, before taking a dramatic downturn in the first few months of 1994.

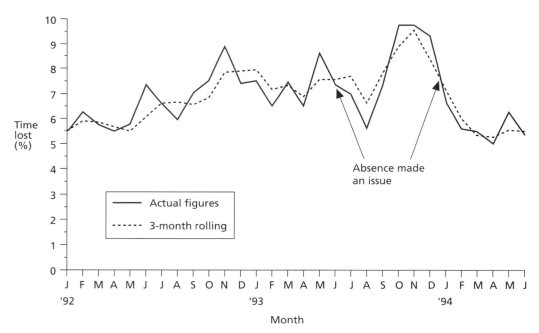

Fig 9.1 Plant absence levels, Jan 1992–June 1994

This corresponds almost exactly with the amount of attention given to absence over this period plant-wide. It was not really considered an issue until 1993, when the new Senior Personnel Manager brought it to management's attention that absence levels were high. A system of spasmodic clampdowns was introduced and prompted drops in absence levels, but not for long. When controls became lax again the absence levels shot up again at the end of 1993, to an even higher level (although this was worsened by an epidemic of flu). The personnel department responded accordingly – this time by instituting a major purge – and the absence rates plummeted dramatically (Jan–Apr 1994). This suggests that absence levels are a direct function of how much attention is paid to absence.

Other factors were considered (such as flu epidemics and restructuring) to see if these might have had an impact on the absence rates to make the connection less obvious, but the pattern can only really be explained by the attention paid to absence, and the connection is so clear that it indicates fairly substantially that simply by making absence an issue, the absence rates will decrease (rather like the Hawthorne Effect).

This important finding does not imply, however, that mere attention should replace permanent control, for clearly this approach is not particularly stable. After both purges the absence percentages started to rise again. Furthermore, the purge only really brought the absence level back down to what it had been in 1992–3, indicating that the attention did little more than curb the excessive absenteeism made possible by the scant attention paid to it in the past. This conclusion is borne out by examining absence rates across the different departments (*see* Fig 9.2). After the 1993 purge there was a substantial drop in all departments except Mouthrinse, where the levels actually rose. Since this is the one department where absence was not felt to be an issue and hence little attention was paid to it anyway, it does lend substantial weight to the hypothesis that absence decreases when made an issue.

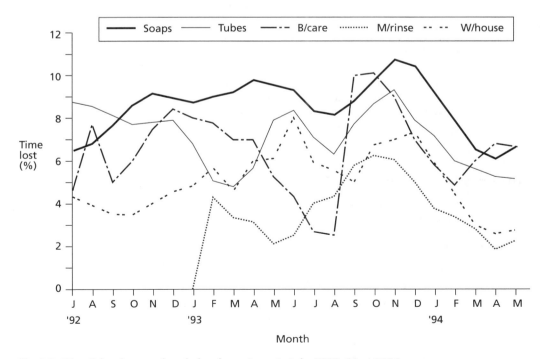

Fig 9.2 Monthly absence levels by department, July 1992–May 1994

Long- and short-term absence

Half of all absence is for less than five days in a single spell. Figure 9.3 shows the distribution of absence spells lasting for 1, 2, 3, 4 or 5 days in 1993 when compared with 1994. This proportion only moved from 51 per cent down to 48 per cent in 1994, when there was the increased attempt at management control. The number of one-day absences generally came down in 1994, yet there has been a corresponding increase in the number of five-day absences. In view of the fact that January 1994 saw the start of a site-wide clampdown on absence, this could easily be one effect of this: that is, firming up on absence control changes one-day absences into five-day absences!

Staff absence

Staff absence levels fluctuated from month to month, with a noticeable drop in the summer months. On average the time lost rate for 1993 was 1.48 per cent, which rose slightly in 1994 to 1.8 per cent. These figures are actually considerably lower than the national averages calculated by the Confederation of British Industry (CBI) in 1987, which had a rate of 4 per cent for professionals and 3 per cent for managers in large establishments. The pattern of absence was also different, with five times as many one-day absences as five-day absences.

Absence levels at Glactel have been a direct function of how much management attention has been devoted to the absence issue. Over 18 months the level drifted up to 10 per cent, which is way above the industry and regional average. Clampdowns on the part of management made this percentage drop dramatically, but it was not a sustained drop, and only really curbed the excesses which had been made possible by the lack of attention. Although attention is clearly a very important factor in the controlling of absence, it does need to be built into a permanent structure to ensure that it does not wane as supervisors move onto other concerns.

The vast majority of absence at Glactel is short term and self-certificated. In 1993 there was a particular problem with one-day absences. When team managers clamped down on absence at the start of 1994, this reduced the number of one-, two- and three-day absences. However, it also had the effect of increasing the number of five-day absences, the number of which almost doubled in one department. This is one effect of control which clearly warrants investigation. While staff are not absent to the same levels as the hourly paid, when they do go absent, the period of absence tends to be much shorter, usually one or two days.

Attitudes to absence

Fifty-seven interviews were carried out at the site and produced the following comments about the absence situation.

Awareness of absence

Senior managers were all acutely aware of absence levels at the plant, but this awareness was not based on fact, and was more thought about than acted upon.

> I know that absence is a problem, but right at the moment there are more pressing problems with production which I need to deal with, so it's not very high on my list of priorities.

Supervisors had much more of a working knowledge of absence. They all knew roughly what the percentage was for their shift and how it compared to the department, but

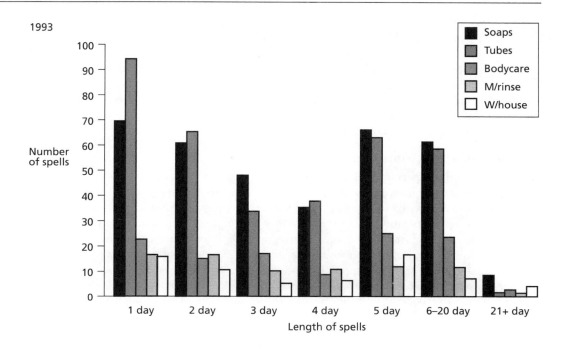

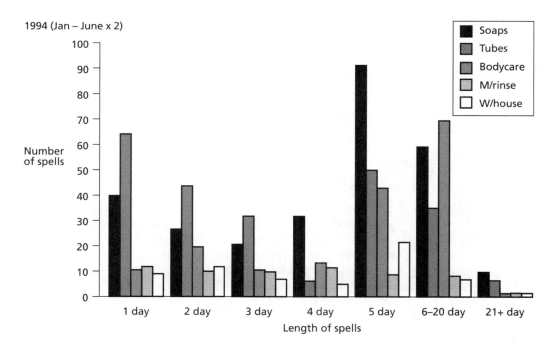

Fig 9.3 Length of absences by department, 1993–1994

seemed to get this information more from a general feeling from their own records than from the weekly time-lost statistics from payroll.

Their informal records enabled them to pinpoint individual 'offenders' and those with long-term sick problems, but they were less concerned with the majority of their workers, and only seemed to know a person's absence record if they 'knew' them to be an offender.

Most of the hourly paid employees had no idea about the percentage of time lost, although all the supervisors claimed that they communicated the official time-lost percentage in regular team briefings!

The effect of absence on work

All the supervisors regarded absence as a 'planning headache', but qualified this by saying that different kinds of absence affected them in different ways. An absence of one day was a major problem because they would only know about it on the morning it occurred, and might not know whether a person was simply late or would be coming in and could be used on a line. Week-long absences, on the other hand, were much less disruptive. If they knew on a Monday morning that someone would be off for the week, they could then plan round them. Once a person phoned in sick for the week, the supervisors did not bother to phone them or encourage them back to work, since they have already planned round them.

Hourly paid employees said the absence of others had little effect on their work, although 25 per cent welcomed absence as it provided them with overtime opportunities to cover for absentees.

Types and causes of absence

When asked why people were generally off work, senior managers all answered in terms of motivation, morale, lack of commitment and unexciting work, or the influence of an absence culture:

> Well, they're not sick are they?

> I don't think sickness is a major part of absence.

> There's still a mentality which sees absence as a holiday entitlement – you have five weeks' holiday and six weeks' sick.

> There's still a culture which says you're a fool unless you have the time off, which says, 'the company's out to screw you, so you might as well screw them back!

> Workers think, 'I don't enjoy work anyway, I'm only here for the money, so I'll take what I can.'

Supervisors, on the other hand, were more inclined to believe that absence could be genuine sickness. They had a strong distinction in their minds between genuine absence and non-genuine absence. There was still a certain amount of cynicism, however, with references again to the idea that absence is seen as a holiday entitlement, to the motivational issue, to unrest at the plant and to overtime as a major factor. Overtime was seen to have three effects. First, that people would rather have their 'time off' during the week rather than at the weekend, since they could get paid time-and-a-half or double-time at weekends. Second, because people work so much overtime, they need time off and do become genuinely ill because they're worn out. Third, people consciously use absence to share out the overtime in the shift.

As far as type of absence is concerned, not only is there is a strong distinction in the minds of the team managers between genuine and non-genuine absence, but there is an assumption that one- and two-day absences are much less likely to be 'genuine':

It's not the people who take weeks off, it's the people who take one or two days off at a time who are abusing the system.

… longer absence will be more obviously sickness whereas a one-day is more likely to be a hangover.

Hourly paid employees were quite flummoxed when asked the reasons for absence and their answers were vague, but still revealing. Tables 9.1 and 9.2 show the answers to two questions.

Table 9.1 Hourly paid employees' replies to the question, 'What are the main reasons for people being off work?'

Replies	%
'Just sickness' (shrugging their shoulders)	26
'Boredom', 'conditions have changed', 'morale and job satisfaction have gone down'	28
A combination of the above two	17
'People skiving'	17
'Sickness is a holiday entitlement'	12

Table 9.2 Hourly paid employees' replies to the question, 'What are the main reasons for one-day absences?'

Replies	%
Overslept	39
Alcohol	24
Family problems	15
Issue at work the day before	7
One-day illness	15

ACTIVITY BRIEF

1 What does the term 'absence from work' mean to you?

2 What do you think of the informal rota for periods of time off work, described by Edwards and Scullion (1982)?

3 In your experience what has been the effect on employee absence of self-certification for short periods of sickness?

4 Analysis of absence data at Glactel shows that absence drops when there is 'a purge', but the effect is only short-lived. Why do you think this is?

5 It appears that staff absence at Glactel is lower than shopfloor absence. What do you think the reason is for this?

6 What is the difference in attitudes to absence revealed among senior managers compared with those of supervisors?

7 What would you do about the management of absence (or attendance) at Glactel?

RECOMMENDED READING

Argyris, C (1960) *Understanding Organisational Behaviour*, London, Tavistock.

Dalton, DR and Mesch, DJ (1991) 'On the extent and reduction of avoidable absenteeism; an assessment of absence policy provisions', *Journal of Applied Psychology*, 76, 6.

Edwards, P and Scullion, H (1982) *The Social Organisation of Industrial Conflict. Control and Resistance in the Workplace,* Oxford, Blackwell.

Finchman, M (1984) 'A theoretical approach to understanding employee absence' in Goodman, PS and Atkin, RS (eds) *Absenteeism; New Approaches to Understanding, Measuring and Managing Employee Absence*, San Francisco, Jossey Bass.

Gibson, RO (1966) 'Towards a conceptualisation of absence behaviour', *Administrative Sciences Quarterly*, 11.

Hammer, TH, Landau, J and Stern, R (1980) *Absenteeism When Workers Have a Voice: The Case of Employee Ownership*, Working Paper, Cornell University.

Hucynski, AA and Fitzpatrick, MJ (1989) *Managing Employee Absence for a Competitive Edge*, London, Pitman.

Johns, G and Nicholson, N (1982) 'The meaning of absence: new strategies for theory and research' in Straw, BM and Cummings, LL (eds) *Research in Organisational Behaviour*, 4, London, JAI Press Inc.

Schein, EH (1980) *Organisational Psychology* (3rd edn), Englewood Cliffs, NJ, Prentice Hall.

Steers, RM and Rhodes, SR (1984) 'Knowledge and speculation about absenteeism' in Goodman, PS and Atkin, RS (eds) *Absenteeism; New Approaches to Understanding, Measuring and Managing Employee Absence,* San Francisco, Jossey Bass.

Southern Marine remunerations and payment systems

Richard Thorpe

INTRODUCTION

Southern Marine is an extremely successful, wholly owned subsidiary of Rockwell Power. Its business is the maintenance and refurbishing of marine engines – a fiercely competitive market on a world scale. Technology and the quality of the employees the company recruits both play their part in ensuring that Southern Marine remains competitive.

BACKGROUND TO THE CASE

Currently, the company specialises in two engine types. They power the freighters as well as the smaller luxury yachts. Its market is literally the world's shipping industry and those companies in this market that are successful and remain so are those that can keep marine delays due to engine failure down to a minimum – the order-winning and order-losing criteria in this industry sector. Although the market is not particularly price sensitive, a conditioning factor remains price.

Southern Marine represents a new player in the engine field. Recognising an opportunity through its parent company and situating itself on the south coast, it is ideally placed to take advantage of the gap it perceives in the market.

The company is non-unionised and has grown quickly, in a classical way, although the procedures and manufacturing processes are 'high tech' and its personnel (approximately 200) are extremely highly skilled. Its wages and salary structure has been unable to cope with the strain of such a rapidly growing concern. When the business employed only 25 to 30 people it wasn't difficult to design and manage a wages and salary strategy that was logical and considered fair. Since its inception in 1989, however, the number of engine makes the company is capable of refurbishing has doubled and still more are planned. Technicians, engineers and clerical staff have all taken on new work as the company has grown and the wages and salary policy, originally not a problem, could potentially now hold back future development, particularly if the number of disputes about pay were to rise, or the frustration felt by many were to increase.

As with many other companies, an important feature of this business is the need to retain the flexibility of its staff so that it can continue to meet the needs of both the customers and market – a key ingredient in the success of the business thus far. Currently there is a great deal of flexibility between operatives and supervisory and technical staff and the management wish to retain this feature in any new scheme, so that the strategic needs of the business can continue to be met.

THE PERCEIVED NEED FOR A NEW WAGES AND SALARY SYSTEM

Although the present system is not completely 'chaotic' or 'irrational' there is a recognition from local management that the company's rapid development will lead to the need for a suitable system of job evaluation to be introduced. With the company's present stability the opportunity is ripe for the consideration of such a system.

The management are also cautious, however, as they have identified that one of the priorities for the success of the business rests in its ability to attract and employ a satisfied, 'dedicated' and motivated workforce. As has already been indicated, the plant is not unionised. It does have a works committee, however, that operates well, and the management is committed to a participatory approach to change. Although the company is primarily in manufacturing, it adds value through the service it offers to the shipping industry. In the eyes of the company, emphasis must be and remain on the high quality of work produced and service offered and this means the fostering of co-operation and commitment in its employees. To this end some of the negative aspects of job evaluation systems need to be carefully avoided. For example, any scheme must be able to accommodate changes in market rates, technology and levels of productivity easily, so any design will need to be flexible and adaptable. Some schemes are better designed to cope with such changes than others and this must be carefully considered.

REASONS FOR IMPLEMENTATION

It is recognised that some companies install job evaluation procedures to avoid conflicts that have arisen, while others install them as a package to remove anomalies. In the case of Southern Marine, both would appear to be good reasons for adoption. Specifically, problems have arisen from two main areas:

1 Problems from administrative grades due to a perceived lack of equity, and concern voiced over the number of incremental rises.
2 Problems in a number of grades (particularly supervisory/technical grades) due to previous merit payments to some members of the workforce and not to others. This practice, although now stopped, has led to claims of unfairness.

EFFECT ON COSTS

Job evaluation usually involves additional costs in the short term, as anomalous jobs are worked through the system and the range of jobs are accommodated. Local management recognise this and they have made it clear in a statement about their wages and salaries policy that it is their intention to pay salaries within the second and third quarter of a wages and salaries survey and that as their price structure is not particularly labour-cost sensitive, additional increases in the short term will not significantly affect profitability. Should orders be jeopardised by strike action or the loss of workforce goodwill, however, the cost to the company would be very much greater and could damage the forecast expansion. This is closely linked with the company's key aspects of competitive advantage which relate to its priorities for success being the quick turnaround of refurbished or repaired engines.

SCOPE OF THE STUDY

The organisation has four working groups: operatives, supervisory and technical grades, administrative grades and managers.

The management recognise that a well thought through scheme could include both operatives and management, but the company is cautious and considers any change should relate initially to only two of the four groups of workers, and be extended later.

Tables 10.1 to 10.5 give information on the number, salary scales and salary levels of the employees at Southern Marine.

Information on numbers and salary scales is given for all grades, but salary levels for individuals is only given for administrative grades Ag1–Ag6 (*see* Tables 10.1 and 10.5) and supervisory and technical grades S/Tg7–S/Tg10 (*see* Tables 10.2 and 10.5)

Table 10.1 Southern Marine Ltd – Schedule of 1995 salary scales for administrative grades

	Start	6 months	1 year
Ag1	£6,244	£6,494	£6,751
Ag2	£6,804	£7,076	£7,360
Ag3	£7,419	£7,712	£8,023
Ag4	£8,086	£8,410	£8,745
Ag5	£8,812	£9,164	£9,531
Ag6	£9,605	£9,988	£10,389

Table 10.2 Southern Marine Ltd – Schedule of 1995 salary scales for supervisory technical grades

	Year 1	Year 2	Year 3
S/Tg7	£10,472	£10,900	£11,325
S/Tg8	£11,414	£11,882	£12,345
S/Tg9	£12,439	£12,948	£13,456
S/Tg10	£13,561	£14,113	£14,669

Table 10.3 Southern Marine Ltd – Schedule of 1995 salary scales for management grades

Mg1	£14,805 – £16,899
Mg2	£16,778 – £19,005
Mg3	£18,752 – £21,122
Mg4	£20,728 – £23,215

Table 10.4 Southern Marine Ltd – Schedule of 1995 salary scales for operator grades

	Start	3 months	6 months
Og1	£ 7,596	£ 7,751	£ 7,904
Og2	£ 8,417	£ 8,520	£ 8,623
Og3	£ 8,929	£ 9,136	£ 9,340
Og4	£ 9,547	£ 9,750	£ 9,956
Og5	£ 9,853	£10,111	£10,366
Og6	£10,470	£10,778	£11,086

Table 10.5 Listing of the employee file for Southern Marine Ltd as of 26 July 1995

Name		Grade	Join date	M/F	Salary	Position
D	Holman	Ag2	25/06/94	F	£6.804	Clerk Typist
H	Arrowsmith	Ag2	10/11/90	F	£7,360	Clerk Typist
C	Woodhams	Ag2	29/03/92	F	£7,360	Clerk Typist
E	Bell	Ag2	20/09/92	F	£7,360	Clerk Typist
J	Hough	Ag2	16/06/90	F	£7,360	Clerk Typist
J	Mercer	Ag2	07/01/90	F	£7,360	A/C Clerk
H	McLaughlin	Ag2	05/07/92	F	£7,360	Clerk Typist
J	Stewart	Ag2	02/06/90	F	£7,360	Telephonist/Receptionist
T	Hines	Ag2	25/06/94	F	£6,804	Purchase Ledger Clerk
J	Major	Ag2	22/02/93	M	£7,360	Computer Operator
IJ	McDonald	Ag2	12/04/92	F	£7,360	Clerk Typist
AA	Pengelly	Ag3	11/01/92	F	£7,701	A/C Clerk
P	Livesey	Ag3	11/01/92	F	£8,024	Senior Tech. Librarian
I	Briggs	Ag3	22/03/92	F	£8,024	A/C Clerk
AL	Masepiece	Ag3	13/06/93	F	£8,024	Secretary
J	Holgate	Ag3	13/04/91	M	£8,024	Security Guard
JW	Hall	Ag3	28/04/90	M	£8,024	Security Guard
FG	Wilkinson	Ag3	29/04/90	M	£8,024	Security Guard
LM	Abbott	Ag3	01/11/89	F	£8,024	Commercial Assistant
R	Rigby	Ag3	28/04/90	M	£8,024	Security Guard
IM	Dunn	Ag3	21/09/91	F	£8,024	Secretary
JC	Warren	Ag3	21/05/91	M	£8,024	Security Guard
WB	Wales	Ag4	02/03/91	F	£8,745	Buyer
AH	Harkins	Ag4	07/01/90	F	£8,745	Cashier
EN	Weir	Ag5	21/04/91	F	£9,531	Executive Secretary
H	Brough	Ag5	16/07/94	M	£8,812	Shipping Co-ordinator
M	Cunliffe	Ag6	28/03/87	F	£11,034	Executive Secretary to MD
J	Haig	S/Tg8	17/10/91	M	£11,414	Provisioner
IF	Couts	S/Tg9	26/01/90	M	£12,948	Eng. Services Tech.
PG	Holt	S/Tg8	25/06/94	M	£11,414	Eng. Services Tech.
DJ	Bainbridge	S/Tg8	19/04/92	M	£12,345	Eng. Services Tech.
RR	Bagley	S/Tg8	23/06/90	M	£12,345	Transport Supervisor
W	Harris	S/Tg8	17/09/89	M	£12,345	Stores Sup.
RC	Shaw	S/Tg8	18/08/90	M	£11,882	Eng. Services Tech.
C	Richards	S/Tg8	30/01/94	M	£11,882	Senior Buyer
RB	Jones	S/Tg8	03/03/90	M	£11,398	Requirements Planning
K	Robertson	S/Tg8	14/04/90	M	£12,345	Quality Tech.
J	Freeman	S/Tg8	28/09/91	M	£12,345	Provisioner
JS	Shawcross	S/Tg9	03/11/90	M	£12,948	Supervisor Bench
EM	Howard	S/Tg8	12/07/92	M	£12,345	Eng. Technician
H	Taylor	S/Tg9	17/09/89	M	£12,948	Product Line Sup.
P	Towns	S/Tg9	17/09/89	M	£13,724	Quality Sup.
J	Ford	S/Tg9	17/09/89	M	£12,439	Supervisor Test Cell

Table 10.5 *continued*

Name		Grade	Join date	M/F	Salary	Position
CR	Rose	S/Tg9	25/09/90	M	£13,456	Senior Buyer
R	Buchanan	S/Tg9	26/01/90	M	£12,948	Product Line Sup.
J	Freymann	S/Tg9	31/03/90	M	£13,456	Sup. Accessory Shop
RC	Gallagher	S/Tg9	14/01/90	M	£13,456	M/C Shop Sup.
DR	Knight	S/Tg9	01/10/89	M	£13,724	Process Sup.
RW	Westwood	S/Tg9	31/03/90	M	£12,948	Prod. Services Sup.
JR	Nelson	S/Tg9	07/01/90	M	£13,724	Senior Quality Tech.
D	Grime	S/Tg9	07/01/90	M	£13,861	Eng. Services Sup.
JH	Banks	S/Tg10	03/09/89	M	£14,669	Projection Facilities Sup.
M	Wilson	S/Tg9	17/09/89	M	£13,591	Welding Sup.
R	Mansfield	S/Tg9	17/09/89	M	£13,456	Sup. Provisioning
M	Coleman	J	09/07/94	F		
E	Howarth	Mg	08/10/89	M		
A	Platt	Mg	26/01/90	M		
P	Hunpheson	Mg	05/01/92	M		
S	Denton	Mg	30/07/89	M		
B	Whickens	Mg	10/01/93	M		
E	Wilde	Mg	16/03/94	M		
S	Adshead	Og	05/03/94	M		
S	MacDonald	Og	04/06/94	M		
M	Boston	Og1	29/11/92	M		
M	Platt	Og2	18/02/90	M		
D	O'Brien	Og2	25/06/94	M		
D	Kelly	Og2	13/10/90	M		
R	Harper	Og2	26/10/91	M		
K	Harrington	Og2	02/07/94	M		
K	Procter	Og2	25/05/91	M		
J	Hacking	Og2	16/07/94	M		
R	Wood	Og2	28/07/90	M		
N	Hancocks	Og3	08/08/90	M		
N	Hogg	Og3	12/01/91	M		
S	Roebotham	Og3	21/09/91	M		
S	Morran	Og3	02/06/90	M		
J	Hurst	Og3	17/11/90	M		
M	Evans	Og3	27/04/91	M		
R	MacDonald	Og	28/04/90	M		
M	Barrett	Og3	31/03/95	M		
M	Bostock	Og3	12/05/90	M		
J	Bostock	Og3	01/10/90	M		
N	Clark	Og3	07/07/90	M		
J	Williams	Og3	05/11/89	M		
A	Law	Og3	26/05/90	M		
E	Cotton	Og3	17/01/93	M		
J	Bengett	Og3	12/05/90	M		
C	Tetley	Og4	12/01/91	M		
A	Whellan	Og4	04/02/90	M		
T	Bridge	Og4	08/09/90	M		
A	Fairclough	Og5	22/09/90	M		
S	Birtwistle	Og5	22/09/90	M		
D	Bottrall	Og5	18/02/90	M		
R	Cook	Og5	26/04/92	M		
H	Laim	Og5	16/07/94	M		
P	Bicker	Og5	18/06/94	M		
D	Williams	Og5	26/05/90	M		
T	Elliott	Og5	14/06/92	M		
C	Beech	Og5	01/11/92	M		

Table 10.5 *continued*

Name		Grade	Join date	M/F	Salary	Position
T	Green	Og5	11/05/91	M		
A	Curtain	Og5	31/08/91	M		
W	House	Og5	01/12/90	M		
P	Apple	Og5	21/09/91	M		
B	Wagner	Og5	01/06/91	M		
M	Cahill	Og5	21/07/90	M		
L	Boat	Og5	24/03/90	M		
P	Flower	Og5	02/08/92	M		
A	Ball	Og5	27/02/94	M		
C	Hurst	Og5	23/08/92	M		
C	Prince	Og5	01/06/91	M		
K	Boyle	Og5	12/01/91	M		
T	Wogan	Og5	19/04/92	M		
L	Neeson	Og5	29/09/90	M		
B	Knight	Og5	26/01/90	M		
R	Geer	Og5	09/06/90	M		
J	Depp	Og5	21/09/91	M		
S	Kennedy	Og5	19/04/92	M		
C	Marsh	Og5	21/09/91	M		
H	Bogart	Og5	22/06/91	M		
L	Bacal	Og5	12/01/91	M		
J	Cagney	Og5	17/05/92	M		
S	Loren	Og5	07/09/91	M		
J	Mack	Og5	10/01/93	M		
O	Simpson	Og5	01/12/90	M		
O	Petersen	Og5	10/01/93	M		
P	Wells	Og5	24/08/91	M		
M	Douglass	Og5	17/01/93	M		
C	Clay	Og5	24/05/92	M		
B	Forbes	Og5	09/06/90	M		
J	Lennon	Og5	18/06/94	M		
P	McCartney	Og5	18/08/90	M		
R	Starr	Og5	11/06/91	M		
G	Harrison	Og5	17/09/89	M		
L	Olivier	Og5	06/07/91	M		
M	Rooney	Og5	22/09/90	M		
B	Blessed	Og5	26/01/90	M		
P	Kerr	Og5	22/09/90	M		
G	Lee	Og5	22/03/92	M		
A	McInally	Og5	18/08/90	M		
J	Priest	Og5	01/08/92	M		
M	Aston	Og5	18/06/94	M		
W	McFarlane	Og5	27/07/91	M		
J	Reid	Og5	22/09/90	M		
R	Willis	Og5	18/06/94	M		
M	Julian	Og5	24/03/90	M		
I	Doherty	Og5	03/11/90	M		
R	Humphreys	Og5	06/05/90	M		
P	McHugh	Og5	09/04/90	M		
R	Douglas	Og5	17/05/92	M		
K	McDougal	Og5	18/08/90	M		
C	Cherry	Og5	18/06/94	M		
D	Francis	Og5	22/03/92	M		
S	Patrick	Og5	31/01/93	M		
L	Donegan	Og5	16/07/94	M		
P	McGann	Og5	03/11/90	M		

Table 10.5 *continued*

Name		Grade	Join date	M/F	Salary	Position
A	Teacher	Og5	10/01/93	M		
P	Johnson	Og5	29/09/94	M		
A	McCabe	Og5	29/09/90	M		
K	Kennedy	Og5	29/09/90	M		
M	Madden	Og5	10/01/93	M		
I	McAuley	Og5	11/05/91	M		
J	Kay	Og6	18/08/90	M		
F	Keenan	Og6	17/09/89	M		
S	McClusky	Og6	26/01/90	M		
P	Danbury	Og6	12/05/90	M		
D	Essex	Og6	17/09/89	M		
A	Leicester	Og6	26/05/90	M		
P	Corby	Og6	18/08/90	M		
D	Kettering	Og6	22/09/90	M		
L	Wellington	Og6	03/03/90	M		
S	Willis	Og6	28/04/90	M		
E	Askew	Og6	17/09/89	M		
M	Bradley	Og6	18/02/90	M		
M	Campbell	Og6	21/04/90	M		
M	Flaherty	Og6	18/02/90	M		
J	Grey	Og6	21/04/90	M		
P	Garner	Og6	17/09/89	M		
I	Roddy	Og6	23/06/90	M		
R	Rizak	Og6	09/06/90	M		

ORGANISATIONAL STRUCTURE

An organisational chart for the company is given in Fig. 10.1 and Board responsibilities shown in Fig. 10.2.

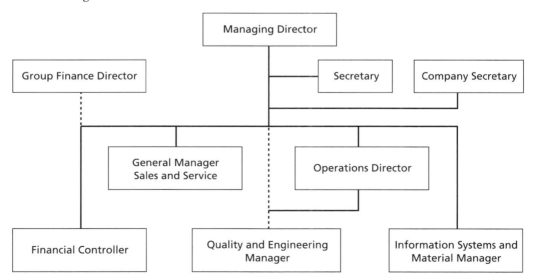

Fig 10.1 Organisational structure of Southern Marine Ltd

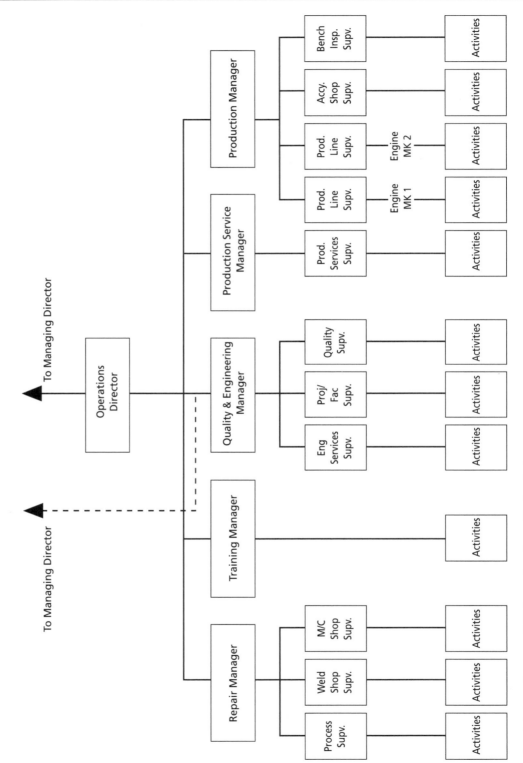

Fig 10.2 Board responsibilities at Southern Marine Ltd

ACTIVITY BRIEF

1 Examine the company's present pay system and make recommendations for a system that will meet the needs of the developing business, while remaining simple to operate and understand and flexible to future needs.

2 Advise on the method by which any change you advocate will be approached, drawing up a critical path of activities and highlighting any change in structure or working parties you may consider necessary to ensure a successful outcome.

3 Consider grade differentials, merit awards and the provision of service increments.

RECOMMENDED READING

Armstrong, M (1993) *Managing Reward Systems*, Buckingham, OUP.

Armstrong, M and Marlis, H (1994) (eds) *Reward Management: A Handbook of Remuneration Strategy and Practice*, London, Kogan Page.

Bowey, AM and Thorpe, R (1988) 'Payment systems and performance improvement: participation in payment system design', *Employee Relations*, 1, 1.

Bowey, AM and Thorpe, R (1986) *Payment Systems and Productivity*, Basingstoke, Macmillan.

Casey, B, Lakey, J and White, M (1992) *Payment Systems: A Look at Current Practice*, London, Policy Study Institute.

Crow, D (1992) 'A new approach to reward management' in Armstrong, M (ed) *Strategies for Human Resource Management*, London, Kogan Page.

Lawler, EE (1971) *Pay and Psychological Effectiveness: A Psychological View*, New York, McGraw–Hill.

Pickard, J (1993) 'Merit and pay taking over job evaluation as a driving force on salaries', *Personnel Management*, 25, 5, 13.

Smith, I (1993) 'Reward management: a retrospective assessment', *Employee Relations*, 15, 3.

Thorpe, R and Bowey, AM (1988) 'Payment systems and performance improvement: design and implementation', *Employee Relations*, 10, 4.

Quaid, M (1993) 'Job evaluation as institutional myth', *Journal of Management Studies*, 30, 2.

Promotion decisions and management diversity at American Manufacturing*

Patricia J Ohlott and Marian N Ruderman

INTRODUCTION

Alex Price, the CEO of American Manufacturing, is committed to developing a diverse workforce within his organisation. To this end, he has worked with his human resource department to provide American Manufacturing's employees with gender and racial awareness workshops, diversity training programmes, mentoring programmes, and company-sponsored associations for women and ethnic minorities. Part of the company's strategy involved the deliberate development and tracking of white women and ethnic minorities of both sexes. The company also set goals regarding the numerical distribution of women and ethnic minorities it wanted to have at various levels in the organisation.

BACKGROUND TO THE CASE

At this point it is unclear how well the company's diversity initiatives are doing. The way job assignments are made ultimately influences the advancement of men and women through the managerial ranks. Thus, a closer look at how promotion decisions are made at American Manufacturing may shed some light on how well the company is working towards its goal of achieving a diverse managerial workforce.

Top management at American Manufacturing conducts a series of annual review meetings to discuss potential candidates for upper-level management positions. Prior to this meeting, key decision makers have the opportunity to review the performance appraisals and other human resource records kept about the candidates over the past several years. At the meeting, these records, as well as the personal experiences of the decision makers with the candidates and input from others who have worked with the candidates, are discussed.

---

* The names of the company and the individuals in this case are fictitious. The scenario presented in the case was developed as a composite of information observed in the authors' study of actual promotion decisions in three large companies (*see* Ruderman and Ohlott 1994).

MAKING A PROMOTION DECISION

Last week Alex Price met with his three Divisional Vice-Presidents – John Cox, Alan Jones, and Steve Bacon – to discuss the opening they would have for an Area Manager in Alan's division later in the year when the incumbent, Sam Evans, retires. The Area Manager job is a generalist position. Managers who have been successful in the position in the past came from different functional backgrounds and entered the job with a variety of different experiences.

The executives' discussion centred on four high-potential managers: two men, Tom McIntyre and Mark Smith, and two women, Marcia Campbell and Susan Sutton. All of the candidates were proven performers, with excellent track records, and had been with the company for at least ten years. They had all followed traditional career paths, moving up the corporate ladder in line positions of increasing responsibility. They all currently held comparable positions as Business Managers, although they worked in different businesses located in different divisions. Each candidate was deemed equally qualified for the candidate pool because he or she had appropriate job experiences which had more than adequately prepared him or her for the Area Manager job. We shall listen in on the discussion.

'Let's talk about Tom first,' Alex suggested. John had worked closely with Tom in the past, and offered:

> Tom's experience as a plant manager means that he knows our products well. I also feel very comfortable with Tom. I know his strengths and weaknesses. I know how he's going to behave. Our relationship was an effective one. I always knew I could count on him being stable and consistent over time.

Steve added:

> I have also worked with Tom and always felt I could count on him; we thought alike. My main concern about Tom is that he seems to have a short-term results orientation, and I'm not sure about his ability to think strategically.

Alex agreed with John's assessment of Tom:

> I find him to be very credible; he presents himself well and performs well consistently. One accomplishment of his that really stands out for me is his management of our new quality programme. He designed, developed, and implemented that programme, which has led to a significant reduction in defects and costs. I think he would be a good, solid choice for the job if we can verify that he does have some strategic ability. However, I'd also like to know what people think of the other three candidates.

Alan said:

> Well, as you know, Marcia works in my division now. Her long experience in this division means that she knows the business in depth. In that respect I think she would be a good choice for the job. She knows the people in the group and has established good working relationships with them. Promoting Marcia rather than bringing in an outsider would foster a sense of continuity in the group. Many of the job's responsibilities would also be familiar to her, since the same products are involved, and that would make the new job easier for her to handle. Marcia has also performed very well in her three previous jobs for us. For example, she developed a plan to improve our sales in Europe and was able to convince senior management that it was a good plan. After we implemented Marcia's plan, our European sales jumped 40 per cent! Marcia has also been to see me several times to ask about her career progress and what she

needs to do to move ahead in our organisation; she is concerned that her career is progressing too slowly.

Alan continued:

My only misgiving is that if we promote her there may be some difficulties with peer relationships. Some people may give her a difficult time if they think she was promoted over other qualified people just because she is a woman, and I don't know if she can handle that.

Alex concurred that Marcia would also be a reasonable choice for the job:

I think Marcia is a person of great personal power. From what I have seen of her work, she shows great enthusiasm and strength of purpose. She seems capable of standing her ground on important issues and is not easily intimidated, as she showed when she presented her sales plan to us.

The group went on to discuss Mark Smith. Steve began:

Even though Mark doesn't work in my division now, I know that he has excellent leadership skills. I worked with him for a number of years some time ago. Remember, I was his boss when he successfully turned around our Center City plant which had been losing money and was plagued with process problems for years. He proved that he could handle difficult situations, which makes him a strong candidate for the Area Manager job. I can be a tough person to work for – some people call me abrasive – but I always knew I could talk frankly and honestly with Mark. I never had to guard what I said or be concerned that what I said would offend or upset him, and this is important because he would have to work with some very difficult people if he got this job. In addition, I think that moving to a new division would be a good developmental experience for him; it would help him develop a breadth of knowledge about the company.

The other executives all knew Mark personally and agreed that they all would feel comfortable working with Mark and that this job would be a good test for him. John had one misgiving:

I have heard some customers say recently that Mark comes on too strong with them. They feel his successes have encouraged him to become arrogant, and I think we ought to give him some feedback on that.

The last candidate to be discussed was Susan Sutton. Steve asked:

Who is Susan Sutton? I've never met her and haven't heard much about her. I just don't see how someone can be successful in this job if they haven't established their reputation among internal and external clients, customers and suppliers.

John was the only one who knew much about Susan, and he volunteered the following about her:

I would endorse Susan for this position in part because she is a very strong person. She did a great job handling our negotiations with the Japanese firm last year. Susan found a creative way to finance the project, which resulted in a new business venture for us. She showed a lot of strength of character and stood by her convictions. In general, she argues very persuasively and enthusiastically. Overall her track record is outstanding, and her international experience is a plus for the Area Manager job. Not only would she be a good fit for the job, but she would help us meet our diversity goals.

Alan was more hesitant:

> My concern is that this position would involve considerably more responsibility than her current job, and I'm not sure if she's ready. Her records indicate that she probably does deserve a promotion, though. Perhaps we could make her a Senior Business Manager and keep her in mind for the next Area Manager position that opens up. I'd like to give her more of a chance to prove herself.

The discussion about the candidates continued for several hours, but the decision makers failed to arrive at a consensus. None of the candidates was clearly outstanding. All had different strengths and weaknesses to bring to the job.

ACTIVITY BRIEF

1 If you were one of the key decision makers in this case, which candidate would you select for the job? Why?

2 Do you see any patterns in the criteria you considered? Are there any patterns in the decision makers' comments?

3 Are the criteria different for men and women? If there are any differences, do they matter?

4 What would happen to the company's diversity initiative if the highly committed CEO were to leave?

5 How could you encourage commitment to diversity throughout the organisation?

RECOMMENDED READING

Morrison, AM (1992) *The New Leaders: Guidelines on Leadership Diversity in America*, San Francisco, Jossey–Bass.

Morrison, AM, Ruderman, MN, and Hughes-James, M (1993) *Making Diversity Happen: Controversies and Solutions*, Report No. 320, Center for Creative Leadership, Greensboro, North Carolina.

Ohlott, PJ, Ruderman, MN, and McCauley, CD (1994) 'Gender differences in managers' developmental job experiences', *Academy of Management Journal*, 37, 1, pp 46–67.

Ruderman, MN, and Ohlott, PJ (1994) *The Realities of Management Promotion*, Report No. 157, Center for Creative Leadership, Greensboro, North Carolina.

Ruderman, MN, Ohlott, PJ, and Kram, KE (1995) 'Promotion decisions as a diversity practice', *Journal of Management Development*, 14, 2, pp 6–23.

Ruderman, MN, Ohlott, PJ, and Kram, KE (1996) *Managerial Promotion: The Dynamics for Men and Women*, Report No. 170, Center for Creative Leadership, Greensboro, North Carolina.

Disabled employees within a local authority

Carol Woodhams and Ann E McGoldrick

INTRODUCTION

The employment of disabled people is often pessimistically viewed as being overly problematic, resulting in their disproportionate exclusion from the workforce (Barnes 1991). Some organisations have now begun to utilise the under-resourced potential of this group of people and are reviewing their policies and practices to ensure that they are not discouraging the employment of people with disabilities. This case focuses on the issues that are current within Southtown City Council, an organisation in the advanced stages of an initiative to integrate increasing numbers of disabled people. It is an illustration of the response of one progressive organisation to the issues raised by the employment of disabled staff at the time of the implementation of new legislation.

Research has established that on the whole disabled employees function well over a range of performance indicators (Du Pont 1990). This case study is an illustration of the rewards that can be realised through the employment of disabled people for all parties involved in the employment relationship. Three individual cases have been chosen to demonstrate this point. It must be said, however, that within this organisation these rewards have not been realised without a very distinctive attitude from the human resources (HR) department and individual line managers. The employment of some moderately to severely disabled people required an educated, determined approach to problem solving and a flexible and adaptable attitude from all parties concerned. It is, therefore, not surprising that problems remain in some areas.

Within the context of a publicly owned organisation in a changing business and legislative environment, it is the task of the reader to find solutions for the HR department to enable an improved quality of working life for these and other disabled staff.

BACKGROUND TO THE CASE

The 1990s have witnessed several developments in the business environment. Many of these changes have impacted in a positive way on the organisational view of minority groups in general, and as a result they have the potential to affect the current and future employment prospects of disabled people. The drive toward equal opportunities for all minority groups has been reshaped as a business necessity and has taken on a new impetus

(Ross and Schneider 1992); disabled people are at last increasingly becoming recognised as a group deserving of access to true employment opportunity.

Demographics

The publicity that surrounded the anticipated effects of the 'demographic timebomb' had led forecasters to predict that the 1990s would become the decade when equal opportunities policies would be vigorously pursued in order to fill gaps in the skills market. It was predicted that recruiting young, qualified people would become increasingly difficult, and employers would be forced to consider traditionally under-utilised sections of the population in order to make up for the decreasing numbers of the under-25s. Disabled people were regarded as a very useful and under-fished pool of potential employees. The recession substantially undermined the effects of this demographic change, and consequently organisational response has been limited.

Technology

It is possible that technological development will prove useful to disabled employees and their employers in two ways. Closely aligned to the increased demand for a more flexible workforce, technology can serve to eliminate employment barriers by facilitating more convenient job design. This includes, for example, provision of a wider range of employment options with the computerisation of jobs, more flexible working arrangements with the possibility of home-based working and less physical demands (Roulstone 1993). Second, a vast range of technological innovations are available to the disabled person compensating for their specific deficits, i.e. enabling the blind to 'see', the speech-impaired to 'speak' and the deaf to 'hear'. Such developments will help to maximise the abilities of disabled people.

The social environment

The rise of movements representing other minority groups and the subsequent passing of anti-discrimination legislation in these areas have influenced the development of the disabled people's movement in the United Kingdom in the last two decades. Wishing to control the design and administration of their own services to more adequately represent their rights, disabled people formed organisations such as the British Council of Disabled People in 1981 and Voluntary Organisations for Anti-Discrimination Legislation in 1985. They started to use direct action and demonstrations to protest their views. A 'Rights not Charity' march was organised in July 1988 and similar direct tactics have been used by the Campaign for Accessible Transport and the 'Block Telethon' Campaign in 1992. Wide publicity surrounded events such as disabled people chaining themselves to buses to protest about inaccessible public transport, and the debacle of the blocked Civil Rights Bill in 1994, while behind the scenes organisations representing the case of disabled people worked hard to ensure that public opinion began to move from charity-based provision toward an acknowledgement of extended rights.

Legislative developments

One of the most influential of the current adjustments to the business environment is the implementation of the Disability Discrimination Act 1995, designed to give disabled people extended employment rights. It replaced one of the longest standing and most derided pieces of legislation on the statute books – the Disabled Persons (Employment) Act 1944 and 1958. That law established a quota scheme where companies which employed 20 or more people were under obligation to fulfil a quota of 3 per cent of registered disabled people. The law had never been comprehensively enforced. Only ten employers had been prosecuted since its enactment for not achieving the quota and not being in possession of a quota exemption certificate, and none at all since the 1970s. This law was beset with further problems. Only registered disabled people 'counted' towards the quota, and many disabled people chose not to register for personal reasons. This meant in practical terms that the quota was unachievable since registered disabled people only comprise approximately 1 per cent of the workforce.

Consistent with their policies of minimalist intervention, the Conservative government resisted legislative solutions, turning instead to a system of education and awareness by issuing a series of Codes of Practice backed up with a programme of financial assistance for employers designed to facilitate the entry of disabled people into the job market. Elsewhere in the world, however, reform was more enlightened and advanced. One group of countries, typified by the United States, Canada and Australia, includes employment rights within very broad anti-discrimination legislation which covers equal access in the areas of housing, transport and the provision of goods and services. Employment practices are only one aspect of a comprehensive policy which recognises the rights of disabled people and attempts to eradicate discrimination against them. The USA, Canada and Australia all have human rights legislation at federal and state level (Lunt and Thornton 1993).

A contrasting approach is found in other member countries of the European Union (EU) (Doyle 1995). Broadly speaking, their approach to employment promotion is similar to the UK 1944 Act, involving legal obligations and compulsion in the form of quota systems and reserved jobs. Despite the fact that the intention of these types of measures is very positive, they have generally been found to be difficult to enforce and results are disappointing. Equal opportunity measures have a higher profile and demand greater respect. The historical development of these policies typified by EU countries have given them their shape and form, the philosophy under which they operate and their current policy prerogatives. Employment policies are determined by a compilation of the policy interests of several government departments. The majority of European countries have recognised the rights of disabled people to equal treatment in all social and economic activities in principle and attempts have also been made to achieve full integration in a number of countries by reconciling divergencies in policies for disabled people. However, it is still fair to say that European disability policies are characterised rather by incrementalism than by radical change (Lunt and Thornton 1993, p 179).

Methods of ensuring adherence to the particular legal obligations also differ between countries. Those with direct human rights provision attach enforcement measures to the conducting of business activity, such as contract compliance. More generally countries promote the employment of disabled people through financial measures, such as compensation to employers for reduced productivity, and help with adaptations to the workplace.

The Americans With Disabilities Act 1990 has informed disability rights advocates in Britain and been particularly influential upon the sponsors of the Civil Rights (Disabled Persons) Bill which achieved renown for its spectacular failure to make progress in the House of Commons in 1994. The movement and pressure on the government had begun, however, and was gathering momentum. Even employers' groups acknowledged that it was time for improved legislative intervention (The Employers' Forum on Disability 1993).

Finally, as a result of the social and business pressures described above, the government conceded to a shift in focus away from the principle of compensation for injury sustained in armed conflict toward the concept of the right to work. Similarly, the rhetoric of most European governments in relation to disability and employment is moving away from paternalistic state intervention to measures that encourage independence and responsibility. Policies are now also starting to encompass all types of disabilities rather than physical disabilities alone. The Disability Discrimination Act legislation takes effect during 1996 (Arkin 1995). This significant piece of anti-discrimination legislation gives disabled people the right not to be discriminated against in employment. It is unlawful for employers with 20 or more employees to treat disabled people less favourably without justification. This includes all aspects of employment from the recruitment and selection process through to the termination of employment, encompassing training, promotion, transfers, etc.

THE LOCAL AUTHORITY

Southtown City Council Local Authority is one of the larger local authorities in the country, employing over 16,000 full-time and 13,000 part-time staff. This case relates specifically to the leisure department of the organisation which has a mix of working environments spread over many sites ranging from park keeping to desk-bound white collar work. It has its own separate human resource function but executes policy decisions that are made centrally. Most of the local authority buildings were built prior to the 1981 Disabled Persons Act, obliging providers of premises to make appropriate provision for disabled people in terms of access. Many of the buildings are old, poorly designed and built on many levels with inaccessible lifts, or with very heavy manually operated entry doors (necessary for security reasons). Some are in listed buildings where permission for lifts and ramps is extremely difficult to obtain. In broad terms reasonable access has been achieved, although sometimes relying on measures which make the disabled person dependent on others, such as the use of a bell and a goods lift. This situation is preferable, however, to that which preceded it when wheelchair users had to be carried upstairs by a security guard. Although these alterations were planned for the sake of the staff, in many cases the public have also benefited. Most of the sites are located in areas which are easily reached by public transport.

The structure of the organisation is traditional and has not been significantly adapted in response to delayering trends. The hierarchy of managerial positions is clear and promotion opportunities are good. The organisation exhibits a paternalistic, caring culture which is often associated with public organisations. The majority of the work is organised into teams, with staff working together to maximise strengths and compensate for any weaknesses.

Equal opportunity strategy

The most recent Chief Executive was very committed to the philosophy of equal opportunities and to this area in particular. The initiative really commenced with the conferring in 1986 of the 'Fit for Work' award from the Employment Service. This further inspired a committed approach that has been slowly translated into progressive measures and has gathered strength in the years since. Five years ago, disability was singled out from among competing equal opportunity groups as a minority group worthy of special attention. An

Equal Opportunities Officer, Mr Brown, was given the task of encouraging more disabled people to join or remain with the organisation and ensuring that procedures were not directly or indirectly discriminatory. He developed this role to the extent that it exceeded all expectations. Previously where a need for job adaptations was identified and the specialist agencies, i.e. the Placement Assessment and Counselling Team (PACT), needed to be contacted, changes had been made very slowly. Managers became disillusioned with the service and disabled people did not apply to the organisation for employment via the job centre or directly in answer to job advertisements in newspapers. Mr Brown was given the task of cultivating a more disabled-friendly image and modifying the service within the human resource department from a reactive problem-solving approach to a proactive problem-detection approach. He undertook this task with vigour and such a high level of personal commitment and enthusiasm that the successor to his position views with some dread the task facing him.

Motivation for equal opportunity initiatives

The authority has strong links with and feels answerable to the local community. The approach to equal opportunities generally, however, has been motivated by a desire to encompass the diverse mix of skills that are available in the area served. This should be distinguished from a charity-based approach motivated by a social conscience to take on a 'burdensome' obligation or a desire to publicise a good public image through the community. The organisation is reportedly persuaded by the benefits that appropriately qualified disabled people can bring to the organisation in under-utilised skills and strengths that are associated with this minority group. While there is a commitment to a gradual increase in the proportion of disabled employees, there is also a determination to avoid the misunderstanding surrounding cases of positive discrimination that have resulted in so much damaging publicity from the popular press and bad feeling from sections of the community. In May 1986, in an attempt to achieve legality in its position (being under the 3 per cent quota and voluntarily without an exemption permit), Lambeth Council began to recruit 'only people who are registered disabled' (Gledhill 1989). *The Sun* subsequently gave the Council its 'Barmiest Council of the Week Award'. Less extreme policies of a similar type have been pursued by Hackney and Manchester City Councils, among others.

Currently at Southtown 2.1 per cent of the organisation's staff are registered as disabled – a figure which has risen gradually over the last eight years. Although this may not seem high in comparison with an estimate that 8.9 per cent of the local population has a disability, it compares very favourably with many other organisations. The results of a recent survey of 208 local authorities suggests that on average 1.2 per cent of their employees are registered disabled people (Woodhams and McGoldrick, 1995).

Unfortunately, the numbers of disabled people decrease at senior levels to more unacceptable proportions (0.6 per cent).

Equal opportunity policy and practices

In 1993 the Equal Opportunities Policy was revised. The equal opportunities statement is comprehensive in its coverage of minority groups:

> Southtown City Council is an Equal Opportunity Employer and is determined to ensure that no job applicant or existing employee is treated less favourably on the grounds of sex, race, disability, religious belief, marital status or age or by any requirement which cannot be shown to be justifiable.

Changes which have ensued cover the range of employment practice including:

1 *Recruitment and retention.* Responsibility for recruitment has been decentralised. Interviewing is generally carried out by line management and a representative of the human resource department to advise them on equal opportunity issues. Everyone who is involved in short-listing or interviewing has attended the in-house training course where financial resources have been provided to train them in disability awareness. Details of the breakdown on recruitment at every stage is forwarded to the central human resource department to be monitored for bias. In some departments psychological testing is compulsory. The list of vacancies published on a weekly basis is circulated to every job centre in the county. The organisation relies heavily on the circulation of this information by the DEA (Disability Employment Advisor). Vacancies are advertised in *RADAR's Bulletin* and the *Arberry Profile* for disabled graduate recruitment. They are generally proud of their fair and progressive recruitment procedures.

   The council also endeavours to retain employees who become disabled or whose condition deteriorates. The adaptation of the original job and environment, if at all practical, is preferred to placing an individual in a new post. Major efforts are made by the human resource department and the line manager to adapt the job. If this is not possible, alternative employment opportunities are investigated. While positive action is allowed, however, positive discrimination is not and if the job holder has to apply for an unrelated job, he or she is given no preference over other candidates. Recently, with the reduction in vacancies and compulsory competitive tendering, it has not always been possible to find alternative employment.

2 *Monitoring.* A recent audit of the whole workforce detailed the representation of minority groups. Only those who were registered as disabled were identified, although those who might be eligible to register but chose not to were encouraged to contact the human resource department. The results were not positive. Few people were prepared to volunteer such information.

3 *Line management.* During the publicity created by the audit it became apparent that not all managers were committed to or even aware of policy regarding disabled applicants. Since a joint Equal Opportunities Working Party meets on a two-monthly basis, it was decided that a prominent task should be to produce a handbook for managers to set out procedures relating to the employment of disabled people. In addition a questionnaire survey of line managers known to be responsible for disabled employees was undertaken. This sought to identify areas in which they could be supported and improve their potential. An annual review of progress was implemented. The human resource department hoped in this manner to encourage line management to take increased responsibility for the individual welfare of their disabled subordinates.

4 *Initiatives.* In an attempt to encourage disabled people to feel that they are appropriately experienced in their job application, Mr Brown proposed a work-shadowing programme. Employees who were six months from retirement would be shadowed by an unemployed disabled person. The post would then be filled in the conventional way, although the disabled individual would be in a strong position. The organisation displays the 'Two Ticks Symbol of Good Practice' on all stationery and is committed to the self-policing obligations contained therein. These include the stipulation that every disabled person who meets the minimum job criteria at the application stage is guaranteed an interview. This local authority has taken the additional step of contacting those

who do not meet the criteria. They are offered a general interview by the equal opportunities department, who will try to assist the disabled person in improving his or her chances in future employment applications.

INDIVIDUAL CASES

Tony, the groundsman

Tony is a groundsman at one of the smaller local authority sites. He does not have the full use of his legs – one of them being a prosthesis – which means that he cannot manage to walk long distances without difficulty. In addition he has a slight learning disability. He was inherited by the local authority when they took over the property. He has adapted to his new employment circumstances very well. He is good at his job, well liked by his colleagues and never causes any trouble to his manager. His strongest asset as an employee is his reliability. He is always early to work getting in at 7.30 am, although he is not contracted to start until 8.00, when he makes tea for his colleagues as they arrive. In the past three years he has taken only one day's sick leave. He is so predictable in his routine that the bus he catches waits for him for a couple of minutes if he is not at his stop on time. Tony works with the aid of a special buggy that cuts out the need for him to walk around the property and carry the tools necessary to do the job. This was obtained with assistance from the local PACT team at no cost to the organisation. His manager knows him well and Tony responds to the individual attention that she is able to give him. One aspect of his employment does give cause for some concern. He is the only employee in the organisation who has a job description which is identifiable by his own name. This situation has arisen because he was unable to adapt to the requirements of a more traditionally defined role and has remained very inflexible to new job requirements. He is not so much limited by his physical impairment but by a stubbornness of character. Fortunately, this characteristic is tolerated by his current team of work colleagues, who have to be even more flexible in their own jobs to absorb parts of his.

Andrew, the computer programmer

Andrew is a computer programmer with cerebral palsy. He is a wheelchair user and has difficulty with speech, making it almost impossible to communicate in the traditional fashion. He is also unable to feed himself. He came to the organisation on a temporary placement and has now been there for nearly six years. He is positively viewed by colleagues and although it is never made explicit, he is regarded as the organisation's 'model' disabled employee. Despite considerable initial scepticism, his employment has been a major success story for both parties.

His employment required multiple adaptations to be made to the building, office layout, his own work station and the equipment he uses in the execution of his job. He has an adapted keyboard and an overhead LCD display on which to type messages and thus 'talk' to colleagues. He was recently promoted and is now in charge of two people. After six years in the same environment he fits in so well that work colleagues tend to forget about his handicap: 'he doesn't count as disabled any more'. Andrew is very dedicated, always enthusiastic and reliable, with an excellent sickness absence record. His manager reports that his productivity is comparable, while his mistakes are less frequent than his colleagues, although his speed is not quite as good.

Social services personnel call in to assist with lunches and most practical obstacles to a normal working life have now been overcome. There only remain a few points on which his manager has to pay any special attention. With Andrew's permission, induction for new staff within the same building involves a briefing about Andrew and his methods of communication. This has served to minimise initial co-worker anxieties. Furthermore, training programmes are held at an inaccessible site where wheelchair access is impossible. As a result all relevant courses have to come to him. In addition, fire regulations have caused some problems. Evacuation points are restricted and he has to be accompanied during fire alarms. The regulations have meant that he cannot be in the building alone and cannot therefore be engaged in overtime without support arranged well in advance.

Susan, the post assistant

The case of Susan demonstrates the necessity for an adaptive managerial approach. Unlike the previous two illustrations, Susan is not on a full contract. She has a job in the post room on a supported place. The Shaw Trust pays 50 per cent of her salary. Like Andrew she is limited by the effects of cerebral palsy. Unlike him, she does not use a wheelchair, nor does she have speech deficiencies, but she does walk with a severe limp and has limited use of her right arm. Her employment experience has not been as satisfactory.

Susan is well liked. She has often been called the life and soul of the office party, but her employment record shows that she is not settled. She has had four transfers to different departments in the last four years. Her job appears to be determined by the access requirements of avoiding steps. Her manager reports that she does not seem to enjoy her job. She is neither skilled nor qualified in any subject to GCSE level. At the same time it is obvious that she is not unintelligent, just not stimulated to advance. The NVQ route is not open as the assessment criteria are not easily adapted to suit people with differently demonstrated abilities.

Health and safety procedures required some thought since her current work site is on the third floor, but Mr Brown and Susan's manager arrived at a solution. A PARAID evac-chair was supplied by PACT and is used in conjunction with trained support from colleagues. Colleagues volunteered to assist in droves. A rota system by the door identifies which of the individuals in the department have responsibility for that day. Although Susan is not on a traditional contract, she gets identical treatment to her colleagues. She receives the same performance reviews, and is subject to the same rules, regulations and procedures as everyone else in the organisation. In practice it may be that she is allowed considerable latitude. She does have a very poor sickness record with hardly a fortnight going by without time off due to illness. Her reduced productivity is not a point of concern to her manager since she is on a supported wage, but it disgruntles colleagues at busy times of high demand. No information is supplied to colleagues at induction since the manager considers the subject to be too personal to be common knowledge. Mr Brown and Susan's manager consulted each other and ordered the design of a customised chair which cost £500 and was built in Germany. It is intended to give her the physical support she needs and is designed to put her at the correct height to do her job. She refuses to use it.

ACTIVITY BRIEF

1 What changes in managerial attitudes will be required by the transition from the quota-based legislation currently prevalent in Europe to the UK's new rights-based legislation?

2 What human resource procedures will have to be put into place, maintained, reviewed or improved within this organisation to ensure equality of opportunity and successful integration for disabled people?

3 What problems is the authority likely to encounter in striving to implement these procedures and how best could they be overcome?

4 Which of the measures would you associate with a more progressive and strategic HRM-linked approach to managing diversity?

5 From an employment perspective, what differences exist between disabled people as a minority group and other more traditional under-represented/disadvantaged groups?

RECOMMENDED READING

Arkin, A (1995) 'Improving access in the workplace', *People Management*, Nov.

Barnes, C (1991) *Disabled People in Britain and Discrimination*, London, Hurst and Co.

Birkett, K and Wormann, D (eds) (1988) *Getting on with Disabilities – An Employer's Guide*, London, IPD.

Doyle, B (1995) *Disability, Discrimination and Equal Opportunities*, London, Mansell.

Du Pont (1990) *Equal to the Task II: Du Pont Survey of People with Disabilities*, Wilmington, Du Pont Corporation.

Gledhill, N (1989) 'Only people with disabilities need apply', *Equal Opportunities Review*, Jan/Feb, pp 22–5

Honey, S, Meager, N and Williams, M (1993) *Employers' Attitudes towards People with Disabilities*, IMS Report 245.

Iles, P and Salaman, G (1995) 'Recruitment, selection and assessment' in Storey, J (ed) *Human Resource Management – A Critical Text*, London, Routledge.

Lunt, N and Thornton, T (1993) *Employment Policies for Disabled People*, Employment Department Research Series, No. 19.

Ross, R and Schneider, R (1992) *From Equality to Diversity*, London, Longman.

Roulstone, A (1993) 'Access to new technology' in Swain, J, Finklestein, V, French, S and Oliver M (eds) *Disabling Barriers – Enabling Environments*, Sage Publications/The Open University.

The Employers' Forum on Disability (1993) *Partnership: A Fresh Approach*, Schneider Ross and The Employers' Forum on Disability.

Woodhams, C and McGoldrick, A *Disability and Employment – The Organisational Response*, Paper presented to the British Academy of Management Conference, Sept 1995.

Justifying an employee assistance programme*

John Berridge

INTRODUCTION

'Where are my worry beads?' thought Christine Powers, as she sat in front of an almost-blank VDU screen. Only the words 'Draft Board Paper – Confidential: Recommendation on Continuance of the Pilot Employee Assistance Programme' glowed back at her, as the winter sun sank, and she realised that the paper had to be completed that afternoon. This was no time for worry beads, thought Christine, or any other executive stress reduction device. Not even for her new decision-making aid – an elegant marquetry dice-box, with two imitation-ivory dice. It had been given to her, tongue-in-cheek, by the Regional Director of her firm's Employment Assistance Programme provider at the end of his visit yesterday. Ostensibly, he had come to help her to clarify any issues in her report. It was clear, however, that his real motive was some keenly needed business – a toehold in a major industrial group. Christine liked the Regional Director's approach, respected his professionalism, but recognised his commercial motives.

BACKGROUND TO THE CASE

The parent company – Spa Domestic Appliances (UK) Ltd

For the last year, Christine Powers had been Human Resources Director of Spa Distribution and Service (UK) Ltd (known as SDS), a subsidiary company of Spa Domestic Appliances (UK) Ltd (known as SDA), the British arm of a major international manufacturer of domestic and industrial white goods. The organisational structure is shown in Fig. 13.1.

---

* This case has been written for pedagogic purposes, and does not imply good or bad managerial or professional practice in the contexts described. The case is based upon real organisations, but has been substantially modified by changing all names, certain aspects and information, by applying a factor to certain figures and by omission of other statistics. No resemblance is made or intended to any existing or former organisation, company or individual.

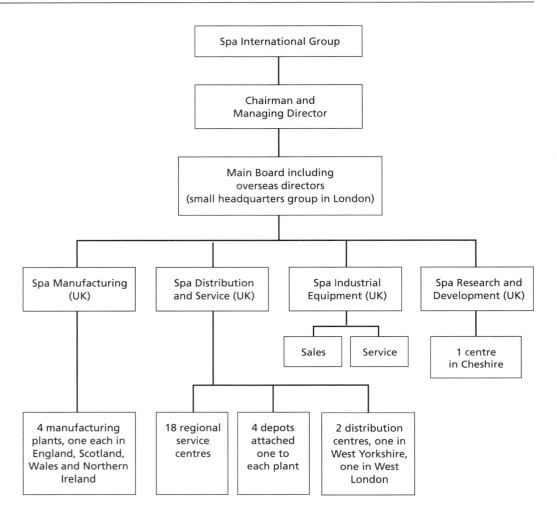

Total employees about 11,000

Fig 13.1 Organisational structure of Spa Domestic Appliances (UK) Ltd (SDA)

The product range covers most domestic electrical appliances, but in particular washing machines, dryers, dishwashers, refrigerators and freezers, vacuum cleaners and carpet shampoo cleaners, mixers, blenders, grinders, mincers and numerous other small appliances. The products from Spa are at the upper end of the market, from the point of view of price and quality, and the company wishes to consolidate this position, while moving from being number three or four in volume terms in most product markets to being number two or three. Spa products are noted for innovation, responsibility in design and safety, ecological consciousness, and the company is anxious to reinforce its reputation for reliability and service. Sales of Spa products were traditionally through electric goods wholesalers and high-street independent retailers, and through the retailing chains of the former regional electricity companies. Increasingly now the majority of sales pass through the specialist high-street electric goods chains of stores, through megastores in out-of-town shopping complexes, and through some mail-order chains. Most customers buy the larger appliances with extended warranties (covered by insurance), in addition to Spa's own exclusive two-year warranty. Both types of repair and subsequent service contracts are handled for the great majority of purchasers by Spa, through its own subsidiary SDS, with service engineers making visits to customers' homes and doing the service or repair work on site.

Spa manufactures around half of its products in Britain, particularly the larger appliances. Within the European group, Spa imports and exports certain products, in line with a sophisticated and integrated business plan on a Europe-wide basis. While the British operation has to be viable on a stand-alone basis, Spa International has a strong identity as a European company, and wishes to both profit from and contribute to European ideals, as the international headquarters is in an EU member country.

The company – Spa Distribution and Service (UK) Ltd

The creation of SDS, as a separate, fully controlled, downstream subsidiary company, following on from manufacturing and import, has been for over 15 years an essential part of SDA's corporate plan for forming strategic business units within the British operation. As its name implies, its two activities are distribution and service. Each was originally headed by a general manager who was a full-time executive member of the SDS Board. In turn, each of the two sectors of activity had a full functional range of specialisms, replicated at service centre level to the necessary extent, and controlled by and reporting to the Service Centre Manager, who was responsible for the centre's financial and quality performance. With four regional managers, each with about ten to twelve service centres, senior managerial control over the service centres was quite tight through routine reporting systems and by frequent physical visits, both announced and unannounced. Nevertheless, some of the service centre managers were known as 'characters' or even 'barons in their fiefdoms', having been in their jobs for up to 15 years in some cases.

An extensive reorganisation took place in SDS, coinciding with Christine's arrival. Following a report from one of the more original firms of management consultants, H and C, a business re-engineering exercise was applied to the comfortable but under-performing service company. A network of some 40 or 50 depots was rationalised to the present structure. Many small depots were closed, selected staff were offered generous voluntary severance or relocation, and a small number were made compulsorily redundant. The change was accomplished without collective conflict and only a very few employees felt aggrieved. It was Christine's first test at SDS, and although acting only as the implementer rather than as the architect, she passed with much positive comment. Following many of the H and C precepts, the Board was slimmed down, with functional specialist directors responsible for *both* service and distribution, instead of having separate structures as before (*see* Fig 13.2). Each director had a very small supporting staff, no longer in London but in northern England next to regional headquarters and adjacent to the largest service centre. Sophisticated IT back-up provided up-to-the-minute information; the headquarters' task was policy and intelligence, macro-issues of control and occasionally trouble-shooting. Below SDS board level, four regional operations managers had full responsibility for running their regions as business units within company policy (*see* Fig 13.3). They directly controlled all regional employees through the service centre managers, each of whom had similar responsibility for his or her centre and territory. The functional directors and their staff at SDS headquarters had no direct control over their specialist – only a professional/advisory relationship.

As will be surmised, the key figures in the delivery of the SDS domestic service to the public are the service centre managers. Selected three years ago from the previous managers of the original smaller centres, with the aid of sophisticated assessment procedures, they were almost all company veterans of ten years or more, and were self-made company men to a man. With full operational responsibility for their centres, their subordinate hierarchy within the service centre was greatly slimmed down (*see* Fig. 13.4), with only four supervisory posts remaining. Below these posts, all employees were organised into work teams, responsible for their own training, work methods, quality improvement and leadership, along with the working team leader. The organisation of the service engineers was even more simplified: all area supervisor posts were eliminated, and each engineer worked individually. A functional responsibility existed for each engineer with the stores team (for parts and equipment), the planning team (for work scheduling) and the accounting team (for invoicing, etc.). The intention was to let each engineer see himself as his own business, thereby instilling responsible behaviour, which was verified (*not* checked up) by the quality assurance team. Any other business functions which were necessary (including personnel – *see* next section) were the duty of the Service Centre Manager to resolve, using in-company resources in the first instance. All service centre managers were remunerated by performance-related pay, allowing a substantial supplement to their basic salary.

The human resources function was greatly revised in the reorganisation. At SDS headquarters in northern England, Christine now had three specialists: one for HRM, one for industrial relations and international matters, and one for HR development. All had been recruited by Christine from outside the company, and like her, had previous HR backgrounds in retailing, engineering and service industries. Their task had three elements:

- to provide an expert intelligence service to board level;
- to write the HR manuals which service centre managers had to follow; and
- (if essential) to act as trouble-shooters on site.

The former structure of regional personnel managers, and their deputies, in each service centre, plus a personnel clerk each, was abolished, and personal severance terms offered, compulsorily.

At service centre level, the manager was responsible for HR matters, via the four supervisors for centre staff, and personally for all service engineers. An administrative assistant (part-time, like many in administration and reception) was responsible for inputting employees' data into the central HR information system. The service centre managers'

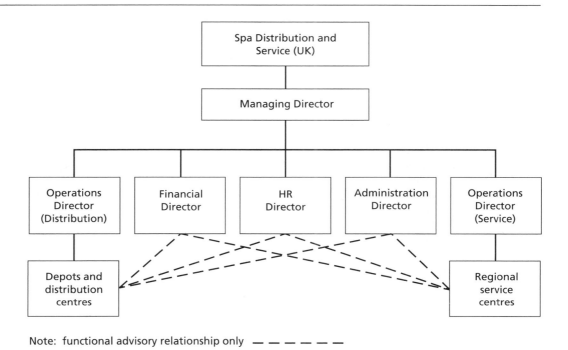

Note: functional advisory relationship only — — — — — —

Fig 13.2 Organisational structure of Spa Distribution and Service (UK) Ltd (SDS) after reorganisation

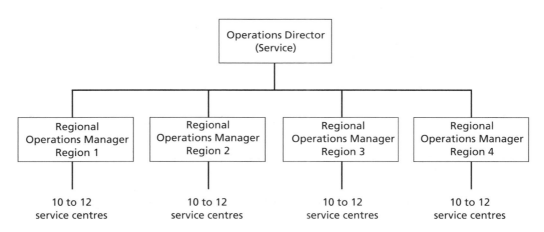

Fig 13.3 Organisational structure of SDS service sector after reorganisation

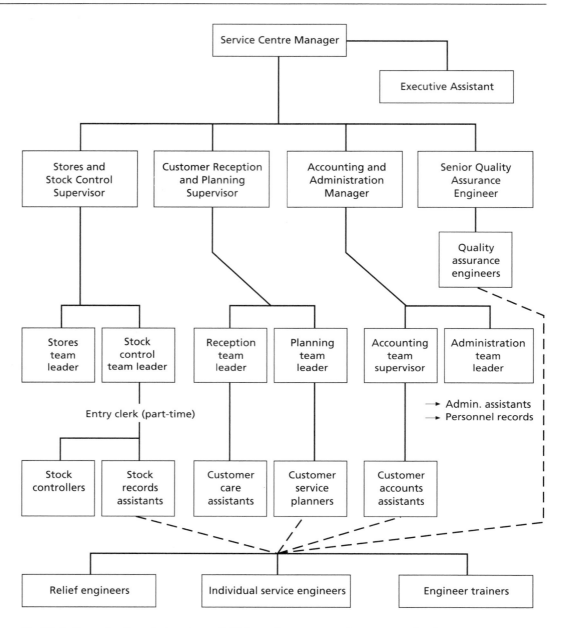

Fig 13.4 Organisational structure of SDS service centres after reorganisation

executive assistants (following Christine's recommendation) were all qualified with the Certificate in Personnel Practice (CPP) and each dealt with routine personnel issues as part of his or her duties. Christine made a point of visiting each service centre every two months and discussing issues with the manager and his assistant. These visits were largely fruitful.

The Employee Assistance Programme did not form part of the HR function in any way, but true to its origin, reported directly to the Managing Director of SDS.

The employee assistance programme

About three years ago, Christine's predecessor (now retired) had persuaded the SDS Board to run a pilot study of an employee assistance programme (EAP) in one region of the company. The region was small, having four service centres, and was geographically isolated from the other regions. Reading the Board paper, Christine summarised the rationale. There was a worryingly high absence problem (especially on Mondays and Fridays, self-certificated), there were still too many complaints about work mistakes and rudeness to customers, and the then Personnel Director felt that EAPs were the employee benefit of the future. Valid though those reasons might be, however, part of the reason for adopting the EAP appeared to be the hard sell by the EAP provider company. Since the total cost over a three-year contract was in the order of £70 per head, the sum was within the limit which required no reference to the SDA main board. Christine suspected that her long-serving predecessor had seen the EAP as updated welfare, particularly since the paternalist style of the old Spa company had been replaced by a sharper business focus. The welfare officers of old had been swept away, occupational health had been pruned and pruned again to a passive relic, and the old-fashioned personnel department had transmuted itself into a small strategic advisory function by devolving its powers to line managers. It was difficult to pin down the precise rationale for the adoption of the EAP, or to find a specific justification, either morally or economically. After a three-year trial run, however, the time was due for the EAP to be appraised at Board level. A decision would have to be made by the SDS Board over continuing the programme (or not) on the present basis, extending it, modifying it or changing the EAP provider firm.

THE INTRODUCTION OF EAP PROVISION

Reading through the files, Christine Powers found it hard to fault the EAP contractor's initial investigation, formulation, introduction and implementation of the EAP – the central philosophies of the EAP, as the provider company (Carus Healthcare) termed them. A thorough employee survey had been carried out by questionnaire and interview (including first-line supervisors) in order to elucidate latent and manifest needs, to identify stressors and document their origins, incidence and severity, and to explore perceptions of the EAP service that could cater for expressed needs. The EAP provision, as it was eventually evolved, was then exhaustively discussed with management and supervisors, individual employees and the two main unions in the service centres. Top management were optimistic that the EAP could foster commitment; service centre managers saw it bluntly as a disciplinary tool; employees were wary about confidentiality; and unions were distrustful of management's individualist motives, but declined to oppose it.

The EAP provision that was eventually adopted was a variant of the standard service provided by Carus Healthcare. It was strongly advocated by a friend of the SDS Managing Director (who had one such in his medium-sized firm). The basis of the EAP was a hot-line, open 24 hours per day, and manned entirely by qualified general counsellors, who dealt with factual matters or short-term counselling, or advisory issues: more specialist topics were passed on to specifically dedicated counsellors, or to regionally based counsellors who could make arrangements to continue the contact by telephone or through face-to-face meetings at regional offices.

The EAP was a full-range service, although the majority of clients presenting were expected to be troubled by alcohol and substance abuse, relationship/marital/sexual problems, financial and legal problems, bereavement, and career/retirement/health matters, in that order of frequency. No limit was placed on the number of sessions which a corporate employee–client might have with a counsellor on a particular issue – in practice, the expertise of the counsellor in assessing the enquiry controlled the number of sessions, and few problems of excessive length or cost were expected to be encountered.

Most referrals to the EAP provided by Carus were (in the British tradition) self-referrals, although no doubt often prompted by family, co-workers, and fellow trade unionists. It was not possible to disaggregate the figures, but the sequence given above is probably accurate for frequency. The referral from confrontation by a supervisor (a major source of referral in the US model, which linked substandard job performance with supervisors who had received training in disciplinary referrals to the EAP, as a condition of suspension of formal disciplinary procedures) was expected to be almost non-existent, on the basis of other British companies' statistics.

The EAP instituted on a pilot basis was broad-brush in scope (eating disorders to job neglect, one might say slightly flippantly), and covered all full-time staff with more than one year's service plus their immediate family, spouses/partners and children. It did not cover temporary employees, short-contract (under one year) employees, under-18 workers, subcontractors, part-timers or pensioners.

In spite of the EAP's wide coverage of staff members, it did *not* include as clients former partners or previous families in case of divorce or breakup, etc., grandchildren, in-laws and parents, and it did not cover overseas issues.

The basis of the EAP was total confidentiality to the client. No details of participation in the EAP were given to the employer, unless there was an extremely urgent need for the company to know (e.g. crime, major fraud, physical danger to co-workers or public) and then only with the client's permission. No such incidence had occurred at SDS. In the case of managerial referral, Carus usually convinced the employee to accept the same confidentiality restriction. The service was entirely free to the client, but he or she normally would have to arrange any conversation or meeting outside working hours.

The annual report to the company from Carus dealt with types and numbers of problems and outcomes, discussion of underlying organisational sources of problems, and a cost–benefit justification. The report was made entirely anonymously to the Managing Director, the Human Resources Director and the company's consultant occupational health physician.

The EAP's introduction was carefully planned, with briefing sessions for all employees, training for service centre managers and quality assurance supervisors in identification, confrontation and then help for troubled employees, and familiarisation for Carus Healthcare employees in the particular culture of SDS. The disciplinary elements were carefully discussed with unions and a workable mutual understanding reached over the treatment of a troubled employee.

THE EAP IN OPERATION

The intended focus of the programme was of course on the repair and service employees, who represented the public face of SDS in the eyes of most of the customers. These service engineers numbered up to 80 or 100 per service centre, and were the core of the service business. Almost exclusively male, over 35 years of age, they were often not qualified technician engineers, but had acquired a practical training and experience in maintenance and repair jobs from a variety of backgrounds, including other repair firms, military service and generally in the engineering industry.

The selection process for service engineers had received much attention over the preceding five years, with the assistance of a leading firm of recruitment consultants. A detailed study of the job had revealed that it required a fairly basic level of technical aptitude competence, and training of about National Certificate (NVQ 3), but more importantly the ability:

- to work independently;
- to diagnose technical problems systematically;
- to rectify faults strictly according to the service manual;
- to have interpersonal skills to handle customers (who may be aggressive or anxious) in their own homes;
- to plan the work day;
- to issue and collect customer accounts; and
- to make out daily work reports.

Additionally service engineers needed to be of presentable appearance and with the social skills to deal with a wide range of customers, and to be of total integrity, since they worked in people's homes (sometimes unaccompanied) and handled cash and credit cards in payment for repairs.

Candidates were put through a test battery at the recruitment consultants' office, interviewed intensively, and screened before being put forward to the Service Centre Manager. He was provided with the consultants' report, interviewed the survivors, and appointed those who met his personal criteria, subject to detailed references. There was always a good response to advertisements for service engineers. These were placed in regional newspapers as and when vacancies arose, and service centre managers rarely had difficulty in selecting good calibre applicants. No 'buffer stock' of trained engineers was held, but each service centre had two or three trainers or relief engineers to cope with holidays, extended sickness or other unexpected vacancies in the short term.

When the newly recruited service engineers joined SDS, they received a two-week technical programme on the firm's product range, followed by a two-week attachment to an experienced engineer on site, to acquire practical experience. Once this training was completed, they were assigned to a geographical territory (usually several postcode areas) and serviced the full range of Spa domestic appliances. In practice, about 80 per cent of calls involved a relatively restricted range of washers, dryers and dishwashers up to about eight years old, although Spa equipment had been known to last 20 years or more.

Each engineer had a small diesel van, bearing company livery, equipped with a standard set of tools and parts, on which no deviation was allowed. The company was anxious to obtain BS 5750 and ISO 9000-type accreditation, and insisted on every repair being done by the standard method, following the service manual exactly to the letter, using official parts and tools, in the interests of high quality. No private tools, unofficial equipment, parts or fixes were allowed – even the box of odd screws, bolts, nuts, old pliers or screw-drivers, tape, etc., beloved of all maintenance engineers, was banned! The quality assurance engineers, attached to each service centre, routinely sampled each service engineer's work (usually where the customer subsequently complained) and occasionally carried out an audit (unannounced) on the status of the company van and its equipment. Woe betide the service engineer who had not done the repair exactly according to the repair manual, or who was found with unauthorised or private equipment on board his van.

The daily routine of a service engineer was to receive a work schedule the previous day, which indicated early and late calls, or any other customer requirements. This schedule was devised by the service centre planning department, who in turn had received the informa-tion from the telephone receptionists, who had taken the information from customers. The detail of the information varied greatly, in terms of the nature of the fault, and accuracy of description of the appliance model and serial numbers. The company repair procedure specified that a first visit was to identify the fault exactly, and to allow repair, providing that the spare parts were held among the standard stock in the company van. This worked in over 80 per cent of calls, but where the procedure did not work, the service engineer ordered the necessary parts, and made a second call when they were available, approx-imately a week later. Occasionally, a third call might be required, but the customer was not charged for the call-out after the first visit. Problems had arisen over this procedure. Although it minimised the holding and distribution of parts, customers found it slow and engineers were frustrated at times when they were not permitted to order unusual parts in advance for machines which they had repaired before and whose breakdown character-istics they knew well.

Each engineer worked from home, being responsible for organising paperwork, and organising the maintenance and servicing of his company vehicle, which was assessed as an employment benefit by the Inland Revenue. The engineer would visit the service centre at least once a week for spares, instructions and liaison with management, but routinely, parts were delivered to service engineers' homes by a service centre van, and left in a shed or outhouse. About one day every three months was devoted to new product and update training.

Service engineers were expected to work until their daily roster of calls was finished – on a good day this could mean a 4pm finish if jobs went well and the road traffic flowed well. On a bad day, it could be 6.30pm, with the paperwork to finish subsequently at home. Normally service engineers were expected to work one evening per week until 8pm on out-of-hours calls for those customers who requested them. This was a distinctive fea-ture of Spa's marketing of appliances, but not popular with engineers who were expected to work this period (as with late finishes on 'normal' days) as a part of their working week without overtime. Usually, engineers knew their sequence of calls at the start of the day, but occasionally they had to vary their sequence to call on a particularly insistent and aggres-sive customer (known to them as a 'screamer') who demanded an unscheduled call – communicated via the paging facility with immediate effect.

Over the last two years, service centre managers had been under pressure to improve performance, and as a result of various organisational changes (such as enhanced van stock levels) and better communications (closer control through paging throughout the day), they had improved the daily call rate by 15 per cent and increased the proportion of successful first-time repair visits by around 8 per cent. More importantly, service centre managers were able to congratulate the service engineers on improvements in the customer satisfac-tion index over each of the last three years, which was now the best in the industry.

Service engineers were apparently attracted to the jobs at Spa by the variety of work, the freedom allowed by the use of one's own company van, the variety of people encountered and, of course, the money and security. The monthly salary was individually determined within quite a narrow band, with rises being given for merit and length of service. Salaries were at a good level for the service industry, and compared well with maintenance jobs in the engineering industry, but without the overtime payment opportunities. After a one-year probationary and qualifying period, permanent contracts included all the usual big-company benefits, such as pensions, life insurance and sickness payment benefits at a good level. While promotional opportunities were slender (there were only the quality assurance positions), there was no supervisor standing by to hassle engineers, the business seemed to expand steadily each year with wider ownership of Spa products, and the company had a premium product market reputation.

The complaints flowed in, however, and reached top management levels in their aggregated form. Service centre managers complained about technical work quality. The major problems were:

- wrong repairs using incorrect parts or methods;
- non-standard repair and service procedures which ignored service manual instructions;
- incomplete daily work schedules (often due to becoming ill during the working day, or domestic urgencies);
- excessive van breakdowns or failures to start in the morning;
- excess time spent on non-reported faults, resulting in unexpectedly large bills for customers;
- a recent rising proportion of repeat (uncharged) calls due to stock-outs on the service van.

Other complaints from service centre managers related to customer care and service quality. There were innumerable complaints about sickness absence lasting several days, or temporary indisposition resulting in non-arrival or very late arrival of service engineers. Several engineers had been put on restricted days due to symptoms of coronary heart disease, reported via their own general practitioners. A small but highly incensed group of customers alleged serious discourtesy, rudeness, unhelpfulness and verbal aggression from sales engineers. Again a different small but very angry group of customers said that they had been wrongly charged; often this was proven (due to the complexity of the bill calculation procedure, carried out in the customer's premises by the service engineer) though no financial irregularity for personal gain had been detected. Owing to last-minute unavailability of service engineers, due to family problems or on compassionate grounds, an increasing number of service calls had to be cancelled on the preceding or actual day; rescheduling was often not possible at once, and the eventual call to effect the repair often took up to an additional two weeks. With increasing service business coming to SDS from the marketing success of SDA, the company had responded to engineers' complaints of workload by engaging additional service engineers. Employees felt, however, that an equilibrium of work and engineers was never attained. One item of information went against these perceptions and statistics held by managers: this was the company-wide independent customer satisfaction survey commissioned annually by SDS. Over the previous three surveys, the division in which the EAP was operating was one of only three divisions in the country in which customer ratings rose overall in each of the three years.

Collectively, employees' complaints were less easy to categorise. Over the last three years, there had been no formal industrial relations conflict, partly perhaps because the two

SDA unions represented in the company (and recognised, other than for collective or individual wage bargaining purposes) were numerically weak, and partly perhaps because the selection screening methods, used by the recruitment consultants and less systematically by managers, tended to identify and eliminate union militants and potential organisers. The unions, as already mentioned, did not oppose the introduction of the EAP, but expressed doubts that it would be used as a substitute for pay benefits for members. Furthermore, unions voiced complaints that the EAP was being used as a smokescreen for management's decisions to increase workloads of service engineers, to increase control over their work pattern and methods, to run down long-established occupational health provisions, and to strengthen disciplinary procedures. In particular, unions' objections were concerned with members being more stressed, with consequent increased health and social problems, especially for older members and those with long service.

At the level of individual SDS employees, the complaints were also very vociferous, and appeared to be increasing in number since the introduction of the EAP. Some complaints were made openly in discussions/arguments with management about the pressure of work making the job intolerably stressful. Issues of contention were:

- the existence of the quality assurance inspection;
- the need to work long hours to finish the day's work;
- the compulsory evening work (built into the monthly salary) once a week;
- the lack of liaison with receptionists as in the 'old days';
- the increasing length of retention in service of the vans resulting in greater unreliability;
- the lack of co-operation with the stores team over pick-up of spare parts;
- the need to call in by telephone when each of the day's jobs was finished and to carry a receive-only radio pager, which (engineers felt) was used by management solely to increase their work-rate;
- the abusiveness of certain customers when jobs were uncompleted or repeated service calls were required to rectify problems;
- the difficulties with obtaining payment from a few customers;
- the increasing complexity of customer invoicing and completion of work reports at the end-of-the-day. Employees denied that any service engineer gave anything but his best to the company, but openly said that physical illness was resulting from the job pressure, resulting in absenteeism and undue worry about job security.

The EAP provider company (Carus Healthcare) and its counsellors saw the complaints in terms of their repercussions in stressed, worried and troubled employees presenting themselves by telephone and in face-to-face meetings. The main categories of problems for which assistance was required were (in order of incidence) alcoholism, personal physical and mental health, family and relationship problems, financial problems, smoking, substance abuse – followed by minor incidence of career development, bereavement, eating disorders, legal problems, etc. It was clear from Carus Healthcare's records that the incidence and severity of the problems raised by employees were higher than might have been expected in a company such as SDS. Second, it was noticeable that a great surge of self-referrals appeared about three to four months after the EAP was put in place; no drop-off had occurred, subsequently, and if anything, there had been a small steady increase in employees using the EAP, especially among the immediate family of employees. Third, contrary to management's expectations, the level of reference to the EAP was as high among service centre staff as it was among service engineers, and the distribution of issues was little different also.

The counsellors at Carus expressed much satisfaction at the broad-brush nature of the programme at SDS, at the open-ended access until problems were resolved with the client (thereby allowing full exploration), and at the resilience of SDS clients in sharing responsibility and in taking control in tackling issues. Due to the relatively intensive nature of utilisation of the EAP, however, the managers at Carus Healthcare made it plain that the annual per capita fee would need to be raised considerably for any continuation of the service. A final interesting point emerged from the annual satisfaction survey conducted by Carus and fed back anonymously to SDS: not only was there high and rising appreciation of the EAP among its clients, but there also was among the employees of SDS a relatively high level of pride, commitment and loyalty to the company – an outcome which continually both baffled and pleased the company management.

THE ISSUES

Christine Powers sharply pulled herself out of her ever-more confusing thoughts and back to the here-and-now. 'Don't confuse yourself with the evidence,' she determined. 'Stick to the issues.' Gathering her thoughts together, she began to list those issues under four headings:

1 Measuring and evaluating the goals, methods and effectiveness of the pilot EAP according to the various stakeholders.
2 Assessing the relevance, utility and value of the EAP to individual employees of SDS in the wider context, as well as in their work as employees.
3 Understanding the impact of the EAP on line managers and the extent to which it helps them, or modifies their managerial styles and behaviour.
4 Exploring the linkages within SDS, and wider within SDA, between the provision of an EAP and other corporate strategic policies related to employee contribution and commitment, quality, organisational change and culture.

She stopped. 'Just a moment, there's a fifth heading. I mustn't forget I am the director of a human resources function after all!' She added:

5 Clarifying the relationship between HR and EAP, the potential for conflict and mutual support, and the operational responsibility for EAP.

'That will do nicely,' felt Christine. 'Now to put the flesh on the bones, and to turn it into a report for the Board.'

ACTIVITY BRIEF

1 Has Christine Powers identified the essential issues in assessing whether to continue with the EAP, and in what form? Are there wider issues? Are there key specific points to be resolved before the decision is taken?

2 How does the Human Resources Director in this case identify and reconcile the viewpoints of the various organisational stakeholders in respect of the EAP? Is it necessary to do so?

3 What worries are created for the organisation by instituting an EAP, especially in terms of dependency, confidentiality and authority?

4 As EAPs also become big business in Europe (in the US, 75 per cent of the *Fortune Top 500* companies have them), how are the competing professional–ethical, commercial and effectiveness pressures and demands balanced out by the organisation, when advised by the HRM function? Compare the external contractor-based EAP with other potential provision methods.

5 With the institution of an EAP in an organisation, what impact is felt, respectively, on the personnel management, industrial relations, occupational health and human resource management functions?

6 Consider the following suggestions for role play.

(a) *Policy issues*
Students are allocated roles (as below) and a common fact base (*see* case study), say, a week before the role play, to allow familiarisation and preparation. They prepare roles by study of the case, personal study of the recommended reading and other sources, and (if possible) on-site investigation.

The roles to be played are shown in Fig. 13.2, and are:

Christine Powers	Progressive, determined HR Director at SDS, but not interested in building an empire for its own sake.
James Russell	Operations Director, 30s, with a keen analytical mind, task-oriented, more cost- than benefit-driven.
Forbes McCann	Financial Director, 40s, possessing a sceptical mindset for any proposal where the bottom line is unclear.
Gloria Simmonds	Administration Director, 40s, brilliant at alternative scenarios and no-nonsense.

Objective: agreement on EAP policy for Spa Distribution and Service (SDS) and a recommendation to the Spa main board.

(b) *Operational issues*
Students' roles as in (a) above in terms of preparation. The roles are listed in Figs 13.3 and 13.4 and are:

Peter Horsley	Service Centre Manager at Checkley, early 50s, served 15 years in SDS, determined yet willing to consider new ideas – nominee of service centre staff.

Greg Longdon   Stock controller and acting stores team leader at Blackbeck, MSF
                 steward there, and company joint union convenor for SDS staff for
                 over ten years.

Christine Powers See above.

Duncan Isbister   Company occupational health advisor and honorary university lec-
                  turer, currently conducting stress and well-being audits in the
                  company.

Objective: discussion and definition of the EAP's operational role at service centre level, if
put on a permanent basis

7 Following one or both of the activities in **6**, either:
  (a) as a group, devise the outline arguments for Christine Powers' Board paper, indicating
      the persuasive and negotiating tactics to be used, with time-scale, and making a
      recommendation for or against adoption of the EAP, with reasons;
  (b) individually, write the Board paper in full (maximum 1000 words or four pages of dou-
      ble-spaced WP text) preceded by a 100-word summary and recommendations.

RECOMMENDED READING

Berridge, JR and Cooper, CL (1993) 'Stress and coping in US organisations: the role of the Employee
    Assistance Programme', *Work and Stress.* 7, 1, pp 89–102.
Berridge, JR and Cooper, CL (1994) 'The Employee Assistance Programme: its role in organisational
    coping and excellence', *Personnel Review.* 23, 7, p 80.
Cunningham, G (1995) *Effective Employee Assistance Programs*, Thousand Oaks, California, SAGE
    Publications.
Davis, A and Gibson, L (1994) 'Designing employee welfare provision' in Berridge, JR and Cooper
    CL, *op. cit.*, pp 33–45.
Megranahan, M (1989) *Counselling – a Practical Guide for Employers*, London, IPM.
Nelson-Jones, R (1995) *Theory and Practice of Counselling*, London, Cassell.
Reddy, M (1986) *The Manager's Guide to Counselling at Work*, London, Methuen.
Roman, PM and Blum, TC (1992) 'The core technologies of employee assistance', *EAP
    International*, 1, 1, pp 4–8.

CASE 14

Stress management interventions in organisations

Margaret Ferrario and Cary L Cooper

INTRODUCTION

This case documents a research project initiated and funded by a Healthcare NHS Trust on stress reduction strategies in the work environment. This was carried out by the authors over a two-year period. The objectives of the project were to obtain the commitment of four participating companies, to identify any major sources of stress within each organisation, to implement stress management interventions intended to reduce or alleviate the effects of stress and to evaluate their effectiveness. The project formed part of a long-term objective of the Trust, which aims to identify sources of stress and to improve employee health as part of a wider initiative of health promotion within the local community.

It has been known for many years that workplace stress is costing the UK economy and organisations an enormous human resource bill (Cooper and Payne 1988). According to the Department of Health and the Confederation of British Industry (1991), the cost of sickness absence for stress and mental disorders has been estimated in the UK at more than £5 billion a year.

There is a growing recognition of work stress as an important occupational health problem. There is an acknowledgement that occupational stress contributes to an increasing proportion of worker compensation claims, health care, disability, absenteeism, and productivity losses. As a result, there is an increasing interest in how stress can be reduced in the workplace. There are few studies to date on the effectiveness of stress reduction strategies in occupational settings. The aim of this case is to evaluate some stress management interventions and the outcomes of such interventions.

A growing number of employers are recognising the existence of stress at work and are taking steps to minimise it. These steps can take several forms. First, and most common, are stress management interventions at the individual level. These include a set of techniques aimed at the individual, such as relaxation, biofeedback, time management, stress awareness programmes and cognitive restructuring, which reflect attempts to alter the ways in which individuals structure and organise their world. Second, many organisations are beginning to introduce stress counselling, or what are being termed Employee Assistance Programmes (EAPs) for their employees. EAPs are counselling resources provided to employees of a particular organisation by an outside agency. Provision of exercise and meditation are other examples of interventions aimed at the individual.

BACKGROUND TO THE CASE

Four companies of varying sizes and occupational sectors agreed to participate in the project. The methodology involved assessing the sources of stress by means of a stress audit. This aided the formulation of corrective measures by means of appropriate stress management interventions. Evaluation of the interventions was then carried out several months later and any improvement in employee stress levels or health was monitored. The measures used included a validated stress questionnaire (Occupational Stress Indicator, Cooper *et al* 1988), biographical information, questionnaires designed to evaluate the effectiveness of the interventions, interviews, analysis of organisational context and sickness absence data. The approach necessitated gaining commitment from both management and staff to the programme. The main objective was to design and implement strategies tailored to specific company needs and/or constraints.

Three out of the four companies participated in an intervention. The fourth company did not go ahead in spite of an intention to do so at the outset, due to a very unstable financial position. It was felt by senior management that an intervention would have little effect on the low morale of the workforce caused through high job insecurity and implementation of changes by senior management. The interventions implemented in the three other companies consisted primarily of individual-oriented interventions involving workshops tailored to address the needs of the employees within each of the organisations.

THE FOUR ORGANISATIONAL CONTEXTS

Company A

Company A is a small financial service company and has 60 employees with a third of its workforce distributed in six small branches and the remaining two thirds at the company's head office. The company has grown over recent years and become profitable under the leadership of its current Managing Director. Staff turnover is low and the majority of employees are female, with most branch staff working on a part-time basis. All policy and administrative decisions are made by the Managing Director who has shaped the culture and direction of the company.

Company B

Company B is a small manufacturer and supplier of a specialist product. It has 143 employees and is sited on a modern industrial estate with good working conditions. This company was a family-run business until a few years ago when there was a management buy-out. The four directors who run the company have introduced many changes and have been successful in making the company very profitable. They have maintained a 'paternalistic' culture which the previous owners cultivated. The management style of the current directors is a participative style giving autonomy to their staff where possible.

Company C

Company C is an old-established clothing manufacturer with approximately 190 staff. Established over 200 years ago, it was run as a family business until a few years ago. Machines, tools and the physical working environment have changed very little and are in urgent need of remodernising. Most staff in the factory are paid on a 'piece-work' basis, i.e. on the basis of work completed. When the company was run as a family concern, it was common to lay off workers for several weeks of the year when business was poor and to re-instate them when needed. This was quite acceptable to staff who would then claim unemployment benefit until re-employed. The present management, accountable to a board of shareholders in London, have stopped this practice and have introduced many changes which the current workforce have been resisting. Because of this resistance, senior management have taken a tougher stance with the workforce and not involved workers in any decision making. 'Troublesome' workers have been eased out through a series of redundancies and voluntary severance.

In spite of management efforts, the company has deteriorated, mainly due to a fall in demand for the product and competition from abroad. The future of the company is uncertain and job insecurity and low morale, coupled with a lack of confidence in the management, are prevalent among the staff.

Company D

Company D is a large transport company. The headquarters which participated in the study employs around 480 staff. Due to increased competition, there have been many changes in working methods and increasing workload. The majority of staff deal with customers on the telephone and the level of skill required by employees varies according to the department. The company's head office is based in the south of England from which decisions are made on the operations of the company's four business groups. The organisation is made up of two main business units. The largest unit (Unit A) accounts for 80 per cent of staff, and deals with customers directly on the telephone and is responsible for the major portion of company income. The smaller unit (Unit B) accounts for 20 per cent of the workforce. Unit B staff also deal with customers on the telephone but, because they are giving specialist advice, most of them are graduates with extensive experience in their field.

OVERVIEW OF METHODOLOGY

The project involved three main stages:

1 Stress audit involving questionnaires and random sample of interviews. The questionnaires were numbered to enable pre- and post-intervention comparisons.
2 Design and implementation of stress reduction strategies on the basis of the results of Stage 1.
3 Evaluation of strategies using questionnaires, a second stress audit, sample interviews, and sickness absence data.

A questionnaire was used to evaluate six sources of workplace stress – the Occupational Stress Indicator (OSI) in addition to personality characteristics (Type A/B behaviour and Locus of Control), and individual coping strategies. Individual stress outcomes included mental and physical health and job satisfaction. The scores were obtained by comparing mean scores of the individuals or groups with the mean scores of a general population of around 8000 individuals (which form the basis of norm scores). The OSI is a highly reliable and validated instrument for identifying the major sources of stress.

Results of Stage 1 stress audit – pre-intervention stage

The results of Stage 1, detailed below, report the results of the stress audit and interviews conducted within each of the four companies. A total of 279 questionnaires were received out of a total of 873 (31.9 per cent response rate) and a total of 95 interviews were conducted. Table 14.1 details the response rate for each of the four companies.

Table 14.1 Response rate at Stage 1

Company	A	B	C	D
Questionnaires received	34	55	57	133
Total sent out	60	143	187	483
% response rate	56.6%	38.5%	30.5%	27.5%

Company A

The OSI results showed that 'career and achievement' was the main source of pressure. The interviews revealed that communication could be improved and that the Managing Director's more autocratic style of management had a negative effect on the organisational climate. The staff stated that he did not offer positive feedback and was quick to criticise staff in front of others. On the positive side, they had confidence in his ability to direct the company and make it profitable.

Interestingly, the MD's OSI scores indicated his main source of pressure was dealing with people, which may account for his style of management. He also claimed that it was hard for him to relinquish any control to his junior managers and that he liked to make all decisions regarding the company. The OSI revealed Company A staff to have high job satisfaction.

Company B

The results showed that the only source of pressure related to 'career and achievement'. The interviews revealed that because of the small size of the company it was difficult to progress. In general, there was high job satisfaction and no negative symptoms of stress. The interviews revealed that people were positive about the company and its directors and felt there was high job security and a senior management who took an interest in them. The OSI revealed Company B staff to have high job satisfaction.

Company C

The OSI revealed that 'career and achievement' and 'organisational structure' were the main sources of pressure. The interviews revealed that the majority of the workforce were resistant to the changes which the new management were trying to implement. Originally, the Managing Director took a sympathetic stance towards the workforce, but as he could not get their co-operation, he adopted a more autocratic management style. Morale is low due to the third year without profit and widespread redundancies. The interviews revealed low job satisfaction as did measures on the OSI. Communication was cited as poor and there was a lack of consultation by management with staff. The OSI scores showed low job satisfaction and poor physical health.

Company D

The results showed that the majority of individuals identified 'career and achievement' as a main source of pressure. This was confirmed by many individuals who were interviewed who felt there was a lack of promotion prospects. The results of the questionnaire also showed that there was a general lack of job satisfaction. The interviews revealed that they were under pressure due to increased workload. Many of the staff who deal with customer information and complaints on the phone described the work as often boring and repetitive. Nearly all of those interviewed felt there was a lack of communication within the company.

For the purpose of this project, one particular department (Unit B) of Company D was selected for an intervention and subsequently became the focus for evaluation.

Stage 2 – stress management interventions

The results of the stress audit in Stage 1 enabled the evaluation of corrective measures regarding stress management interventions in Stage 2. The following is a brief description of the recommendations and implementation or non-implementation of interventions designed to reduce stress.

Company A

There were two main recommendations to the Managing Director of the company. The first was that he should re-evaluate his style of management. It was suggested he relinquish some decisions to his managers and praise his staff more for good work rather than concentrating on the negative aspects. His profile was fed back to him which showed that his major source of pressure was dealing with others at work – which he acknowledged. Due to external regulations he is being forced into relinquishing some control and has started to do this but admits he finds this difficult.

The other main recommendation was that the researcher and another consultant run a one-and-a-half day session with a sample of staff, including the MD, in order to enhance communication and team-building. This was initiated, but the MD did not attend. This was at the request of the researcher as members of staff had grave concerns about his attendance as they felt they would be too inhibited by his presence. The workshop was designed to improve communication and enhance team skills and there was an input on stress management. Individuals were paired to discuss action plans on how they would reduce a major source of stress over the next two to six months. Participants completed an evaluation of the workshop. The evaluations showed that most participants had felt the workshop was useful. A brief outline of the workshop content included:

- Practical exercises in groups highlighting communication and team-building.
- Evaluation of various types of leadership styles.
- Group discussions on their organisational context.
- Discussion on the causes and symptoms of stress.
- Awareness of individual stress management initiatives.
- Development of three- to six-month action plans to alleviate a major cause of stress.

Company B

The results of the analysis showed the only source of pressure for the majority of staff were 'career and achievement' issues. The management acknowledged that progression in the company was limited and were aware that they had some highly skilled staff who should have moved on to other companies in order to pursue their careers. There was little they could do, however, but they did acknowledge this to staff after feeding back the results of the survey and promised to try to address this problem further.

Many of the staff did not report being under pressure. There were individuals in the company with high stress profiles, however, and it was decided that the researcher run two one-day workshops. A random sample of staff was targeted which included those with high stress profiles. However, management also let staff know that anyone who felt they would benefit from such a workshop would be entitled to attend.

Two one-day sessions consisted of informing participants of the nature of stress, its effects and a discussion of stress reduction strategies. Individuals were encouraged to discuss any problems and the session involved participants separating into pairs and discussing a two- to six-month action plan on how they would reduce one major stressor either in their work or home environment. Participants completed a short questionnaire regarding the evaluation of the session. This revealed that most had found the workshop useful. A brief outline of the workshop included:

- Highlighting the causes of stress and eliciting which stressors exist in the organisation.
- Symptoms of stress.
- Questionnaires and exercises designed to elicit any stress-producing symptoms within individuals.
- Group discussions on what can be done to alleviate the causes of stress within their own environment.
- Development of three- to six-month action plans to alleviate a cause of stress and encourage co-mentoring in order to provide support for pairs of individuals to carry through these plans.

Company C

Company C was informed about the results of the survey and a series of recommendations for reducing stress was documented for the MD to consider. These included a mixture of organisational and individual-oriented interventions.

At a subsequent meeting between the researcher and the MD, the MD claimed that the company was not doing well and that he was taking a harder line with staff because they were resisting planned changes. Communication had worsened between staff and management. He had implemented a series of redundancies and many had been persuaded to leave through voluntary severance.

It was ultimately decided that due to low morale, poor sales figures and a series of redundancies including managers, no intervention should take place. However, the MD agreed that a final stress audit could take place.

Company D

The main source of pressure was related to a lack of promotion prospects within the company as the organisation had steered toward a flatter management structure. The interviews also revealed that there was a lack of communication in the company between management and staff. One department became the focus of the study.

The staff in this department were highly skilled with most holding university degrees. They dealt with customers on the telephone providing specialist advice and information. Career progression was limited unless staff were prepared to move to another geographical location which many were reluctant to do. The manager had already recently implemented more participation in decision making by organising staff into quality groups in order to both help improve the business and provide more autonomy to staff. He was also keen to introduce some sort of multi-skilling in order to enrich current jobs.

It was decided that the manager would make use of the company's occupational health advisor based at the company headquarters in the south. A series of one-day sessions was organised away from the office in a hotel. The entire 48 staff attended these one-day sessions over a period of a month, i.e. one day per week with around 12 people at each session. The session was run jointly by the occupational health advisor and the manager.

The sessions consisted of providing information on stress at work and remedial measures individuals might try to alleviate stress. The manager spent some of the time inviting staff to tell him their problems at work and a discussion ensued on how these problems might be alleviated. The session ended with the advisor involving the group in relaxation techniques. A brief outline of the workshop content included:

- Provision of information on what causes stress and stress symptoms by company occupational health advisor.
- Encouragement by department manager for group discussions on what particular stressors are experienced by employees in his department.
- Group feedback elicited to suggest ways of alleviating the causes of stress at work.
- Relaxation and exercise to combat stress demonstrated by occupational health advisor.

Results of Stage 3 stress audit – post-intervention stage

All four companies were sent a final OSI six months after the interventions. There was a much lower response rate to the final audit, as obviously not everyone who completed the first audit would complete the second one for various reasons.

Company comparisons on stressors and stress outcomes for the intervention groups – pre- and post-intervention

Statistical analyses of the intervention groups in all three companies were conducted between stressors and outcomes, pre-intervention compared to post-intervention. Although very few stressors significantly differed statistically between the two stages, there was a tendency for the stress levels to be lower at the post-intervention stage six months later. Interestingly, the no-intervention company, Company C, had higher stress levels at Stage 3, which is not surprising considering the lowered morale and higher job insecurity. The results are shown in Fig. 14.1 which show the stressors of each of the four companies pre- and post-intervention in relation to the normal population denoted by 0. This illustrates stress factors for each company which fall below or above the normal population given as a percentage.

Similar analyses were conducted on the stress outcomes for each of the four companies at the pre- and post-intervention stage. Figure 14.2 (on page 152) shows the results in relation to the norm scores denoted by 0. It can be seen that job satisfaction is even lower at the final audit stage in Company C (the no-intervention group). Job satisfaction improved in Company A but fell in Companies B and D. With regard to health, the intervention group in Company A, who originally reported poor physical health scores, showed improved physical health scores in addition to a slight improvement in mental health. The groups in the other three companies did not report much improvement on their original health scores.

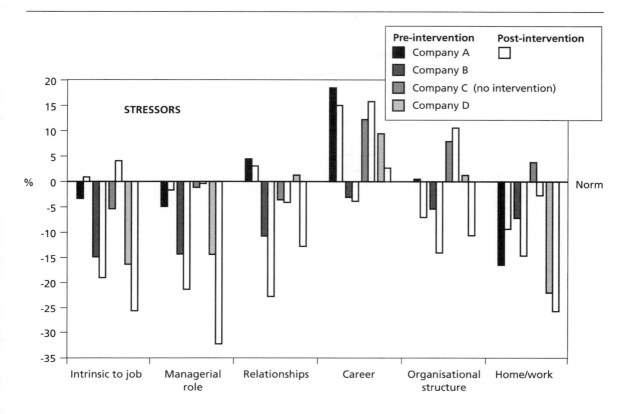

Note: with stressors, high score = high stress

Fig 14.1 Stressors pre- and post-intervention – intervention groups' OSI mean scores compared to norms

Comparison of sickness absence data – pre- and post-intervention

Sickness absence was compared in the intervention groups in all four companies between six months prior to intervention and six months after the intervention. Access to data was obtained in Companies A and B, but not in Companies C (due to lack of upkeep) and D (where this resided in the south of England and access was denied). Therefore, the sickness absence figures for Companies C and D were obtained through their self-report data in the biographical questionnaires. Table 14.2 indicates the mean number of sickness absence days for each company. The figures show how sickness absence was reduced post-intervention with the exception of Company C.

Table 14.2 Comparison of mean no. of days re sickness absence pre- and post-intervention

	Company A	Company B	Company C	Company D
6 mths pre	2.2	3.4	3.0	7.1
6 mths post	1.8	1.6	5.4	4.4

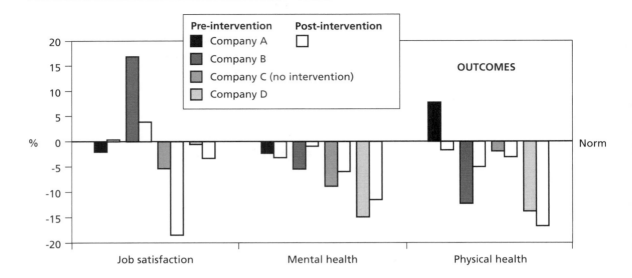

Note: with job satisfaction, high score = high satisfaction
with health, higher score = poorer health

Fig 14.2 Outcomes pre- and post-intervention – intervention groups' OSI mean scores compared to norms

ACTIVITY BRIEF

1 Develop alternative stress management interventions for each of the companies described above. Provide two alternative interventions, one aimed at the individual level and one at the organisational level.

2 The results indicated that the stress levels were generally lower at the post-intervention stage. What other factors might account for this?

3 Identify at least five major problems associated with conducting and evaluating applied research.

RECOMMENDED READING

Cooper, CL, Cooper, R and Eaker, L (1988) *Living with Stress*, London, Penguin.
Cooper, CL, and Payne, R (1988) *Causes, Coping and Consequences of Stress at Work*, Chichester, Wiley.
Cooper, CL, Sloan, SJ and Williams, S (1988) *Occupational Stress Indicator*, NFER Nelson.
Cooper, CL and Williams, S (1994) *Creating Healthy Work Organisations*, Chichester, Wiley.
Sutherland, VJ and Cooper, CL (1992) *Understanding Stress: A Psychological Perspective for Health Professionals*, Basingstoke, Macmillan.

PART 3

Employee Development

Important issues relating to the development of employees are the subject of 'Slogan Stores PLC', where Sally Messenger, Christoph Williams and John Davison assess their potential impact on key performance ratios. This includes the concept of competence-based education and training, exemplified by NCVQ in the UK, whilst placing employee development generally within the framework of the company profile and the need to develop competitive advantage.

Changes in business strategy which require the further development of skills and knowledge at management level are the subject of 'Strategic choice for management training and development in "Aerospace"'. Nicholas Kinnie and Martin Ridley consider company commitment to training and evaluate an existing programme, weighing the extent to which course objectives have been met in respect of understanding of wider business perspectives, the development of management skills and confidence, to assess requirements for the company's future.

In 'Developing a staff training culture in a retail organisation', John Guthrie reports the experiences of the manager of a retail store in New Zealand when attempting to react to operating inefficiencies which appeared to be reflected in the attitudes and morale of staff, including full- and part-time workers. A minimal and spasmodic training philosophy, driven by a profit rationale has to be countered in order to establish an appropriate range of skills through a new training programme.

The crucial importance of management development in the face of times of radical change underlies the case of 'Management development at ARCO Ltd', which examines the appropriateness of existing development models and the manner in which they are implemented. Michael Doyle delineates the design and delivery of a programme by the Personnel Co-ordinator, evaluating its failure to meet expectations and permitting readers to review current approaches.

The next case relates to an important initiative which was set up to encourage the development of staff through an award and regular reassessment of standards. Peter Critten explores the extent to which investing in the development of each member of staff can really be measured in business terms. 'Investors in People three years on: Torquay Leisure Hotel Group's experience' provides the opportunity to follow the process engaged in, while also reflecting on questions arising relating to this organisation's specific experience and questions of HRM strategy.

The final case in the section brings together again wider aspects of the organisation surrounding the development of employees. It details a four year case study relating to 'New Zealand Breweries: what is the future of the HRM function?' Ian Glendon, David Simmons and Greg Bamber investigate the desire to add value to the company and improve organisational performance. Strategic initiatives are accompanied by instituting training as a major responsibility of the HR group.

Slogan Stores PLC

Sally Messenger, Christoph Williams and John Davison

INTRODUCTION

The newly appointed Managing Director of Slogan Stores PLC, Max Margins, has contracted a consultancy firm to provide him with recommendations for a new training and development strategy. Max Margins is a member of an industry working party which is concerned with national and international trends and developments in the retail sector. He is therefore aware that the government has recently indicated a willingness to sponsor company initiatives that encourage the uptake of national competence-based education and training qualifications.

A team of three consultants is working on this project. Initially the plan is to focus the training and development strategy on store management and sales floor staff. One consultant has undertaken the desk research stage and produced an overview of the company and its activities together with a summary of the concept of competence-based education and training (CBET). The second member of the team, Lucinda Sharp, has undertaken Phase 1 of the field work and conducted a range of interviews with a sample of staff to gather feedback regarding current education and training activities within the company. Last week she made an initial presentation to the Board of Slogan Stores PLC.

The reader is invited to be the third member of the project team and is asked to analyse the material produced by the desk research, to study the transcription of Lucinda Sharp's presentation to the Board and to gather together any further information available before formulating a set of draft recommendations and issues for the organisation to consider and debate.

BACKGROUND TO THE CASE

Slogan Stores PLC, a mixed goods retailer, was established as a family-owned business in 1955. Mixed goods retailers are defined as those with less than 80 per cent of their business sales, or 50 per cent in the case of food retailers or hire or repair business, generated from the sale of one major commodity. This group of retailers includes department stores, variety stores and general mail order houses (Keynote Publications 1990). Typical product ranges would be clothing, footwear, leather goods, household goods, toiletries, etc. The company became publicly owned in 1972, following successful flotation on the stock market. Since then the company has expanded from a turnover of £225 million to £1.5 billion and has over 23,000 employees. This growth has been achieved mainly organically, with the number of stores in the UK rising from 32 to 137 over this period. Five years ago the company, anticipating a slowdown in its domestic growth, embarked on tentative expansion into Europe, acquiring a regionally based chain of 15 stores in France in 1990.

The company's core markets are ladieswear and childrenswear, in both of which the company holds the second largest market share in the UK. In ladieswear, however, the company's product offer is often seen as staid and aimed at an older market. Market share is declining and only just heads a pack of other retailers whose individual market shares are dwarfed by that of the leading player who accounts for 42 per cent of the market. In childrenswear, an expanding market, Slogan Stores PLC, by contrast, is seen as something of a trend-setter with a wide and innovative product range that appeals to parents and children across a broad socio-economic scale. Other major product ranges include menswear, footwear, household textiles and furnishings, lighting, home entertainment and toiletries.

In the past three years, with foreign-in-origin, discount and off-price retailers entering the UK, the company market share has fallen from 8.5 per cent to 6.3 per cent. The expansion into France has also presented a number of problems: no significant profits have been accrued so far and plans for further expansion are being put on hold. This is partly due to the slightly downmarket image of the acquired stores. Repositioning these stores has proved more difficult than at first anticipated and this has been hampered by initial attempts by the company to superimpose the existing organisational management culture and ethos onto the French stores. Slogan Stores PLC is now in the process of implementing a devolved organisational structure which will allow greater autonomy to the management of the French operation.

The financial markets have lost faith in the company in recent years. It is thought that this led to the recent and sudden departure of Conan Terry, doyen of the City during the phenomenal expansion of the company in the late 1970s and 1980s. During the slowdown in the company's organic growth in the latter part of the 1980s and early 1990s, however, Mr Terry's management style came in for much criticism both from within and outside the company, resulting in his recent ousting as Managing Director.

Table 15.1 presents selected key performance ratios for Slogan Stores PLC for the current financial year.

Table 15.1 Comparative performance ratios for current financial year

	Industry average	*Slogan Stores*
Stockholding (days)	7.5	11.2
Net margin (%)	8.1	6.2
Profit per employee (£)	8,400	6,600
Sales per employee per year (£)	65,108	64,429
Labour turnover		
Store management (%)	40%	48%
Shopfloor staff (%)	65%	79%
Senior executives (%)	11%	15%

Table 15.1 gives the staff turnover ratios at executive, store management and shopfloor staff levels. Over 70 per cent of turnover at this level is accounted for by managers with less than 18 months' service with the company. Conversely, there is a large proportion of managers, particularly at Departmental Manager level, who have long service with the company and among whom labour turnover is negligible. Within the shopfloor workforce there is a very small and declining proportion of staff who have more than five years' service with the company. A large proportion of the labour turnover at this level occurs

among staff with six to twelve months' service. At executive level, i.e. Area Controller and above (*see* Fig. 15.1) the greatest proportion of long-serving managers are found. Most positions at this level are filled by people who have been with the company for a minimum of ten years and longevity of company service is generally found to increase as one moves up the executive ladder. In fact few people at the very highest levels within the organisation have been with the company less than 20 years.

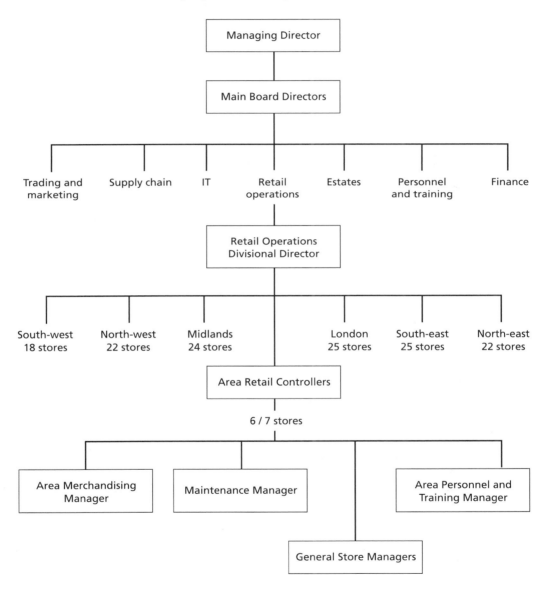

Fig 15.1 Slogan Stores PLC retail operations organisational chart

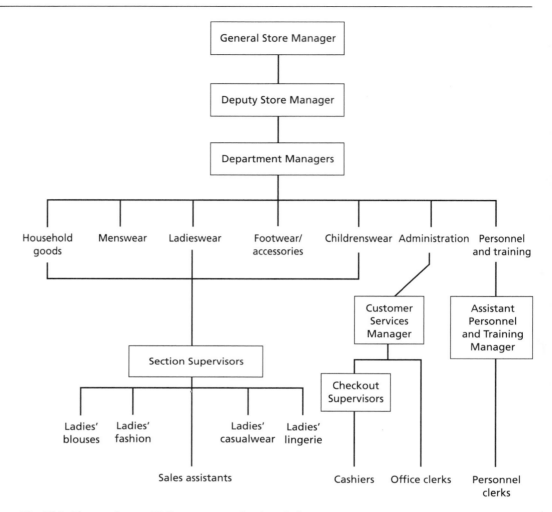

Fig 15.2 Slogan Stores PLC store organisational chart

The organisational structure of the company's retail operations is presented in Figs 15.1 and 15.2. Strategy and policy is determined at director level and implemented on a centralised basis across the company's retail divisions. The divisions are organised on a regional basis and, below that, are divided into areas. At divisional level, Divisional Directors are responsible for the broad implementation of all company policies and the financial performance of 18 to 25 stores within the division. Area Controllers report to Divisional Directors and they themselves have responsibility for the day-to-day implementation of company policies and practices for six or seven stores within each division. In this they are assisted by Area Managers for merchandising, maintenance and personnel and training. The Area Personnel and Training Manager, for example, would be responsible for ensuring that all company personnel and training policies are implemented and adhered to in stores, that training and development is planned and takes place in accordance with individual stores' needs, and for providing specialist advice to the Area Controller and Store Managers, Store Personnel and Training Managers within the area.

It should be noted that names of divisions are nominal only and do not necessarily correspond with exact geographic regions of the UK. Furthermore, the French operations are not included within this organisational structure. These stores have their own Divisional Director who, while reporting to the Retail Operations Director of Slogan Stores PLC, has considerably more autonomy, particularly in formulating policy on issues of trading and marketing and personnel and training, than his UK counterparts.

THE CONCEPT OF COMPETENCE-BASED EDUCATION AND TRAINING (CBET)

Although currently in vogue, competence-based training systems have been developed and implemented, at company level, in the retail industry for a number of years. It is, however, only in more recent years that a national attempt has been made to identify the competence requirements of the different industry sectors in the UK.

Desk research has indicated that despite the widespread use of competences in the retail industry, there is still much debate concerning the conceptualisation of the approach. For example, there is a distinction between personal and occupational competence. Personal competence concerns the identification of characteristics (or orientations) that differentiate effective retail managers from those which are less effective. This approach is concerned with the latent or potential capability of individuals to act in their roles as managers. In contrast, occupational competence concentrates on measuring the actual performance of managers (i.e. what managers actually do rather than what they can do) in order to be effective.

The development of CBET in the UK has been prompted by a series of White Papers in the 1980s and the subsequent establishment of the National Council for Vocational Qualifications (NCVQ). As an accrediting body, NCVQ has overall responsibility for the provision of competence-based vocational qualifications and the maintenance of quality assurance mechanisms.

It should be noted that the government has invested significant sums of money in the development of competence-based qualifications and through funding arrangements has been actively encouraging their implementation. For example, Training and Enterprise Councils (TECs) are involved in the initiative.

NCVQ has prescribed the structure of the new National Vocational Qualifications (NVQs) and the method of analysis which identifies the standards and outcomes against which individual performance is assessed. The philosophy of NVQs is that assessment is ideally undertaken in the workplace and that achievement is not tied to time-serving. In addition to direct observation on the job, a variety of other techniques may be used to assess knowledge and understanding, such as written and oral tests or the completion of portfolios of evidence.

In order for a company to offer NVQs it needs to set up a framework involving the training of staff to undertake assessments and the establishment of procedures to ensure the system is meeting external national criteria. These procedures should not be underestimated in terms of resource requirements.

At the end of the 1980s the retail industry began developing national standards which would form the basis of NVQs. To date the Distributive Occupational Standards Council (DOSC) has been highlighted as one of the most successful in terms of the number of people who are working towards or have gained an NVQ.

THE BOARDROOM PRESENTATION

Lucinda Sharp, a member of the team of consultants researching the new training and development strategy for the company, has interviewed staff regarding current education and training within the company. She presents her findings to the Board of Slogan Stores PLC:

'First, may I begin this presentation by thanking the Board for agreeing to attend this meeting, which was called at short notice, to outline the progress which has been made to date in developing a new training and development strategy for Slogan Stores PLC.

'As you know from the research plan, I have spent the last month undertaking Phase 1 of the field work and as such have now completed a range of interviews with senior management, the training and development department and a number of store-level staff. I am now able to report to you, therefore, the current perception of training and development within your company and to offer some thoughts on the possible way forward.

'Before I embark on highlighting the key findings to emerge so far from the field work it is important to appreciate the organisational context in which this research is being conducted. The recently published half-year results indicated the company's financial performance was poor relative to that of its competitors. Productivity and sales ratios per employee were exceptionally low. In addition, staff turnover at all levels within the organisation was high and a recent employee attitude survey indicated that job satisfaction and staff morale were at an all time low. Leakage figures had also increased, further compounding the difficulties being faced at the operational level.

'When the data gathered from Phase 1 of the training and development interviews was analysed, the following issues emerged:

1 Both store managers and operational staff are unhappy about the delivery of inappropriate and irrelevant training and development programmes. Store managers are increasingly reluctant to allow staff to attend courses (which last between two and four days each) at the company training centre in Eastbourne. As is to be expected, a number of the staff are discontented with the lack of opportunity to follow a course and when they do they complain that they spend a few days in a classroom hearing about what should be happening in the stores and sometimes wonder if they are all working for the same company – added to which there is no real recognition that they have attended a course besides the fact that the details are kept by the store manager.

    Personnel and training staff feel that their resources are stretched and that it is therefore difficult to make any changes to the current training and development systems. They are aware, for example, that training needs to be made more relevant to today's business but they feel they need direction from senior management in the form of an organisational policy for training and development particularly now the company has European interests.

2 Tensions exist between shopfloor staff and store management, with the managers viewing the salesforce as not being competent enough to perform their operational activities. In addition, senior executives view store managers as lacking in the capability to deal with long-term business problems in a manner that takes the business forward and prevents the re-emergence of the same problems. Their ability to identify and respond to industry trends in order to identify market opportunities was also questioned.

    The salesforce do not have a high opinion of their managers. They feel that managers are only concerned about meeting sales targets and that there is an atmosphere of 'them and us' in the company. A number expressed their intention to leave the organisation once the economic climate looks healthier. There was a general feeling that other companies in the retail industry are focusing on staff as their greatest resource in the increasingly competitive market place.

3 The company's organisational structure is generally perceived as being overly bureaucratic. Staff at all levels complained that this led to slow and inefficient communication, both within the organisation and when responding to customers and suppliers. While detailed figures are not available, there appears to have been an increase in the number of complaints received about the level of customer service across all stores.

4 The training and development department reported how a recent industrial tribunal had highlighted problems concerning career progression routes. These were perceived as being unfair and more closely linked to an employee's length of service as opposed to his or her performance. A similar problem was associated with the existing salary scales.

'As a result of these preliminary findings it is possible to make some broad recommendations.

'First, there is a need for a corporate restructuring and cultural change programme. This should result in increased productivity, quality and overall business performance by focusing upon:

- the identification of individual and organisational training needs;
- the development of a framework for training design and delivery;
- the specification of job profiles and descriptions;
- the development of succession plans and career progression routes;
- the design of performance-linked pay schemes;
- the enhancement of motivation, morale and confidence of employees;
- the building of teams;
- the improvement of communications.'

Mr Margins interrupted at this point:

'I am sure we all appreciate your outline recommendations but I have not convened this special meeting for you to waste the time of my Board members. Quite frankly, everyone sitting around this table could have made those suggestions without doing any research and spending any money.'

Ms Sharp continued:

'Well, these are of course only preliminary suggestions, as you requested. The development of a strategic plan would be the next stage of this initiative. This would need to consider issues such as flattening the organisation's structure, multi-skilling staff and job rotation. Such changes would involve encouraging empowerment and teamwork, job evaluation and identifying and defining competence statements. These would then be related to training and development activities, appraisal and succession planning, recruitment and selection systems and pay scales. The strategy would also have to focus upon a host of potential difficulties associated with implementation and the impact on the public's perceptions of Slogan Stores PLC.'

Mr Margins conceded:

'OK, you've got an understanding of the situation. Having listened to your comments, I would now like you to concentrate on the three key issues in preparation for our next meeting which takes place in three weeks' time.'

ACTIVITY BRIEF

1 Identify the key issues which Slogan Stores PLC needs to consider when deciding whether or not to operate a competence-based assessment system. In particular identify the advantages and disadvantages of operating a national system as opposed to developing and implementing an in-house programme.

2 Company training policies are often strongly influenced by the government. How could this affect the development of a new training and development strategy for Slogan Stores PLC?

3 Discuss the advantages and disadvantages of implementing a training and development programme that concentrates more on personal or occupational competence.

4 Discuss the importance of company culture in developing and implementing a competence-based training system.

5 Prepare a set of recommendations for the next meeting of the Board on the future strategic direction of training and development within the company. You should include guidelines and contingency plans to ensure effective implementation.

RECOMMENDED READING

Burke, J (ed) (1989) *Competency-based Education and Training*, Lewes, The Falmer Press.

Fletcher, S (1991) *NVQs, Standards and Competence – A Practical Guide for Employees, Managers and Trainers*, London, Kogan Page Ltd.

Hodkinson, P and Issitt, M (1995) *The Challenge of Competence: Professionalism through Vocational Education and Training*, London, Cassell.

Jessup, G (1991) *Outcomes: NVQs and the Emerging Model of Education and Training*, London, The Falmer Press.

Keynote Publications (1990) *Retailing in the UK: Market Review*, Hampton, Middlesex, Keynote Publications.

Truelove, S (ed) (1995) *The Handbook of Training and Development* (2nd edn), Oxford, Blackwell Business.

Wolf, A (1995) *Competence-based Assessment*, Buckingham, Open University Press.

Strategic choice for management training and development in 'Aerospace'

Nicholas Kinnie and Martin Ridley

INTRODUCTION

The case examines the implications of changes in the business strategy of the 'Aerospace' company for the skills and knowledge of its managers and considers how the resulting training and development needs might be met.

BACKGROUND TO THE CASE

Company structure and history

'Aerospace' employs approximately 6600 people engaged in the design, manufacture and sale of finished products and components for the aerospace industry. The head office and largest plants are based on a single site in the UK in the Midlands, although there are three other smaller operating locations spread throughout the south of England. 'Aerospace' was founded in 1910, and has for the last year been owned by a large conglomerate, 'M Group', which has its head office in the north of England. 'M Group' employs approximately 35,000 people in 30 countries, although over three quarters of them are based in Europe. 'Aerospace' sales totalled £300 million in the last financial year, with an operating profit of £19 million, while the parent group's sales were £3000 million with a pre-tax profit of £222 million.

'Aerospace' is broken down into five divisions as follows:

Division A   Builds and sells finished products mostly for the Ministry of Defence (MOD) and employs 2829 people.

Division B   Operates in several businesses related to the supply of specialised assemblies and services for the aerospace industry and employs 1250 people.

Division C   Carries out work for both the civil and military markets and employs 1370 people.

Division D   Produces components for the civilian aerospace market and employs 606 people.

Division E   Includes a mixture of services and manufacturing subsidiaries and employs 556 people.

Each division has a Senior Management Committee which is headed by a Managing Director who reports to the Chief Executive of 'Aerospace' who is in turn responsible to 'M Group'. The recently appointed 'Aerospace' Personnel Director, William Shears, sits on the Company Board and heads up the 'Aerospace' resourcing and development activity which includes the Training and Development Manager, Peter Strachan. Each of the divisions has a Personnel Director, with his or her own staff, including a Head of Training in all the Divisions except E. The divisional staff are responsible for all day-to-day matters concerning personnel, while the 'Aerospace' staff deal with strategy and management training and development.

'M Group' is divided into three broad business areas: vehicle components, aerospace and industrial services. Each of these is headed by a Managing Director who sits, along with the Chief Executive, the Finance Director and the Human Resources Director and four non-executive directors, on the Main Board of 'M Group'.

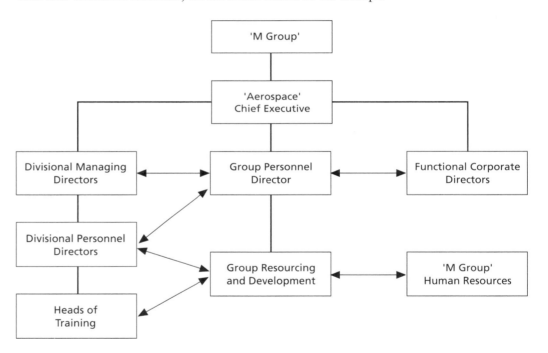

Fig 16.1 'Aerospace' HR working relationships

'Aerospace' began to produce aircraft during the First World War and in the 1950s manufactured under licence to an American design. During the 1960s and 1970s it formed a highly successful alliance with another European manufacturer and sold many products to the MOD in the UK and throughout the world. The military market began to decline during the early 1980s, however, and the company tried to move into the commercial market. By the mid-1980s 'Aerospace' experienced a gap in its order book and suffered severe financial difficulties. As a result the company was financially restructured in 1985 and reorganised into its present, more diversified form. There followed a period of five years of severe economic pressure resulting from increased competition, over-capacity and the introduction of competitive tendering by the MOD. Consequently, 'Aerospace' was subject to virtually continuous change as the company grappled with the need to remain internationally competitive and to reduce costs.

Recent events

Since the reorganisation, the strategy of 'Aerospace' has continued to shift away from the military markets and towards the civilian business. This has been achieved by developing commercial versions of existing products and by moving into new markets. These changes have exposed the company to new market conditions and to customers who are placing new demands on the company. This, in turn, has created enormous pressures to reduce costs which has been achieved by plant closures and reductions in the number of employees by voluntary means. Consequently, employment has fallen to its present level from approximately 13,500 ten years ago.

MANAGEMENT TRAINING AND DEVELOPMENT

'Aerospace' has traditionally devoted considerable time and attention to its employee training and development activities. The employee development policy seeks to:

> develop employees in a cost-effective manner that matches the business plan and personal development needs and maximises individual contributions towards achieving the business and departmental objectives.

The policy states in detail the training and development responsibilities of the Chief Executive, directors, line managers and personnel and training staff.

An extensive range of training and development opportunities has been provided by 'Aerospace' for its employees:

- part-time MBA courses;
- senior executive programmes in the UK and abroad;
- specialist courses for functional managers, e.g. in commercial contracting;
- leadership workshops;
- collaborative courses on changes in the aerospace industry;
- negotiating skills workshops;
- General Management Programme.

These courses are either taught in-house or subcontracted to specialist training centres. One of the longest established providers is 'Arcadia' which is a large training and development institution with an experienced staff. 'Arcadia' offers courses ranging from tailor-made programmes for companies such as 'Aerospace' up to MBA degrees.

General Management Programme

The General Management Programme (GMP) has been running for the last seven years and is a two-week off-site course based at 'Arcadia'. Initially aimed at the top managers in the company, it is now available for senior and middle-level managers. These managers are drawn from all the functions of 'Aerospace' including manufacturing, purchasing, sales, systems, finance, quality, personnel and legal. Virtually all of these managers have formal qualifications of some kind and many have degrees, some higher degrees. Most have a technical background with very limited previous exposure to management training.

The course is taught both by staff from 'Arcadia' and 'Aerospace' human resources specialists. The two weeks are run separately, but for common cohorts of approximately 20 managers. A wide variety of methods is used including traditional lectures, case studies, role play exercises and discussion groups.

The typical content of a course is described below.

Week 1

The emphasis is on knowledge and skills directly related to the main activities and functions of the business including:

- Company strategy
- Total quality
- Commercial and marketing strategy
- Business planning
- Finance

Teaching methods during this first week involve formal lectures and case studies.

Week 2

The emphasis is on interpersonal skills related to the management of tasks and teams at work with an emphasis on role plays, discussion groups and practical exercises. Typical course content would include:

- Managing change
- Coaching and counselling
- Leadership styles
- Negotiation and collaboration
- Managing teams
- Action planning

Each session of the course is evaluated by the delegates using a simple form which records their responses using a five-point scale under the following headings: new information, relevance, enjoyment and duration. The mean scores and range are then calculated and displayed. In the last year the delegates have been invited to a 'Debrief Day' at which their learning during the course and experiences since their attendance are discussed with training centre and in-house staff.

Review activities

William Shears, the newly appointed 'Aerospace' Personnel Director, has decided to conduct a review of management training and development activities with particular attention given to the GMP since this is by far the biggest commitment. This task has been delegated to the Training and Development Manager, Peter Strachan, who has decided to conduct two main activities:

- an analysis of training and development needs as perceived by senior managers in the organisation;
- a survey of all the past participants of the GMP to collect their views.

IDENTIFICATION OF MANAGEMENT TRAINING AND DEVELOPMENT NEEDS

The aim of the first review activity was to identify what 'Aerospace' requires over the next five years in terms of development needs and how this dovetails into the business and organisation needs and the future strategy. These needs were identified through discussions with around 24 senior managers conducted by both 'Aerospace' and 'Arcadia' staff. These interviews indicated that, although 'Aerospace' had several different businesses ostensibly addressing different customer bases, the development needs were very similar – in the order of 80 to 90 per cent. They also helped to produce a number of initiatives not specifically concerned with training solutions. Individually it became much easier to establish where parts of the organisation had common needs and also to make comparisons on issues such as appraisal, open learning, succession planning, negotiating skills, and recruitment of trainees and graduates.

The results of the review were divided under three headings: current business issues, organisational issues and possible solutions.

Business issues

The senior executives identified a series of key issues confronting the business over the next five years.

- There was increased pressure on costs as customers were seeking better value for money and no price increases.
- Greater responsiveness to customers' requirements was needed in order to gain new business. This, in turn, put pressure on the speed of responsiveness within the organisation.
- The implications of the move to the globalisation of markets had to be understood and the opportunities for growth identified. Particular attention was drawn to the concept of 'multi-cultural' management.
- All employees should understand the implications of the strategic repositioning of the business associated with the move towards the civilian markets.
- It was essential to retain the reputation 'Aerospace' had for technical excellence in key parts of the market and that these strengths were exploited further.
- Further business partnerships had to be established with other suppliers to provide the products and services required by the major customers.

Organisational issues

These changes in the business were seen to have various implications for the organisation and its workforce.

- Multi-skilling was essential not just for shopfloor employees, but also for managers because of the move away from a functional-based approach towards a team-based focus.
- The commercial market demanded a greater preparedness to take risks and to have a better awareness of the business as a whole. More self-confident attitudes and behaviours were needed to initiate change and to challenge existing assumptions.
- Previous practices had tended to be responsive whereas a much more pro-active approach was now required. Managers needed to take greater responsibility for their own jobs and their careers.

- Much greater attention was required to management skills particularly those appropriate to the new environment such as teamworking, leadership, communications and the more sophisticated use of IT.
- Managerial competences had to be much more closely aligned with the needs of the business and integrated within project teams.

Possible solutions

Various possible future developments were put forward by the senior executives.

- Establishment of cross-functional teams taking responsibility for particular projects.
- Greater emphasis on personal career planning and maximising opportunities for self-development.
- An emphasis on the skills and attitudes appropriate to innovation and change management.
- The development of a wider view about the business among all employees with particular attention to commercial awareness.
- Consideration of the specific skills involved with managing both subordinates and superiors.
- Awareness of the issues associated with globalisation and the establishment of further strategic partnerships.

EVALUATION OF THE GMP

Managers who had attended the course were contacted and asked to complete a three-page questionnaire which asked questions about their experience of the course, the extent to which the objectives were achieved and suggestions for future changes.

Experience of the course

Of the 353 managers who attended the GMP between 1987 and 1993 approximately a fifth subsequently left the company through redundancy, retirement or for other reasons. Three quarters of respondents had experienced some kind of change in their job following their attendance, with 'early delegates' (those who attended between 1987 and 1990) more likely to have changed than 'recent delegates' (those who attended between 1991 and 1993). Of these, just over half had taken up new positions within the organisation, while the remainder had extra workload or responsibilities within the same position.

Three quarters of delegates reported they had a meeting with their manager before the course and in two thirds of cases this meeting led to objectives being set. Follow-up interviews also took place in two thirds of the cases, but they were found to be useful in less than one in two cases.

Positive comments were made about both the 'hard' (directly business-related) and 'soft' (behavioural) content. Interpersonal skills were the most frequently mentioned soft skills, followed by personal skills and greater self-awareness. Finance and marketing subjects were the most commonly mentioned hard skills. Approximately 80 per cent of respondents made positive comments about the learning methods used, and, in particular, positive comments were made about the use of case studies and the mix of course members.

Typical comments were:

The learning approaches and methods used ... were varied, prevented boredom and ensured the messages were received and digested.

The opportunity to do presentations with little time to prepare is useful.

There was very strong support for the practice of holding the programme off-site, with frequent references to the importance of being away from the work and home environment and the contribution the location made to team spirit. There were a number of positive comments as to the suitability of the facilities and location of 'Arcadia'. Just over half of the respondents specifically said they did not want the location to be changed to one closer to home, while approximately one quarter had no preference for location. Only one in six actually wanted a change, usually to a site nearer to home, but maintained that this should remain off-site.

The attainment of course objectives

The report considered first the extent to which the GMP was achieving the principal aim of the course and then looked at the extent to which the sub-objectives were achieved. The principal aim of the course was:

To provide individual managers within 'Aerospace' with the opportunity and means to improve their contribution to the achievement of corporate objectives and the implementation of change.

There was widespread evidence that the GMP had an impact on the managerial style of participants. Nine out of ten respondents said that the course had an impact, with the remainder saying that the impact of the course had faded or it had not been what they had expected. Just over two thirds of the respondents said they had used various business skills learnt on the course. Particularly useful areas were finance and marketing, interfaces with other departments, self and team development. There were some comments amongst these that it was, of course, difficult to disentangle the impact of the GMP from other courses and the experiences on the job.

OBJECTIVE 1: BROADENING THE BUSINESS PERSPECTIVE OF PARTICIPANTS TO EMBRACE OTHER FUNCTIONS AND HOW THEY RELATE

There was clear evidence that managers became more aware of a whole range of other business functions after attending the course. In particular, two thirds of the respondents said they found the financial knowledge useful at work, and one in five mentioned marketing knowledge specifically.

Some typical quotes:

I found the course very beneficial – I feel I greatly improved my performance as a manager and the knowledge gained on other business subjects has been useful.

The programme has made me very much more aware of how I related to my colleagues and company customers.

OBJECTIVE 2: SHARPENING MANAGEMENT SKILLS AND ENHANCING CONFIDENCE OF INDIVIDUALS IN THE MANAGERIAL ROLE

There was some evidence that this objective was being achieved. Attention was drawn, in particular, to the value of role plays, case studies and discussions which improved personal confidence in an environment where little risk was involved.

For example:

> I found (the methods) an aid to boosting confidence; it was also useful to be part of a team whereas at the time I was a specialist working on my own.

The evidence of change was weaker from other interviewees, however, who mentioned that a great deal of ground had to be covered in a short space of time and there were doubts about the opportunities to put these skills into practice:

> It's like moving from basic arithmetic to differentials in an afternoon.

> 'Arcadia' was wonderful. But, it's like having a tool kit so packed that you only half understand how to use it. You come away with a lot of knowledge, but few skills. You may deal with appraisal or coaching, but you don't get a chance to put it into practice.

> Training courses in their own right are good, but when you get back the phone rings ... With a bit of luck you might practise one or two things. The real key is development coaching as well as formal courses to pursue the same themes as 'Arcadia'.

OBJECTIVE 3: UNDERSTANDING THE RANGE OF ACTIVITIES WITHIN 'AEROSPACE' AND APPRECIATING EACH COMPANY'S CONTRIBUTION TO ACHIEVING CORPORATE OBJECTIVES

There was strong evidence that the participants learnt a great deal from the formal input about the group and had the opportunity to compare and benchmark their performance. Just under one quarter of the respondents specifically mentioned that their interfaces with other departments had been improved. There were also signs that learning took place informally as part of the simple act of bringing managers together from different parts of the group. Indeed, some delegates said that useful business contacts were made during the course which had been maintained since then.

Typical quotes were:

> I feel the event was a valuable occasion for 'Aerospace' managers to come together to review their skills against national and international standards and benchmark the cultures of both the individual group companies and the overall business culture.

> It was good to be part of a diverse team drawn from different parts of the group and to begin to appreciate the different activities, problems and concerns and challenges that exist within 'Aerospace'.

OBJECTIVE 4: RECOGNISING THE ROLE OF LEADERSHIP IN ACHIEVING GOALS, THROUGH THE BUILDING OF EFFECTIVE TEAMS AND THE NEED FOR INTER-TEAM CO-OPERATION AND SUPPORT

There was evidence that team-building had improved as a result of the course with one third of the respondents drawing attention to this. In addition, a quarter said their style was now more appropriate to their managerial task and one in six said they were more reflective of their own strengths.

For example:

> I believe I have learnt to delegate responsibility for tasks more appropriately ... while my communication and leadership behaviour now fits my position more readily.

> It has improved the way I interact with my team. It gave me a better understanding of making the most of an individual's skills in a team and helped me to delegate more effectively and to coach and develop my staff.

However, the dangers of trying to implement a new team-based approach in a work environment which was not conducive to such changes were noted by some managers. One view held by managers was that the GMP raised expectations about their future way of working which could not be met back in the workplace:

> I have sensed a de-motivation that comes after people attend 'Arcadia'. They return fired up with advice on good practices that they wish to exploit, but do not have the budgets or supporting culture to make any serious change to their pre-'Arcadia' practices. Many people see 'Arcadia' as offering an ideal that 'Aerospace' does not readily turn into practice.

> The methods and cultural messages of the course are fine, but they will have little impact on the company generally unless the ground back at the ranch is fertile.

> The culture and ethos promoted by 'Arcadia', while commendable, does not fit comfortably with the 'Aerospace' style.

Indeed, one manager put the same point more bluntly saying:

> People return from the course with high expectations, but it then gets beaten out of them.

OBJECTIVE 5: PROVIDING A FRAMEWORK WITHIN WHICH INDIVIDUALS CAN PLAN AND TAKE ACTION AND CONTINUE THE PROCESS OF SELF-DEVELOPMENT

Many respondents stressed there were insufficient opportunities to continue the learning outside the course itself. Indeed, as noted above, one quarter of the respondents specifically asked for follow-up activities after the course. Respondents said they felt unsure where 'Arcadia' fitted within their own development and, on some occasions, in their career paths. They suggested the need for a longer term map or plan which placed various training and development activities in their wider context.

> Interest and follow-up at management level has not proved forthcoming; hence while some aspects of management could have been usefully applied, any attempts to change have been stifled by opposing views. 'Aerospace' needs to decide whether it wants training to result in improvements or whether it's just a holiday.

> We need to extend learning and development past the last day of the course. Although there are some attempts to do this it needs to be more systematic.

> The real problem is how to bring the GMP out of the classroom and into the workplace.

> Why don't we implement all the good things we learn? If we don't intend to learn the lesson, why bother spending the money?

Future changes

The respondents identified a number of changes which might be made to the subjects and techniques which are covered in the course and were very keen to stress the need for the course to reflect changes in organisation structure and culture. There were three types of suggestion for changes, the common theme of which was well expressed by one manager who said that there was a need to *'make the course closer to the job'*.

REFLECT CHANGES IN STRUCTURE AND CULTURE

Almost one third of respondents said the course content needed to reflect the changes in the company more closely. This was reflected particularly in the demand for more strategic and analytical skills and job-related personal knowledge.

Some relevant quotes:

How do you understand what are the critical business issues, and how do you get people to buy into these?

There was minimal content on the solving of practical problems either as part of the course, or in the follow-up activities.

It's very interesting to know how to read a set of financial accounts, but it is far more practically relevant to learn about job costing and project planning.

We're faced with a quantum leap from matrix management to business unit responsibility, and the course needs to reflect this.

PREPARATION AND FOLLOW-UP

One quarter of respondents suggested the need for better preparation and follow-up:

More in-depth and formal preparation pre-course on company needs and personal needs must be of value.

'Arcadia' felt like (and was) a start of a management development process. It needs to be followed up.

FUTURE COURSES

Approximately one in four respondents made positive comments about the course and stressed the need for there to be some kind of follow-up course for more senior managers:

We need to keep the learning and development process active continuously and evaluate how we are changing our style and effectiveness and how we could develop further.

A similar style course going on from where 'Arcadia' left off would be interesting.

I would suggest this 'Arcadia' course (or a derivative) be compulsory for all our management team.

Following the course review and interviews with key directors Strachan has to put forward plans for future management training and development for discussion with his boss, William Shears. Formal proposals will then be presented to the 'Aerospace' Company Board.

ACTIVITY BRIEF

1 Comment on the actions taken to review management training and development in 'Aerospace'.

2 What conclusions do you draw from the findings of these reviews?

3 What are the possible changes which 'Aerospace' might make to its provision for management training and development? Which of these do you suggest and why?

4 How might your suggested changes be put into place?

RECOMMENDED READING

Bickerstaff, G (1993) 'Measuring the gains from training', *Personnel Management,* Nov, pp 48–51.

Fombrun, CJ, Tichy NM and Devanna, MA (1984) *Strategic Human Resource Management*, New York, John Wiley.

Hamblin, AC (1974) *Evaluation and Control of Training*, Maidenhead, McGraw–Hill.

Kolb, DA (1984) *Experiential Learning: Experience as a Source of Learning and Development*, Englewood Cliffs, New Jersey, Prentice Hall.

Pedler, MJ, Burgoyne, JG and Boydell, T (1991) *The Learning Company*, London, McGraw–Hill.

Sloman, M (1993) 'Training to play a lead role', *Personnel Management*, July, pp 41–5.

Storey, J (1991) 'Do the Japanese make better managers?' *Personnel Management*, Aug, pp 24–8.

Storey, J (1994) 'Management development' in Sisson, K (ed) *Personnel Management. A Comprehensive Guide to Theory and Practice in Britain*, Oxford, Blackwell, pp 365–96.

Developing a staff training culture in a retail organisation

John Guthrie

INTRODUCTION

The following case addresses the problems facing the manager of a retail store in New Zealand when she attempts to develop a staff training culture in her store. Students are required to evaluate the role of training, and the types and levels of training in the context of an environment where training is not always given a high priority.

BACKGROUND TO THE CASE

Adrienne Gittus is the Manager of Wickliffe Traders, a department store in Dunedin, New Zealand. Wickliffe Traders has 42 branches throughout New Zealand. The stores range from being very large, with more than 300 employees, to relatively small, with fewer than 20 employees. In the last ten years the company has been the target of a series of take-overs. In the mid-1980s it was bought by a high-flying property investment company, primarily for the value of its extensive real estate holdings. The 1987 share market crash destroyed the property company and Wickliffe Traders was subsequently bought by a consortium consisting of managers from Wickliffe Traders, a group from a Maori Trust, and a large Australian retailer. It is suggested that each of the new partners had different motives for being involved in Wickliffe Traders: the managers for job continuity and investment; the Maori group for investment; and the Australian retailer to expand into New Zealand and benefit from greater purchasing and promotion power. In the course of ten years, therefore, Wickliffe Traders had gone from being owned by a family company run by dedicated retailers, to an investment opportunity for non-dedicated retailers, and back to being a combination of ownership by non-retailing investors and ownership by dedicated retailers.

Adrienne has been with the company for nine years and has been part of all of the changes. Her previous position, which she had held until six months ago, was at a smaller regional store with 30 employees. The relationship with the small group of employees had been very friendly and she was finding it difficult to adjust to a larger store with a larger staff. This was not helped by the fact that her performance and rewards were based totally on financial measures.

The Dunedin store has 110 employees, 10 of whom are management, with the remainder being in sales positions. Of the 100 sales personnel 10 are full time (more than 40 hours per week), 40 are part time (30 to 40 hours per week), and 25 are part time (less than 30 hours per week). The last group is made up largely of students from the local university who work at weekends. It should be noted that in New Zealand it is only in the last ten years that shops have been able to open at weekends. At the time of writing most shops open on Saturdays, but less than half would open on a Sunday.

Adrienne had been appointed to the Dunedin store on the basis of her profit performance at the regional store. She was somewhat stunned to find that many of the systems she had put in place in Timaru that contributed to her profit figures, were not in place in Dunedin. In fact the shop appeared to be operating inefficiently and she felt this was reflected in the attitudes of the staff. Because she was judged on financial performance, her first priority was to put in place the appropriate systems. This included a thorough audit of pricing, purchasing and personnel. She had to change the way many of the staff operated, and reported. There were no job losses resulting from the audit but there was considerable uncertainty and suspicion. This was particularly evident in certain departments, and with a number of the older female staff, many of whom had been employed by the store for more than 15 years. The situation was compounded by a mystery shopping exercise that was carried out soon after Adrienne's arrival. The objective of the exercise was to evaluate the level of customer service provided by Wickliffe Traders' staff. The exercise and subsequent focus groups with staff identified the following areas of concern:

- communication problems between top management and sales staff;
- low employee morale, and negative attitudes;
- lack of formal, ongoing training;
- a need for uniformity of employee appearance;
- more efficient use of employees to cater for peak periods, with the possibility of rotating staff around the departments;
- store layout.

The report was disappointing for Adrienne as she had hoped that the staff would accept a settling-in period for a new manager, and understand the importance of improving the operational systems and the store profitability. When she looked at the mystery shopper report and list of concerns it was clear to her that staff morale was the number one problem.

TRAINING PHILOSOPHY

Being driven by profit, it is not surprising that Wickliffe Traders' approach to training was both minimal and spasmodic. Staff training was generally regarded as a luxury that could only be offered when times were good. Training was the first expense trimmed when times were tough. Training levels were also influenced by the attitudes of head office management and by individual store managers. Adrienne had access to an area training officer based in Christchurch, 200 miles north of Dunedin, but for the most part his role was to provide training material as requested by managers, and to facilitate product training from suppliers. He didn't ever run training courses in individual stores. Training was often given to managers, but more often than not the training was oriented towards the financial side of the store's operation. This meant that Adrienne had had very little training on managing and motivating staff.

RESEARCH

Adrienne participated in a survey being carried out by the Retail Studies Group at the nearby University of Otago. The objective of the survey was to identify and evaluate retailers' attitudes towards training. Adrienne felt that if the response from her company was more negative than other companies, she could possibly use that information to impress upon her employers the importance of training, which in turn could result in more training being offered to her staff.

When she received the results (*see* Table 17.1) she was surprised to see how low training was rated by employers in terms of relevance at different levels. She thought it would have been higher. While not being surprised that most training for pre-employment and entry-level staff was provided by high schools and polytechnics, she wondered why the university was not regarded as a provider of training, especially in the areas of strategy. In her situation she had often reflected on how beneficial it would be if she had other people around her with whom she could discuss more than just merchandising. This was reflected in the results of the survey where retail marketing was considered to be the domain of senior management only. She also acknowledged the importance of training staff in the areas of motivation, leadership and team-building but knew that her company did not provide such training.

Table 17.1 Summary of results of university survey into retailers' attitudes towards training

	Pre-employ		*Entry level*		*Supervisor mid-management*		*Senior management*	
Relevance	Very relevant	66%	Very relevant	72%	Very relevant	80%	Very relevant	73%
	Marginal/		Marginal/		Marginal/		Marginal/	
	not relevant	33%	not relevant	27%	not relevant	20%	not relevant	27%
Delivery	High Sch.	31%	High Sch.	25%	High Sch.	0%	High Sch.	0%
	Polytech.	50%	Polytech.	21%	Polytech.	14%	Polytech.	20%
	Univ.	0%	Univ.	0%	Univ.	1%	Univ.	17%
	Private	19%	Private	9%	Private	36%	Private	41%
	Employer	0%	Employer	44%	Employer	49%	Employer	19%
Use of existing programme			Qualif.	12%	Qualif.	14%	Qualif.	17%
			Non qualif.	55%	Non qualif.	36%	Non qualif.	24%
			Nil	33%	Nil	49%	Nil	59%
Key skills: core			1 Customer care aware		1 Communication		1 Communication	
			2 Communication		2 Decision making		2 Decision making	
			3 Personal presentation		3 Problem solving		3 Problem solving	
Key skills: functional					1 Store operations		1 Financial control	
					2 Loss prevention		2 Retail marketing	
					3 Profit control		3 Budgeting	
Key skills: human resources					1 Motivation		1 Motivation	
					2 Team-building		2 Leadership	
					3 Leadership		3 Team-building	

She was somewhat stunned to discover that on average retailers spend less than $500 per employee per year, and that more than half of those surveyed spend nothing on training. She was not aware of the total figure spent on training by her company but was sure that in her own store the figure was less than $500 per employee per year. When comparing her opinions with those of other chain stores she could see that while they agreed on the importance of training, and on the most important areas for training, especially for senior management, her company's commitment to training was significantly less than others. She knew that rival retail chains had recently employed specialist staff trainers, and in one case the rival company had employed two of her senior managers.

She then took part in a survey carried out by the university that sought the opinions of employees. In particular the questionnaire asked employees about previous training they had been given, and how relevant and effective the training had been. It also asked employees what training they would like. The survey involved three major chain stores so Adrienne was able to receive a report on her store. Her initial reaction was one of disappointment when she discovered that only 30 per cent of her staff had responded. Subsequent discussions revealed that many of the staff felt threatened. Others felt that they had made suggestions in the past and nothing had happened. Most of her employees felt that the training they had been given was relevant and the quality of the training was reasonable. The limited number of employees who had been involved in training courses outside of the company that resulted in a qualification appeared to be more perceptive about the relevance of training. They also felt that the training provided by outside trainers was more effective than those courses offered by her staff. This made Adrienne think that future training should be provided by people outside the company, and where possible should result in the employee gaining a qualification in the form of a certificate or a diploma.

She considered the following information on how important different areas are to employees as a good guide to developing her training programme (*see* Tables 17.2–17.4).

Core skills

Table 17.2 Relative importance of individual core skills to employees

Core skills	Mean importance	Very important (1) (%)	Important (2) (%)	Not so important (3) (%)
Customer care awareness	1.211	80.7	17.5	1.8
Communication	1.254	76.3	22.0	1.7
Problem solving	1.400	65.5	29.1	5.5
Personal presentation	1.458	62.5	29.2	8.3
Decision making	1.517	58.6	31.0	10.3
Prioritising	1.600	46.0	48.0	6.0
Planning	1.604	52.8	34.0	13.2
Time management	1.607	48.2	42.9	8.9
Negotiating	1.719	42.1	43.9	14.0
Total	1.486	59.2	33.1	7.7

Customer care awareness, communication, and problem-solving skills are perceived by employees to be the most important core skills. This is relatively consistent with those skills considered to be important by Adrienne who perceived customer care awareness, communication, and personal presentation skills to be most important for entry-level employees, and communication, decision-making, and problem-solving skills to be most important for mid-management and senior-management level employees.

Functional skills

Product knowledge, selling, loss prevention, and cash-handling skills are perceived to be the most important functional skills by the employees. These skills were considered by Adrienne to be of moderate importance for entry-level employees – all four skills being approximately in the middle of the ranked skills. Store operations, loss prevention and profit control skills were perceived by retail managers/owners to be the most important skills for mid-management level employees, while financial control, retail marketing, and budgeting were considered to be most important for senior managers.

Table 17.3 Relative importance of functional skills to employees

Functional skills	Mean importance	Very important (1) (%)	Important (2) (%)	Not so important (3) (%)
Product knowledge	1.161	85.5	12.9	1.6
Selling skills	1.269	76.9	19.2	3.8
Loss prevention	1.396	66.0	28.3	5.7
Cash handling	1.449	61.2	32.7	6.1
Telephone skills	1.521	52.1	43.8	4.2
Merchandising	1.577	48.1	46.2	5.8
Sales promotion	1.582	49.1	43.6	7.3
Stock control	1.647	43.1	49.0	7.8
Performance management	1.667	42.6	48.1	9.3
Store operations	1.679	39.3	53.6	7.1
Industrial and employee relations	1.686	43.1	45.1	11.8
Retail marketing	1.700	44.0	42.0	14.0
Budgeting	1.750	37.5	50.0	12.5
Legal and ethical considerations	1.750	40.4	44.2	15.4
Computer/keyboard skills	1.754	36.8	50.9	12.3
Purchasing/buying	1.776	42.9	36.7	20.4
Numeracy	1.780	36.6	48.8	14.6
Profit control	1.830	36.2	44.7	19.1
Purchase planning	1.860	32.0	50.0	18.0
Operations management	1.896	33.3	43.8	22.9
Financial control	1.958	33.3	37.5	29.2
Resource management	1.958	31.3	41.7	27.1
Total	1.666	46.0	41.5	12.0

Human resource skills

Motivation, team-building, and leadership were regarded as being very important to both the supervisor/mid-management and senior management. While they also regarded training as being very important neither group felt that appraisal and counselling were as important. It occurred to Adrienne that the emphasis on leadership and motivation could be attributed to the existing climate within the company. In her opinion the centralisation of power had removed much of the confidence from her managers and in part contributed to the lack of respect employees had for management. She did feel some concern for the fact that it appeared that her managers did not regard appraisal, coaching and counselling as components of leadership, motivation and team-building skills.

Table 17.4 Relative importance of human resource skills to employees

Human resource skills	Mean importance	Very important (1) (%)	Important (2) (%)	Not so important (3) (%)
Leadership	1.259	75.9	22.4	1.7
Motivation	1.264	77.4	18.9	3.8
Training	1.346	69.2	26.9	3.8
Team-building	1.350	70.0	25.0	5.0
Goal setting	1.389	64.8	31.5	3.7
Delegating	1.556	50.0	44.4	5.6
Appraisal	1.596	51.9	36.5	11.5
Coaching	1.698	43.4	43.4	13.2
Counselling	1.735	42.9	40.8	16.3
Total	1.466	60.6	32.2	7.2

At the end of the questionnaire employees were asked to give their opinions on their company's attitude to training and on their perceptions of the quality of communication between employees and senior management in their company. While initially being cautious about allowing these questions to be included, Adrienne decided that they could give some insight into how well their training is regarded and how well the communications are between staff. She had been very concerned about the negative attitude of staff not just to training but to other staff and to the company.

The feedback she received on employee perceptions of their company's attitude towards training is presented in Table 17.5. The majority of employees considered their company's attitude toward training to be relatively positive, with 72.3 per cent perceiving it to be either 'good' or 'very good'. This is reinforced by a low mean of 2.108. Only 14.4 per cent believe their company's attitude to be either 'poor' or 'very poor'. While this was not disappointing, Adrienne was concerned that her company performed less well than the other companies involved in the survey.

The following feedback she received on employee perceptions of the quality of communication between employees and senior management is presented in Table 17.6.

It was this result that was of most concern to Adrienne, especially as these results were for the three companies. She was provided with a breakdown for her own store and was disappointed that none of her employees had considered that the quality of communication was very good, and a greater percentage (relative to the other companies) had the opinion that the communication between senior management and staff was poor.

Table 17.5 Employee perceptions of their company's attitude towards training

Attitude	Frequency	Valid (%)	Cumulative (%)
Very good	8	9.8	9.8
Good	28	34.1	43.9
Neutral	26	31.7	75.6
Poor	18	22.0	97.6
Very poor	2	2.4	100.0
Missing	4		
Total	86	100.0	

Table 17.6 Employee perceptions of the quality of communication between employees and senior management in their company

Communication quality	Frequency	Valid (%)	Cumulative (%)
Very good	8	9.8	9.8
Good	28	34.1	43.9
Neutral	26	31.7	75.6
Poor	18	22.0	97.6
Very poor	2	2.4	100.0
Missing	4		
Total	86	100.0	

Having successfully put in place the systems for improved operations, Adrienne now felt she was in a position to address the staff attitude and staff training problems. She knew that failure to do so would quickly negate the work she had done to date. Her problem was knowing where to start, and how to change the corporate culture.

ACTIVITY BRIEF

1 How would you evaluate the situation Adrienne is now in?

2 What action is appropriate and why?

3 Prepare a draft training programme suitable for Adrienne's organisation, identifying methods, outcomes and evaluation criteria.

RECOMMENDED READING

Arkin, A (1995) 'Breathing fresh air into training', *People Management*, 1, 15, pp 34–5.

Chain Store Age Executive (1995) 'Preparing for the new millenium', 71, 5, p 132.

Evans, J (1995) 'Exploring aisles of opportunity', *People Management*, 1, 21, pp 46–7.

Keep, E (1989a) 'A training scandal?' in Sisson, K (ed) *Personnel Management in Britain*, Oxford, Blackwell.

Keep, E (1989b) 'Corporate training strategies: the vital component?' in Storey, J (ed) *New Perspectives on Human Resource Management*, London, Routledge.

Perry, A and Cottrell, D (1995) 'Leadership courts at Sears', *Training and Development*, 49, 7, pp 32–4.

Reid, MA, Barrington, H and Kenney, J (1992) *Training Interventions: Managing Employee Development* (3rd edn), London, TPM.

Management development at ARCO Ltd

Michael Doyle

INTRODUCTION

There is now a pressing need for organisations to respond rapidly and decisively to the changes being wrought by an unforgiving, and at times even hostile environment. Many organisations are now coming to the view that managerial effectiveness is now a 'critical success' factor. This is prompting them to reconsider and redefine their expectations in respect of required managerial values, attitudes, skills, behaviours and levels of performance (Jackson and Humble 1994, Fulop 1991). For example, as public sector organisations have sought to adapt to the effects of transformative changes such as privatisation, the organisational expectation has been that managers will begin to acquire the entrepreneurial, innovative, business-oriented values, attitudes and behaviours necessary to manage effectively in the new context. In the private sector a similar pattern is emerging. For instance, the quest for greater efficiency, quality and improved customer service – coupled with an increase in the pace and complexity of technological change – has encouraged organisations to devolve greater autonomy and control to employees. In line with these measures, managers are now expected to adopt attitudes and behaviours that are consistent with and supportive of an 'empowering culture'.

However, expectations will only be met if managers are properly educated, trained, and developed. From an organisational perspective, this requires a commitment to the provision of appropriate levels of organisational resources, support and guidance (Coulson-Thomas 1989). It also necessitates a lessening of the gap between the rhetoric of management development and what is actually going on in the 'reality' of the workplace (Molander and Winterton 1994 (p 89), McClelland 1994).

This last point is significant when the strategic nature of management development is considered. Although there is an espoused recognition and commitment among commentators and senior managers that management development has a strategic role to play, the evidence suggests that in practice there are barriers and difficulties as it seeks to fulfil this role (McClelland 1994). For example, the successful implementation of strategic 'culture change' initiatives such as Total Quality Management (TQM) and Business Process Re-engineering (BPR) is often conditional upon achieving significant shifts in managerial attitudes and behaviours. This can be problematical, however, as managers 'cling' to their traditional attitudes and behaviours which may often be incompatible with the new cultural requirements and, indeed, may prove to be dysfunctional to the overall change process. Recent evidence certainly points to managerial issues as being a significant contributor in the lack of success of TQM initiatives (Redman, Snape and Wilkinson 1995, Kaye and Dyason 1995).

But this appears somewhat paradoxical. Negative managerial attitudes and behaviours are often cited as a significant contributory factor in the failure of these culture change initiatives and yet there appears to be little attention paid by organisations to the underlying cause(s). Indeed, there is a strong suggestion that dysfunctional attitudes and behaviours may stem from the 'failure' of strategic management development policies and practices to address wider structural and cultural issues and lend sufficient support and guidance to those managers having to come to terms with the implications that such changes hold for their roles, managerial competence, status and careers (Miller and Cangemi 1993).

That management development may somehow be 'failing' in the context of radical and transformative change initiatives is an issue that is explored more fully in the following case study. The case study highlights a number of important issues:

● the way management development is perceived in organisations and the way it is implemented in the mid-1990s;
● the appropriateness of existing models of management development during a time of radical change;
● the role and contribution of management development in assisting the organisation to transform and develop itself.

BACKGROUND TO THE CASE

Although ARCO Ltd and Eurochem are fictitious companies, the scenario is a synthesis of two 'real-world' case studies in which the author was involved, both as a management development consultant/advisor, and as a participant observer of management development policies and practices during a time of major change.

After an extensive market research exercise conducted in the early part of the 1980s, the multinational company, EuroChem, identified a potentially lucrative niche in the market for chemical dyes and took a strategic decision to invest in a new processing plant. With the aid of generous grants from the European Community and attractive UK tax and capital allowances, a new company, ARCO Ltd, was formed and an investment of £20 million was made to build a modern chemicals complex at a greenfield site in the West Midlands where it now employs some 150 people.

The intention from the outset was to design a plant incorporating state-of-the-art chemical processing technology. This meant recruiting a high calibre team of scientists and technicians to build and commission the plant. EuroChem scoured the industry to find the right individuals and eventually recruited a general manager and chief engineer who both had an exceptional track record in the industry. Their first task was to recruit and train a new team of technical, scientific and engineering personnel who would eventually form the core management team of an expanding and successful company.

Throughout the 1980s, the plant proved to be highly efficient and profitable and a decision was made to expand the existing site. As ARCO grew, so it began to specialise and differentiate in terms of functional organisation. Eventually, a new management structure emerged and, as originally envisaged, many of the new managers were promoted from within the original core team of technicians and scientists who by now had built up a considerable body of technical knowledge and processing expertise – an asset the company did not want to lose.

By the beginning of 1990, the plant was working up to and, at times, beyond full capacity and the strain on both the equipment and people was beginning to tell. Overall levels of efficiency and quality were falling and unit costs were increasing remorselessly. The relationship between the new processing managers and their staff became more formalised and their managerial style more autocratic, even confrontational, as the managers strove to maintain existing performance levels.

In marketing terms, the 'honeymoon period' of the 1980s was over. ARCO now found itself losing market share to other companies who had developed a more attractive product range and had become more competitive as they invested in newer technology. A number of ARCO's products were now becoming obsolete and others were being priced out of the market by increased operating costs. Inventory levels were too high and this was placing an added burden on an already difficult financial situation. The company was approaching a crisis. Simultaneously, it was having to reduce costs, increase efficiency, invest in new technology, diversify into new products, and win new business.

It was during a EuroChem Group Board meeting in early 1991 that the depth of ARCO's predicament became clear to Mike Dawson. Mike had joined the company as Chief Executive in 1989 to replace the retiring General Manager. He was concerned and frustrated that despite his best efforts to motivate and encourage his managers, change was proving difficult to manage and the company's performance levels were not improving. The reason for this became clear to him when he was presenting ARCO's three-year business strategy to the Board and was promptly put on the spot by the Group Chairman who turned to him and said, 'That's fine Mike, but are you confident that you have got the right level of commercial and managerial skills to see it through?'

There then followed an intense discussion among the other Board members. Agreement was reached that one of the major contributing factors to ARCO's current problems was the lack of commercial and managerial competence among its existing management team. One member of the Board seemed to put his finger on it when he pointed out the existence of a dominant 'techno-culture' where technical considerations and priorities among managers subordinated the need to acquire complementary commercial and people-management expertise. He further pointed out that because ARCO's managers were now lacking the entrepreneurial, innovative and motivational skills necessary to deliver the required levels of customer service and quality in a tough commercial environment, the company would find it increasingly difficult to maintain profitability and take advantage of commercial opportunities as and when they presented themselves.

The meeting ended with a general agreement that until the issue of management competence was resolved, it was unlikely that ARCO's overall performance would improve. The Board made a strategic decision that ARCO should embark upon an urgent management development programme – one that was designed to engender the management styles, behaviours and competences that were consistent with the delivery of ARCO's agreed business strategy and its survival in a rapidly changing environment. By the end of the meeting, Mike was left in no doubt by his fellow Board members about the changes they expected to see in the management of ARCO Ltd.

THE IMPLEMENTATION OF A MANAGEMENT DEVELOPMENT PLAN

Management skills at ARCO

The Personnel Co-ordinator, Janet Davis, was elated. She had just finished a hastily convened meeting with Mike Dawson in which Mike had asked her, as a matter of urgency, to produce a development plan for the whole of the management team. Mike would present the plan to senior managers at ARCO's next management team meeting in two weeks' time. After constantly arguing that ARCO must improve the level of its management skills, Janet now felt confident that at last things were going to change!

Janet Davis is in her mid-forties. She joined ARCO in the mid-1980s as a quality engineer but as the company grew, she increasingly found herself taking on an informal training role with more and more responsibility for various aspects of personnel administration. It was then decided to appoint Janet to the new position of Personnel Co-ordinator but, in practice, Janet found most of her time was spent organising technical training and routine personnel and administrative paperwork. Nevertheless, Janet was keen to make her mark and set out to familiarise herself with personnel systems, procedures and good practice. Whenever she proposed new ideas to improve ARCO's HR systems, however, she discovered that she was banging her head against the proverbial 'brick wall' of a technical, production-focused culture which at times seemed to have difficulty in distinguishing between its people and the inanimate objects in the processing plant!

Despite these difficulties, Janet made a point of keeping in touch with most of the managers and employees in the plant. Many of them trusted her and valued her opinion on a range of issues. As a result of these informal discussions, Janet began to realise that it was the neglect of 'people issues' and the confrontational behaviour of a number of managers that lay behind many of ARCO's problems. She also realised that the managers were not wholly to blame. The majority were good technicians but lacking in the broader skills required to manage in a rapidly changing environment where commercial and people skills were now just as valuable as technical expertise. As these managers came under pressure to improve their own performance, their deficiencies were increasingly being exposed. To cover for these weaknesses, their instinctive response was to adopt an autocratic, confrontational, fear-inducing style of management. While this achieved the required short-term results, it was having a catastrophic effect on employee motivation and morale – the very things that Janet knew were vital to ARCO's longer term survival.

Designing and delivering a management development programme at ARCO

Janet wasted no time in producing a detailed management development plan. The plan comprised a comprehensive analysis of current perceived weaknesses among ARCO's managers using data drawn from an analysis of past performance reviews and informal discussions with a number of managers and their bosses. The plan also detailed recommendations for improvements over the short and long term and the budgetary and resource implications of implementing the plan.

The plan was presented to Mike Dawson two weeks later. Janet was disappointed by Mike's initial reaction. Mike expressed concern about the time that managers would have to spend away from their workplace on courses and in the classroom of the local college. He also found some of the costs unacceptable in the present financial climate. Janet agreed to modify the plan and when she returned a week later, Mike accepted it without reservation. As she left the office, Janet reminded Mike that he had agreed to present the plan at the next senior management team meeting to gain their approval and commitment which, she pointed out, was vital to the successful implementation of the plan. Mike confirmed he would do this but warned Janet that it would be in a much abbreviated form as there was a heavy agenda to discuss. Back at her office, Janet began to organise the programme of management development activities.

A few days later, Mike confirmed that the plan had been approved by the senior managers and Janet started to implement her plan. First, she wrote to all of the middle managers explaining that she had been in contact with a local Further Education (FE) college and places were available on a Certificate in Management Studies (CMS) course starting the following month. In her letter, she pointed out that the course would lead to a recognised national qualification in management and that the company would provide full financial support. A number of managers expressed an interest and subsequently enrolled on the course.

For many of the less experienced or newly promoted junior managers, basic management skills training in areas such as communication, motivation and leadership was an urgent priority. Many had been promoted from within the company and because they were from a technical or scientific background had little experience of managing people. Janet decided that a number of short, in-house courses would give them the essential skills to manage in a reasonably competent fashion. The other priority was to improve the relationship between some managers and their teams which had deteriorated alarmingly in recent years. Janet had already identified this as being the result of poor management and work pressures. A programme of team-building activities was arranged to forge a new co-operative spirit and bring the managers closer to their teams.

Janet had discussions with a number of external consultants who subsequently agreed to organise and deliver the required training in core management skills and team-building.

As the plan unfolded, Janet began to turn her attention to the human resource systems and procedures in the company. The annual performance development review was updated to take account of the criticisms she had received from managers who said it was not 'user friendly'. A series of workshops was organised in which all managers, including the senior managers, received practical training in appraisal skills. Other changes and improvements included the introduction of a new discipline and grievance procedure, a staff handbook, and alterations to selection and induction procedures.

A failure to meet expectations?

In the first few months things went well. There was considerable enthusiasm and support across the company for the various activities. In her informal discussions with managers, many remarked that they found the management training 'interesting' and 'useful'. As one manager said, 'this was something that should have been done years ago'. Then the problems began to appear, however.

The first sign of unease came when Janet read the post-course evaluation forms from the supervisory training and discovered that although many of the supervisors had found the course interesting, they questioned its relevance to many of the specific problems and issues they had to face and deal with at ARCO. When she discussed this with some of the supervisors, they pointed out that it was one thing to learn about the basic principles of topics such as motivation and leadership, but what do you do when your boss refuses to let you take any responsibility for managing people? One even remarked that his boss had told him to ignore what he had learnt on the course and 'concentrate on keeping product quality within specification'!

Around the same time, a phone call was received from the CMS Course Leader at the FE College expressing concern at the poor levels of attendance which she felt stemmed from the attitudes of some students who appeared to be 'anti-theory', especially when it came to the subject areas that dealt with the 'management of people'. Some also appeared to be resentful of the time they were having to spend in the classroom, producing assignments and preparing portfolios (one student likened it to management 'stamp collecting').

The problem wasn't helped by the fact that when the managers returned to the site they faced a considerable backlog of technical problems, compounded by the need to commission a new section of the plant to produce a range of dyes for the emerging European market. Production was already three months behind schedule. This was mainly due to poor design, installation errors and poor operator training. On top of all of this, the processing managers were coming under intense pressure from the sales department. They had to 'get it right first time or else'.

The modifications to the performance development review were well received by ARCO's managers but following the initial training period, a number of managers warned Janet that time and resources were going to be a major constraint and the company must make adequate provision for this. Janet was now becoming alarmed at the low rate of reviews being carried out. Without the feedback from the reviews, she would have difficulty in preparing a training plan and budget for the next financial year. More worryingly, however, were the excuses that managers were now making to avoid conducting the reviews with their employees. Some pointed out that a recruitment moratorium had led to increased workload for them and their staff and they could not spare the time to conduct the reviews. Other managers gave the distinct impression that they lacked the required commitment to the process while still others found the process threatening to their managerial position and had no intention of participating. Indeed, the worst offenders appeared to be the senior management team!

The consultants who operated the team-building workshops came to see Janet with some disturbing information. The workshops had gone well and participants had remarked how useful they had found the experience. However, the consultants were astonished to discover the 'gap' that existed between those who were managing the teams and their senior manager colleagues who were accused of being 'remote', 'autocratic' and 'uncaring'. It transpired that the senior management team had largely alienated managers at the middle and junior levels from all but the most routine and mundane management processes. Communication and teamwork were non-existent and they felt they were excluded from virtually all forms of policy or decision-making processes within their departments. The consultants advised Janet to approach Mike Dawson and recommend to him that the issue be discussed among the senior managers, perhaps beginning with a detailed survey and analysis of the company's culture and management style.

Nine months have now elapsed since the implementation of the management development plan and Mike is shortly due to report progress to the EuroChem Group Board. When he hears of the problems now being experienced in the management development programme, he stands up and walks across the room to look out of the window. 'Do you know, Janet, I knew this would happen. We have got the wrong type of people managing this company and until we change that, we are wasting our time investing in any form of management development.'

ACTIVITY BRIEF

1 Imagine you are a Personnel Manager in EuroChem, ARCO's parent company. Over the years you have become friendly with Janet and have given her advice on a number of occasions. Last week, she came to see you and explained that she was confused and perplexed by the apparent failure of her management development plan at ARCO. You listen to what she has to say and promise to help her.

   Prepare a short report (about 1500–2000 words) outlining the possible causes of failure of the management development plan and make suggestions for improvement.

2 What do you think Mike Dawson was getting at when he stated 'We have got the wrong type of people managing this company and until we change that, we are wasting our time investing in any form of management development'?

3 Within the context of ARCO Ltd, there were a number of internal and external factors that were exerting (or had the potential to exert) either a positive or negative influence on the management development process.

   Identify these influencing factors. In what way and to what extent did they affect the management development process? In your view, what action was needed to remove or reduce the negative influences and reinforce those having a positive influence?

4 During a time of radical change, organisations are constantly urged to become more flexible and adaptable – to become 'learning organisations'.
   (a) Assess the extent to which existing management development approaches (such as those being used in this case study) were contributing to organisational learning, development and renewal.
   (b) Based on the evidence presented in the case study, how far do you believe existing perspectives, models or approaches to management development might have to be 'reframed' so that they remain effective in an era of profound and often traumatic organisational change?

RECOMMENDED READING

Coulson-Thomas, C (1989) 'Human resource: the critical success factor', *Leadership and Organisational Development Journal*, 10, 4, pp 13–16.

Doyle, M (1995) 'Organisational transformation and renewal: a case for reframimg management development?', *Personnel Review*, 24, 6, pp 6–18.

Fulop, L (1991) 'Middle managers: victims or vanguards of the entrepreneurial movement?', *Journal of Management Studies*, 28, 1, pp 25–43.

Jackson, D and Humble, J (1994) 'Middle managers: new purpose, new directions', *Journal of Management Development*, 13, 3, pp 15–21.

Kaye, M and Dyason, M (1995) 'The fifth era', *The TQM Magazine*, 7, 1, pp 33–7.

McClelland, S (1994) 'Gaining competitive advantage through strategic management development', *Journal of Management Development*, 13, 5, pp 4–13.

Miller, R and Cangemi, J (1993) 'Why TQM fails: perspectives of top management', *Journal of Management Development*, 12, 7, pp 40–50.

Molander, C, and Winterton, J (1994) *Managing Human Resources*, London, Routledge.

Redman, T, Snape, E and Wilkinson, A (1995) 'Is quality management working in the UK?' *Journal of General Management*, 20, 3, pp 44–59.

Investors in People three years on: Torquay Leisure Hotel Group's experience

Peter Critten

INTRODUCTION

Investors in People (IIP) was launched in October 1991. Since then the standard has been awarded to over 3,300 companies (at the time of publication) that have shown evidence of how investing in the development of their staff has contributed to their business objectives. Each company awarded IIP is required to be reassessed every three years. This case study explores the extent to which investing in the development of each member of staff really can be measured in business terms and the extent to which this change is permanent.

This case study is based on the experience of the first hotel group to be awarded IIP in 1992 – Torquay Leisure Hotel Group (TLH). The group is now preparing itself for its forthcoming reassessment. The context of TLH's original application for IIP status in 1992 and the strategy and procedures implemented to meet the respective criteria are outlined. The situation three years later is then examined and the issues to be tackled when applying for reassessment are discussed. The wider strategic issues the case study raises about the ability of IIP to bring about lasting change are explored and a number of questions are posed relating back to TLH's experience.

BACKGROUND TO THE CASE

Torquay Leisure Hotels (TLH) was the first hotel group to receive the Investors in People award which was presented to them in November 1992 by Devon and Cornwall Training and Enterprise Council. TLH is a family-owned business which started in 1948 with just one hotel. Since then it has acquired three more hotels – all adjacent to each other on a six-acre site in Torquay. The fourth hotel was purchased in 1992.

Acknowledgement
I would like to express my appreciation to Laurence Murrell, MD of Torquay Leisure Hotels, for agreeing to be the subject of this case study and for so freely providing the information on which it is based.

As the owner of resort hotels, the Group's objective is to have 'a full house 365 days of the year'. In order to achieve this, a key strategy for the Managing Director, Laurence Murrell, when he took over the business from his father in 1981, was to develop a range of accommodation and leisure facilities to 'generate revenue and employment all year round, not just in the summer months'. Facilities currently include an outdoor pool, indoor bowling rink, two tennis courts, croquet lawn, and two ballrooms (dancing holidays is a key feature).

The four hotels between them offer 400 bedrooms in addition to which there are 36 self-catering apartments. TLH employs 250 staff. While the MD's strategy to 'generate revenue and employment all year round' has worked, in 1990 profitability was progressively falling and reached a low which prompted the MD to take action. The action he took resulted in a dramatic 25.19 per cent increase in gross profits between 1990 and 1992. The remedy was to embark on a review of the way staff were trained and developed and to link this with the newly introduced Investor in People award. A summary of the action that was taken to meet each of the four IIP principles follows. (*See* Appendix 1 for the full list of assessment indicators which employers must demonstrate they can meet to comply with the four principles of Commitment, Planning, Action and Evaluation.)

TORQUAY LEISURE HOTEL GROUP'S APPLICATION FOR IIP STATUS

Commitment

In line with this first IIP principle, the MD began with a review of his own management style and how this related to his senior management team. Directly reporting to the MD is a Group General Manager and the General Managers (GMs) of each of the four hotels which are run as independent companies. In addition, central support departments have been established to offer a resource to each hotel in the fields of maintenance, purchasing, sales, accounts, entertainments and personnel and training.

Criterion 1

With the help of an external consultant the culture of the senior management group changed from being run by two men (the MD and his deputy, the Group General Manager) to 'a collective approach to running the business'. There were two particular consequences of this stage.

1 The business plan was broken down into specific target areas where performance needed to be improved:
   ● Conditions of employment
   ● Standards of performance
   ● Customer service
   ● Health and Safety
   ● Sales
   ● Maintenance
2 Responsibility was delegated to each GM to achieve particular targets. Furthermore all staff received a copy of the business plan.

This met the first criterion of the principle of commitment:

Every employer should have a written but flexible plan which sets out business goals and targets, considers how employees will contribute to achieving the plan and specifies how development needs in particular will be assessed and met.

Criterion 2

The second criterion assesses how well the organisation communicates its vision to and involves employees:

Management should develop and communicate to all employees a vision of where the organisation is going and the contribution employees will make to its success, involving employee representatives as appropriate.

This is what ultimately drives the whole initiative – the success of the communication process. These were just some of the ways the MD communicated to staff his vision of where the company was going and their place in it:

1 The business plan was 'cascaded' down from MD to the General Managers who each produced a 'Hotel Operational Plan' which in turn went to Departmental Heads who produced their own departmental plans which in turn were communicated to all departmental staff. The final stage was for an individual development plan to be drawn up for each member of staff when he or she was appraised (*see* below). In this way there was tangible evidence that the development of each employee was linked to the overall business plan.

2 General Managers responsible for particular targets (sales, etc.) produced specific action plans for achievement of these targets and publicly displayed these throughout the hotels.

Planning

Criterion 1

The resources for training and developing employees should be clearly identified in the business plan.

Right from the outset the decision was taken that managers should be responsible both for the design and implementation of all training. The business plan made this clear and confirmed that the primary role of each manager was to be a 'coach' to his or her staff.

A Training Officer was appointed not so much to carry out the training but to be a support and facilitator to the managers. Her role was to co-ordinate the training needs, produce a company-wide plan and ensure that each member of staff got information prior to the training taking place and that it was 'followed up' afterwards. She also helped to produce learning materials, OHPs, etc.

Criterion 2

Managers should be responsible for regularly agreeing training and development needs with each employee in the context of business objectives, setting targets and standards linked, where appropriate, to the achievement of National Vocational Qualifications (or relevant units) and, in Scotland, Scottish Vocational Qualifications.

There are three ways in which training needs identified at TLH were inextricably linked with the company's business objectives:

1 The Supervisor Management Programme, run by General Managers for their Heads of Department, focused heavily on the importance of standards of performance for meeting business objectives. Though the company did not produce standards of performance for all operational staff, as a first step all managers were trained to carry out a performance review with all staff. As the MD subsequently observed:

> Of all the initiatives that we've introduced, I think this is the one which has had the most dramatic impact. When you think about it, it's obvious – it involves all operational staff. Somebody who had worked here for six years came up to me and said 'Isn't it wonderful that somebody sat down with me after six years just to hear my views!'

The consequence of each review was that the individual had an opportunity to identify development needs which were then confirmed in writing.

2 The company then went through a process of targeting each Head of Department to work with his or her staff to set standards of performance (SOPs). What is unique about these standards is that they are perceived to be 'the main method of managing quality in any establishment'. Each SOP 'describes who, how, what, where, when and why needs to happen in order that the customer gets a consistent level of product and service every time'. What is more each member of staff was asked:

- to describe how he or she carries out a particular task at that moment;
- to consider whether there were ways in which he or she could improve on what was done;
- to agree with colleagues how the standard should be described.

In this way the staff had ownership of the standards which they had defined. Even more importantly, the standards were driven by what would have an impact on the customer so they could not fail to be business driven.

As to the incorporation of NVQ standards, the MD was initially cautious. His approach was to set standards that were appropriate to his business and then to consider to what extent the standards staff had achieved could be accredited within the NVQ framework.

3 Every six months there is a special meeting of the MD with his four General Managers and the Training Officer to review the company's training needs in the light of changes as a result of which the training plan is amended.

Action

Criterion 1

Action should focus on the training needs of all new recruits and continually developing and improving the skills of existing employees.

Before Investors in People focused attention on the need for some kind of staff handbook, there was no standard description of the range of benefits TLH offered employees. Now each new member of staff – whatever his or her level – has to attend a company induction programme within two weeks of commencement of employment. This is just one of no less than 36 programmes of training, many of which have been developed by managers supported by the Training Officer.

In addition to company induction the new member of staff will already have received a departmental induction programme which follows a standard pattern but is given by the

Departmental Head. Thereafter there are a range of programmes (35 in all), some of which are mandatory. A number of these will be run by departmental heads and managers who have themselves received training as on-the-job trainers/coaches and instructors. In this way training becomes as much a part of the routine as opening the bar on time. It also signals to every member of staff that training is an ongoing process.

Criterion 2

All employees should be encouraged to contribute to identifying and meeting their own job-related needs.

This was one area where the MD recognised more work had to be done with operational staff to make them confident enough to articulate their own aspirations and development needs. The company had met the IIP criterion because it had instituted an appraisal system and given each member the opportunity to discuss his or her own needs and how they could be met. Not everyone was able to describe exactly what their needs were, however.

The Training Officer assisted managers to help their staff agree their own personal development plans.

Evaluation

Criterion 1

The investment, the competence and commitment of employers and the use made of skills learned should be reviewed at all levels against business goals and targets.

There are three indicators attached to this criterion all of which put the onus on the organisation to provide the necessary evidence that the outcomes of training have been reviewed against the following criteria:

- against 'business goals and targets';
- against the objectives of the respective training programmes implemented;
- against 'individual, teams and organisational levels'.

Criterion 2

The second criterion puts the onus finally on senior management to review and make sense of the information in the context of the organisation as a whole:

The effectiveness of training and development should be reviewed at the top level and lead to renewed commitment and target setting.

The MD recognised that establishing systems and procedures was not enough in itself:

It was particularly the evaluation that pushed us on further and changed our culture, the way we are as a company. It pushed us into a way of thinking which is now becoming the norm. We are actually evaluating the results of what we do and using that evaluation. It has reinforced the planning process.

Following the running of any training event, delegates complete a 'Course Review' sheet rating such things as the relevance of the course for them, the amount and quality of information provided, the way it was presented, etc., together with any comments for improvement. Each delegate is asked to return the form to the personnel department within seven days of completing the training.

The second stage is that within three months the delegate's line manager is required to complete a 'training effectiveness sheet' and return it to personnel. It is a simple A4 sheet, one side of which requires the assessor to make observations about the member of staff's work; the other side reproduces the outcome of a discussion with the employee summarising the benefits derived from the training input.

The third stage is that after collecting all the information from the two forms, the Training Officer then compiles a report which is sent to senior management.

The final stage is that every six months the regular weekly senior management meeting between the MD and the General Managers of the hotels is devoted solely to a review of training carried out over the last six months, what conclusions can be drawn when comparing benefits with the overall business results and what lessons there are for the future. The Training Officer will also be present.

Conclusions

The more you can provide evidence that change is taking place, so people aren't relying on just gut feel, the more it actually gives them confidence in what they are doing. Investors in People is a great way of illustrating to people that we are actually achieving something in what we're doing.

Having invested so much of his time and that of his managers in achieving the culture of support that brought to TLH the Investors in People award, Laurence Murrell identifies two key factors. First, that of customer service:

The future lies in quality and you can only get at quality by involving everyone and getting them to work as a team.

He clearly feels that the process of achieving Investors in People helped bring everyone together in achieving a common purpose.

The other factor relates to the amount of money that is invested in people in so far as:

Payroll for hotel operations is the single largest expense. If managers invested anything like the same amount in plant and equipment they would be keen to evaluate their options. Compared to the amount of investment in property and plant the amount of time spent on performance review is minimal.

He ends with a common reflection:

It seems so obvious – you wonder why you haven't done it in the past.

PREPARING FOR REASSESSMENT

The MD is now preparing for a reassessment of IIP. What lessons has he learned from implementing the practices described above over the last three years? What changes still need to be made? What will be the key focus for the 1995 review?

Just as three years ago, preparation for IIP has been driven by the need to improve business profitability overall by developing individual members of staff so that they can make a bigger contribution. Three years on, therefore, lessons for reassessment have been driven by commercial reasons and not by training and development *per se*. A key influence has been the latest review of staff pay compared with one year ago when all staff received a bonus on the basis that they were all contributing to company targets. Though the company is still a thriving and successful enterprise, levels of profitability have made Laurence Murrell realistically review the wisdom of paying out a company bonus without linking it in some way to individual performance. As he says:

> However hard a person may have worked, the company still has to generate profit to pay for any pay increases.

The MD has agreed with all staff that in future a portion of the annual bonus will be linked to company performance.

> In simple terms this means that if TLH has not made sufficient profits, we will not be able to afford to pay out the whole bonus.

How, then, does this link with IIP? For Laurence Murrell, 'profitability is driven by improved standards' and improved standards can only come about through raising awareness of the importance of setting and surpassing standards of excellence. This brings us back to training and development, which is at the heart of IIP.

The big lesson for Laurence Murrell over the last three years is that he thinks the 'balance' in the equation of investing in training to improve performance has swung too far towards training and development *per se* without tangible evidence that performance has indeed improved. The need to redress this balance is at the heart of his strategy for re-applying for IIP. He intends to approach reapplication in rather a different way from the first time round, however, when the whole company's efforts were directed at ensuring it had addressed each IIP indicator in turn and providing sufficient evidence in a massive portfolio. This time round the focus will be on getting the business plan right. The business is very much tied up with the staff in it, and so Laurence sees this effort as being synonymous with what IIP is trying to achieve.

The focus for reassessment, therefore, is on changing the balance towards more specific measurement of achievement.

Implicit in the thinking behind IIP is that if every member of an organisation is clear about a business's objectives and is developed in such a way to help achieve them then the business as a whole must benefit as a result.

When Laurence Murrell first embarked on IIP in 1992 he was clear that investing in people by involving and developing them had to be good for business. As he prepares for reassessment for IIP he is still as enthusiastic as ever about the development of people, but recognises that somehow this has not been matched by awareness of business policy and action necessary to make it work. His action plan for the next round of IIP reflects a 'balancing of the equation'. (*See* Appendix 2.)

ACTIVITY BRIEF

1 Look back over what the MD did under each of the four areas – commitment, planning, action and evaluation – and suggest what changes he might make under each of the headings to ensure that investment in development has a tangible measurable outcome under the control of the management of TLH.

2 Given the details of how TLH met the criteria of IIP first time round and the MD's comments on priorities for the future, on which of the IIP indicators would you advise TLH to concentrate in its bid to get recognition for another three years?*

3 What lessons do you draw from TLH's experience which can be applied to your own organisation, if it were to apply for IIP?

4 What advice would you give to Investors in People UK Ltd for amendments/additions to the IIP indicators to strengthen the link between individual development and achievement of an organisation's business objectives?

RECOMMENDED READING

Critten P (1993) *Investing in People – Towards Corporate Capability*, Oxford, Butterworth–Heinemann.

Campbell D, Coldicott T and Kinsella K (1994) *Systemic Work with Organisations: A New Model for Managers and Change Agents*, London, Karnac Books.

Finn R (1994) 'Investors in People: counting the dividends', *Personnel Management*, May.

'Firms queue up for Investors status', *Personnel Today*, February 1995.

Fowler A (1994) 'How to obtain an Investors in People award', *Personnel Management Plus*, June.

IRRR (1994) 'Investors in People: an IRS survey of employers' experience', *Employee Development Bulletin 52*, April.

'Quality control for Investors in People standard', *Personnel Today*, August 1994.

---

* Torquay Leisure Hotels were successfully reassessed in November 1995.

APPENDIX 1
INVESTORS IN PEOPLE: THE INDICATORS

1 Commitment

An Investor in People makes a public commitment from the top to develop all employees to achieve its business objectives.

Every employer should have a written but flexible plan which sets out business goals and targets, considers how employees will contribute to achieving the plan and specifies how development needs in particular will be assessed and met.

Management should develop and communicate to all employees a vision of where the organisation is going and the contribution employees will make to its success, involving employee representatives as appropriate.

1.1   There is a public commitment from the most senior level within the organisation to develop people.
1.2   Employees at all levels are aware of the broad aims or vision of the organisation.
1.3   There is a written but flexible plan which sets out business goals and targets.
1.4   The plan identifies broad development needs and specifies how they will be assessed and met.
1.5   The employer has considered what employees at all levels will contribute to the success of the organisation and has communicated this effectively to them.
1.6   Where representative structures exist, management communicates with employee representatives a vision of where the organisation is going and the contribution employees (and their representatives) will make to its success.

2 Planning

An Investor in People regularly reviews the training and development needs of all employees.

The resources for training and developing employees should be clearly identified in the business plan.

Managers should be responsible for regularly agreeing training and development needs with each employee in the context of business objectives, setting targets and standards linked, where appropriate, to the achievement of National Vocational Qualifications (or relevant units) and, in Scotland, Scottish Vocational Qualifications.

2.1   The written plan identifies the resources that will be used to meet training and development needs.
2.2   Training and development needs are regularly reviewed against business objectives.
2.3   A process exists for regularly reviewing the training development needs of all employees.
2.4   Responsibility for developing people is clearly identified throughout the organisation, starting at the top.
2.5   Managers are competent to carry out their responsibilities for developing people.
2.6   Targets and standards are set for development actions.
2.7   Where appropriate, training targets are linked to achieving external standards and particularly to National Vocational Qualifications (or Scottish Vocational Qualifications in Scotland) and units.

3 Action

An Investor in People takes action to train and develop individuals on recruitment and throughout their employment.

Action should focus on the training needs of all new recruits and continually developing and improving the skills of existing employees.

All employees should be encouraged to contribute to identifying and meeting their own job-related needs.

3.1   All new employees are introduced effectively to the organisation and are given the training and development they need to do the job.

3.2   The skills of existing employees are developed in line with business objectives.

3.3   All employees are made aware of the development opportunities open to them.

3.4   All employees are encouraged to help identify and meet their job-related development needs.

3.5   Effective action takes place to achieve the training and development objectives of individuals and the organisation.

3.6   Managers are actively involved in supporting employees to meet their training and development needs.

4 Evaluation

An Investor in People evaluates the investment in training and development to assess achievement and improve future effectiveness.

The investment, the competence and commitment of employers and the use made of skills learned should be reviewed at all levels against business goals and targets.

The effectiveness of training and development should be reviewed at the top level and lead to renewed commitment and target setting.

4.1   The organisation evaluates how its development of people is contributing to business goals and targets.

4.2   The organisation evaluates whether its development actions have achieved their objectives.

4.3   The outcomes of training and development are evaluated at individual, team and organisational levels.

4.4   Top management understand the broad costs and benefits of developing people.

4.5   The continuing commitment of top management to developing people is communicated to all employees.

APPENDIX 2
PLANNING TO MEET IIP CRITERIA – CONTRASTING STRATEGIES

	1992	1995
COMMITMENT	Collective company approach to development of company business plan within which each of the four hotel managers had specific targets to achieve. Influence was 'top-down' with a company-wide rather than hotel-specific commitment.	Each Hotel Manager produces a business plan for his/her hotel and agrees that with MD. Influence is therefore more 'bottom-up' with each manager and member of staff committed to and directly responsible for achieving their own targets.
PLANNING	Company training plan devised based on assessment of individual needs within framework of standards of performance which was the responsibility of one General Manager to agree across all hotels.	Each Hotel Manager agrees with own staff standards of performance needed to achieve its own business plan and what is most appropriate way of assessing these standards. Development needs resulting from this process then written up as hotel training plan subsequently agreed with MD and Training Officer.
ACTION	Key focus was to ensure each new member of staff had induction training within two weeks of starting and then attended standard company courses organised by the Training Officer.	Onus is on each Hotel Manager to ensure each new member of staff is inducted within two weeks of starting and thereafter that the Training Officer is brought in to advise on individual development plan to meet development needs identified in hotel training plan.
EVALUATION	A company-wide system of evaluation forms was instituted which followed up effectiveness of training and were reviewed every six months at a senior management meeting attended by the four Hotel Managers, the MD and the Training Officer.	Each hotel is responsible for continuous monitoring of standards which are reviewed every month at separate meeting between each Hotel Manager and the MD.

APPENDIX 3
IMPLEMENTING IIP – TWIN CYCLES OF A SYSTEMIC APPROACH

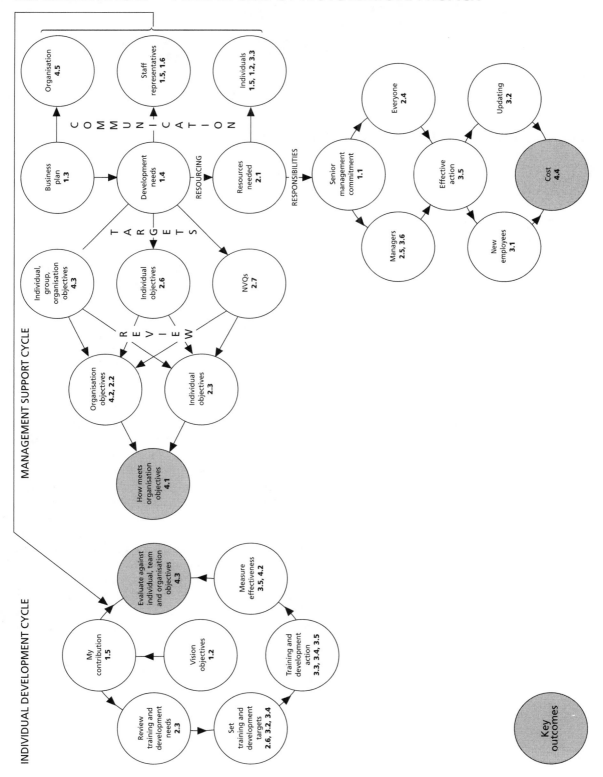

CASE 20

New Zealand Breweries: what is the future of the HRM function?

A Ian Glendon, David E Simmons and Greg J Bamber

INTRODUCTION

By the end of the four-year period of the case study, the company New Zealand Breweries (NZB) had introduced a series of human resource (HR) initiatives. The case study considers whether there is definitive evidence that NZB's HR practices are actually adding value to the company. In addition, there are questions about the influence of HR on the organisation. How can the effects of the HR initiatives on the culture of NZB be assessed?

The case initially provides background on NZB before examining key corporate strategic initiatives and their HR implications. The case focuses on specific aspects of HR, including objectives, HR records and statistics, performance management, organisation structure and staffing. Data from organisation climate surveys and illustrative analyses of strengths, weaknesses, opportunities and threats (SWOT) are provided to assist in assessing NZB's organisational culture.

One aspect of the modern approach to human resource management (HRM) is the integration of HR functions with line management responsibilities rather than maintaining HR within a separately identifiable 'staff' role, as tended to happen with the traditional personnel management function (Storey 1989, Guest 1991, Boxall 1992, Schuler 1992). Other features of an HRM approach are a greater than hitherto emphasis upon strategic drivers for HR procedures and processes (Dyer and Holder 1988, Storey 1989, Schuler *et al* 1993, Snape *et al* 1994) and the integration of the main components of HRM – selection, performance appraisal, employee relations, rewards and training and development (Fombrun *et al*, 1984, Hendry and Pettigrew 1986). Despite all the models and rhetoric extolling the benefits of an HRM approach, however, few organisations actually practise a fully fledged HRM regime (Storey 1992, Patrickson *et al* 1995). This case study describes an attempt to implement a suite of HR practices in an organisation, driven not through exposure to the theoretical literature, but rather by experience of market pressures. Two objectives of these initiatives were to add value to the company and to improve the culture of the organisation.

BACKGROUND TO THE CASE

NZB is part of the Lion Nathan Group, which has four divisions:

- New Zealand Liquor, which includes NZB;
- Australian Brewing, which includes Castlemaine Perkins, Tooheys, Swan and other brewers;
- the soft drinks business, in which Lion Nathan has the franchise for bottling Pepsi-Cola brands in Australia and New Zealand;
- Lion Nathan International, export and overseas operations including a substantial investment in China.

By Year 4 of the case study, NZB had 197 employees – 6.2 per cent of the Group's total workforce of 3175. The Group has undergone a massive downsizing exercise to reach this figure from around 18,000 employees in Year 1.

Lion Nathan is financially strong with profits of NZ$209.7 million on a turnover of NZ$2514.1 million for the year ending 31 September 1994*. Turnover for the previous trading year was $2288.6 million and there was similar growth in the two previous years. Despite this strong performance, Lion Nathan is in a mature industry, so it has attempted to expand domestically and internationally.

To support growth, the corporate executives hold that internal systems must meet or exceed world's best practice which they characterise as 'A Class'. A Class is the best performance indicator from a series of benchmarking measures (for details *see* Souza *et al* 1993). The 1994 Annual Report reflects strong management confidence by reporting that:

> All Lion Nathan companies are in the process of adopting an international system that incorporates the best of International Standards Organisation (ISO) documentation standards with Total Quality Management philosophies and streamlined work processes, benchmarking Lion Nathan not only against leading overseas breweries, but also against the very best international companies.

NEW ZEALAND BREWERIES (NZB)

NZB represents a small percentage of Lion Nathan's total operations, however, it is at this enterprise that Lion Nathan adopted and refined HRM strategies that would become benchmarks for the rest of the Group.

The Managing Director (MD) of NZB is supported by a Board comprising directors for marketing, sales, finance, operations, business development and HR. The Master Brewer is also a Board member. An initial indication of the priority accorded to HR is that NZB includes the HR Director on its Board of Directors.

NZB operates two plants on New Zealand's South Island: in Christchurch, The Canterbury Brewery and in Dunedin, Speight's Brewery. The main brands produced are Canterbury Draught, Speight's and Guinness. The major market is the South Island of New Zealand in which the company has a 51 per cent share. Canterbury Draught is a strong regional brand and won a gold medal at the 1994 Monde Selection Awards in Belgium.

---

* NZ$1 = £0.45 in April 1996

NZB strategic initiatives

In 1994 NZB adopted several forward-thinking strategic initiatives. It opened a new PepsiCo bottling plant on the Canterbury Brewery site to take advantage of the management infrastructure and support services there. This was the first major production synergy between Lion Nathan's soft drinks and brewery operations, which the company saw as a 'model for future development'. NZB identified a series of six key issues related to strategic business initiatives for the forthcoming year:

- build Canterbury Draught's 'momentum and soul';
- innovate in product, package and technical services;
- maximise productivity;
- broaden distribution to extend availability;
- nurture the 'cult status' of the Speight's brand, with the objective of delivering strong volume growth;
- identify and counter competitors' programmes.

NZB saw HR strategies as integral to the implementation of these broader strategic initiatives. Therefore, it developed HR policies to support each of the six initiatives. For example, training programmes were specifically tailored to facilitate the success of each initiative.

The HR Director argued that there was an onus on the HR group to support the efforts of the company to increase productivity. This reflected the goal that HR must add value to the company. To maximise productivity the following HR initiatives were considered:

- *Retain 'A Class' personnel* (those rated by employee assessments as being above average and therefore the most valuable to the company).
- *Allocate a NZ$100 budget for each individual member of staff*. Staff were allowed to spend the NZ$100 budget at their discretion on a company-related activity. According to the HR Director, this policy was an important step in generating a more trusting culture within the enterprise.
- *Promote from within the company*. This policy helped to foster cohesion within the enterprise and it reinforced the notion that high-performing employees could expect to be rewarded by promotion.
- *Conduct regular 'organisational climate' surveys*. These reflected the belief that culture is changeable in the short term and that the HR group must constantly help to improve the climate of the enterprise.
- *Increase training to a minimum of five days per employee per year*. Training was a major focus for the HR group.
- *Focus training on teams*. Teamworking was adopted as a method for fostering a more participatory organisational culture.

NZB adopted HR policies that were complementary and mutually reinforcing. While senior management accepted prime responsibility for designating strategic policies, each of the main functions (sales, marketing, finance, operations, brewing) also produced its own action plans against HR priorities.

A major role of the HR function at NZB is measuring and trying to improve its organisational culture. To review employee perceptions of the organisational culture, NZB carries out an annual organisational climate survey. While the term 'organisational culture' is more commonly used these days, here we use the term employed by the company. Although

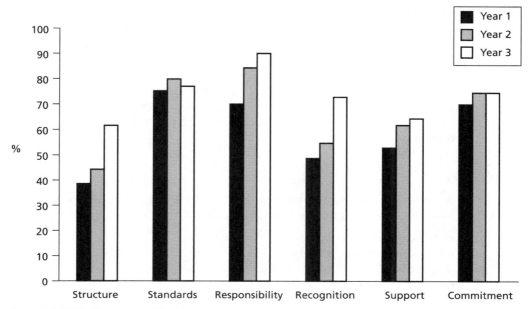

Fig 20.1 NZB climate profile, Years 1 to 3

the two terms have different meanings (Furnham and Gunter 1993), in this case they are used interchangeably. A climate questionnaire with questions covering six key areas – structure, standards, responsibility, recognition, support and commitment – is distributed annually to all NZB employees. Fig. 20.1 shows data for Years 1 to 3. The organisational climate profile provides management with information on which aspects of organisational climate may need attention as well as indicating the extent to which earlier interventions are likely to have been successful. For example, it might be inferred from Fig. 20.1 that interventions on employee perceptions of the structure of the organisation have had some degree of success and that perceptions of responsibility and recognition have also been improving over the three-year period. NZB management recognised that it was important to 'get the downsizing right', or the climate scores would show the result (of getting it wrong).

The HR Director argues that soon after conducting the first survey, managers were able to initiate an almost immediate improvement in the culture of NZB. Does this perhaps tend to contradict a widely held belief that it can take several years to change an organisation's culture?

SWOT analyses

As part of its continuing HR planning, through the HR function the company carried out SWOT analyses – reviews of strengths, weaknesses, opportunities and threats – on all its main functional areas, as well as for the company as a whole. These were done separately for 'People capability', 'HR systems' and 'Culture and organisation'. With advice from the HR Director, line managers were responsible for undertaking the SWOT analyses. The HR Director argued that this policy forced line managers to incorporate HR considerations into their daily decisions. Data generated by the SWOT analysis exercises are useful for illuminating various aspects of HR.

HUMAN RESOURCE MANAGEMENT IN NEW ZEALAND BREWERIES

Until 1990, the HR function was directed centrally from Lion Nathan Group Headquarters in Auckland (which most employees saw as remote from them – 750 km away from Canterbury, towards the north of New Zealand's North Island). Since 1990, however, the function had been led by a strong and influential change-agent, NZB HR Director, Mr Dennis Finn, based at the Canterbury Brewery. The HR Director is supported by two HR officers – one for sales/marketing/finance and the other to cover office and operations staff.

HR objectives

A major focus of the HR objectives for Year 4 was improvement in organisational culture. In setting objectives for the business to achieve by Year 4, priorities were identified as:

● Achieve 'A Class' (world-class benchmark).
● Unify the recruitment system.
● Refocus sales team under new direction.
● Achieve increases in all climate survey dimensions year by year.
● Reinvigorate NZB's training and development.

Records and statistics

The HR Director argued that to demonstrate the value of the HR function, it is essential to gather and quantify HR information. This approach can be contrasted with the view of HR that has been offered by other commentators (e.g., Peters and Waterman 1982). Such writers extol the 'soft' attributes of HR, such as the style in which senior management deal with staff. While not discounting the importance of the 'soft' elements of HR, Dennis Finn attempted to make HR initiatives measurable, recordable and actionable with clear linkages to strategic performance indicators, such as earnings before interest and tax (EBIT).

In keeping with attempts to link HR with broader business strategy, the performance of the company's HR activities is very well documented. The HR department keeps detailed statistics in respect of the company's HR activities and how these relate to company performance.

Table 20.1 provides statistics on HR issues. Information from the SWOT analysis can be used to supplement the statistics in Table 20.1 to provide a richer picture of the HR systems in NZB. A summary of data that were generated as part of the HR Department's SWOT analysis follows. In general, it was found that all systems were in place and that the overall picture was satisfactory. However, further work is needed in training and development.

Table 20.1 Key HR results and financial priorities

Criterion	Year 1	Year 2	Year 3	Year 4
Headcount	250	201	197	197
Employment costs as percentage of sales	18%	16.9%	14.8%	13.7%
EBIT (NZ$)	8.5m	12.8m	16.6m	20.4m
EBIT per employee (NZ$)	34,000	63,681	84,264	103,553

- *Strengths.* The industrial relations component of the HR Plan is in place; strong incentives apply to all staff; Individual Development and Feedback (ID&F) Plans are in place; appraisals are aligned with the Annual Operating Plan (AOP) focus; HR insights are discussed at Board level; NZB's results and recruitment; regular organisational climate audits are undertaken.
- *Weaknesses.* Training and development needs focus and direction; the HR Officer needs further guidance and support in this area; NZB needs to devote attention to its policy on economic rewards and should set up continuous improvement teams.
- *Opportunities.* Improving NZB's sales training; quality circles and the contribution of its HR function.
- *Threats.* The HR Director moving on to a sister company within the Lion Nathan Group, possibly heralding a reduction of the momentum of NZB's HR initiatives.

Performance management

Performance appraisals and feedback are at the heart of HRM in NZB. They are included in the accountabilities of senior managers, which is reflected in their pay. These accountabilities specify areas for improvement, objectives for the coming year in terms of people management and other areas specific to that position. Feedback at NZB is 360 degree. For example managers are assessed from above, below and from the side (by other managers at an equivalent level in the hierarchy). Performance management is an HR tool that has a powerful influence at NZB. NZB staff are given regular performance feedback designed to enhance their performance. According to the HR Director, all staff receive so much feedback that, 'there is nowhere to hide in NZB'. He means that once everyone knows what is expected of them and how they are performing, they simply have to get on with the job and deliver results.

In addition, the climate survey is linked to the performance management system. For example, if the climate survey reveals that there are problems in the satisfaction of employees in the finance area, then managers and staff will develop specific action plans that could improve job satisfaction. For managers this could include leadership development, training in team facilitation or focusing on recognition of their staff, as one way of helping to win their commitment.

Individuals' accountabilities and performance evaluations are weighted and summed to produce an overall performance rating. The performance evaluation form is signed by the employee and his/her manager and endorsed by a member of the HR department.

NZB's HR plan includes each individual's personal profile and his or her development plan plus an identification of key talent which supports a broader goal of recruiting from within. During the previous year, 13 staff were promoted, a further eight were 'broadened' (given other roles to perform), five were transferred (including one promotion) and six left the company (two retired, two resigned and two were made redundant). Five managers considered to have high potential talent were recruited and three key executives were provided by NZB to the parent company.

Development assessments are carried out by team leaders and managers in January and February and training development starts in May at the start of a 9 to 12 month plan for each individual. A Lion Nathan Group ex-employee acts as external consultant for the training, which typically includes sessions on supervision, leadership skills and team-building.

Remuneration for NZB staff is good by local standards. There is a link between pay and performance, with 2 per cent being related to development appraisal for individuals who are 'on target', which increases to up to 10 per cent for those who are assessed as outstanding, as shown in Table 20.2. In addition, individuals can receive up to another 10 per cent annual bonus, which is related to company performance.

Table 20.2 Performance related pay

Development appraisal	Pay supplement
Below target	0%
On target	2%
Above target	5%
Outstanding	10%

Organisation structure and staffing

Organisation structure and staffing is a primary responsibility of the HR team. Dennis Finn argues that the company is 'hard driving' and with 'virtually no fat'. There is a maximum of four layers of management – including the Managing Director – and considerable responsibility is devolved to line managers. A maximum of 10 to 12 people report to a manager; 6 to 8 is typical. Table 20.3 shows staffing levels and staff movements ('churn and turn') during a 12-month period.

Table 20.3 Staffing levels and staff movements over a 12-month period

Function	Staff number	Staff movements
Sales	57	11 (19%)
Operations	94	7 (7%)
Marketing	7	3 (43%)
Finance/Admin.	16	3 (19%)
HR	4	–
Distribution	15	2 (13%)
Other	4	1 (25%)
Totals	**197**	**27 (14%)**

One SWOT analysis explored several issues relating to company staffing. In general there is a strong team, but perhaps it is changed too often at senior levels.

- *Strengths*. There is a strong sales team; new young talent; NZB acts as a team unit; solid reliable Finance Director; MD's excellent style; NZB is capable of 'self-reproduction'.
- *Weaknesses*. There are changes to the senior team – sales, marketing and HR; operations is still the weakest link; Business Development Director is not part of the team; marketing team lacks depth.
- *Opportunities*. There is much new talent in the local universities; NZB is installing a trade marketing function and injecting new life into business development with a new Sales Director.
- *Threats*: Business development is not integrating; the new team doesn't 'gel'; the Master Brewer is becoming 'stagnant'; can NZB operatives rise to the 'A Class' challenge?

ORGANISATIONAL CULTURE

The results of NZB's climate surveys were part of a series of reinforcing strategies that were intended to deliver rapid results. Other data used to measure culture include results from the 360 degree performance management appraisals. The SWOT analyses also provide an indication of NZB's culture. In summary, the SWOT analyses revealed generally positive findings but there appeared to be a need to be beware of potential complacency.

- *Strengths*. Excellent organisation climate survey results; NZB team spirit; innovation from within; an open approach to HR; an excellent reward system; promotion from within.
- *Weaknesses*. Turnover in operations is low; operations culture needs improvement; marketing lacks focus.
- *Opportunities*. Build on outstanding climate survey scores; one system for all – achieve 100 per cent participation in these voluntary surveys; achieve 'A Class'; once marketing structure is settled, a new direction will be seen.
- *Threats*. Constant pressure to improve organisational climate scores; complacency.

ACTIVITY BRIEF

1 To what extent can HR initiatives such as those described be shown to add value to the organisation? What are the best methods for measuring the impact of HR on the value of the organisation?

2 What are the most appropriate methods for measuring organisational culture? Can organisational culture be changed in a short period of time? How effectively can organisational culture be measured?

3 After Dennis Finn moves on, should NZB
   (a) recruit another NZB HR Director?
   or
   (b) ensure that line managers take full responsibility for HR issues with any necessary assistance from the Group's HR Director based in Auckland?

RECOMMENDED READING

Boxall, PF (1992) 'Strategic human resource management: beginnings of a new theoretical sophistication?' *Human Resource Management Journal*, 2, 3, pp 60–79.

Dyer, L and Holder, GW (1988) 'A strategic perspective of human resource management', in Dyer, L (ed) *Human Resource Management: Evolving Roles and Responsibilities*, Washington DC, The Bureau of National Affairs.

Fombrun, C, Tichy, NM and Devanna, MA (1984) *Strategic Human Resource Management*, New York, Wiley.

Furnham, A and Gunter, B (1993) *Corporate Assessment: Auditing a Company's Personality*, London, Greenfield.

Guest, DE (1991) 'Human resource management and the American dream', *Journal of Management Studies*, 27, 4, pp 377–97.

Hendry, C and Pettigrew, A (1986) 'The practice of strategic human resource management', *Personnel Review*, 15, 5, pp 3–8.

Patrickson, MG, Bamber, VM and Bamber, GJ (eds) (1995) *Organisational Change Strategies: Case Studies of Human Resource and Industrial Relations Issues*, Melbourne, Longman.

Peters, T and Waterman, R (1982) *In Search of Excellence*, New York, Harper & Row.

Schuler, RS (1992) 'Strategic human resources management: linking the people with the strategic needs of the business', *Organisational Dynamics*, 21, 1, pp 18–32.

Schuler, RS, Dowling, PJ and De Cieri, H (1993) 'An integrative framework of strategic international human resource management', *International Journal of Human Resource Management*, 2, 4, pp 717–64.

Snape, EJ, Redman, T and Bamber, GJ (1994) *Managing Managers: Strategies and Techniques for Human Resource Management*, Oxford, Blackwell.

Souza, SA *et al* (1993) *The Oliver White ABCD Checklist for Operational Excellence* (4th edn), Essex Junction, Vermont, Oliver White.

Storey, J (ed) (1989) *New Perspectives on Human Resource Management*, London, Routledge.

Storey, J (1992) *Developments in the Management of Human Resources*, Oxford, Blackwell.

PART 4

Employee Relations

The final section starts with a notable case at the Timex Plant in Dundee. Martin Dowling and Graeme Martin describe this bitter and highly publicised case in 'Employee relations, trade unionism and HRM: lessons from Timex', showing how the cost-competitive trading environment, and in particular the HRM approach adopted in response, led to dispute, negotiation, deadlock, workforce lock-out, picket-line violence and eventual closure.

This is followed by a topical case dealing with 'Changing employee relations at Powerco'. Powerco is a regional electricity company now facing choices in respect of their HR decision making in a competitive climate, and the need to meet shareholder interests and to satisfy customer expectations. Hamish Mathieson enquires how this affects employee relations issues in terms of the mix between individualism and collectivism, bargaining and consultation processes, reward systems and the need for workforce flexibility.

'Managing employee relations in a local authority building works section' focuses on the HR issues arising for managers as a result of the introduction of compulsory competitive tendering. David Farnham and Lesley Giles explore the impact this has for the employment of local authority staff, job terms and conditions and employee relations. The case revolves around the attempt to secure future contracts to protect jobs, while facing necessary cost reduction.

The advent of NHS trusts has caused problems in respect of the appropriate machinery to be adopted for local pay determination, recognition of union bargaining, forms of negotiation or consultation adopted and the remuneration system to be instituted. In 'Establishing a pay regime in an NHS trust: prescribing the treatment', Susan Corby evaluates such a situation, which necessarily raises questions regarding the advantages and drawbacks of job evaluation and performance-related pay.

It has sometimes been claimed that Japanese management is more efficient than Western systems, with greater worker commitment. Rick Delbridge and Mike Noon utilise the case of a Japanese-owned consumer electronics plant in the UK to investigate 'Formal communication and worker representation in a Japanese transplant'. While the company appears to be a model of best practice, ambivalence and scepticism were encountered at shopfloor level. This case permits readers to make their own evaluation.

'Bargained flexibilisation: the dynamics of change towards new work organisation' by John Salmon examines a dominant theme in HR literature and debate. The case relates the change a company makes in the face of increased competition, moving from mass production to flexible manufacturing and developing a leaner, more diversified work organisation. The employee relations implications are assessed in terms of both trade union influence and the need for social flexibility within the organisation.

To complete the section, Fintan Hourihan and Patrick Gunnigle introduce the case of Marks and Spencer (Ireland) Ltd where recognition of trade unions contrasts to other countries in which the company is located. The focal question is whether this can be a strategic move from control to commitment, enhancing the company's effectiveness, provision of quality and labour force flexibility. The background of employee relations in Ireland is linked to corporate policy and operations in the Irish stores.

Employee relations, trade unionism and HRM: lessons from Timex

Martin Dowling and Graeme Martin

INTRODUCTION

This case is concerned with events surrounding the closure of the Timex plant in Dundee in 1993 after a highly publicised and at times violent dispute. The dispute and eventual closure of the factory raised many social, economic and political issues and caused widespread debate in the country and beyond. At a *societal* level, the points at issue included the very nature of industrial enterprise in the late twentieth century, the relationship between industry and society, and the future shape of employment relations in mature economies like Britain. Violence on the picket line – the like of which had not been seen in Britain since *The Times* Newspaper dispute and the Miners' Strike of the mid-1980s – attracted massive media publicity and public outrage. At an *organisational* level, events at Timex raise many questions about the dynamic relationship between corporate and human resource strategy, particularly within the context of multinational decision-making processes (Chakravarthy and Perlmutter 1990, Hendry 1994, Tyson 1995, Purcell 1995) and about the management of change and the application of a particular style of human resource management within a strongly unionised environment (Pettigrew and Whipp 1991, Sisson 1993, Guest 1995).

BACKGROUND TO THE CASE

The Timex Corporation is a privately owned, US-based multinational which forms part of the business empire of Norwegian Fred Olsen, who took over the running of the conglomerate from his father in the mid-1950s. Timex has its headquarters in Middlebury, Connecticut and currently has an estimated annual turnover of $640 million. It employs 7000 people in the US, Europe and the Philippines, marketing and assembling watches.

The Timex Corporation was one of a number of multinationals attracted to Dundee at the end of World War Two and it began producing mechanical watches in the city in 1946. For the next twenty-five years, despite the inevitable ebbs and flows arising from the economic cycle, production and employment levels gradually increased so that by the early 1970s the size of the workforce had increased to approximately 6000 employed in three factories across the city. Although employment declined somewhat in the years that followed, the company still employed over 4000 in 1978. At this point, a period of change was ushered in that for the Dundee site took the next 15 years to unfold. It began with the company changing the *technological* base of its watch production from mechanical to electronic technology and changing the *geographical* base of that production from Dundee and its other production centres in Europe and the USA to the Far East, principally the Philippines. A related aspect to these changes was Timex's integration forwards into retail outlets for watches in order to take advantage of the larger margins associated with retailing. (The value chain for wrist watches shows the vast bulk of added value is created at the wholesaling and retailing stages (Gilbert and Strebel 1992).)

For the Timex Corporation as a whole these changes have been successfully managed in the sense that the new technological, geographical and marketing features of its watch production have provided the basis for renewed growth and profitability. For the Dundee site, however, the period of change was less successful. It ended with the closure of Timex's one remaining factory in the city in August 1993 following a bitter industrial dispute that had lasted eight months.

TIMEX AND DUNDEE: THE EARLY YEARS AND THE DEVELOPMENT OF AN IR CULTURE

The company set up the first of its plants in the city in purpose-built accommodation to produce low-priced, value-for-money wrist watches. Buoyant post-war demand conditions, the adoption of Fordist-type volume production methods coupled with innovative product development (the company was the first to introduce self-winding and battery-operated watches) and heavy promotional expenditure led to a gradual expansion of the workforce. Timex became the largest single private sector employer in the city of Dundee and, apart from major redundancies in 1971, Timex enjoyed a positive image in the city until the early 1980s. It was considered by many of its staff and potential recruits to be an organisation which offered relatively secure, well paid employment in an area dominated by traditional but declining industries such as shipbuilding and jute manufacture.

The Dundee operation also became the largest production facility in Timex's worldwide operations, which a former senior and long serving manager suggested was an extremely important factor in explaining the attention paid by the US management to the plant's manufacturing strategy and industrial relations. At the same time, the Dundee operation was always a manufacturing/assembling facility. It had little product-design tradition or capacity itself – most product innovation being developed in the US.

Operating in a traditionally unionised industrial environment, Timex found itself from the outset employing a unionised workforce and was obliged therefore to recognise and deal with powerful trade unions for most sections of both its blue and white collar workforce. In particular the engineering union (today called the Amalgamated Engineering and Electrical Union) became the dominant union force in the plant. Over the years a traditional pattern of employment management via strong collective bargaining with the unions was established (Purcell and Sisson 1983). With the Dundee facility operating a volume strategy based on cost-plus financing, it soon became something of a cash cow for the Timex Corporation. This in turn also became a source of union bargaining power which was used to secure economic benefits and job controls at the point of production – concessions which the management seemed willing to give to secure continuity of output.

A former manager confirmed:

The union controlled many aspects of life on the shopfloor and built up lots of overtime earnings for its members. Management seemed powerless to resist.

A senior shop steward commented:

Yes we wanted involvement and used our power to get it ... but it was always used in a co-operative way. When management wanted changes we always co-operated but we made sure our members were protected.

Over time it seems the situation began to resemble something of an 'indulgency pattern' (Gouldner 1954). Both sides came to an accommodation with each other and whether through co-operation or conflict secured their objectives. The engineering union especially was able to secure a strong position over both the *content* of the employment relationship and the *process* that led to its features for the typical worker. This industrial relations tradition was later to be of great significance in the months leading up to closure but before this came about, Timex attempted for over a decade to transform its business in Dundee and it is to this attempt that we now turn.

THE DECLINE OF MECHANICAL WATCHMAKING AND THE MOVE INTO SUBCONTRACTING ELECTRONICS

Timex's fortunes in Dundee began to change in the late 1970s, following the decline in demand for mechanical watches – the sector of the wristwatch market in which the company had traditionally been dominant. The competition from electronics-based watches from the Far East led to Timex setting up new plants, initially in Taiwan and subsequently in the Philippines, to produce the cheaper more innovative watches using the newer technology.

It is from this point in the late 1970s that the importance of the Dundee business in Timex's global operations began to decline. However, the commitment to remain in Dundee was still very evident – a commitment personally guaranteed at the time by owner Fred Olsen. In a change of product-market strategy, the Dundee business entered into the first of a number of subcontracting agreements with electronics companies – initially with the entrepreneur, Clive Sinclair, to assemble the ZX computer range and then with Nimslo to manufacture the Japanese-designed 3D camera. Such a change was not as fundamental as it first appears. As explained by a former senior manager, the plant's competence lay in component manufacture and/or assembly rather than in integrated processes of design/test/manufacture. Although there was a brief flirtation with a small new product design project, Timex management in both the US and Dundee decided that to begin to develop a set of new products from scratch lay neither in the site's capability nor in the time frame available to maintain plant utilisation. Contract electronics thus seemed a workable solution as it required neither extensive development in skills for many of the existing workforce nor a great deal of investment in new plant.

A former shop steward agreed:

The move from mechanical to electronics gave us no problems over the changeover. Good eyesight and manual dexterity are needed and so the skills needed for electronic work were the same as for mechanical work.

However, these initial subcontracting ventures did not prove to be long-term successes for the Dundee plant. The ZX computer range was taken over by Amstrad and production of the Nimslo camera was moved to Japan. Meanwhile in the early 1980s, the company decided to relocate its remaining mechanical watch assembly to production facilities in France. As a result, employment levels in Dundee began to fall continuously from 1978 when Timex employed 4200 in the city. In 1983 a major redundancy of 1900 was declared. Workers undertook a sit-in but the compulsory redundancies went ahead and the union failed to halt the transfer of work away from Dundee. In addition to its success on the issue of the redundancies, the company was also able to secure flexibility changes among the remaining workforce. As a former shop steward explained:

> We had to agree to 1900 jobs going in order to save the rest. We also agreed to a two-tier wage structure with temporary contracts paid at £20 to £25 per week less than the full-time equivalent. There was a lot more flexible use made of labour in response to the needs of the company.

The pursuit of a 'hard contracting' human resource strategy by the company (Tyson 1995) was in keeping with the traditional adversarial characteristics of employment relations at the site. It was a strategy that no doubt took advantage of the weakened market position of unions and workers at the time and clearly signalled the type of employment regime that was to feature in the years ahead.

Timex's operations in Dundee continued throughout the 1980s to develop in the field of contract manufacturing and providing other ancillary services to original equipment manufacturers (OEMs) such as the major computer companies. When IBM took over the Sinclair ZX computer range, Timex's association with IBM began with it producing metal frames for the company's PCs and, later, printed circuit boards. In 1986 contracts were also secured from Amstrad to assemble PCs and then printers for the company. Other developments saw electronic control units manufactured for Minolta, Bang and Olufsen and Creda Cookers. By the late 1980s, then, Timex had secured a place for itself within the contract electronics manufacturing market – but the move was to have the greatest significance for the management of employment at the factory.

THE CONTRACT ELECTRONICS MARKET AND ITS IMPLICATIONS FOR EMPLOYMENT MANAGEMENT AT TIMEX

During the late 1980s favourable demand conditions for contract electronic manufacturers (CEMs) existed. Many of the original equipment manufacturers (OEMs) began to focus on their core competencies/business activities, seeking new markets and providing them with management solutions. This led to much of the OEMs' subassembly work being contracted out to the CEMs and by 1988 the estimated annual growth rate of the contract electronics market had reached 45 per cent. Although this declined during the recession, by 1993 demand had increased by 21 per cent over the previous year's level (*Scotland on Sunday*, 30 May 1993). In addition to the contracting-out policy of the OEMs, European Union rules on the content of finished equipment that had to be sourced in the host country also augured well for the prospects of European-based CEMs like Timex.

In 1993, just prior to the factory closure, the *Financial Times* (16 March 1993) reported a glowing future for the contract electronics manufacturers which had become the fastest growing sector of the European electronics industry and worth, in global terms, an estimated $22 billion by the mid-1990s. It depicted the industry in terms of strategic alliances between the OEMs and the CEMs that could provide fast response times, flexibility and high quality as well as low-cost manufacture. As Timex discovered, however, the reality was a commercial relationship in which, as one of many possible suppliers in a worldwide competitive marketplace, they were very much at a disadvantage compared to the buyer.

By the early 1990s, IBM was supplying 70 per cent or more of Timex's Dundee business, principally the production of printed circuit boards, and took advantage of a highly competitive market environment, intensified by Far Eastern competition, to set exacting cost and delivery standards. The Scottish plant of IBM was aiming to secure the monitor production for the whole of IBM and was seeking a 25 per cent reduction in inventory at their Greenock plant. For their component suppliers such as Timex they specified how much they were willing to pay for subassemblies, the cost and source of bought-in parts, and could insist on strict JIT-related delivery schedules.

Moving into the contracting market had major implications for the Dundee plant's management. IBM, in particular, not only exercised strict control over price but also over conformance to design, quality and production standards and, during the initial stages of the contract, had a permanent group of production staff resident in Dundee. The nature of employment management in Dundee was also to change as a consequence. As one of Timex's former managers explained:

> The company had lived for years in a situation where compromise with the unions was the name of the game because it could pass on the costs. Moving into subcontracting meant that this was no longer possible and the unions didn't like it.

Despite some successes in the new market it had moved into, however, the company was still having difficulty in adjusting fully to the cost and employment requirements of the industry. The cost structure of the Dundee plant was estimated to be some 20 to 30 per cent higher than the main competitors in the contract electronics industry and continued to remain so for much of the period in question. The issue of the high and relatively fixed cost structure of the company's Scottish operation was identified by management as a major obstacle in competing effectively in the market. This evidence did not dissuade the management team from continuing to penetrate the market, however. A former HR manager explained the problems that Timex faced in moving into the electronics market in the following way:

> ... a strategy based on competence in assembly and manufacturing seemed eminently possible if a labour run-down, new contracts and (changes in) labour practices could be managed. The company achieved the first two but was always going to find it difficult to overcome the union practices and influence and accommodating style of union–management relationships developed during the high volume/high margin watch manufacturing days of the 1960s and 1970s.

> (Contract electronics) was a low margin industry. Rapid technological change, fluctuating programmes, quality and delivery demands of customers made it a difficult market for us. This was mainly a non-union industry with a younger workforce, much lower fringe benefits and greater flexibility.

Redundancies at the Timex plant had continued throughout the 1980s but provoked no industrial action since they were achieved by voluntary means for the most part. By 1985 employment was down to 1000 and by 1990, 580. In that year a further major review of work organisation at Timex and 'Fresh Start' – as it was called – resulted in more voluntary redundancies together with changes in working practices. Those who remained received

£2000 for accepting the new agreement and in addition an employee share-ownership scheme was introduced and a worker director elected to the Board of Timex UK. A saving scheme and a profit-sharing scheme were also proposed. These employment changes marked something of a departure from the traditional approach of previous years and can be seen as an attempt by management to develop a more 'soft contracting' human resource strategy (Tyson 1995). However, whether it was going to be sufficient to overcome the legacy of a well established adversarial relationship was much less than certain.

By 1993 Timex had become one of the 'big six' CEMs in the UK, although it had also seen massive reductions in its workforce, the closure and demolition of two of its three factories in the city and the concentration of all production in one part of its original factory. Moreover, the cost of restructuring had contributed to the accumulation of losses of £10 million since 1987.

As we have seen above, the move to subcontract work from the early 1980s onwards was marked by several attempts by the company to change its approach to work, employment and industrial relations (Gospel 1983). Both 'hard' and 'soft' variants of HRM practice can be detected (Storey 1992, Tyson 1995) as can attempts to move away from a traditional 'personnel and IR/pluralist' approach to a more general 'HRM/unitarist' approach although the extent of this was never strong given the presence of a sceptical, unionised workforce that had been subjected to a decade of retrenchment (Guest 1989).

It is clear that for Timex management, workers and unions alike, however, the 1980s had witnessed a change in the nature of the characteristic features of employment. For many years mechanical watch production had 'cocooned' the two sides, but the harsher cost and production realities of the contract market were forcing changes that each found difficult – in the event – to fully come to terms with.

COST REDUCTION, CHANGE AND EMPLOYMENT POLICY: STRIKE AND CLOSURE IN 1993

The final part of the attempted transition began in June 1991 when the company recruited Peter Hall to manage the Dundee plant and to turn the factory around given its poor financial record in recent years. Many seemed to agree that it was make-or-break time for the Dundee factory. Speaking on BBC radio, Timex's Employee Director commented after the closure:

> When Peter Hall was hired to take over as the manager in Dundee it was made clear to the local trade union officials and to everyone in the plant that Peter Hall was the last throw of the dice.

His initial actions also seemed to be approved by the local management team. As one senior manager put it:

> Hall came in with lots of good ideas on how to run a company of this size ... he seemed to know what he was doing and saved us quite a bit of money in the short term by replacing an expensive mainframe computer system with networked PCs and by cutting out a lot of unnecessary overtime.

Other views differed, however. A senior shop steward commented:

> He came in with a very aggressive style in discussions. The man had no industrial relations background and had very fixed views. Management should dictate and any concessions made

by the union were immediately seen as weaknesses by Hall. This was a great misreading of the signals.

Late in 1992 major problems arose over the IBM delivery schedule and there would need to be a severe production cutback in the first half of 1993. Hall developed a plan for cutting costs in the Dundee plant in conjunction with his management team and also with advice from two US-based Vice Presidents of Timex. It was this plan and in particular the approach to employment management that it implied which eventually led to the dispute and later closure of the Timex factory.

In December 1992 Timex proposed to lay off 190 workers for 26 weeks. Under a previous union agreement those laid off would be entitled to a payment equivalent to the basic daily wage rate for 12 weeks but the company argued it could no longer afford to honour this agreement. In negotiations the union proposed rotational layoffs so that the economic hardship could be shared out among the entire workforce. The company rejected this claiming it would take too long to train workers in the various jobs they could be rotated to and so would disrupt production. Layoff notices were distributed to 170 workers on 7 January 1993 and this provoked a half-day sit-in by the workforce. Further talks over the next three weeks failed to produce a breakthrough and the workforce voted in favour of industrial action which commenced on 29 January 1993. Within days the company issued letters to all strikers (who consisted of the vast majority of manual workers; supervisory, technical and managerial staff continued to work) warning them that unless they returned to work by 8 February 1993 they could face dismissal. The message was largely ignored although a few strikers returned to work.

At further talks in the middle of February 1993, the company proposed a four-point peace plan:

● arbitration on the original question of layoffs;
● a 10 per cent cut in fringe benefits;
● a wage freeze for 1993;
● the workforce to share 50 per cent of any profits made by Timex in 1993.

The union objected to these new conditions but the company argued that cost reductions had always been on the negotiating agenda, although the union had refused to discuss them until the issue of the layoffs had been settled. The strikers agreed to return to work 'under protest' but found themselves 'locked out' when they turned up for work on 15 February 1993. The company was unhappy that workers were not prepared to accept fully the cut in benefits and appeared concerned that a sit-in might result. On 17 February 1993 all 340 striking workers were sacked and the same evening recruitment notices appeared in the local press. Speaking on BBC local radio later in the dispute, Peter Hall argued that the company couldn't afford continued discussions on the matter as seemed likely given an 'under-protest' return to work.

By early March 1993 Timex had recruited over 100 workers to replace those dismissed. Violence on the picket-line outside the factory increased as strikers and their supporters tried each day to prevent the replacement workforce being bussed in. As the dispute wore on, numerous third parties appealed to the two sides to reopen negotiations. Attitudes began to harden, however, and the room for compromise narrowed. John Kydd Jnr., union convener at the plant, speaking at a rally in Dundee in support of the strikers declared:

The first option is what we all want. We go back in there with our heads held high all 340 workers together, united and underneath the banner of the AEEU, or they close Timex for good in Dundee.

For his part Peter Hall declared himself happy with the quality of work being provided by the new workforce (which had grown to 270 by the end of May 1993):

> We have a recovery plan in place that is going very well and our customers are satisfied. Timex will survive and grow ... As far as we are concerned, the disputes with the union is at an end ... We cannot turn the clock back now.
>
> (*The Courier*, 14 April 1993)

During May 1993 a number of secret meetings were held in London between senior union officials and Timex management. As a result the company proposed a 'peace plan' consisting of a 27 per cent cut in pay and benefits. (This compares to the 10 per cent cut workers were asked to accept at the beginning of the year.) The offer was put to a mass meeting in early June 1993 and was unanimously rejected by the strikers. The AEEU Executive Officer for Scotland, Jimmy Airlie, had felt duty bound to put the offer to his members following his negotiations with management. The overwhelming rejection, he declared, '... shows our members are not prepared to accept such a draconian cut in benefits and wages' (BBC Local Radio). Mr Airlie was also quoted in the city's evening paper as saying:

> ... the dispute is now in a very entrenched position ... It seems to me that if there isn't a negotiated settlement I can't see how Timex can do their business in Dundee.
>
> (*Dundee Evening Telegraph*, 3 June 1993)

Fred Olsen, the owner of Timex, visited the besieged plant in late May 1993 and indicated his personal wish that the plant remain open. Many believe that it was his personal intervention in 1983, following the demise of mechanical watch production, that saved the Dundee factory. Speaking on local radio, Olsen declared:

> You must understand that we have kept this place going. And you might say we had no reason to because after the mechanical watch went out and we went to electronic watches the whole artistry of making watches changed. Some of you remember we had the Sinclair computers, we had the 3D camera, we did everything we could to put something in to keep it going because we had a history of being here since 1946 and we failed in many of them. Now we seem to have built up a niche making these boards for other people. But it takes a lot of effort.

In the middle of June 1993 it seemed that a breakthrough had come with the sudden announcement of Peter Hall's resignation 'for private reasons'. More talks were planned but by now Timex was only interested in offering the strikers a financial inducement in order to facilitate an orderly rundown of the plant. This was rejected by the union and on 15 June 1993 Timex announced it was to close its operations in Dundee before the end of the year. Two months later, on 19 August 1993, the factory closed. Announcing the decision, Mohammed Saleh, Timex Vice-President for Human Resources said:

> Well I feel personally very bad, I feel sad ... on a personal level I've been involved with Dundee for 20 years. I've been with this company that long. I wanted it to remain open. I did everything – I'm not the only one who wants it to remain open. We did everything we could and from a personal standpoint I'm very unhappy about it. I'm sad about it but I really feel I and my colleagues did everything we could. I pleaded personally sometimes with the union to consider the situation and tried every creative way (sic) to find a solution, every creative way, just

as much as we tried creative ways when we introduced the Fresh Start. But in spite of all this effort I'm afraid we couldn't make it a go.

(BBC Local Radio)

The union announced the dispute would continue and the strikers continued with their attempt at a consumer boycott of Timex products. Applications for unfair dismissal to an industrial tribunal had been lodged by all the sacked workers and these would not be withdrawn, it was said. By mid-October 1993 however, Timex offered all strikers a cash settlement if the boycott and industrial tribunal applications were withdrawn and the strike fund (some £180,000) was disposed of in a way not likely to harm Timex. This was agreed by the strikers and the dispute was declared officially over.

AFTERMATH OF CLOSURE

Inevitably claim and counter-claim were soon being exchanged as an attempt was made to try to explain the reasons for closure. Some blamed the intransigence of the unions or the management or both and maintained that a settlement could have been negotiated given goodwill from all sides. Managerial tactics over the way the issue was handled from the outset came in for severe criticism in some areas of the mass media. The personalities and styles of Peter Hall and John Kydd Jnr (the union convener at the plant) were said to clash so much that the dispute was almost inevitable from the start. Perspectives differ and inevitably explanations will too. However, two quotes are illustrative. Asked why he thought closure had occurred, Mohammed Saleh replied:

> I would say certainly this dispute aggravated it. I think the fact that the subcontract manufacturing is a competitive thing and I think the fact that the cost base in Dundee is very high which you could say created that dispute in a way or in a big way. So it is in the competitive nature of the business and the individual dispute contributed to the closure.

(BBC Radio News)

In answering the question, Bill Spiers, Assistant General Secretary of the Scottish Trades Union Congress, argued:

> It does look as though at some stage the company thought that they could get by with the, as they call it, replacement labour – I would call it a scab workforce – that they thought they could get by with it, they weren't serious about negotiating and by the time they realised that the workforce they'd recruited didn't have the skills to maintain the quality of service that you have to maintain in the electronics industry these days it was really too late ... I think really the responsibility does lie with management. It was the same people they were dealing with that they'd always dealt with before and there was no reason why they couldn't have come to an agreement that could have got them through what we hope is a short-term downturn in the electronics market. What the company seem to have done when they brought in Mr Hall from the south is to have misjudged the situation and I think it's a classic example of bad management misjudgment that has led to tears all round.

(BBC Local Radio)

ACTIVITY BRIEF

1 Analyse the corporate and employee relations strategy pursued by Timex in the period to 1983.

2 In terms of human resource strategy, what was required following the move by the company into the contract electronics market after 1983?

3 Following the move into the contract electronics market, evaluate management's approach to human resource strategy in the period to 1992.

4 Consider the course of events and the actions of both sides during the dispute in 1993. What might have produced a more positive outcome? Was closure of the plant inevitable?

5 In the context of Timex's global strategy after 1983, account for the company's failure to bring about successful organisational change at its Dundee plant.

RECOMMENDED READING

Chakravarthy, BS and Perlmutter, HV (1990) 'Strategic planning for a global business' in Vernon-Wortzel, H and Wortzel, LH (eds) *Global Strategic Management: the Essentials* (2nd edn), New York, Wiley.

Courier (Dundee) (1993), 14 April.

Evening Telegraph (Dundee) (1993), 3 June.

Financial Times (London) (1993), 16 March.

Gilbert, X and Strebel, P (1992) 'Developing competitive advantage' in Mintzberg, H and Quinn, JB (eds) *The Strategy Process*, London, Prentice Hall.

Gospel, HF (1983) 'Managerial structures and strategies', in Gospel, HF and Littler, CR (eds) *Managerial Strategies and Industrial Relations*, London, Heinemann.

Gouldner, A (1954) *Patterns of Industrial Bureaucracy*, New York, Free Press.

Guest, D (1989) 'Human resource management, its implications for industrial relations and trade unions' in Storey, J (ed) *New Perspectives in Human Resource Management*, London, Routledge.

Guest, D (1995) 'Human resource management, trade unions and industrial relations' in Storey, J (ed) *Human Resource Management, A Critical Text*, London, Routledge.

Hendry, C (1994) *Human Resource Strategies for International Growth*, London, Macmillan.

Pettigrew, A and Whipp, R (1991) *Managing Change for Competitive Success*, Oxford, Blackwell.

Purcell, J (1995) 'Corporate strategy and its links with human resource management' in Storey, J (ed) *Human Resource Management, A Critical Text*, London, Routledge.

Purcell, J and Sisson, K (1983) 'Strategies and practice in the management of industrial relations' in Bain, G (ed) *Industrial Relations in Britain*, Oxford, Blackwell.

Scotland on Sunday (Edinburgh) (1993), 30 May.

Sisson, K (1993) 'In search of HRM', *British Journal of Industrial Relations*, 31, 2.

Storey, J (1992) *New Developments in the Management of Human Resources*, Oxford, Blackwell.

Tyson, S (1995) *Human Resource Strategy*, London, Pitman.

Changing employee relations at Powerco

Hamish Mathieson

INTRODUCTION

The following case is concerned with the employee relations policy choices faced by managers in a regional electricity company. The creation in 1990 of 12 privatised regional electricity companies (RECs) in England and Wales set in motion changes in the organisational and cultural context framing the management of employee relations. Prime elements in the new context are the introduction of competition, pressure to reduce operating costs and the companies' perceptions of themselves as separate businesses in which meeting shareholder and customer expectations are accorded high priority. The case focuses on decision making in three key areas: bargaining and consultation arrangements, pay systems and workforce flexibility.

BACKGROUND TO THE CASE

The essential tasks of the industry are the generation of bulk electricity in a network of power stations, its transmission via the high voltage National Grid, and its ultimate distribution and supply to consumers on a local basis. Prior to the passage of the Electricity Act 1989 which triggered the privatisation process the industry was structured (at least in England and Wales) on the basis of a 'vertical separation' between the 'upstream' generation and transmission activities undertaken by the Central Electricity Generating Board (CEGB), and the 'downstream' distribution and retailing functions fulfilled by a collection of regional area boards. The industry in Scotland, on the other hand, demonstrated full vertical integration of generation, transmission and distribution functions undertaken by two 'regional' electricity boards. An analogous arrangement applied in Northern Ireland.

So far as England and Wales are concerned, the postwar pre-privatisation era, set in train by 1947 legislation nationalising the industry and further legislation a decade later, was characterised by two important features.

1 *There was little competition.* Successive governments prioritised continuity of supply and capital investment in hardware ahead of measures to enhance competition. Moreover, the prices charged to consumers by area boards were heavily influenced by the tariff terms upon which the monopoly generator, the CEGB, sold bulk electricity to the boards. Some commentators likened the relationship between the CEGB and the area boards as one of 'domination and subservience'.

2 *The industry was production-driven.* The statutory duty to 'keep the lights burning' and meet demand from the consumer rested with the CEGB. As a consequence the industry became 'engineering-led' and also acquired a reputation for extensive procedural bureaucratisation.

None of this, however, should mask the sustained expansion and success of the industry in terms of capital investment, technological change and productivity growth.

The 1989 Electricity Act has brought substantial changes in the organisation and operations of the industry. In introducing the government's plans for the industry's privatisation the Secretary of State for Energy declared that his proposals were aimed at transforming a 'producer-dominated' industry into a 'consumer-led' industry. This has subsequently entailed the break-up of the CEGB and the creation in its place of three competing power-generating companies in England and Wales – National Power, Powergen and Nuclear Electric. In Scotland the successors to the 'integrated' area boards are Scottish Power and Hydro-Electric, together with the nuclear generator, Scottish Nuclear.

Privatisation also created 12 regional distribution companies in England and Wales (the RECs), whose powers and responsibilities significantly exceed those of the former area boards. They exercise control over the transmission grid through joint ownership of the separately constituted National Grid company; they are able to buy bulk electricity from whichever generator they wish; and they may enter the field of generation themselves. The RECs operate under a public electricity supply (PES) licence which places upon them the statutory obligation to meet demand formerly held by the CEGB. Compliance with the terms of the licence, which also requires the companies to separate different businesses (distribution, supply, appliance retailing, electrical contracting, telecommunications, etc.), is monitored by the Director General of Electricity Supply (DGES) at the Office of Electricity Regulation (OFFER). A principal role carried out by the DGES – the Regulator – is to supervise the prices charged by the RECs to their customers for the distribution and supply of electricity in which they have regional monopolies. These so-called 'regulated' businesses are responsible for the management and operation of the physical distribution network in the franchise area and the purchase of electricity from generators and its sale to consumers respectively. Taken together the distribution and supply businesses may typically account for 90 per cent of profits with the non-regulated activities (appliance retailing, electrical contracting, telecommunications, etc.) accounting for the rest.

Several implications arise from the regime imposed as a result of privatisation so far as the RECs are concerned.

1 Decisions by the DGES to cut the future allowable level of prices the RECs may charge their customers for electricity are likely to affect the companies' projected income and profits levels. Consequently, managers are under pressure in such circumstances to cut operating costs and increase efficiency to compensate. A strategy of diversification involving expanding non-regulated businesses may also be chosen as a route to top-up profits.

2 Although the RECs are less exposed to competition than the generators by virtue of the regional monopolies in their distribution businesses, they nevertheless face competition for the supply of electricity to non-domestic large consumers of which there are estimated to be 50,000. A further spur to competition is the plan due to be realised in 1998 allowing domestic electricity customers to choose between alternative suppliers.

3 The responsibility placed on the RECs to meet demand by their holding of PES licences requires managers to be vigilant in ensuring responsiveness to customers and quality of

service. To this end the DGES's brief includes monitoring the companies' efficiency in dealing with customer requirements.

4 Company managements cannot ignore the fact of their companies' stock exchange quotation; sensitivity to shareholder and 'City' expectations and, since April 1995, the possibility of take-overs and mergers, act as a stimulus to management practices which never lose sight of the 'bottom line'.

EMPLOYEE RELATIONS IN THE INDUSTRY

Employee relations in electricity supply have been characterised by sophisticated collective bargaining and consultative machinery, stability and relative industrial harmony. In many respects the arrangements introduced following the legislation nationalising the industry in 1947 and surviving until privatisation mirrored the classic Whitley pattern. Negotiations were conducted at national, i.e. industry, level in four separate collective bargaining machines covering different sections of the workforce. These bodies were made up of senior members of the electricity boards together with senior trade union officials. They were:

● the National Joint Industrial Council (NJIC) which covered the largest group of employees, industrial manual staff including foremen, represented by the craft-based EETPU and AEU (merged in 1992 into the AEEU) together with the GMB, TGWU and UCATT;
● the National Joint Council (NJC) covering professional, administrative, clerical and sales staff, including the majority of female staff in the industry and represented largely by NALGO (incorporated into Unison in 1993) and GMB/APEX;
● the National Joint Board (NJB) covering the 'strategically' powerful professional engineers represented by the Electrical Power Engineers' Association (EPEA); and
● the National Joint Managerial Committee (NJMC) covering managerial staff up to executive level and also represented in the main by EPEA and NALGO.

Below the national bodies there existed district (regional) and local (works) level committees for each bargaining group responsible for ensuring the proper implementation of national agreements and resolving any difficulties. In addition, there were formal disputes procedures with stages at local, district and national levels plus arbitration and a parallel three-tier union-based machinery of consultation.

Several important outcomes resulted from such arrangements.

1 Collective agreements tended to be highly formalised and comprehensive in scope, given the intention of their framers that the terms would apply to the complex circumstances and eventualities of an entire industry.
2 The strong commitment of the employers to a centralised, collective model of industrial relations entrenched the trade unions while also concentrating union power in the hands of full-time officials. This together with the tendency of the disputes machinery to refer issues upwards removed a stimulus for workplace union organisation.
3 The arrangements delivered benefits to both parties: employers achieved significant changes in working practices, reductions in manpower and productivity improvements with remarkably little union resistance through industrial action. Employees experienced pay and conditions terms which were superior to the norm in many cases.
4 The role of central government cannot be overlooked, as ultimate paymaster to the

industry and being directly responsible for 'keeping the lights on', given the potentially devastating industrial strength of the power workers. Balancing these roles ensured that political influence in the industrial relations affairs of the industry was always present whether in blatant forms or via 'backstairs whispers'.

Overall, however, the traditional pattern of employee relations management conformed closely to the 'good employer' model in which collective bargaining and widespread union recognition was central. The trade-off for union recognition was an expectation of union co-operation in issues such as increasing productivity and in introducing new working practices and new technology. This was largely delivered.

The advent of privatisation

The fragmentation of the industry into 19 separate companies after privatisation has provided an impetus and a vehicle for change in the management of employee relations. As companies respond to the post-privatisation market-oriented climate in which they are responsible for their own destinies, managers are faced with a range of employee relations issues and choices:

● What is to be the mix between individualism and collectivism?
● How is bargaining and consultation to be conducted?
● What reward systems are to be introduced?
● How might the workforce become more flexible in order to meet quality and service performance targets?

It is to these questions that we now turn in considering the case of Powerco plc.

POWERCO PLC

The company, in common with the other former area electricity boards, was floated on the Stock Exchange in 1990 in its new guise as a regional electricity company (REC). As one of the larger RECs, it employs approximately 8000 people in its seven businesses, reflecting the company's strategy of becoming established as a diversified utility services group. At the core of the company are its electricity distribution and supply businesses which together employ around 5000 in tasks such as the maintenance of the distribution network and in billing and meter reading, and which make by far the biggest contribution to Powerco's profits (approximately 85 per cent). Clearly the performance of these businesses is critical to the success of the company. These are also the 'regulated' businesses subject to the scrutiny of the government-appointed Regulator who conducts periodic reviews of the allowable charges which the company may make to its domestic customers for electricity. In a recent review, the Regulator ordered that distribution charges be cut by 14 per cent in the next financial year, followed by four years in which charges must be reduced by the Retail Price Index (i.e. the rate of inflation) minus 2 per cent. Powerco has calculated that the price caps will have the effect of reducing company income by £300 million over the next five years. In a recent statement the Chairman responded by declaring that unless the company significantly reduces its costs there will be a substantial loss in profits which would be 'unacceptable' to shareholders who might shift their investments elsewhere to the long-term detriment of the business and job security. Given that the pay bill accounts for the largest proportion of the company's controllable costs, Powerco has announced the shedding of 1200 jobs over a five-year period, almost a quarter of current core business staff numbers. As part of the restructuring five area offices will be replaced by three regional offices. A voluntary severance scheme has been introduced to assist in the avoidance of compulsory redundancies. Other requirements specified by the regulator involve the setting of more demanding standards of service to customers. In response Powerco is developing a number of 'customer centres', dealing with customers' electricity enquiries, which have opening hours extending into the evenings.

The core business workforce is heavily unionised with union density standing at 85 per cent. Industrial (manual) staff are organised by the AEEU, GMB and TGWU, with the former union accounting for three quarters of the membership. Clerical, administrative and support staff are organised mainly by Unison while professional engineers are represented by the EPEA (part of the Engineers and Managers Association, the EMA). In terms of the proportions of total union membership in the core business, the AEEU and Unison account for approximately 75 per cent, divided equally. The EPEA has 15 per cent with the GMB and TGWU sharing the remaining 10 per cent between them.

In sum the business priorities in the core or 'main' businesses are to retain and build on the traditional base by a combination of cost reduction, increased efficiency and improved standards of customer service.

The non-regulated businesses

A second plank in company strategy is to vigorously pursue the exploitation of potentially profitable opportunities in 'non-regulated' business areas. Such an approach is designed to reduce the dependence of Powerco on profits from the regulated business, particularly at a time in which it will be increasingly exposed to competition in these traditional markets as a consequence of the decision to permit domestic consumers to buy their electricity from competitor power companies in 1998. A major element in the strategy for the non-regulated sector of activities is the expansion of electrical appliance retailing. The company inherited a string of high street 'electricity showrooms' from its predecessor area board but has since embarked on an ambitious strategy of opening up 'out-of-town' superstores located in retail parks, a number of which are outside its heartland area. Moreover, Powerco has acquired additional such stores plus a number of high street shops from another REC, again geographically remote from company HQ. Plans have been announced for further expansion. As a result of such growth almost 60 per cent of sales come from superstores, and the losses in electrical retailing chalked up in pre-privatisation days have given way to growing profitability. This turnaround in fortunes has been against a background of intense competition and PES licensing rules which prohibit the cross-subsidising of retailing operations by the much more profitable distribution business. A key factor has been the employment of managers from the retailing sector who have sought to change the culture from being an arm of a state-owned industry to a free-standing business which can compete with the established giant electrical goods retail chains. In addition, however, staff have been subject to a pay freeze on basic rates for the past year.

Powerco's retailing operations are less well unionised than the core business – around 50 per cent of staff are in membership. Membership has been falling following privatisation, particularly as a result of the company's expansion into the poorly unionised 'superstore' sector. The vast majority of union members are in either the AEEU, covering groups such as delivery drivers and after-sales service staff, or in Unison which organises shop sales staff. The share of total membership is two thirds to Unison, one third AEEU.

While Powerco continues to recognise unions for bargaining purposes in its high street locations it has yet to follow suit in respect of its retail park stores.

The survival of the retailing business would seem to depend to a large degree on an aggressive market-place presence and sustained pressure to drive down costs, which inevitably focuses on staff deployment and pay, given the labour-intensive nature of the operation.

Powerco maintains a contracting business which undertakes a range of industrial, commercial and domestic electrical work and has recently added to its portfolio the supply of double-glazing and cavity wall insulation. Trading conditions have, however, been very difficult on account of recessionary conditions in the construction industry and in the housing market. The company has 'wielded the scalpel' and staff numbers have been reduced by 20 per cent as part of a restructuring exercise. This has returned the business to profitability following several years of losses. The contribution of a 36-month pay-freeze and an increase in the length of the working week from 37 to 41 hours negotiated with the AEEU – the union which represents the mainly electrician membership – must also be noted. In addition, new staff have been recruited on terms and conditions negotiated nationally for the electrical contracting industry. Nevertheless there is no room for complacency and continued progress depends on tight control over costs (especially labour costs which comprise two thirds of a typical contract), competitive pricing and quality of service.

Two other businesses have recently been started, telecommunications and gas, in order to exploit the liberalisation of markets in telecoms services and in gas supply. These are at an embryonic stage but are expanding rapidly. Finally the company has made its first foray into electricity generation via a number of investments and joint ventures in environmentally friendly generation schemes at home and abroad. A significant percentage of staff in these businesses have personal contracts.

EMPLOYEE RELATIONS IN POWERCO

The employee relations inheritance

At the time of privatisation Powerco, in common with the other regional electricity companies, depended upon the long standing national collective bargaining arrangements for the orderly determination of pay and conditions. Pay bargaining, therefore, took place against a background of pay data relating to national trends, supplied by the employers' industry association (the Electricity Council, later Association). Four separate bargaining groups existed: industrial workers (ranging from unskilled labourers to skilled time-served craftsmen), professional engineers, clerical and administrative staff, and managers. The resulting highly detailed and prescriptive agreements were designed to try to minimise the risk of disruption to electricity supply in what was seen as a single vital industry. Industry agreements, however, each of which had a different annual review date, did not provide for an integrated pay structure or common terms and conditions across the bargaining groups. Nor did they specify common procedures for handling disputes, grievances and disciplinary matters. Instead each agreement contained its own grading and pay structure; consequently Powerco inherited a pay structure with, in total, nearly 30 grades and over 200 salary points.

Moreover, agreements varied in relation to the length of pay scales measured in terms of the number of salary points, in degrees of overlap and in minimum and maximum salary levels. Salary ranges within grades also tended to vary in width. In addition, there were differences in staff entitlements in relation to holidays, in standby, call-out, meal and car allowances, in travelling expenses and in premium payments for overtime and shift working. Some of these disparities gave rise to rankles among the industrial staff in particular centring on what they saw as their inferior status in comparison to the professional engineers. Tension between the craftsmen and the engineers also surfaced in respect of work demarcation; for example, engineers guarded their 'right' to authorise the isolation of power lines prior to work being undertaken by manual staff. Craftsmen felt that such duties were well within their competence range. The ensuing restriction on the ability of top-graded craft workers to move into areas of work traditionally the preserve of professional engineers impeded the progress of workforce flexibility. More generally technological change has tended to remove some of the traditional rationale for the strict classification of the workforce into 'manual', 'staff' and 'professional' categories.

The vulnerability of the traditional pay determination structure to claims under the 'equal pay for work of equal value' amendment to the Equal Pay Act has been demonstrated by a series of legal cases and other claims against electricity companies, including Powerco. NALGO (now Unison), which represents the majority of female staff who are concentrated in the clerical and retail sales grades, claimed that pay inequities were sustained by the operation of the separate bargaining machines. This led to comparisons being made between jobs in the clerical structure, and those mainly undertaken by men in the industrial pay structure in which the grades have both shorter numbers of salary points from bottom to top and higher minimum and maximum salaries. The success of the union campaign has been reflected in a series of favourable reports from independent experts and also the verdict of an industrial tribunal that the jobs compared were of equal value. As a result the company is anxious to avoid further equal pay claims.

Several other significant features of the traditional collective bargaining arrangements may be mentioned.

1 Progression within grades was related to service; although progression was dependent on 'satisfactory service' the absence of explicit criteria meant that 'failures to progress' were a rare occurrence.
2 The salary scales specified in the pay structures applied throughout the company as a 'unified entity'; thus the pay rate and other terms and conditions of employment of a person in a given grade would be identical whether he/she worked in electricity distribution or retailing.
3 All national agreements fixed the basic average working week at 37 hours; they also specified, however, that these hours would be worked on a rigid day-working pattern, Monday to Friday. Any time worked outside the '9 to 5' pattern attracted overtime payments.
4 Senior managers and engineers had their pay and conditions determined collectively.
5 The national negotiating machines spawned separate local (district and in-company) joint management/union 'works', 'staff' and 'technical staff' committees whose role was to police the operation of the national agreements, dealing with such matters as working schedules and shift rotas. A company-wide Joint Consultative Council including reps from all unions met to discuss non-negotiating issues ranging from welfare matters to technological change.

Management and unions

The traditional pattern of employee relations in Powerco accorded trade unions a central position. This derived in part from the unions' strong claim to representativeness of staff interest based on very high membership levels. It also reflected prevailing management attitudes, however. A culture of almost automatic consultation with union representatives characterised relations; thus prior to negotiations management would tend to 'quietly' consult union negotiators about its proposals, to gauge reactions. Communication of these proposals to the wider membership was left to the discretion of the unions. Following the conclusion of negotiations the results would be communicated to the workforce via a joint management/union communiqué. Another reflection of management style was in relation to the facilities afforded to shop stewards: the procedural agreement provided that 'time-off' would be granted in relation to 'electricity industry' industrial relations business, thus allowing facilities for attendance at cross-industry union meetings and geographical mobility in the local district. In individual workplaces, such as depots, shop stewards had the freedom to represent all union members irrespective of their possible employment in different divisions of the organisation.

Privatisation and new employee relations strategies

Powerco is moving to devise employee relations strategies in order to facilitate its business objectives. The company's priority in an increasingly competitive market place in all its businesses is to continue to be profitable by developing a more commercial approach and by becoming more customer-service oriented. The cost, quality and productivity of staff are identified as the major factors in remaining competitive. Moreover, the company is concerned to adopt strategies which match the particular product and labour market circumstances of the core distribution business on the one hand, and the developing non-regulated businesses on the other.

In common with all the other RECs, Powerco has given notice to the trade unions of its intention to withdraw from national bargaining arrangements and move to company bargaining. The move is justified by the obsolescence of national bargaining in a situation in which the company is an independent business in competition with others in the industry (and elsewhere). The advantages are seen to lie in the 'customising' of pay and conditions to business objectives and local markets, the streamlining of bargaining machinery and pay structure and the facilitation of greater workforce flexibility. The move is also seen as an opportunity to overhaul joint consultative arrangements.

The company has recently restructured its personnel function. A new Personnel Director has been appointed at the slimmed down corporate centre with responsibility for developing human resources strategies. Each business has in turn set up its own personnel office with responsibility for day-to-day policy implementation. Apart from the strategic move to devolve bargaining, the personnel function has recently made public the framework of Powerco's employee relations strategies in other important areas. Among these are:

- *Reward.* The company will develop pay and benefits arrangements which are appropriate to business needs and which are sufficient to attract, retain and motivate staff. In addition to market rates, pay and benefits arrangements will be based upon flexibility, equity and objectivity, merit/competence-based progression and the relation of reward to business performance. Salary adjustments will henceforth be subject to periodic review of company performance and ability to pay, external salary data on the employment market, and pay claims submitted by the trade unions.

● *Communications*. The company will ensure that everyone understands where the company is going and how it is doing. It will encourage people to behave as if Powerco were their own company.

ACTIVITY BRIEF

Mindful of Powerco's dual strategy of shaping employee relations arrangements to the circumstances of its regulated distribution and supply business and its non-regulated businesses (in particular electrical appliance retailing):

1 Consider the policy choices facing managers in devising new arrangements for staff representation, including trade union recognition, bargaining and consultation arrangements and the role of workplace union representatives.

2 Consider how the company might take maximum benefit of the opportunity to carry out a major overhaul of pay and rewards. Attention should focus on the means by which pay systems and structures might be re-modelled and also the steps to be taken to link pay with measures of individual, team and business performance.

3 Consider how the company might amend its working time arrangements in order to respond to its goal of enhanced customer responsiveness and service quality.

RECOMMENDED READING

Armstrong, M and Murlis, H (1991) *Reward Management: A Handbook of Remuneration Strategy and Practice*, London, Kogan Page.

Blyton, P (1994) 'Working hours', in Sisson, K (ed) *Personnel Management* (2nd edn), Oxford, Blackwell, pp 95–126.

Ferner, A and Colling, T (1993) 'Electricity Supply' in Pendleton, A and Winterton, J (eds) *Public Enterprise in Transition*, London, Routledge, pp 100–33.

Gall, G (1994) 'The rise of single table bargaining in Britain', *Employee Relations*, 16,1, pp 62–71.

Incomes Data Services (1990) *Profit Sharing and Share Options*, Study 468.

Incomes Data Services (1992) *Integrated Pay*, Study 509.

Kessler, I (1994) 'Performance Pay', in Sisson, K (ed) *op. cit.*

Marchington, M (1994) 'The Dynamics of Joint Consultation', in Sisson, K (ed) *op. cit.*

Storey, J and Sisson, K (1993) *Managing Human Resources and Industrial Relations*, Buckingham, Open University Press.

Managing employee relations in a local authority building works section

David Farnham and Lesley Giles

INTRODUCTION

This case focuses on the people management and employment relations issues typically confronting managers working in a local authority contracting services section in the 1990s – the building works section. The case explores the preparations undertaken by managers in one authority to meet the requirements of Compulsory Competitive Tendering (CCT) introduced by Conservative governments after 1980. This case provides an insight into how authorities are responding to the challenges of increasing competition and how they aim to secure contracts and achieve tendering success. The case focuses on the major human resources issues that authorities need to consider when preparing a tender. It explores the implications that a highly competitive tender can have upon the employment of local authority staff, their unions, jobs and terms and conditions. In evaluating the human resources issues and their likely implications, the case considers the roles of key individuals in the people management process, such as line managers, personnel managers and trade union officials. The case also discusses the formal personnel and employment practices and mechanisms involved in the people management process, such as the employee communications system.

BACKGROUND TO THE CASE

Local government

Local government is responsible for the provision of a wide range of public services to the community, including education, housing, social services, personal health services, leisure, environmental health, fire services and, until 1995, police services. These services are provided through democratically elected local authorities. The emerging local government structure in England, which is currently being reformed, is a hybrid one consisting mainly of unitary authorities in the larger urban areas and county and district authorities in the rural areas.

The duties and powers of local government are discharged through Acts of Parliament.

Although the precise administration and interpretation of the use of these statutory powers may vary from one local authority to another, all authorities broadly operate in the same fashion. Hence, council business is commonly conducted through a series of council meetings, committees and subcommittees, comprising elected council members. In practice much of the day-to-day management and policy implementation is undertaken by permanent salaried chief officers or 'directors' and other officers. Many of these officers advise the elected councillors and, therefore, are usually highly qualified, professional people, who are specialists in the particular departments and committees within which they work. Chief officers generally head council departments. The principal chief officer responsible for managing and co-ordinating the activities of all council employees is usually the Chief Executive. A typical local government committee and departmental structure is shown in Fig. 23.1.

(a)

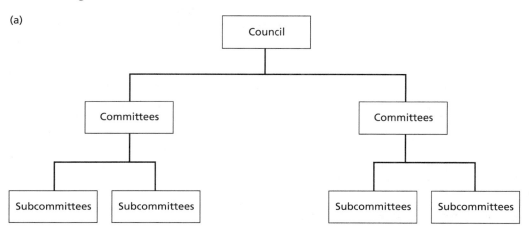

(b)

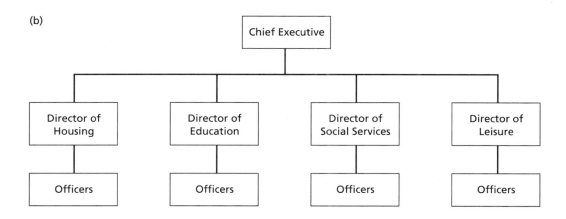

Fig 23.1 Organisational chart of typical local authority: (a) committee structure; (b) departmental structure

With origins in the nineteenth century, local government has experienced a long evolution and, for some considerable time, has enjoyed an effective monopoly as the primary service provider in the community. With few checks traditionally on local government expenditure and the effectiveness of service provision, local authorities, particularly through much of the post-war period, had a relatively free rein to expand and develop services as they saw fit. In recent years, however, especially after the Conservatives came to office in 1979, traditional systems of local government have come under growing constraint. Local authorities have been increasingly criticised for having high spending commitments, providing inadequate services and being largely inefficient bureaucracies, with little or no regard for their consumers in the community (Mallabar 1991, Elcock 1993, White and Hutchinson 1996).

As a consequence, throughout the 1980s, local government was subject to greater central intervention and extensive reform imposed by successive Conservative governments. These reforms reflected wider public-service policies, centred on the belief that private-sector management techniques, commercial criteria and market competition are the key to more efficient and effective public services. In line with other public-sector organisations, local government has been exposed to privatisation, decentralisation, deregulation, market testing and CCT. These have been aimed at increasing competition, securing tighter controls over public expenditure, enhancing value for money, improving the overall quality of public-service provision and, in so doing, meeting and being more responsive to the needs of consumers in the community. Such programmes have had a considerable effect on the functions of local authorities, their organisation, administration and management – not least their people management. CCT has been considered to be one of the most radical of these 'market-based' programmes (Elcock 1993).

Compulsory Competitive Tendering

The Conservative government first introduced Competitive Tendering (CT) into local government through the Local Government Planning and Land Act 1980. CT is the process whereby local authorities are empowered to put out to tender and hence to invite outside contractors to compete for services that they had provided directly. These services were traditionally referred to as in-house services or Direct Labour Organisations (DLOs). Under this Act, CT was largely voluntary. Initially, therefore, authorities could choose whether they wanted to put services out to tender. Building works and highway maintenance, where CT was made compulsory, was the one exception to this. Through the 1980s take-up was not as extensive amongst authorities as government would have liked, however, and as a result CCT was extended to other manual services, under the Local Government Act 1988. These included refuse collection, cleaning of buildings and other cleaning, catering, ground maintenance, repair and vehicle maintenance, and leisure. In 1992, CCT was also applied to professional and technical services such as IT, legal and financial services and personnel. Making CT compulsory has meant that it has become unlawful for authorities to use DLOs in certain designated services, unless the specified areas of work are won in competition, usually with private sector firms. In-house workforces, awarded services through open competition, have generally become known as Direct Service Organisations (DSOs).

CCT has been phased in since 1989, with specified minimum and maximum contract periods, ranging from three to seven years. Different authorities may, therefore, have the various services they provide at different stages in the tendering process. Under the CCT guidelines produced by government, authorities should only award contracts for manual services and most professional services on the basis of commercial criteria. Hence, contracts should always be allotted to the lowest tender and, unless in exceptional circumstances, they cannot usually be refused or terminated solely on the basis of, for instance, health and safety, race relations, sex discrimination or general employment matters. Authorities can only override the lowest tender for professional services, where it can be shown the tender does not provide the necessary technical or specialist expertise required. Authorities have gained an important function in defining the exact level and quality of the services to be provided, usually known as the 'client' function. In the monitoring and evaluation of service performance, authorities have had to draw up detailed specifications for each area of work. It remains difficult to refuse a tender on the basis of quality alone, however, especially if the tender is commercially competitive.

CCT has, therefore, had dramatic consequences. It has made it harder for authorities to promote non-financial objectives or to shield inefficient DLOs. Authorities, now permanently exposed to competition, have been forced to restructure and reorganise their services and are increasingly having to manage their operations on a more commercial, cost-conscious basis. This has put local authority managers under increasing pressure. Authorities were initially quite successful at winning contracts, with 75 per cent awarded nationally to authorities in the first round of tenders in 1989 (Elcock 1993). As government has continued to enhance competition and to favour private-sector contractors in the tendering process, however, there has been a general decrease in successful tenders among DSOs (LGMB 1993, Elcock 1993). For example, in 1989 cleaning DSOs won 56.3 per cent of contracts. By 1993 this had reduced to 18.2 per cent. Likewise grounds maintenance won 73.1 per cent of contracts in 1989 but by 1993 this had reduced to only 3.3 per cent. As more contracts are lost, a lot of DSOs have been forced to close. This has led to major reductions in staffing and extensive manpower streamlining programmes, involving redundancies, retirement, staff redeployment and retraining. As local government is one of the largest areas of public-sector employment, providing work for some 2.6 million people, the cost of labour has become a major consideration in local government planning and administration. CCT has thus had vital implications for the management of human resources. Authorities have been required to develop and reform their human resources strategies and to deploy their labour more economically, flexibly and efficiently.

The Council

Seaview City Council (SCC), which was formerly a non-metropolitan district council in the south of England, is now a unitary authority covering a geographical area of approximately 20 square miles and representing just over 200,000 inhabitants. It has been Labour-controlled since the early 1980s. Important council business is conducted by 45 councillors, representing 15 wards. Elections are held over a four-year cycle, with 15 elected council members retiring each year. Since 1980, SCC, like all other authorities, has had to meet the challenge of CCT.

Shortly after CCT legislation was introduced in 1980, SCC reorganised its internal departmental structure to form 'directorates': technical services, leisure and tourism, personnel and management services, finance, central services, housing services, and contracting services. Each of these became headed by a 'director', whose principal function was to ensure the efficient running of the directorate for which he or she was responsible, as well as to advise councillors on specific directorate business. The directorate of contracting services (DCS) became the new DSO, responsible for all services put out to tender. At the time of its creation a new internal system of 'service level agreements' was also set up. This system was established between the DCS and other directorates and required each directorate to cost and develop formal agreements for the internal services provided to the DCS.

The Council was determined, through the development of the DCS, to sustain all the services it had always provided, defend jobs and develop a more efficient, cost-effective approach to CCT, which would enable it to outsmart its competitors, meet increasing operational pressures and ultimately achieve tendering success, while preserving high service standards. Reforms had to be carefully planned and implemented within a tight time scale if these objectives were to be achieved; legislation was to be complied with and contracts for all tendered services were to be developed on time. Most importantly, the authority had to ensure it won contracts 'fairly' and avoided at all costs any 'anti-competitive' behaviour, which could threaten the success of the tendering process and, hence, the employment security of the DCS workforce. Such behaviour, being unlawful, was known, at best, to stimulate external investigations of the in-house tender by the Department of the Environment, signified with the issuing of a Section 13 Notice, and, at worst, to result in the withdrawal of the contract – marked by a Section 14 Notice.

The DCS currently employs approximately 1000 people and in 1994–5 it had an annual turnover of £25 million. It comprises six operational sections: building works, highways services, refuse services, horticultural services, cleaning services, and catering services. The Director of DCS is assisted by three deputies: the Assistant Director of Finance and two Assistant Directors for Operations. The day-to-day management of each of these sections is delegated from the Assistant Director to a section manager (*see* Fig. 23.2). The DCS has achieved much success in the tendering process over the last five years, securing 85 per cent of its contracts. However, the present Director of DCS, Richard Sandell, has recently become concerned about the problems presented by the forthcoming tendering process, particularly within the building works section (BWS), and has been monitoring developments there closely.

THE SITUATION

The building works section

The BWS is essentially responsible for undertaking repairs to council homes and providing a general building and mechanical maintenance service to the Council, local housing associations and other directorates within the authority. Since CCT legislation was introduced in 1989, the BWS has been forced to put out to tender the day-to-day maintenance of over 22,000 council houses in 11 housing areas. In the first two rounds of tenders, the section was quite successful, losing only two of the 11 areas to private contractors. For the past six years, it has therefore been able to operate without any major structural reorganisation in nine of the housing areas and to avoid the need for staff streamlining and redundancy. In recent years, however, the BWS's economic position has been growing more insecure.

In an ever-more competitive environment and a period of serious recession in the building industry, private contractors have increasingly looked to local government service contracts as an attractive source of guaranteed income. Many private-sector firms in the area have worked hard to develop their building operations and, in particular, to exploit all available opportunities in contracting work. Richard Sandell is only too aware of the recent success of local firms and the extent of the challenge they now present to the authority's building works' team. He hopes that William Smith, the current BWS general manager, headhunted twelve months ago from a large private-sector contractor, can help the BWS secure future contracts and thus protect jobs. William is an ambitious, well qualified individual, with an impressive track record in the building trade and Richard believes he has the necessary experience and expertise in building contract work to raise the section's performance to meet the growing intensity of local competition.

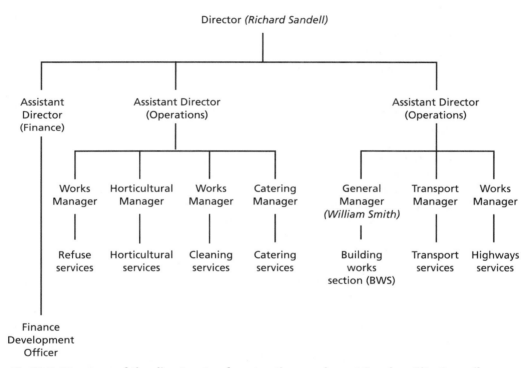

Fig 23.2 Structure of the directorate of contracting services at Seaview City Council

Over the past year, since his appointment as head of the BWS, William has worked very hard to enhance section productivity, develop the skills and competences of his management team and establish a competitive tendering strategy, which can secure future tendering success. Detailed research has been necessary to establish current cost levels, in-depth market knowledge and undertake cost comparisons of service provision, based on regional competitors' rates and local market conditions. To enhance the tendering process in the BWS, William has organised training for his management team and has called upon the expertise of local management consultants, specialising in tendering assessments. He and his colleagues have also attended Institute of Building Works and Maintenance Conferences, where they have been able to consult with other DSO managers. Complex computer-based modelling has been employed to develop overall financial projections for the BWS and to assess the impact of varying tender strategies upon financial performance and profitability. Throughout the whole process, regular meetings have been called of the section's management team to cross-check information, review progress and discuss the development of the strategic business plan.

With the market rate largely fixed by local economic factors, the main emphasis of the BWS management team has been tightening expenditure, increasing efficiency and identifying ways of reducing costs, while retaining a high service quality. Cost management has focused on two broad areas: direct costs and overhead costs. Direct costs include materials, vehicles and labour; overheads include the costs of computing, administration, finance and other personnel. In the past year, all section procedures and practices have been subjected to considerable scrutiny and the management team has implemented modifications in operations to cut costs. With the cost of the workforce consuming some 70 per cent of the section's entire expenditure, managing labour costs, in particular, has attracted considerable attention.

Over the past few months, William has explored cost reduction options with the authority's long-serving Personnel Manager, Jack Magee, who is based in the directorate of personnel and management services, and discussed a number of key personnel considerations. Jack has grown concerned about William's rather dictatorial approach to people management within the BWS and the implications this may have for the future tendering process. Although recognising that William's hard line and ruthless attitude have been essential to his general business success, Jack has sensed that such an authoritarian manner has been less effective in William's dealings with the workforce.

Jack Magee has worked for SCC for over 20 years and has accumulated invaluable expertise as a local government personnel professional. He knows the local authority has for some considerable time been committed to a 'model' employer approach to people management and industrial relations and that this has given rise to very specific personnel policies and employment practices. These policies have essentially been paternalist, welfare-centred and collectivist. The authority has traditionally accepted union recognition and employee consultation and espoused collective bargaining as the best method of regulating employee relations. The BWS, in line with all the authority's services, has subsequently experienced a long history of good management–union relations. These have largely been free from industrial conflict and labour unrest and management has adhered to collective agreements, negotiated nationally by local authority employers and the unions in the Whitley Council. Jack strongly believes the authority's model employer personnel practices, seeking employee co-operation and rooted in employee welfare and employment security, are the key to a competent highly motivated workforce and this, in turn, is the key to high productivity and consistent, high quality service provision. Indeed, this participative approach to people management has been espoused by national bodies, such as the Institute of Personnel Management (now Development) (1988) and the Local Government Training Board (1988) in their early CCT management guidelines. He therefore feels it is wrong to value employees purely in cost terms, as William seems to be doing.

Despite the considerable changes in local authority control and management in recent years, Jack has worked hard to sustain traditional participative employment practices and to maintain good relations with all trade union representatives, where union density is over 80 per cent of the workforce. In the BWS, in particular, he has developed a long association with representatives from all the main manual unions, including Michael Main, the shop steward from the Transport and General Workers' Union (TGWU), Fred Clay, from the Union of Construction, Allied Trades and Technicians (UCATT) and George

Bradley, the steward representing members of the Amalgamated Engineering and Electrical Union (AEEU). All the shop stewards, having held their posts for some time, have served their members effectively and are well versed in local employment practices and union matters. Furthermore, they are all deeply committed to their union roles and securing the best terms and conditions for their members. They have, therefore, appreciated the good working relations they have developed with Jack and their employers, under the model employer approach within the authority.

Jack has found it increasingly difficult to maintain this level of involvement with the union representatives, however, and to sustain a consensus approach to industrial relations. The situation has been aggravated by William's management style. Indeed, for the most part, William and his management team have largely chosen to bypass traditional employment mechanisms and communication channels. Although William is aware that the prospect of CCT is threatening to employees, who fear job losses and redundancy, he has done little to communicate with shop stewards and staff to inform them of the stage-by-stage developments and to allay their concerns. Apart from a few mass meetings with the workforce, the odd employee circular and basic 'briefing' sessions with the union representatives, William appears to have been more intent on taking management decisions in secrecy, with limited direct consultation with the unions, section employees or indeed the personnel department. William has stated that detailed staff consultation is being delayed, until the final stages of the tendering process, to conceal the finer details of the bid from competitors. This has been of little reassurance however, and has only served to foster a growing scepticism and resentment amongst the workforce, especially amongst the union representatives – Michael Main, Fred Clay and George Bradley – who have begun to distrust the motives behind managerial behaviour. Recently, Jack has heard rumours that union representatives are exploring the possibility of balloting their members for industrial action. He knows at best such activity will disrupt working relations and threaten service provision and, at worst, will greatly hamper the tendering process and the future of the BWS. Sensing growing disaffection among the workforce, Jack has encouraged William to hold a series of union–management meetings, in an attempt to resolve the situation. William is using this forum to present his human resources proposals.

The human resources plan

In consultation with the BWS management team, William has developed a human resources (HR) plan. In this plan he has identified what he considers are the key human resources strategy areas and the actions necessary to achieve the required cost reductions for tendering success. The key areas proposed are workforce reduction and terms and conditions of employment.

Workforce reduction

Workforce reduction has been seen as a necessary component of the new human resources strategy. It is believed the efficiency and effectiveness of human resources management can be greatly enhanced in this area through four mechanisms.

1 *A workforce analysis.* This is proposed in the BWS, involving the systematic collection and analysis of detailed employee information. As well as collecting general information, including workforce numbers, labour turnover, length of service and age profiles, such an analysis will establish employee preferences, skills and experience. This information will form the basis of all subsequent mechanisms working to reduce the labour force.

2 *Recruitment controls.* These will be introduced to ensure vacancies are managed more efficiently and equitably. These new controls will mean that in future all BWS vacancies will be processed through a central panel consisting of unions, personnel and equal opportunities officers. Having taken local factors into consideration, the panel will collectively decide whether vacancies should be advertised, frozen or filled through internal redeployment. Every effort will be taken to consider the best options for existing employees.

3 *Redeployment and retraining opportunities.* These will be actively pursued to provide job opportunities for those 'surplus' employees to avoid, as far as possible, the necessity for redundancy and staff streamlining. This may, where appropriate and feasible, involve redeploying staff to another service within the DCS. Retraining programmes will be developed for employees redeployed to areas requiring new skills, wherever appropriate.

4 *Early retirement and redundancy.* Redundancies seem increasingly likely, although the main intention of the BWS has always been to avoid them as far as possible. With stringent economic conditions, however, this can no longer be guaranteed. Where 'surplus' employees cannot be redeployed/retrained, redundancy may be necessary. Redundancies will commence on a voluntary redundancy/early retirement basis and progress to compulsory redundancies as and when appropriate.

The BWS management team has carefully reviewed and scrutinised existing workforce statistics and information to identify where cost savings can be made. At the present time, it feels opportunities for redeployment and retraining are limited. On this basis it is proposed there is a need for at least a 10 per cent reduction in the workforce.

Terms and conditions of employment

Although the BWS wishes to continue implementing national conditions of service, certain local conditions will have to be amended. Similarly it is deemed necessary to make certain amendments in pay. It is felt these modifications will serve to greatly enhance efficiency and worker productivity. The following amendments are proposed:

● terminating pay for the first three days' sick;
● increasing hours by 10 per cent;
● reducing holidays by one week;
● reducing pay for holidays to basic rate;
● terminating overtime bonuses;
● restraining basic pay at its 1995–6 level.

In response to these human resources proposals, a meeting has been convened among the union representatives and officials to discuss the management team's human resources strategy and to consider their implications for staff. The union representatives, having strong reservations themselves, are aware the proposals in their present form are unlikely to win the support of the workforce and need to be renegotiated. With the tender deadline approaching, they appreciate the need to act quickly and work hard if they are to save jobs, resist what they see as moves to work intensification and negotiate a more acceptable package for their members.

ACTIVITY BRIEF

1 Critically evaluate William's human resources plan. In your evaluation, assess the full implications of all the proposals and consider possible alternatives.

2 What do you understand by the 'model' employer approach to people management practised at this local authority and more widely in the public services? What are the features of the 'new model' employer approach now emerging in local government and the public services in association with government reforms since 1979? Compare and contrast the two approaches.

3 Develop a negotiating strategy on behalf of the management team, which you can employ in future meetings with the union representatives.

4 Identify the issues and processes that might be involved in a workforce analysis.

5 What do you think will be the likely outcome of this negotiation process? In other words, how do you think the situation could be resolved in the BWS?

RECOMMENDED READING

Elcock, H (1993) 'Local government', in Farnham, D and Horton, S *Managing the New Public Services*, Basingstoke, Macmillan.

Farnham, D and Giles, L (1996) 'Human resources management and employee relations', in Farnham, D and Horton, S *Managing the New Public Services* (2nd edn), Basingstoke, Macmillan.

Farnham, D and Horton, S (1996) 'Traditional people management,' in Farnham, D and Horton S *Managing People in the Public Services*, Basingstoke, Macmillan.

Farnham, D and Horton, S (1996) 'Towards a new people management?' in Farnham, D and Horton, S *Managing People in the Public Services*, Basingstoke, Macmillan.

Fredman, S and Morris, G (1989) *The State as Employer*, London, Mansell.

Institute of Personnel Management and Income Data Services (1988) *Competitive Tendering in the Public Sector* (rev. edn), London, IPM.

Local Government Management Board (1993) *Compulsory Competitive Tendering Information Service, Survey Report No. 8*, Dec.

Local Government Training Board (1988) *Competition and Contracting Out: Issues for Local Government*, London, LGTB.

Mallabar, N (1991) *Local Government Administration in a Time of Change*, Sunderland, Business Education Publishers.

White, G and Hutchinson, B (1996) 'Local government', in Farnham, D and Horton, S *Managing People in the Public Services*, Basingstoke, Macmillan.

Establishing a pay regime in an NHS trust: prescribing the treatment

Susan Corby

INTRODUCTION

This case concerns local determination of pay in a National Health Service trust. At the outset the trust has to decide what machinery to adopt for local pay determination. This covers the method of pay determination – for example, by collective bargaining or unilaterally by management. It raises union recognition issues as well as issues surrounding the format/constitutions of pay determining bodies – that is, a single table or multi-tables. These choices in turn have implications for the remuneration system to be adopted – that is, a single pay spine or different pay arrangements for different staff groups. In addition, strategic choices have to be made about procedures for handling conflict and about the basis of the pay regime – for example, whether it is based on competences or job evaluation – and finally, whether performance is rewarded and, if so, whether it is on an individual, group or organisation basis.

BACKGROUND TO THE CASE

Under the National Health Service and Community Care Act 1990, the government introduced proxies for the market – that is, an internal market – into the NHS. Thus it separated the purchasing of healthcare from its provision and enabled NHS trusts to be formed from the units providing healthcare. These trusts, in line with the government's drive to devolve power away from the centre, were given some autonomy on financial matters and considerable autonomy on personnel matters, including the freedom to set their own terms and conditions.

Nevertheless, trusts' theoretical autonomy on personnel matters is constrained in practice in three main ways.

1 It is constrained by political initiatives, as the government is the paymaster. Currently the government is encouraging trusts to determine their own pay and grading systems. Accordingly, with varying degrees of enthusiasm and at different speeds, trusts are moving towards fully fledged local pay regimes.

2 Trusts' new-found autonomy on personnel matters is limited in practice by the collectivist and pluralist traditions dating back to the NHS's inception. There are over 20

staff organisations which have certificates of independence and are recognised nationally and they can essentially be divided into two categories: trade unions and professional associations. Trade unions in the NHS recruit from both inside and outside healthcare and are all affiliated to the TUC. The professional associations, in contrast, are specific to the health sector and are rarely TUC affiliates. The largest TUC affiliate is Unison and the largest non-TUC affiliate is the Royal College of Nursing. Union density in the NHS as a whole is just over 60 per cent (Bird and Corcoran 1994).

All the staff organisations are in favour of the NHS's well embedded national pay determination arrangements under which terms and conditions for each functional group are set in one of two ways. Over half the NHS staff, namely doctors and dentists, nurses, midwives and health visitors and professions allied to medicine have their pay determined by government on recommendations of pay review bodies with their other terms and conditions determined by collective bargaining in the joint, so-called Whitley, machinery. Nearly all the remaining staff – for example, administrative and clerical workers, ancillaries, scientists, ambulance staff – have *all* their terms and conditions determined in the Whitley system. The main exceptions to any national arrangements are general and senior managers and healthcare assistants (Seifert 1992).

3 Trusts' autonomy on personnel matters is constrained by the Transfer of Undertakings (Protection of Employment) Regulations 1981 – the so-called TUPE Regulations. Under its provisions staff, previously employed by the district health authority but working in a hospital which has become a trust, can continue to receive nationally negotiated terms and conditions and/or pay rates arising from pay review body awards for as long as they choose to do so, provided they stay in the same job and are not promoted.

NETHERDENE HOSPITAL NHS TRUST

Netherdene Hospital became an NHS trust in April 1993. It is a general acute unit on one site with a turnover of £100 million. So far it has met its three financial duties: it has made a rate of return of 6 per cent on net assets; it has stayed within the external financing limit set by the Department of Health; and it has broken even on income and expenditure. It has 4200 employees of whom 1680 nursing staff form the biggest group (40 per cent). Administrative and clerical staff comprise 15 per cent of Netherdene's employees, as do support staff, while at the top of the hierarchy, medical staff comprise 9 per cent and managers 2.5 per cent. Situated in the north-west of England, labour turnover is relatively low. It varies by staff group: 10 per cent for ancillary staff and 5 per cent for nurses. There are 12 unions active in the trust. These are:

Amalgamated Engineering and Electrical Union (AEEU)
British Association of Occupational Therapists (BAOT)
British Dental Association (BDA)
British Dietetic Association
British Medical Association (BMA)
Chartered Society of Physiotherapy (CSP)
Manufacturing Science and Finance Union (MSF)
Royal College of Midwives (RCM)
Royal College of Nursing (RCN)

Society of Radiographers
Unison
Union of Construction, Allied Trades and Technicians (UCATT)

Union density overall is 65 per cent, slightly above the NHS average, but there are variations by occupational group. For instance, 80 per cent of nurses are unionised but only 50 per cent of administrative and clerical staff.

The Personnel Director, Rose Evans, is worried about the cost implications of local pay determination – both the developmental costs and the costs of introduction – as there will have to be provisions for staff to be assimilated and their old pay protected for a period, especially if they are going to be persuaded to give up their rights under the TUPE Regulations. She knows her concerns about costs are shared by the Finance Director. She also believes that introducing a fully fledged pay system is time consuming. She considers that her energies could be better spent on skill mix changes and increasing the ratio of support staff to professionals. This could include, for instance, developing new jobs such as ward assistants, to combine domestic and portering duties, and assistants for paramedical staff, and would help to reduce the cost of the hospital's paybill. Furthermore, she has picked up mixed messages from the NHS Executive about the importance of local pay bargaining. On the one hand its HR Director emphasises that the paybill, which amounts to some 70 per cent of a trust's costs, must be directly controlled by the trust. On the other hand, trust personnel directors have been warned not to rock the boat or antagonise the staff organisations, who all support the national arrangements.

Rose knows her scepticism about local pay is privately shared by the Chief Executive, Peter Hughes. Yet publicly, Peter Hughes agrees with the Chairman of Netherdene's Board, Sir Adrian Greenhow, and the non-executive directors. They adopt the government's view that the trust should make every effort quickly to develop its own pay regime, tailored to its needs and business strategy and reflecting the local labour market.

THE MACHINERY FOR DETERMINING A LOCAL PAY REGIME

Union recognition?

Before Netherdene became a trust it consulted with all its unions through a joint staff consultative committee and recognised them for the purpose of representing individuals in discipline and grievance cases. In addition, it sometimes negotiated with them on minor matters, such as shift systems or ancillaries' bonuses. Withdrawing union recognition, or recognising the unions only for consultation, not negotiation, on pay has advantages. It gives management a free hand in determining the reward framework and underlines the message that remuneration is determined by management. Consultation is also generally quicker than negotiation as an agreement may at best be difficult, and at worst impossible, to achieve. Indeed the Personnel Director of South Tees Acute Hospital justified consultation on the grounds that agreement of all the unions involved 'would have been extremely difficult to achieve' (*Personnel Management* 1994). Rose Evans, however, would ideally prefer a less confrontational approach. She wants to try and achieve employee ownership of a new pay regime and believes the involvement of staff representatives in negotiation could be helpful in securing employees' acceptance. Her view is supported by her Chief Executive.

A single table?

While she would prefer to recognise all the unions for collective bargaining purposes, the format or constitution for pay bargaining is far more problematic. Essentially she is unsure whether to opt for single-table bargaining – that is, all the occupational groups together – or for bargaining separately for each occupational group – that is, multi-table bargaining. Trusts that have opted for single-table bargaining have in the main chosen what has been termed a 'prime union' system. They have recognised all the unions for collective bargaining but specified a small number of seats (typically eight) on the main negotiating executive. Thus not all the recognised staff organisations are at the main bargaining table. Such a system establishes a simplified bargaining structure, an important consideration in view of the multiplicity of unions in the NHS; there are 12 at Netherdene, for instance. Managers, have in the main left it entirely to the unions to determine among themselves who should fill the seats and thus have the key negotiating roles, however, and to sort out the mandating and reporting back arrangements. This saves managers from the opprobrium of decisions which are unlikely to please all the staff organisations. Yet managers' freedom to negotiate with an organisation which is not at the single table about a discrete group of staff is preserved. Moreover, as all the unions are recognised, none can complain. A single table, whether or not there is a 'prime union' system, also brings other advantages. It saves management time, as there is only one set of pay negotiations and helps in the harmonisation of terms and conditions, which under the national arrangements vary widely – for instance, hours range from 35 to 39. Furthermore, it ensures that staff representatives are aware of each other's agendas.

Nevertheless, a single-table bargaining system is not problem free. Unison represents ancillaries, clerical and administrative staff and nurses at Netherdene. It could stake a claim to several seats and then, possibly, it would dominate. Conversely, there is a danger that a vociferous, but small union may hog the agenda. Some 120 of Netherdene's nursing staff are midwives, who are in the RCM. Their steward, Anne Jones, is experienced and capable.

Moreover, the corollary of single-table bargaining is a single pay spine going from cleaner to consultant. This is a marked departure from the national arrangements, whereby terms and conditions are determined on the basis of functional groups. On the one hand, it can signal a culture change and an orientation to the trust. On the other hand, a single pay spine in a complex organisation, such as a general acute unit, is bound to be complex and it may be difficult to obtain agreement on a deal which is suitable for all staff. A single pay spine also tends to be inflexible in that it is difficult (although not impossible) for management to give special treatment to a group of staff who are difficult to recruit. There is also a risk with single-table bargaining that a powerful union, such as Unison, could negotiate a relatively large pay uplift, dragging weaker unions, such as the CSP, along on its coat tails. Moreover, often harmonisation is expensive, as there is pressure to harmonise to the level of the highest.

Rose Evans is aware that some trusts argue that bargaining on a multi-table basis – that is, by occupational group – represents an option that may be more acceptable to the staff organisations because it is closer to the national arrangements. It represents a less dramatic break with tradition, even though a trust might amalgamate some of the groups that are separate under the national arrangements – for example, pharmacists and radiographers. She is also aware that an occupational group system may be easier to introduce piece by piece, as it would enable the trust to tackle groups in isolation, one by one, leaving the powerful doctors until the last. For instance several trusts have set up a new pay system already for nurses and midwives only. Another practical consideration is that a multi-table system makes comparability by unions between different groups of staff harder.

The big drawback with such a system, however, is that it fails to encourage flexibility between groups. Strict job demarcations – for example, between nurses and doctors or between nurses and ancillary staff – have been a hallmark of the NHS. They are not conducive to the most efficient use of staff and skill mix changes. Finally, multi-table bargaining is expensive in terms of management time as there are various sets of negotiations. Furthermore, Netherdene will probably still need a trust-wide joint body, to deal with matters of common concern – for instance, job sharing or pensions.

Procedures for handling conflict

Whether Netherdene adopts a single table or multi-tables, thought has to be given to procedures for handling failure to agree. One option is for nothing to be agreed in this area. Accordingly, management has a free hand and can decide how to play it in the circumstances prevailing at the time. It could either force through its proposals without consent, set up a working party to explore other steps or ask ACAS to conciliate. (Conciliation is where a third party talks to both sides, separately or together, and tries to get them to identify common ground and reach a solution.) Leaving the mode of conflict handling to be determined at the time, however, is unlikely to be attractive to the unions. At best, it can lead to uncertainty and, at worst, exacerbate the conflict over the substantive matters at issue.

Alternatively, conciliation by ACAS could be written into the negotiating procedure, or even mediation by ACAS. Under mediation the conciliator plays a more active role and suggests proposals. Another option is for the procedure to provide for both conciliation and arbitration. The latter is morally (but not legally) binding on the parties and, in practice, obviates industrial action as the dispute is settled by a third party who determines an issue on which the parties are unable to agree. This is obviously an advantage and it also enables both management and/or the unions to save face, if the award is unpalatable, because they did not freely enter into an agreement on the terms awarded. This could foster good industrial relations. On the other hand, the disadvantage is that the matter is determined by a third party. Hospital managers have long complained of pay decisions being taken by those who do not have to implement them (Warlow 1989), and, unlike conciliation or mediation, the decision no longer remains in the hands of the parties. Thus, for instance, there is a danger that an arbitrator might make a pay award that the trust could not afford. Even if the procedure specifies that arbitration cannot be entered into unless management and unions jointly agree on a reference, this is hardly a protection. If management repeatedly prevents the unions making a reference to arbitration, this in itself can provide a source of conflict. Furthermore, as most staff perceive arbitration as a fair way to resolve differences, blocking a reference might cut away the moral ground from management's position.

If arbitration is the preferred option, a decision has to be made whether it should be of a pendulum or conventional kind. Generally with conventional arbitration, the arbitrator tends to suggest a compromise between the positions of the two parties. With pendulum arbitration, however, the arbitrator chooses between the final positions on offer from each side. Because of the all-or-nothing nature of the solution, pendulum arbitration tends to encourage the parties to adopt more moderate positions. Fearing that they may lose, the parties only choose it as a last resort, whereas they may resort more frequently to conventional arbitration which often gives something to both parties. The arbitrator has no flexibility in pendulum arbitration, however, and as a result awards may not necessarily stand the test of fairness or improve industrial relations in the longer term.

THE BASIS OF THE LOCAL PAY REGIME

Job evaluation?

Job evaluation is a system for comparing jobs. It can range from simply ranking jobs in order of importance through to analysing jobs against factors such as the amount of decision making involved. These so-called analytical job evaluation schemes can be used to compare dissimilar jobs within an organisation.

Job evaluation has several potential advantages. It can provide the basis for a unified trust-wide pay structure which is accepted as fair by employees, particularly if the more rigorous analytical approach is adopted. It is particularly useful where a single pay spine is being introduced as it provides a system for locating widely different jobs. An analytical job evaluation scheme can provide a block to a claim to an industrial tribunal for equal pay for work of equal value. Furthermore, a job evaluation scheme can be ready made, with consultants, such as Hay, able to provide a system.

Nonetheless, there are a number of drawbacks. It costs money. Consultants are expensive but so is doing it in-house. Indeed one general acute trust is said to have spent £100,000 developing a bespoke job-evaluated pay regime for nurses. There are other drawbacks in job evaluation, however. It can lead to considerable upheaval and staff may be suspicious of the trust's motives in job evaluation, particularly if long standing differentials are altered. If disputes are to be avoided, Rose Evans considers it will be vital to communicate effectively and to involve staff representatives. Moreover, job evaluation, if it is systematic, can result in much paperwork. It also serves to emphasise hierarchy (some jobs are more important than others) and reinforces the traditional view that the only way to bigger and better remunerated jobs is by climbing the structural hierarchy.

Of course, Netherdene could move away from job-based pay towards person-based pay, including rewarding people according to their competences. The unions, however, are unlikely to welcome judgements without the benefit of any form of job analysis.

Performance-related pay

Performance-related pay is the explicit link of financial reward to individual, group or company performance. The NHS Executive is strongly encouraging trusts to adopt a performance pay system of some kind and has held workshops on performance pay and given some trusts (but not Netherdene) money for pilot schemes.

Individual performance-related pay (IPRP) is based on some form of appraisal of the job holder measured against inputs (traits, skills, competences) and/or outputs (objectives) and can take a number of forms, such as progression up a pay structure with additional increments for high performers, or an annual lump sum, whether consolidated into basic pay or not. In the UK as a whole (Kessler 1994, p 473), there is evidence of its growing popularity. In the NHS, IPRP is common among senior managers and among ancillaries, whose traditional output-based bonus schemes have been replaced by qualitative measures

(Health Service Report 1994). It is not common for most NHS staff, however.

Its proponents argue that it is a mechanism whereby the organisation's priorities and strategic objectives can be directly linked to the way the employee does his or her job. Many managers may see this as a more logical approach than linking pay to seniority. IPRP also has the advantage that at least part of pay is seen as dependent on management action, not agreement with the unions.

Nonetheless, IPRP has its critics. They argue that it is difficult to make sufficiently objective judgements about performance. Performance assessments will always be subjective to a degree, especially in non-profit organisations like the NHS and not all managers, even with training, are adept at appraising staff. IPRP can be an expensive option, both administratively and because it can lead to salary drift. Especially if the amount earmarked for performance pay is small, far from increasing commitment, it can be a demotivator. Indeed the evidence that IPRP increases commitment or improves organisational performance is equivocal.

In NHS terms, perhaps, the most serious charge is that IPRP can have a negative effect on co-operation and teamwork. One way round this is to limit IPRP to discrete groups of staff who do not work in teams – for instance, managers. Alternatively, a team-based approach to performance pay could be adopted or even the linking of part of the reward package to the overall performance of the trust, either on the basis of a flat rate or on a percentage of salary. A trust-wide scheme, however, may do little to motivate the individual. Yet it avoids divisiveness, is relatively simple to measure and administer and introduces the notion that rewards are linked to performance. Moreover, whereas unions have campaigned against IPRP, they have not done so in respect of an organisation-based performance award.

Of course, any performance-related pay scheme, whether based on the individual, the group or the trust, is founded on the premises that money motivates and that good performance is not the norm. Arguably that is not a notion that Netherdene wishes to transmit. Rather it could reward individuals who make an outstanding contribution to corporate goals by training and personal development opportunities, not money.

Rose Evans realises that making these strategic decisions is only the first stage. She needs the endorsement of the Chief Executive and then, if that is obtained, she needs the approval of the Netherdene Board. Furthermore, once strategic decisions on the issues raised above have been taken, there are other, mainly operational decisions to be made.

ACTIVITY BRIEF

1 Prepare a report for the Chief Executive, outlining the machinery Netherdene should adopt for the negotiation of terms and conditions at trust level and the procedures for handling conflict. Give full reasons for your choices.

2 Will job evaluation (either job ranking or an analytical scheme) form a central part of the design of Netherdene's reward system? Give full reasons for your decision.

3 Consider the options open to management in respect of performance-related pay and decide which, if any, are most appropriate to Netherdene.

RECOMMENDED READING

Bird, D and Corcoran, L (1994) 'Trade union membership and density 1992–93', *Employment Gazette*, June, pp 189–97.

Corby, S (1992) 'Industrial relations developments in NHS trusts', *Employee Relations*, 14, 6, pp 33–44.

Health Service Report (1994) 'Ancillary and hotel service staff: a survey of 58 trusts', Summer, pp 1–8.

IRS Employment Trends (1993) 'Job evaluation in the 1990s', 546, Oct, pp 4–12.

IRS Employment Trends (1995) 'Single-table bargaining, an idea whose time has yet to come?', 577, Feb, pp 10–16.

Kessler, S (1987) 'The swings and roundabouts of pendulum arbitration', *Personnel Management*, Dec.

Kessler, I and Purcell, J (1992) 'Performance related pay: objectives and application', *Human Resource Management Journal*, 2, 3, pp 16–33.

Kessler, I (1994) 'Performance pay' in Sisson, K (ed) *Personnel Management*, Oxford, Blackwell.

Marsden, D and Richardson, R (1994) 'Performing for pay? The effects of "merit pay" on motivation in a public service', *British Journal of Industrial Relations*, 32, 2, pp 243–61.

Personnel Management (1994) 'Trust revamps pay and grading system', May, p 5.

Seifert, R (1992) *Industrial Relations in the NHS*, London, Chapman and Hall.

Warlow, D (1989) *Report of the Conditions of Employment of Staff in the National Health Service*, London, Department of Health.

Winchester, D and Bach, S (1995) 'The state: the public sector', in Edwards P (ed) *Industrial Relations: Theory and Practice in Britain*. Oxford, Blackwell, pp 304–34.

Formal communication and worker representation in a Japanese transplant

Rick Delbridge and Mike Noon

INTRODUCTION

This case will describe worker representation and the communication practices to be found in a Japanese-owned consumer electronics plant operating in the south of England. Japanese companies and their management practices have attracted considerable attention during the past decade or so. Certain Japanese companies have been seen as 'role models' for the West, although debates surrounding the extent, appropriateness and efficacy of the transfer of 'Japanese' management techniques and systems to the West have been extensive and highly varied in their conclusions (for example, Elger and Smith 1994, Oliver and Wilkinson 1992, Womack *et al* 1990). Proponents claim that Japanese management is technically more efficient and engenders greater worker commitment through offering greater participation and encouraging a 'shared destiny' between management and labour. Critics have argued that manufacturing techniques such as just-in-time (JIT) intensify work on the shopfloor while quality initiatives, such as suggestion schemes and group problem solving, allow management access to the tacit skills and knowledge of their workforce which weakens labour's position in the organisation.

This case is set in a Japanese manufacturing transplant and is based on actual events, characters and conversations witnessed by one of the authors during a period as a participant observer at the plant.

BACKGROUND TO THE CASE

Nippon CTV (UK) is owned by a large Japanese transnational corporation. The plant is the major manufacturing facility for this corporation in the United Kingdom and employs around 1000 people. The plant assembles coloured television sets, which involves three basic operations. *The machine shop* is the most capital-intensive process involving the computer-controlled automatic insertion of small components into printed circuit boards (PCBs). In contrast, *the panel shop* is highly labour intensive, involving the manual insertion of larger components and those too awkward for automatic insertion. In *final assembly*, the PCBs are assembled into the TV cabinet with the tube and other components. The finished TV sets are packed and held in a small finished goods area until they are despatched to the retail arm of the organisation.

Nippon CTV (UK) took over the sole operation of the facility 15 years ago, after a period of joint ownership with a European-owned consumer electronics company. Before Nippon CTV (UK) was established as the sole owner, the joint venture was shut down and the workforce of 3000 was laid off. The company selectively re-hired 300 employees and operations were consolidated at a considerably reduced level. The company committed itself to creating a new structure and style of work organisation, developing employee participation, and establishing a high quality reputation in order to compete in the increasingly competitive consumer electronics industry.

At this time, the plant was very much in the spotlight because it was one of the first major examples of Japanese foreign direct investment in the UK. Particular attention focused on the introduction of flexible teamworking and the requirements and expectations the company had of its union. The plant management, which was predominantly British, signed a single union deal to recognise the Electrical, Electronic, Telecommunication and Plumbing Union (EETPU), now the Amalgamated Engineering and Electrical Union (AEEU). This single union agreement was one of the first to be signed between newly investing companies and trade unions during the 1980s. The deal includes a no-strike agreement, a commitment to pendulum arbitration and single-status conditions including a common sickness scheme, company union, cafeteria and parking. Union membership at the plant is currently around 70 per cent of those eligible to join.

Over the past 15 years the organisation has been a successful, but small, part of its Japanese parent's expanding business. At Nippon CTV (UK) the workforce has more than trebled to 1000 employees and a second small plant has been established to assemble microwave ovens. The main plant now produces over half a million colour television sets a year and has been acclaimed by the Japanese owners as the most successful of its audio visual division's investments outside Japan.

The plant itself has the appearance of an orderly and modern manufacturing facility. It is clean and in good decorative order. There are notice boards, posters and numerous information points throughout the plant. The plant is large, well lit and reasonably spacious and is laid out along flow lines. Materials and work-in-progress are stored and transferred on wheeled trolleys around the separate parts of the main plant building which houses the automatic insertion shop, the panel shop, and the final assembly area (*see* Fig. 25.1).

The basic unit of organisational structure for the manufacturing areas is a team, run by a team leader with the support of senior members (*see* Fig. 25.2). The team leaders are in charge of all production-related activities on their line and they are also responsible for control and personnel issues. The senior members work off-line, but do not play a supervisory role. The teams are typically quite large; in the panel shop they will be the equivalent of one line which is often 40 people. The plant is run with very wide spans of control for its management; for example, the panel shop of around 400 people has a single manager responsible for all its activities and she is supported by one superintendent and the nine team leaders. As part of the single-status policy of the company, every employee is known as a 'member' and all members at the plant are expected to wear the uniform blue jacket, including management. The company has an 'open policy' and manufacturing team leaders and managers each have desks on the shopfloor, and so spend most of their time working close to operations. The rest of the indirect staff are situated in offices on the first floor of the main building. The majority of members on the shopfloor are women. In the panel shop, 90 per cent of the workers are women and this

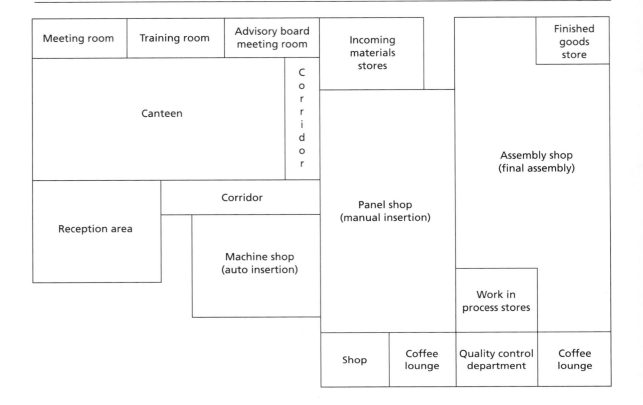

Fig 25.1 Plan of ground floor – Nippon CTV (UK)

includes all of the team leaders. Only one of the four senior production managers is a woman.

The plant is run in the archetypal Japanese manufacturing style. There is very little buffering of processes, with low inventories on the shopfloor, tight time schedules for production and very little spare or 'float' labour. Quality is the key concern for the organisation and the plant has a highly sophisticated quality control and information system. The quality control department produces very detailed information on the previous day's production. In keeping with the individual accountability characteristic of total quality management, this information will pinpoint mistakes to individual members of a single line.

Many of the materials and components are bought in from overseas and consequently stocks are held. However, inside the plant there is very little inventory. There is less than one day's stock between the auto insertion and panel shops. Each main panel line in the panel shop supplies a single final assembly line. The buffer between these lines will be one-and-a-half day's or less. The inventory of panels is kept on trolleys in an area between the panel shop and the final assembly area and this makes the level of inventory very visible to managers and team leaders. The plant management seeks to maintain productivity by setting targets for output for each of the lines. The achievement of these productivity targets is the responsibility of the team leader. Each of the operators is paid on a straight time

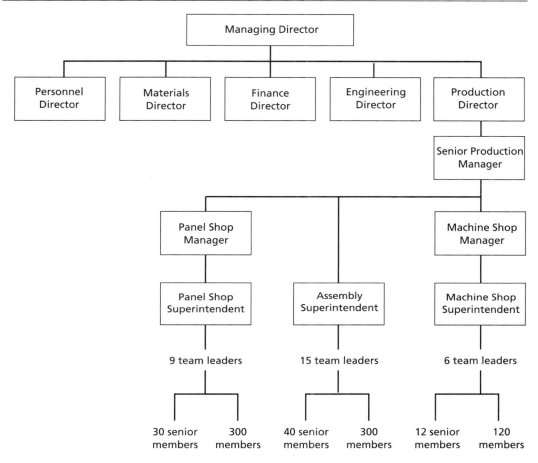

Fig 25.2 Organisational chart for Nippon CTV (UK)

rate, with no individual bonus for either productivity or quality performance. The pace of work is unremitting for operators. In the panel shop, panels travel down a conveyor belt and each operator must insert 10 or 11 components in a 30-second cycle. Gaps are left in the line every two hours so that operators may take a three-minute 'toilet break'. There are two ten-minute breaks during the morning and afternoon, with a half-hour break for lunch.

Every line has information which records the performance against an efficiency target on a daily basis. This information is monitored by the management team and, where appropriate, feedback will be given to the team leaders. The team leaders are held accountable for team performance against the targets and take responsibility for all operational aspects of their lines' activities. They are also responsible for the day-to-day management of the people on their lines. The quality system incorporates individual responsibility and accountability for defects. All the operators have a colour-coded chart above their heads indicating their individual performance on quality – red denotes 'danger', yellow for 'warning' and green 'good'. In the panel shop, the typical cycle time for an operator is 30 seconds or less and they will repeat this time and again for more than seven hours every day. Each operator will insert a total of over 200,000 components in a typical month and the company's target is 20 mistakes or less. Any operator with more defects may be disciplined by his or her team leader.

FORMAL COMMUNICATION

Nippon CTV (UK) appears a model of best practice. The plant runs an induction programme for new recruits, has single status conditions, flexibility and teamworking. Management themselves claim that one of the keys to the plant's success is communication. Formal communication and information displays at the plant take many forms.

- There are charts and programmes on public display at lineside and in the rest areas.
- The team leader holds a team meeting each morning.
- Every month the entire workforce is formally presented with the monthly plant results by senior management.
- Every six months there is a meeting which presents the financial performance of the organisation.
- The individual attendance and quality performance of each member over each month is displayed on charts at the end of each line. The company is very strict on attendance and time-keeping because there is no spare labour to cover absences.

The communication processes at Nippon CTV (UK) are considered by the management to be crucial to the effectiveness of production, and therefore they commit considerable time and resources to the various methods. The verbal communications presented during the morning meetings and the monthly meetings are backed up by the use of notice boards and various information displays throughout the plant. Specific campaigns are reiterated at meetings and emphasised through banners, printed materials and publicly displayed records.

The morning meeting

Every morning before production starts each team of workers in the plant assembles at the end of its line for the team briefing. At this meeting the team leader will read out a statement prepared by management and distributed earlier that morning. The information begins with the previous day's performance on quality and output volume for that line. The team leader will normally pass a comment on whether this performance level was acceptable. Achievement will be recognised as a 'good effort' while failure to reach the appropriate levels of quality or output will be condemned. There is no individual feedback at this meeting. The team leader will inform the team of any visitors to the plant and reiterate any messages that the plant is promoting, such as a 'clean-and-tidy' campaign. At the end of each briefing which takes place between 8.00 am and 8.05 am, the team leader will ask if there are any questions or problems but this is usually met with silence. All members must be at their work stations by 8.05 am because the lines start up automatically.

The monthly meeting

Each month the entire shopfloor attends a presentation by the senior production managers. This meeting is held in the canteen and the workers file in and take their seats while pop music plays over the PA system. At the front, using a small platform and overhead projector, first the Production Director and then the Senior Production Manager present information on the performance of the plant over the preceding month. The meeting lasts an average of 45 minutes. The Production Director gives the aggregate plant position and thanks the workers for their efforts. If there is a failure to reach targets then he will stress the importance of achieving both quality and quantity and urge the shopfloor to improve. He emphasises the need for care and commitment and calls for people to 'do better'. Then the Senior Production Manager will provide a detailed presentation of each line's performance. Each line's actual performance is compared to its monthly targets and achievements are acknowledged while those not reaching their targets are warned. This feedback is very detailed and includes reviews of specific areas so individual workers can be identified (although they are never named). The shopfloor is told of the new targets for the following months and the planned volumes while being urged to make every effort to attain these. 'It's up to you to secure your own jobs into the future' is the rallying call. Workers are asked if they have any questions before they file out, but it is almost unheard of for anyone to speak up.

At individual level

The most common form of communication to individual workers is through displays of individual performance regarding quality and individual attendance records which are displayed on each line. Other individualised communication will typically come through the team leader. Any members who do not perform to a satisfactory level of quality performance are counselled by their team leader regarding any problems or any difficulties they are experiencing, either in the workplace or at home. The team leader explains that their performance is not satisfactory and that they will need to improve in order that they and the company continue to be successful. This 'counselling' procedure is undertaken by team leaders in the coffee lounge area adjacent to the line. At these counselling sessions, operators will be invited to make comments and to raise any questions or problems that they may have. This opportunity is very rarely taken up by the members on the shopfloor.

Management have made a number of attempts to encourage employee participation and to incorporate workers' ideas through a suggestion scheme or through problem-solving activities. The plant ran a SMART scheme which awarded a 'smartie' badge and a bar of chocolate to anyone making a suggestion. At the instruction of a Japanese manager, the company used to present a pink origami swan to any operator who went a week without a defect but this practice was stopped. The Japanese Assistant Director promoted a campaign of quality circles but these did not work well and the scheme was abandoned. Workers have been loath to participate in any improvement effort and the various schemes have proven unsuccessful and been discontinued. Even the sports and social club at the plant is poorly attended.

WORKERS' REPRESENTATION

If a member has a problem or wants to raise a question with management, the first point of contact is his or her team leader. This is stressed to all newcomers during the induction programme. Should the individual member feel that this is proving unsatisfactory, then he or she is advised to see a more senior member of management. There are formal procedures available for individual members and the management team has a very clear set of procedures from which it does not waver. Alternatively, members can approach their trade union steward who will contact the manager on their behalf. Management expect these stewards to work with middle and senior managers in dealing with problems that cannot be resolved by the team leaders.

The company's advisory board

One of the most important structures for communication is the company's advisory board. While the plant management recognises the right of the AEEU to organise at the plant, all formal exchanges between the company and its employees are conducted through the advisory board. There is no separate forum for collective bargaining procedures between union representatives and management. Indeed, the company does not bargain with the union; pay is set by the company in line with the upper quartile level for equivalent employment in the area.

The company advisory board meets monthly and has 12 members. The Chief Steward of the union is one of those members, and his other stewards may stand for election as representatives of their area of the plant. However, there is no guarantee that these stewards will be elected to represent the members on the shopfloor; indeed, anyone has the right to stand for election and become a representative. There are representatives of senior management on the advisory board and a representative of middle management who is responsible for the interests of the superintendents and team leaders. The advisory board's remit is to discuss and debate aspects of employment relations and the general operation of the plant. The remit for discussion at the advisory board is wide-ranging but senior management make it clear that the board's function is 'advisory' and that, while the board may make recommendations to senior management, there is no guarantee that these will be taken up. Apart from the designated membership, a number of shopfloor members are invited to attend each meeting as 'observers'. This allows individual members to witness first-hand the activities of the advisory board.

The advisory board represents a major communication mechanism between management and the shopfloor. Through organised feedback by representatives to their constituencies, the decisions of the board are relayed to the plant: personnel produce a written document which details the decisions of the meeting and each representative is required to read out this document to his or her constituents at an extended morning coffee break the day after the advisory board meeting. All advisory board members are expressly forbidden to discuss the meeting until the official report has been presented.

THE MEMBERS

Monday lunch times had become a regular moaning session for many of the women from the panel shop. After the relief of the weekend, the relentless pace of the assembly line returned their thoughts to the grim reality of their tedious working lives. Kathy, Joanna and Molly were typical of most of the women who worked at the factory – they needed to work to support their families, and this was one of the few factories in the area. As 'old hands' they had been initiating Louise (a new recruit) into 'the way things are', while they ate lunch. Let's listen in on their conversation.

'You want to watch out for that Mandy! She's always booking me for defects, even when they're not my fault,' said Kathy. 'She books everything. I got taken into the coffee lounge because of her.'

'You should speak to Annie [the team leader] about it. Bring it up at morning meeting' suggested Molly.

'No way, I'm not doing that. She's not interested in us, just her numbers. Anyway, you know what she's like, she's always interrupting. We've got to get her on her own and get her to listen.'

'Couldn't you go to the union?' inquired Louise, hesitantly.

'They're useless. They've got Nippon CTV tattooed across their foreheads that lot,' scowled Kathy. 'This toilet break business is disgusting. It's degrading being told when to go to the toilet, but what do they do about it? Nothing. They just turn up to their cosy [advisory] board meetings, say nothing and clear off down the pub.'

'The advisory board is a joke,' agreed Joanna. 'Last week, they changed the rules on sickness pay so that you can only claim it twice a year. By the time that useless Melanie [the panel shop representative] had read out all that crap on quality and monthly targets and whether there are going to be more lights in the car park, she didn't have time to tell us about the sick pay. And only one or two of them there have the guts to say anything. And as for that Dick [the senior steward], he's the MD's pet mouse.'

'Why do they tell us that stuff about targets and quality?' inquired Louise. 'I nearly dozed off in that monthly meeting the other day.'

Molly shrugged and said, 'It's a right waste of time, it's so boring. Still it's a break from working. I never listen. It's the same in those morning meetings. Annie stands there telling us off for our quality and she's the one who keeps turning up the line speed. We've only got one pair of hands. You can't get quality at the speed they want us to go, it's ridiculous.'

'Yeah, I always try and come out of the loo just as she's finishing that meeting,' laughed Kathy. 'You think, "Why tell us this rubbish?" Still, then you think, "Well, at least they are telling us. Lots of firms don't."'

'Annie was round asking if I had any suggestions for improvements this morning,' said Joanna. 'I thought they'd stopped all that business.'

'I hope she asks me. I've got a few suggestions I'd like to make,' muttered Molly. 'For a start she could cut the line speed and give us a few more people.'

'I don't think that's quite the idea somehow. Anyhow, what's the bribe this time? Some more chocolate or a nice paper swan?' said Kathy, sarcastically.

'Is there a suggestion box here then?' asked Louise. 'They never mentioned anything at the induction.'

'Oh, it's much grander than that!' said Kathy. 'They've tried the works here – prizes for suggestions, these quality circle get-togethers, that "smartie" scheme. No one takes any notice though. I mean, why should we? We're not paid to think. We're here to stick pins in a board.'

Molly furrowed her brow and said, 'The problem is we don't really get a chance to have our say. They are not interested in listening to us.'

It was at this point that Mandy walked from the canteen servery, stood with her tray of food and surveyed the room. She glanced at the women before heading towards an empty table in the corner.

'Look at her sitting over there like "Lady Muck"! She really thinks she's something. We're not good enough for her,' said Kathy in disgust.

'Well, I wouldn't want her sitting with me. She'd be watching how quickly you eat your food!' quipped Joanna.

'And she'd be inspecting your chips for defects!' added Molly.

'Mind if I join you lovely ladies?' It was Dick, the Senior Steward.

'Are you slumming it then?' said Joanna, mustering her most sarcastic tone. 'Where are your management mates?'

'Needs must when the devil drives!' he chuckled.

'What are you on about?' asked Molly in utter bewilderment.

'Hob-nobbing! Nowadays its called "networking". It keeps me in touch with the management's plans. Ear to the ground and all that!'

'It's called networking now, is it?' said Joanna. 'That's not what I would call it.'

Kathy and Molly laughed, but Louise glanced down with embarrassment.

Dick looked across the table to Louise and said, 'I hope you are not letting these cynics taint your view of things, young lady. After all, it's up to us to secure our own jobs for the future.'

'"Eek, eek, eek!" went the mouse,' said Joanna.

ACTIVITY BRIEF

1 What benefits do you suppose the managers are hoping to derive through direct communication with employees?

2 (a) Assuming the views of the women are typical, why are the employees uninterested in the information put out by management?

(b) Suggest ways their interest could be stimulated.

3 (a) Identify the various mechanisms that allow employees to have a say, and evaluate the effectiveness of each one.

(b) Molly comments, 'The problem is we don't really get a chance to have our say.' Do you think she is justified?

4 Evaluate the role of the union. Is it an effective form of representation for the employees?

5 It might be argued that the communication process is being cynically manipulated by management. What examples are there to support this view?

6 To what extent does the communication system act as a form of management control?

7 What aspects of the work process might be leading to suspicion and ambivalence among the employees?

RECOMMENDED READING

Elger, T and Smith, C (eds) (1994) *Global Japanization? The Transnational Transformation of the Labour Process*, London, Routledge.

Oliver, N and Wilkinson, B (1992) *The Japanization of British Industry: New Developments in the 1990s*, Oxford, Blackwell.

Womack, J, Jones, D and Roos, D (1990) *The Machine that Changed the World*, New York, Rawson Associates.

Bargained flexibilisation: the dynamics of change towards new work organisation

John Salmon

INTRODUCTION

Flexibility has become a dominant theme in much of the recent discussions surrounding human resource management and debates about the deregulation of labour markets and even corporate strategy. Academics as well as practitioners have given voice to the nature of the current changes taking place in management practices in relation to establishing greater organisational flexibility. One of the most important areas of discussion has centred around the new forms of work organisations that are claimed to be bringing into place radical innovations in industrial efficiency and changes in the social organisation of work. Much of the analysis has been developed from within global models of post-Fordist manufacturing with regulation theory (Aglietta 1979, Boyer 1988, Lipietz 1992) and flexible specialisation (Piore and Sabel 1984) being the leading schools, and at a company level by the theory of the flexible firm (Atkinson 1984, Atkinson and Meager 1986).

Although the use of the term flexibility has come to span a wide area of modern employment behaviour, far less attention has been paid to the way in which the restructuring of work organisation brings forth different expectations and interests as well as fears and opportunities that come to shape the bargained relationship between the employer and the workforce. Drawing upon the experience of fundamental change that took place in a leading electronics manufacturer in the UK, this account explores not only the technological but also the social implications of the firm abandoning mass production in favour of flexible work organisation. Readers are invited to construct an equitable bargained outcome that seeks to balance the gains in industrial efficiency with distributional justice between the management and the workforce.

BACKGROUND TO THE CASE

In general terms, flexibility may be viewed as the capacity by which a diverse collection of existing arrangements prove to be capable of adapting to a changed situation. Over the past decade, however, the term flexibility has come to be used across a broad range of activities that go far beyond the conventional adjustments and minor piecemeal responses through which firms have sought to cope with the short-term fluctuations in the business environment.

Flexibility spans a wide area of activity. Its modern application not only embraces labour markets and differences in contracts of employment, but also industrial relations and new computerised technologies as well as changes in working practices. Flexible working is to be seen in the changing patterns of working hours, shiftworking, the growth of part-time, temporary and fixed-term contracts, as well as the increase in subcontracting. The emphasis upon creating flexible or multi-skilled operators has resulted in a greater consideration of training and has brought into question the traditional shape of job demarcations in the workplace.

For some, flexible working has been seen as marking an employer offensive not merely designed to enable the firm to cope with conditions of uncertainty about future growth, market changes, output and productivity, but also a means for eliminating rigidities in employment and bringing about a new industrial relations climate. Theorists of flexibilisation have sought to conceptualise the current period as one of radical change embodying a fundamental transformation within the international economy. This in turn they see as ushering in widespread innovations in the established mode of industrial efficiency that have implications for skill and the quality of working life.

The theorists of post-Fordism, flexible specialisation and the theory of the flexible firm see this search for greater flexibility among the leading industrial nations as representing a movement of profound change. Despite variations in approach, they generally share a common claim that the period of slower economic growth and rising unemployment represents a structural crisis that has undermined the former pattern of the early post-war prosperity. Rather than simply judging this condition as a temporary phenomenon or a regular cyclical movement within the trade cycle that will eventually 'naturally' readjust itself, it is seen as a structural crisis of the world's mass production economy (Lipietz 1992, Ch. 2). Flexibilisation appears as a central means for overcoming the rigidities of the Fordist system of industrial organisation.

As Leborgne and Lipietz (1989), leading proponents of the French regulation school of post-Fordism, see the situation in the European Union (EU) countries:

> Like all advanced capitalist economies, the countries of the Community have been facing for more than 15 years the crisis of the model of work relations which became the standard general model in the 1950s and which is known as Fordism.

In similar vein we find the flexible specialisation theorists, Piore and Sabel (1984) stating:

> Our claim is that the present deterioration in economic performance results from the limits of the model of industrial development that is found on mass production: the use of special purpose machines and semi-skilled workers to produce standardised goods.

The theory of the flexible firm developed by Atkinson largely developed out of the same historic period that lays claim to a fundamental shift taking place in the business environment. Its particular focus, however, is confined to employment flexibility within the individual firm and more specifically the type of flexible configurations occurring within the UK as opposed to the global preoccupation of regulation theory and flexible specialisation.

The extent to which different theoretical models elevate the concept of flexibility to a generalised model of industrial crisis of the whole mode of industrial efficiency clearly sets them apart from the more conventional analysis of the change functions of labour markets or the behaviour of the firm. To associate the question of flexibility and innovations in work organisation to a crisis of Fordism is not only to define the crisis as a historic stage of industrial development but also comes to shape the direction and possibilities for industrial renewal. In short, nothing less than a radical transformation of the mass production mode of industrial efficiency and its prevailing social relations is being called for.

The crux of this new thinking centres around a number of propositions which claim that Fordist principles of industrial efficiency have become sources of productive rigidity and inflexibility.

Five propositions underpinning radical change from Fordism

1 Firms no longer operate in circumstances that are favourable to the production of high volumes of a standardised product. The 'golden age' of the post-war boom years is now seen as the high point of a historic era of mass markets and the domination of mass production which has now come to an end.
2 Employers, as well as trade unions and workforces, whether in the United States, Europe, Japan or the Far East, have had to learn to cope with managing not only in conditions of increased international competitiveness but also in a much more uncertain business environment.
3 The nature of competition and the benchmarks for corporate performance have changed substantially. The terms of the 'new competition' include non-price features such as product quality, reliability, design, a wider range of choice and a broader range of consumer taste – in addition to price competition.
4 The mass production of a standardised product is giving way to batched production of greater differential product types.
5 The search for new types of flexible production systems centres upon overcoming the inflexibilities of Fordist mass production. The productive limitations of mass assembly line technology, low skilled inflexible labour forces, and the doubts about principles of efficiency based around an extreme division of labour, whereby job tasks are designed and measured according to the scientific techniques of FW Taylor, are now all considered as sources of restrictive rigidity.

The transformation of work?

Since Adam Smith's account of the division of labour in the pin factory, the development of specialisation through subdividing work tasks has been widely held to be a necessary, though far from a socially fulfilling condition, for the creation of manufacturing efficiency. The endorsement of these principles into scientific management and their application to the mass production techniques of Henry Ford saw the establishment of industrial efficiency through the organisation of work becoming a process of rationalisation, simplification and routinisation (*see* Littler and Salaman 1984, Ch. 5). For authors such as Braverman (1974), the resulting 'degradation' of modern factory labour became the dominant feature of the labour process in the twentieth century through a twin combination of tighter managerial control and the progressive deskilling of work.

The adverse impact of working on assembly lines became a *cause célèbre* of a growing social critique of technological progress. Moreover, it came to be regarded as an underlying factor in adversarial industrial relations (*see*, for example, Walker and Guest 1952, Blauner 1964, Goldthorpe *et al* 1968, Ch. 2, Linhart 1981). By the 1970s, experiments in job enrichment, job enlargement and a debate about the quality of working life (QWL) had developed as a movement throughout a number of leading industrial economies. During the last few years, however, these arguments have come from within the flexibilisation debate (Dankbaar 1988). A pivotal role in a number of discussions on the flexible work organisations has been attached to the upskilling of labour.

Rather than simply an attempt to mitigate the excesses of the Fordist division of labour, the creation of multi-skilled flexible workers is seen as corresponding to the new demands of the more diversified production system. Reversing the process of rationalisation and deskilling, Piore and Sabel (1984) regard the adoption of flexible specialisation as resulting in the revival of craft skills. Child (1985) refers to the new production skills of 'polyvalence workers' who are able to operate beyond skill boundaries. Kern and Schumann (1987) see the new production concepts in German mass production industries requiring new forms of professionalisation of work, with considerable emphasis being placed upon formal qualifications and independent skills.

In the British context, somewhat more prosaically, Atkinson (1984) sees a more polarised flexible labour force developing within the flexible firm. He distinguishes the functional flexibility of a set of core workers who have a capacity to undertake a greater variety of tasks from the numerically flexible worker who remains peripheral, low skilled and insecure. The former comprise the regular employees, while the latter are formed from part-time, temporary, self-employed or agency workers.

Flexibilisation has not been without its critics. Doubts exist about a generalised model of post-Fordism. There remains the lack of empirical evidence and the absence of detailed comparative studies to support a single conceptual paradigm (Reed 1992, pp 230–6). For Pollert (1991), the attempt to confine the complexity and diversity of change within a typology called flexibility obscures rather than clarifies management approaches to work and employment. There are problems of basic interpretation. Changes in working practices, for example, may signify increased job enrichment or they could indicate greater exploitation and labour intensification (Elger 1991). Similarly, labour market deregulation might well be paving the way from full-time security towards insecure patterns of employment (Standing 1990, Walsh 1990). A further question centres upon differences in industrial relations systems and in particular the extent to which trade unions may have an interest in maintaining their past achievements against the uncertainties of change (Boyer 1988, Ch. 11).

One overriding difficulty confronting most theories of post-Fordism is how existing national differences in political, institutional and legal frameworks of individual nations come to be telescoped into a single future model of post-Fordist society. In Britain, for example, in contrast to its EU partners, labour market flexibility has centred upon changes in working practices and the legal reform of trade unions. Rather than the European approach of regulation through the 'social partnership' of state, employers and unions, the opt-out from the EU Social Chapter has been part of an attempt to create a freer environment for employers to negotiate over employment contracts, resulting in greater occupational mobility of employees with fewer restrictions upon the hire and fire of labour.

Against a background of the international debate about flexibilisation, the British case has been largely overshadowed by major recession and a sharp contraction in manufacturing employment. Some 2.6 million jobs, or about one third of full-time jobs have been lost in the 11 years to 1990. According to the Workplace Industrial Relations (WIRS) survey, about 18 per cent of employees are now part-time (Millward *et al* 1992, p 18). A

TUC analysis of the Labour Force Survey suggests that 85 per cent of all new jobs were temporary or self-employed, with only 10 per cent being permanent, in the 12 months preceding the autumn of 1994 (TUC 1995).

Clearly there are many difficulties in evaluating the 'explosion' of interest in flexibility. In the case of Britain, where the lack of strongly embedded institutionalised forms of regulation leads to employment policies being shaped by the strength of national employers' organisations and centralised national union organisations, there is clearly much greater room for diversity in approach towards flexibilisation and less inclination for the emergence of a generalised standard model.

This case study explores one such experience of a leading British firm seeking to shift from mass production towards a flexible work organisation.

THE BACKGROUND TO ELECTRICAL PRODUCTS (EP)

EP manufactures electrical circuit breakers for both industrial and domestic buildings. Until the mid-1980s, the firm held a dominant position in the UK market and a healthy export trade confined largely to the countries where British electrical standards were practised. The firm had a very limited product range. Its strong market share, however, had been conducive to high-volume mass-production methods. Consequently, EP relied heavily upon the assembly line system for its principal source of efficiency with the extensive division of labour. The simplification and organisation of job tasks were largely in accordance with the work measurement techniques of FW Taylor's scientific management.

The new competition

During the second half of the 1980s, the trading position at EP came under severe challenge both at home and abroad. From the Far East, EP began to face local competition in its Asian markets. In the UK, new entrants from the countries of the European Union (EU) threatened the firm's domestic market share. Moreover, the nature of these challenges changed the character of competitiveness. The new competition introduced new products and developed a wider product range that marketed circuit breakers not only on cost, but also by non-price features such as quality, reliability, style and personal taste. The limited choice of EP between white or brown standard casing in either metal or plastic had been dramatically extended.

EP responded to the new terms of competition by appointing a new senior management team. They were charged with revitalising the declining position of the firm. With regard to manufacturing strategy their key decision was to abandon their mass production assembly system and to introduce a flexible work organisation that could cope with a more diversified product range so as to address the new competition. This change was preceded by a rigorous examination of the deficiencies of the assembly line at EP.

Mass production at EP

Mass production had been central to the work organisation at EP since the 1950s. Plastic, metal and electronic parts were produced in four of the company's component plants before being transferred to the final assembly plant at the nearby main factory. Here parts and semi-finished goods were routinely put together along the line (Fig. 26.1). The final line comprised 32 semi-skilled female operators. There were two visual inspectors to check the quality of the work in progress. After leaving the assembly area the completed breakers were subject to final tests against pre-set standards for operational safety, quality and performance, before being placed into warehouse stock prior to shipment from the plant.

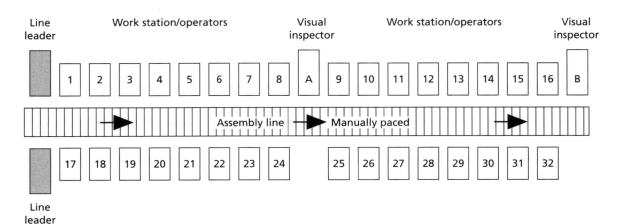

Supervision:Operator ratio

Departmental foreman: 1:250 operators
Line leader: 1:12   operators

Fig 26.1 EP single product mass assembly line – semi-skilled operators

Each section of the line had a line leader appointed by the factory management. These were responsible for ensuring an adequate level of buffer stock of components sufficient to sustain the continuity of production. The line leader also worked on the line and sometimes helped workers who fell behind in their work. They had, however, no formal responsibilities for worker discipline. This was the sole task of the Departmental Foreman.

The management team came to recognise a number of fundamental social and organisational weaknesses in their mass assembly system that led them to abandon its use as a principal source of EP efficiency.

Diseconomies of scale

In contrast to much of the established wisdom in the company that specialisation through the division of labour remained the primary source of high efficiency, the EP management discovered a number of limitations in the firm's mass production system.

1 Unlike the mechanically controlled Fordist production line, the line at EP was not machine paced. Completed job tasks were transferred from work station to work station and operator to operator manually on a non-mechanical roller system. As with the Ford system, each station was wholly dependent upon the preceding station; line speed

was ultimately determined by the speed of the slowest operation. In the absence of a pre-set mechanical line, the speed of assembly at EP was set by human effort. The line therefore moved only as quickly as the slowest or least efficient operator. The management found that at any one time the majority of workstation assembly operators were achieving a sub-optimal level of efficiency. In other words, there was a chronic state of line imbalance between operating skills and output efficiency.

2 The visual inspectors checked the work in progress but contributed no direct value to the labour productivity of the line, yet they received a higher wage rate than the line workers.

3 The EP wage system was based upon a fixed hourly rate – that is, 39 hours' pay for 39 hours' work. Actual take-home earnings were in fact greatly complicated by additional increments that over a long period of time led to distorted differences in the weekly wage. Both between and within the component plants and the main assembly shop there were 15 different wage levels for semi-skilled workers. Among the craftsmen there were two basic grades.

These differentials, particularly among the semi-skilled, were often quite small in actual money terms, but the growth of the supplementary payments had been quite arbitrary – an *ad hoc* development affecting various groups of workers across different sections, workstations and departments and between plants. These were, nevertheless, a particular source of bitterness and a regular issue of dispute in annual wage negotiations for the Engineering Union (AEU) which had sole recognition rights for the whole manual labour force. The decay of the wage structure was believed to lower morale, particularly among the semi-skilled female workers.

For the union, the complexity of the differentials created difficulties in formulating a company wide wage claim that would command both membership agreement and union solidarity. The management also began to recognise that wage differentials were a factor in resistance to the deployment of labour across different parts of the firm.

The new management regarded two further issues as affecting the efficiency of the production line. *Absenteeism* was seen as being 'too high'. It frequently averaged 10 per cent in the assembly section among the predominately female workers. On occasions it reached 19 per cent. Moreover, *lateness* was quite common. The combination of the effects of the wage system, absenteeism and lateness compounded the inflexibilities of the assembly line. The regular attenders objected to being moved at short notice to different job tasks that they were unfamiliar with to cover for the absent or late workers. Not only did they not receive any additional payments for their efforts, but they were also reluctant to leave their social groups and informal social networks that they were party to in their regular place of work.

The constant reorganisation of work at the beginning of the morning shift exposed additional weaknesses in the assembly line. Operator training was quite minimal. All jobs were broken down into routine repetitive tasks that required limited worker skill and avoided the expense of costly investments in training. Simple assembly tasks required either manual dexterity or the use of hand or power tools. Some jobs required soldering skills. There was no systematic policy to train for multi-skilling nor evidence of creating a flexible worker for assembly. As a consequence, the movement of workers at short notice to other assembly tasks as cover for absenteeism or lateness further reduced job completion times that in turn lowered the manually paced assembly line. In effect, the combination of high absenteeism, lateness and low morale, arising out of the wage payment grievances, along-side the lack of flexible labour, were social features that were yielding diseconomies of scale in the mass production at EP.

The central problem facing the new management at EP was how could they develop an efficient form of flexible manufacturing to enable the production of a wider product range yet overcome the social sources of discontent and rigidity of the assembly line system. In other words, how could EP manage social flexibility in terms that might produce a degree of consent and co-operation from its workforce in a way that would address the new competition?

FLEXIBLE WORK ORGANISATION

For the new management team, the planning of the reorganisation of the work process at EP had to meet two guiding principles for change: a more diversified product range and increased efficiency. However, the total focus of reorganisation was directed solely to the female assembly workforce. There was no attempt to change the work practices of the male craft workers.

Figure 26.2 illustrates the new pattern of flexible work organisation adopted at EP. The single mass assembly had been replaced by two distinct assembly processes. Much of the routine, simple assembly tasks such as handfitting, basic wiring and those requiring the use of hand tools such as screwdrivers were to be undertaken on sub-assembly lines. These would produce semi-finished circuits in different model batches for the round-table final assemblers. The final assembly process would now comprise six of the more complex tasks that included power tools for soldering, welding and final wiring. All of these were to be completed by a single operator who could rotate each task on the round-table machine by the use of a foot pedal. Instead of one mass assembly line producing a single product in high volume there were six round-table assembly machines that each could produce a different circuit breaker.

In terms of flexibility, the new flexible work organisation introduced functional flexibility that increased the skills of the operators and replaced the former reliance upon the extreme division of labour of the Fordist type whereby an industrial operator only undertook one simple short-cycle repetitive task. For the sub-assembly lines, each worker had to train to acquire an equal level of competence for all job tasks on his or her particular line. To ensure optimum deployment each assembler was regularly job rotated between all tasks. The round-table operators, however, had to be specially selected for dexterity and ability to use power tools. These tasks were more complex and required a higher level of training. All operators were eligible to apply but only those who could reach the required standards were selected for round-table training. Some three months were required to acquire the total skill competence required.

EP had devised a way of producing six types of circuit breakers at any one time, where before it produced only one. The production flow was also greatly enhanced by flexible workers who could be moved along the sub-assembly lines so as to prevent bottlenecks and delays that plagued the old assembly lines. As multi-skilled workers they were now more competent to cover for absent colleagues. Overall plant capacity, however, remained at a broadly similar level. Flexible working not only saw an increase in product diversity but there was also a massive increase in labour productivity compared with the old assembly line. The sub-assembly and round-table lines required only 18 operators whereas there had been 32 on the assembly line. The achievement of a leaner, efficient and diversified

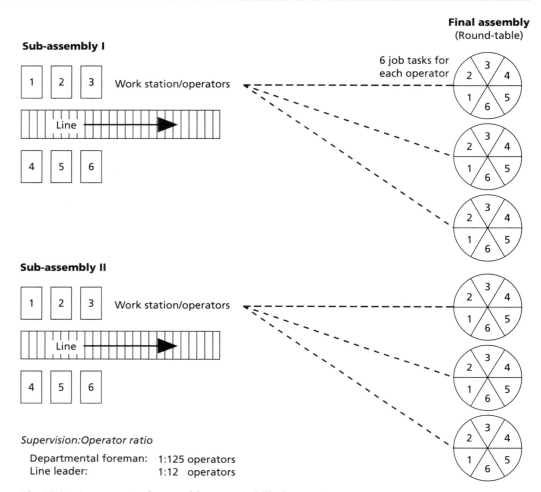

Fig 26.2 EP segmented assembly – semi-skilled operators

flexible work organisation, however, became much more dependent on a higher level of worker co-operation and commitment than was the case with the old line.

The success of the flexible work organisation was, with a smaller workforce, far more vulnerable to the impact of absenteeism and levels of lateness than the assembly line. Moreover, it was questionable how far it could operate within a climate of discontent over the wage structure. The remaining problem for EP management was how they could insulate themselves from the problems with labour discipline and wage structure discontent in order to achieve the required worker commitment and co-operation. Flexibilisation, in other words, had brought into place a more fragile and dependent relationship between the company and its workforce than had hitherto existed.

BARGAINED FLEXIBILITY

The abandonment of mass production and attempts to restructure the organisation of work clearly represent an important way to enhance the flexibilisation intended to meet the international terms of the new competition in a more intensive business environment. As Boyer (1988), the French regulation scholar, makes clear, however, it is not simply a matter of overcoming technological rigidities of production that is up for debate in the post-Fordist analysis. Of considerable importance is how social flexibility comes to be managed. This may ultimately have a significant influence that can shape the outcomes of long-term change. What is much more problematical is what role trade unions will play in influencing the shape of social flexibility.

From an industrial relations point of view, many of the consequences of economic change that have taken place since the early 1980s have had adverse implications for trade union membership and organisation (Baglioni 1992, Ch. 1, Salmon and Stewart 1994). By contrast to the era of post-war growth, in which a progressive strengthening of organised labour saw the economic and political influence of unions extended, the past decade and a half has seen a decline in the aggregate level of union membership occur across most of the OECD nations, including Britain (OECD 1991). Much of this reflects a general compositional shift that has taken place in the structure of the labour market and the effects of developments in new sectors of employment. The traditional highly unionised industrial sectors where male manual employment dominated have been in sharp decline. Areas of new employment have been particularly difficult for unions to organise.

The growth of non-manual workforces, the increase in small firms and the downsizing of large companies as well as the notable increased participation of female workers have been common throughout the advanced economies and have been factors influencing the general level of union membership. Conversely, the evidence of sharp divergences between national rates of unionisation suggests that the actual level of unionisation may also be influenced by country-specific factors. These appear to include changes in public attitudes towards trade unions, employer attitudes, government public policy, particularly regarding protective or restrictive labour law, as well as the extent to which the price of unionised labour exceeds that of the non-union wage (Blanchflower and Freeman 1992). Many of these factors represent national institutional differences that impact upon the popularity of unionisation.

The British context

British trade unions in particular have experienced a rapid decline in membership and an equally notable fall in the level of union recognition and collective bargaining during the past decade and a half. Since 1979, membership has fallen by over a half to its current 7 million. Although the actual number of those in employment remains broadly what it was in the mid-1970s the proportion working in the key manufacturing sector – a previously fertile ground for union recruitment – has fallen dramatically from 35 to 23 per cent of total employment. The WIRS study reveals that the number of establishments with union recognition in this sector dropped from 65 per cent to 44 per cent in the decade to 1990 (Millward *et al* 1992), while the extent to which pay is negotiated through collective bargaining was found in only 45 per cent of establishments compared to 65 per cent in 1980. Nevertheless, the WIRS data reports that the degree of decline tends to be least where union recognition has been present over a long period and where the actual level of unionisation has been high. EP fits into this latter classification. Union negotiations have been conducted with the firm for several decades while the level of plant unionisation has been virtually 100 per cent since the late 1970s.

Determining social flexibility at EP

While the new management at EP brought about the strategic restructuring of the production system, they had yet to decide policy for ensuring the basis for promoting the required level of social flexibility. They had still to resolve, for example, the questions of regular attendance which would be a far more critical issue than they had been under the old assembly line. Moreover, it appeared unrealistic to expect positive behavioural changes among a workforce so dissatisfied by the weakness of the existing wage structure. Furthermore, the burden of change fell unevenly across the workforce. Unlike the Atkinson flexible firm thesis, it was not a core group of male craft workers who became functionally flexible but the semi-skilled female operators. Rather than a bipolar divide between core and periphery at EP, there emerged a more segmented workforce. The craft status of electricians, fitters, toolmakers and machine setters remained largely unaffected by change.

The upskilling, investment in training and the attempt to increase the value of the human resource of labour all centred upon the relatively low-skilled assembly workers. The simple single-task specialisation of the mass assembly line in which individual abilities, aptitudes, and learning potential were severely restricted gave way to a new social division of work within the semi-skilled. Round-table operators received high levels of training and had to meet a skill threshold in order to fulfil the new production demands. They experienced the integration of their tasks plus wider skill and product quality responsibilities. They thus acquired a level of functional flexibility that segmented them from their sub-assembly colleagues by different recruitment, selection, training, job responsibility and skill criteria. The sub-assembly operators became segmented by their lower aptitudes, poorer dexterity and nimbleness, from the round-table tasks and were thereby confined to job rotation among a larger range of simple handfitting work. Nevertheless, for both groups their work skill and intensity was far greater than when confined to one repetitive simple task on the old assembly line.

While this training and upskilling increased their functional flexibility that, for the new management, was intended to contribute to higher company performance, it could also be expected that the expectations and evaluations of the rewards from work would not remain unchanged. The EP management, therefore, proposed to use the forthcoming annual negotiations with the AEU as the basis for negotiating a two-year agreement in order to determine a stable framework for social flexibility, so as to complement their flexible manufacturing system.

ACTIVITY BRIEF

Students should divide themselves into two groups: representatives of EP management and union representatives.

Each side must prepare its case for resolving the issues of social flexibility that continue to exist following the introduction of the new flexible work organisation. Each side must then set out its own recommendations for inclusion in the forthcoming annual wage negotiations – the reforms required to produce a stable settlement. Each side should do the following.

1 Provide a solution to the lateness and absenteeism questions that will enhance commitment and stability.

2 Produce a reformed wage structure that provides a more equable outcome to the changed conditions of work for the functionally segmented labour force.

3 Analyse the advantages and disadvantages of the changes from mass production to flexible manufacturing at EP in terms of:
   (a) company performance
   (b) union members.

4 Assess how useful the theories of flexibility are in accounting for the events that took place at EP.

Both sides must then present their recommendations at a joint reconvened meeting of the whole group. Their own approaches can then be discussed in the light of the final management–union agreement signed at EP.

RECOMMENDED READING

Aglietta, M (1979) *A Theory of Capitalist Regulations*, London, New Left Books.

Atkinson, J (1984) 'Manpower strategies for flexible organisations', *Personnel Management*, Aug, pp 28–31.

Atkinson, J and Meager, N (1986) 'Is flexibility just a flash in the pan?', *Personnel Management*, Sep, pp 26–9.

Baglioni, G (1992) 'Industrial relations in Europe in the 1980s', in Baglioni, G and Crouch, C (eds) *European Industrial Relations: The Challenge of Flexibility*, London, Sage.

Blanchflower, DG and Freeman, RB (1992) 'Unionism in the United States and other OECD countries', *Industrial Relations*, Winter.

Blauner, R (1964) *Alienation and Freedom: The Factory Worker and His Industry*, Chicago, Chicago UP.

Boyer, R (ed) (1988) *The Search for Labour Market Flexibility: The European Economies in Transition*, Oxford, Oxford UP.

Braverman, H (1974) *Labor and Monopoly Capital: The Degradation of Work in the Twentieth Century*, New York, Monthly Review Press.

Child, J (1985) 'Managerial strategies, new technology and the labour process', in Knights, D, Willmott, H and Collinsen, D (eds) *Job Redesign*, Aldershot, Gower.

Dankbaar, B (1988) 'New production concepts, management strategies and the quality of work', *Work, Employment and Society*, 2(1), pp 25–50.

Elger, T (1991) 'Task flexibility and the intensification of labour in UK manufacturing in the 1980s', in Pollert, A (ed) *Farewell to Flexibility*, Oxford, Blackwell.

Goldthorpe, JH, Lockwood, D, Bechhofer, F and Platt, J (1968) *The Affluent Worker: Industrial Attitudes and Behaviour*, Cambridge, Cambridge UP.

Kern, H, and Schumann, M (1987) 'Limits of the division of labour. New production and employment concepts in West German industry', *Economic and Industrial Democracy*, 8, pp 151–70.

Leborgne, D, and Lipietz, A (1989) 'How to avoid a two-tier Europe', *Labour and Society*, 15, 2.

Lipietz, A (1992) *Towards a New Economic Order: Postfordism, Ecology and Democracy*, London, Policy Press.

Linhart, R (1981) *The Assembly Line*, London, Calder.

Littler, C and Salaman, G (1984) *Class at Work*, London, Batsford.

Millward, N, Stevens, M, Smart, D and Hawes, WR (1992) *Workplace Industrial Relations in Transition*, Aldershot, Dartmouth Publishing.

OECD (1991) Organisation for Economic Cooperation and Development, *Employment Outlook*, July.

Piore, M and Sabel, C (1984) *The Second Industrial Divide*, New York, Basic Books.

Pollert, A (1991) 'The orthodoxy of flexibility' in Pollert, A (ed) *Farewell to Flexibility*, Oxford, Blackwell.

Reed, MI (1992) *The Sociology of Organisations: Themes, Perspectives and Prospects*, Hemel Hempstead, Harvester.

Salmon, J and Stewart, P (1994) 'Unions on the brink? Themes and issues', *Employee Relations*, 16, 2, pp 8–23.

Standing, G (1990) 'Labour flexibility and insecurity: towards an alternative', in Brunetta, R and Dell'Aringa, C (eds) *Labour Relations and Economic Performance*, London, Macmillan.

TUC (1995) *Britain Divided – Insecurity at Work*, London, TUC Economic and Social Affairs.

Walker, CJ and Guest, R (1952) *The Man on The Assembly Line*, Cambridge, Massachussetts, Harvard.

Walsh, J (1990) 'Flexible labour utilisation in private service sector work', *Employment and Society*, pp 517–53.

HRM and trade unions: Marks and Spencer (Ireland) Ltd

Fintan Hourihan and Patrick Gunnigle

INTRODUCTION

The compatibility of human resource management (HRM) policies and trade union recognition has been the source of considerable academic debate. Organisational commitment is placed at the core of models of HRM (Beer *et al* 1985, Guest 1987). If the four key HRM policy goals are strategic integration, quality, flexibility and commitment, then only commitment to the organisation need present a direct challenge to trade unionism (Guest 1989).

But moving the company's relationship with its employees from control to commitment throws up questions about the place of trade unions in such a strategy: can trade unions become partners in developing a committed workforce or is their presence inimical to such an aspiration?

The case of the Marks and Spencer Group has been chosen because of its decision to recognise trade unions in the Republic of Ireland from day one; why has it chosen to recognise trade unions in Ireland alone of all the countries in which it is located? What does this imply for the paternalistic policy which is central to its founding philosophy and is attributed as being a key factor in its success? Does dealing with trade unions impact on securing the commitment of employees to the company's distinctive policy approach with its emphasis on quality, innovation, flexibility and an open and involved relationship with its employees?

BACKGROUND TO THE CASE

The Marks and Spencer Group is a major worldwide retailer, employing 62,000 and returning turnover in 1994 of £6.5 billion. As one of the most admired businesses in Europe among the business community and among consumers generally, the Group, which has 300,000 shareholders, is the only retailer in the world with a 'triple A' credit rating.

The Group's retail activities are complemented by new financial services units. The main retailing activities comprise the Marks and Spencer stores worldwide, Marks and Spencer franchises, the Brooks Brothers chain in the US and Japan and Kings Supermarkets in the US. In total, the group had 612 stores worldwide at the end of March 1994, of which 285 were located in the UK and Republic of Ireland.

The Marks and Spencer Group operates on the basis of the following company principles:

- to sell merchandise of the highest quality and outstanding value;
- to offer the highest standard of customer care in an attractive shopping environment;
- to improve quality standards continually through operations by investment in modern technology;
- to support British industry;
- to pursue mutually rewarding long-term partnerships with suppliers;
- to ensure staff and shareholders share in our success;
- to nurture good human relations with staff, customers and the community;
- to minimise the environmental impact of operations and merchandise.

Corporate employee relations policy

The employee relations policies employed by the Marks and Spencer Group have usually been simplistically described as paternalistic. In 1984, the centenary of the Group's establishment, its then chairman, Lord Sieff (also a grandson of Mr Michael Marks, one of the co-founders of the business) outlined the company's personnel philosophy:

> The development of good human relations in industry is one of the main foundations of success and is therefore vital for the maintenance of free enterprise and democracy.

He emphasised that he used the term 'good human relations in industry', rather than 'industrial relations' because 'we are human beings at work not industrial beings'. Good human relations is not just about wages and conditions but also awareness of, and reaction to, employees' needs, he added.

Tse (1985) claims that it is misrepresentation to describe the company's approach as paternalism:

> ... the company's human relations policy also includes a respect for the individual, attention to the problems of individuals at work, full and frank communications, the recognition of people's effort and contribution and continuous training and development.

The company invests considerable resources in 'good human relations'. Typically, there is one personnel executive responsible for every 60 employees. The company also invests heavily in staff development and in elaborate communications structures.

In terms of its stance towards trade unions, the company has best been described as non-union rather than anti-union. Management say that trade unions are welcome to send representatives to address workers in the company's staff lounges and say they do not actively oppose attempts by trade unions to recruit members from among the workforce. Management at the British stores would see people joining trade unions as a reflection of communications problems.

Marks and Spencer are particularly renowned for the non-pay benefits available to employees. All employees are entitled to become members of a non-contributory pension scheme and to medical benefits such as chiropody, physiotherapy, dental care and cervical screening. Other non-medical perks include the provision of hairdressers and heavily subsidised canteens. Paid sick leave stretches from two weeks for those with less than three months' service, to eight weeks after twelve months' service and to twelve weeks after five years' service. After five years' service, sick leave entitlement rises by one week for each added year's service. The company also operates a very generous death benefit scheme.

Furthermore the company operates a profit share scheme in its British stores and this has been offered to Irish workers, although negotiations on its introduction in Ireland have not been concluded.

Irish Employee Relations

The system of employee relations in Ireland is founded on a pluralist tradition characterised, primarily, by reliance on adversarial collective bargaining. In recent times the state has become more directly involved in employee relations by joining with trade unions and employers in centralised, all-encompassing collective bargaining (Gunnigle 1992).

Successive Irish governments have largely been supportive of trade union organisation. The state also plays an important role in providing dispute resolution agencies such as the Labour Court and the Labour Relations Commission as well as the quasi-judicial Employment Appeals Tribunal. The system of Joint Labour Committees which sets legally binding minimum wage rates in certain sectors following negotiations between employer and trade union representatives also provides for enforcement by state inspectors.

The main employer and trade union confederations are well established as 'social partners' and can be said to be representative of both sides of industry given the numbers and the spread of their membership. The emphasis on centralised collective bargaining has merely reinforced the central role played by these organisations in the consensual approach to economic management which is favoured by the majority of political parties.

The most up-to-date (1993) official figures suggest total trade union membership in the Republic of Ireland of 485,700, equivalent to 47 per cent of all employees at work. After considerable growth in trade union membership from 312,600 in 1960 to 527,200 in 1980, the 1980s witnessed the greatest decline in union numbers since the 1930s. Total membership fell by over 51,000 members – almost 10 per cent – between 1980 and 1987. The fall in union membership was arrested in 1988 when the total stood at 470,000 and since then most years have seen a slight rise in overall numbers.

The contrast in levels of trade union representation among employees (excluding the self-employed) in the private and public sectors is striking. In 1993, the number of trade union members in the private sector stood at 220,300 representing just under 36 per cent of all private sector employees, while in the public sector union membership levels of 200,600 represented a density level of 76 per cent (*Industrial Relations News*, 13 April 1995).

Recent research undertaken at the University of Limerick has established that over half of the greenfield operations established in Ireland from the mid-1980s to 1992 and employing more than 100 people opted not to recognise trade unions for collective bargaining purposes (Gunnigle 1995). Country of origin was the critical explanatory factor: of the 27 US-owned companies, 23 were non-union, whereas over 80 per cent of Irish companies decided to recognise unions. This trend has continued in recent times and presents an important new dimension to Irish employee relations.

Despite Ireland's significant level of unionisation, there are no specific statutory processes to govern the process of collective bargaining or trade union recognition. The Irish Constitution confers on individuals the right to join associations or unions. This provision has been interpreted by the Supreme Court to include an implied right not to join trade unions where individuals do not wish to do so.

The most significant development in Irish employee relations in recent times has been the negotiation of corporatist-style agreements covering not just levels of pay increase but also broader socio-economic policies which are linked to the state's desire to exert control over public finances. These agreements are not legally binding but compliance with the pay terms has been consistently high. The main dispute-settling agencies – the Labour Court and the Labour Relations Commission – have also played an important part in ensuring that the agreed pay increases are not exceeded.

These new agreements, beginning with the Programme for National Recovery in 1987, have contained voluntary industrial peace clauses aimed at ending attempts to improve on nationally agreed terms and conditions. Coinciding with these agreements has been the most significant decline in the numbers of days lost due to strike action in the history of the state.

MARKS AND SPENCER IN IRELAND

Marks and Spencer (Ireland) Ltd is a wholly owned subsidiary of the Marks and Spencer Group. The first store in Ireland opened in 1979 when the company opened in one of Dublin's premier retail districts – Mary Street. Soon after, a second store was opened in what is probably Ireland's busiest shopping location – Grafton Street in Dublin – and subsequently another store was opened in Cork in 1989.

In 1993, the turnover of the group in the Republic of Ireland was £50 million but this is estimated to have risen to £90 million within two years. The company has committed £50m to store expansion and a development programme: the main part of this expenditure will be spent on new premises in Grafton Street in Dublin but the group is also known to be considering the opening of a new store on the outskirts of Dublin which would entail expenditure of around £20 million.

The company currently employs 550 permanent workers. Just over three quarters (77 per cent) of the workforce are female. In terms of the organisation structure, managers account for 4 per cent of the total, supervisors make up a further 12 per cent and general operative grades account for 84 per cent.

From the very first day of operation in Ireland, the company has agreed to recognise trade unions. The vast majority of workers are represented by MANDATE – the main union for the retail sector – while a number are also represented by the Services, Industrial, Professional and Technical Union (SIPTU) – Ireland's largest general trade union which accounts for about 40 per cent of all trade union members in the country. MANDATE represents almost 90 per cent of unionised staff in the Irish stores.

Ireland is unique in that it is the only country among the 20-plus countries worldwide where Marks and Spencer has voluntarily agreed to formally recognise trade unions, although small groups of employees hold trade union membership in some countries.

The company also deals with the main dispute-settling agencies provided by the state – the Labour Relations Commission and the Labour Court – though they operate on an entirely voluntary basis, as well as the quasi-judicial Employment Appeals Tribunal. This contrasts with the policy in the United Kingdom where 52,000 of the group's total workforce of 62,000 are employed. In the UK, the company does not as a matter of policy attend the main voluntary dispute-settling agency – ACAS – which is similarly funded by the state, though it does, of course, participate in hearings at the Industrial Tribunal which has a statutory basis.

In deciding to recognise trade unions in Ireland from the beginning, the company was conscious of a number of factors which swung the decision towards recognition. Foremost among these was the fact that the company is British owned and management were conscious of the delicate relationship between Britain and Ireland. Considerable emphasis was put on having the company fit in unobtrusively in Irish society. The Irish retail sector is dominated by Irish-owned retail chains, though one of the biggest, Quinnsworth, is part of a British-owned conglomerate – Associated British Foods. All of the larger retail chains, including Quinnsworth, recognise trade unions.

The most recent official figures suggest that just over 96,000 workers (with equal numbers of male and female employees) are employed in retail distribution, of which 24,000 hold trade union membership – a union density rate of 25 per cent. This figure is largely explained by a lack of penetration by unions in smaller retail units which account for the majority of employment, while there is evidence of greater union penetration among larger retail operations.

Before Marks and Spencer opened in Ireland, company management undertook extensive research and consulted with officials from the main employers' organisation – the Irish Business and Employers' Confederation (IBEC). It is likely they would have been advised by IBEC that consideration be given to recognising trade unions in Ireland because of their established presence among the larger retailers primarily and within Irish industry generally.

Company representatives would also have examined the successes and failures of British businesses in Ireland. One company which had considerable trading difficulties was British Home Stores. These difficulties were attributed by some commentators to the fact that BHS had made limited efforts to tailor its employee relations arrangements to accommodate Irish traditions. The view was taken that the custom and practice in the sector was to recognise trade unions and to have gone against this pattern may possibly have drawn unwelcome and unnecessary problems for the company.

Another factor which influenced the decision to recognise trade unions in Ireland was the experience the company had when opening its first store in continental Europe some years previously. When opening its first store in France, the company found itself running into difficulties because not enough effort was being put into tailoring operating arrangements to fit with French customs and practices. Working patterns and attitudes to weekend working would have been examples of issues where French workers diverged in their attitudes from British staff. Lessons were learned from that experience and managers decided to emphasise the need to take on board host country practices when opening future overseas operations. When opening in Ireland the strongly held tradition of trade union recognition in the sector was clearly an important consideration.

The company has concluded an extensive procedural agreement with the two main trade unions. Apart from covering issues such as pay rates, overtime working and the working week, it also contains a disputes procedure outlining the steps to be followed where differences over the agreement itself, or pay and conditions generally, remain unresolved.

The procedural agreement also sets out agreed procedures with regard to the employment of part-time workers and temporary staff. The agreement with MANDATE provides for the union to maintain a list of people seeking temporary and part-time work in the retail trade. The company gives first preference to people on this list but reserves the right to reject anyone deemed to be unsuitable.

The company also operates a check-off system, whereby union membership dues are automatically deducted from the pay packets of union members and remitted to the unions. Union representatives are allowed to meet all new recruits and to outline the benefits associated with union membership. While a closed-shop agreement does not operate, the vast majority of workers belong to one of the two unions represented in the shops.

EMPLOYEE RELATIONS IN THE IRISH STORES

The management in the Irish stores are essentially left with considerable discretion in managing the stores on the basis that they are likely to know best how to direct operations. Of course, the managers in the Irish stores – many of whom would have worked in the Group's British stores previously – operate within the company's broad policy guidelines and report regularly to senior management in the UK.

In addition to the focus teams which operate throughout the rest of the Group, Irish employees elect representatives to what are known as house committees which comprise shop stewards, their deputies and other elected representatives. The house committee is involved in negotiating pay and conditions with management.

The focus teams, which comprise employees from all levels and sections within the company, discuss with management operational issues such as store layout, staff purchasing procedures and health benefits. In Ireland, a very clear line is drawn between the roles of the focus teams and the house committees – the latter concern themselves solely with negotiating pay and conditions and these issues will not be discussed through the focus teams.

The house committee meets the store manager monthly. Twice every year full-time union officials sit alongside shopfloor representatives and review overall employee relations with management as part of a national house committee. Agreed numbers of worker representatives are entitled to paid time off to attend union conferences and training courses.

In broad terms, the pay and benefits package for workers in Ireland and the UK is as similar as it can be. The company's stated policy in the UK of being 'the best payer in the High Street' is also adhered to in Ireland. Interestingly, however, the basic rates of pay for the Irish workers are to some extent determined outside the company.

Representatives of the main retail employers and trade unions in Dublin and the adjoining district of Dun Laoghaire meet to review pay rates annually. The Dublin and Dun Laoghaire Footwear, Drapery and Allied Trades agreement is then registered with the Labour Court, at which point its terms become legally binding. Representatives of Marks and Spencer would contribute to formulating the position of the employers in negotiations to adjust the agreement. All the main retail stores, even those which do not have a direct role in such negotiations or formally recognise this process, adhere to the terms and conditions set out in the agreement. This eliminates the possibility of excessive mobility of staff between stores in a sector where turnover is traditionally high.

It is the policy of the Marks and Spencer Group, however, to pay rates 20 per cent ahead of those agreed as part of this agreement even though all the other main retailers pay no more than the agreed terms.

Where Marks and Spencer consolidates its position as the 'best payer in the High Street' in Ireland is through its non-pay benefits. And, for the most part, the same benefits are available to the British and Irish workers. They each receive a Christmas bonus – equivalent to four weeks' salary for staff with over twelve months' service – and the same health care, hairdressing services and subsidised canteen benefits apply.

The Irish trade unions have negotiated a career-break scheme which does not apply in the UK. Irish workers also have greater holiday entitlements, but in part this is due to the existence of legislation in Ireland which sets out minimal leave entitlements. The Irish workers' holiday entitlements (six weeks annually for those with between 10 and 25 years' service) are also ahead of those available to workers in the other main retail stores (four weeks annually in the main).

A profit-sharing scheme has been offered to the Irish workers along the lines of that available in the UK but the company's offer has not been accepted by the Irish workers because of changes sought in return for its introduction.

Agreement has also been reached on minimum hours for temporary workers following discussions with the Irish trade unions. Over 90 per cent of the workforce are permanent employees. Temporary workers are mainly taken on to cover peak trading periods: some temporary workers have Saturday-only contracts while the majority of temporary workers are guaranteed at least 15 hours work every week and a maximum of 32 hours. Rosters are prepared well in advance and there is no use of so-called 'zero hours contracts' where workers have no guaranteed minimum hours and are offered minimal notice of their work schedules.

The company and the trade unions have also agreed a 1:1 ratio of full-time and part-time employment – a feature which also contrasts with the lack of any such regulation of the numbers employed on a part-time basis in the UK.

Again in contrast to the UK, where rostering and greater use of part-time workers minimises the need to work beyond the contractually agreed working week, agreement has been reached in Ireland between the company and the trade unions on conditions relating to overtime working. All overtime working is optional though part-time staff may be contracted to work if necessary where the stores engage in late-night trading.

For full-time staff working in excess of 37.5 hours in a week, a standard overtime rate of time-and-a-half is paid. Part-time staff do not qualify for this overtime rate until they have worked the basic weekly hours appropriate to their category. However, they are entitled to overtime at double-time rate on the same basis as full-time staff. This would include working between midnight and 8.30 am where this has not been contractually stipulated, work on Sundays and public holidays, and working after normal finishing times when the store is trading after normal closing times. When stores are open for late-night trading, part-timers benefit the same as full-time staff in receiving double time for working beyond seven and a half hours for that day. Furthermore, a range of allowances are payable in the Irish stores to cover work during 'unsocial hours'.

The company has also reached agreement with the trade unions on acceptable standards in terms of conduct and attendance (the acceptable absenteeism level is 4 per cent).

The main trade union in Marks and Spencer, MANDATE, has played a prominent part within EuroFiet – the Europe-wide federation of retail unions – in campaigning for the establishment of a works council within the Group. An international conference was organised in Dublin in March 1995 with retail union officials from the UK, Belgium, France and Ireland in attendance. The decision to hold the conference in Dublin was seen in part to reflect the unique position held by the Irish trade unions – as the only unions voluntarily recognised by the Group. The unions said the purpose of the meeting was to initiate negotiations with the company with a view to establishing a European Works Council.

The company issued its own proposals, however, for the establishment of a Marks and Spencer European Council just prior to the Dublin conference. The company said this new forum would be in addition to the focus teams and house committees and would present 'an exciting opportunity for everyone to become more aware of the European and international dimension of the business'. The move was seen by the company as 'a natural extension of our policy towards communicating with staff'. It was also noted that the Board of Directors had decided to introduce its European Council ahead of the requirements set out in the EU works council directive, which allows companies until 1999 to introduce information and consultation procedures.

The Council would allocate one place for countries where up to 1500 are employed and two places for countries where there are between 1500 and 3000 employees. This would mean 15 Council places for the UK workforce, two for France and one each for Ireland, Belgium, the Netherlands, Spain and the company's Financial Services subsidiary. A maximum of 30 places were allowed for by the company to allow for future expansion.

Employees interested in nominating themselves for places were advised to discuss the matter with their personnel managers and where there were a number of applicants the selection procedures would be decided by the house committees, focus teams and management.

These proposals were criticised by EuroFiet on the basis of a claimed lack of consultation with workers on the part of the company. In Ireland, MANDATE instructed its members to defer making any nominations to the proposed European Council, pending clarification of a number of issues. The matter was still unresolved as this case study was written.

In terms of collective bargaining practices, the biggest difference perceived by management in the Irish operations, compared with the UK operations, relates to the expectation among the Irish workers for higher levels of compensation to be paid when operational changes are suggested. Whereas in the UK the company would pay compensation for up to 26 weeks in recognition of changes in working time practices, for example, the Irish workers would have expectations of higher levels of compensation. Recently, the company agreed to pay two years' compensation to 26 workers who were losing their car parking spaces and part of an early morning supplement as well as some overtime as a result of the company's decision to introduce operational changes.

Another difference seen by management in Ireland is the length of time taken to complete negotiations. Whereas in the UK the company would have given employees three months' notice of the operational changes mentioned in the example above and then paid the compensation of up to 26 weeks' pay, talks on the same change in Ireland took over nine months to complete and resulted in a three-week strike by 70 workers in spite of the company's acceptance of Labour Court settlement proposals.

The company also makes use of the services of the main employers' body, IBEC, in collective bargaining and for research purposes. This also contrasts with the situation in the UK, where store managers would consult the company's central employees relations section for advice and guidance.

In terms of business and operating performance, then, does the fact that trade unions are recognised have any bearing on the performance of the Irish shops? As we have seen the company is trading very well and has major expansion plans. Management in Ireland are happy to report that shopfloor relations with staff are very good – a view which is shared by union officials. There is agreement that management operate with a very open upfront policy.

In terms of standard indicators, such as staff turnover and absenteeism, the Irish shops are said to compare with the best in the UK. Of the 200 workers employed by the company in its first store in 1979, 100 are still with the company 16 years later.

ACTIVITY BRIEF

1 What do you believe are the key advantages and disadvantages for the Marks and Spencer Group in recognising trade unions in its Irish operations?

2 (a) Compare and contrast industrial relations in the UK and the Republic of Ireland.
  (b) Based on your analysis, which factors do you believe were most important in the decision of Marks and Spencer to recognise trade unions in Ireland?

3 Based on your insights from this case, what do you believe are the critical employee relations considerations for organisations locating in a country outside the UK?

RECOMMENDED READING

Beer, M, Spector, B, Lawrence, P, Quinn Mills, D and Walton, R (1985) *Human Resource Management: A General Manager's Perspective*, Glencoe, Illinois, Free Press.

Berridge, J (1992) 'Human resource management in Britain', *Employee Relations*, 14, 5.

Brunstein, I (1995) *Human Resource Management in Western Europe*, Berlin, De Gruyter.

Guest, D (1987) 'Human resource management and industrial relations', *Journal of Management Studies*, 24, 5, pp 503–21.

Guest, D (1989) 'Human resource management: its implications for industrial relations and trade unions', in Storey, J (ed) *New Perspectives on Human Resource Management*, London, Routledge.

Gunnigle, P (1992) 'Changing management approaches to employee relations in Ireland', *Employee Relations*, 14, 1.

Gunnigle, P (1995) 'Collectivism and the management of industrial relations in greenfield sites', *Human Resource Management Journal*, 5, 3.

Gunnigle, P, McMahon, G and Fitzgerald G (1995) *Industrial Relations in Ireland: Theory and Practice*, Dublin, Gill and MacMillan.

Hourihan, F (1996), 'Employee relations and collective bargaining: Ireland' in Burgess, P (ed) *Employee Relations and Collective Bargaining*, London, European Management Guides, Incomes Data Services/Institute of Personnel Development.

Keenoy, T (1990) 'HRM: a case of the wolf in sheep's clothing', *Personnel Review*, 19, 2.

Salamon, M (1992) *Industrial Relations: Theory and Practice*, London, Prentice Hall.

Sieff, M (1984), 'How I see the personnel function', *Personnel Management*, Dec, pp 28–30.

Tse, K (1985), *Marks and Spencer*, Oxford, Pergamon Press.

INDEX